The Middle East in the World

"Pitched at ... tly the right level to provide a many-faceted introduction to the study of the modern ...dle East, this book will be a must for all those who aspire to understand and to teach ... background to contemporary events in this troubled region of the world."
—**Roger Owen**, Harvard University

"This is the ... book I have been waiting for! It covers a lot of ground in terms of history, politics, and ...ltures of the Middle East, but also goes deep into several very important topics repre ...tative of issues faced by peoples and societies across the region. It will work perfec ... for my classes that have a mix of students, some with knowledge of the region and ...ers completely new to it. The book is also sophisticated in introducing students to ... many ways different disciplines approach the study of the Middle East, both today ... in the past, and the problems that arise with each of them. Finally, its blended lea... ng approach provides plenty of opportunities for students to pursue additional kno ...dge, calling their attention to online resources and examples from media around the ...d. This textbook will satisfy a need for undergraduate courses on the Middle East ...m diverse perspectives and in a variety of disciplines."
—**Amy Young Evrard**, Gettysburg College

The Middle Ea... in the World offers students a fresh, comprehensive, multidisciplinary entry point to the broader Middle East. After a brief introduction to the study of the region, the early chapters of the book survey the essentials of Middle Eastern history; important historical narratives; and the region's languages, religions, and global connections. Students are guided through the material with relevant maps, resource boxes, and text boxes that support and guide further independent exploration of the topics at hand. The second half of the book presents interdisciplinary case studies, each of which focuses on a specific country or sub-region and a salient issue, offering a taste of the cultural distinctiveness of the particular country while also drawing attention to global linkages. Readers will come away from this book with an understanding of the larger historical, political, and cultural frameworks that shaped the Middle East as we know it today, and of current issues that have relevance in the Middle East and beyond.

── FOUNDATIONS IN GLOBAL STUDIES ──

Series Editor: Valerie Tomaselli, MTM Publishing

The Regional Landscape

South Asia in the World: An Introduction
Editor: Susan Snow Wadley, Syracuse University

The Middle East in the World: An Introduction
Editor: Lucia Volk, San Francisco State University

East Asia in the World: An Introduction
Editor: Anne Prescott, Five College Center for East Asian Studies

The Middle East in the World

An Introduction

Edited by Lucia Volk

Routledge
Taylor & Francis Group

NEW YORK AND LONDON

First published 2015
by Routledge
711 Third Avenue, New York, NY 10017

and by Routledge
2 Park Square, Milton Park, Abingdon, Oxon, OX14 4RN

Routledge is an imprint of the Taylor & Francis Group, an informa business

Library of Congress Cataloging in Publication Data
The Middle East in the world : an introduction / editor, Lucia Volk ; contributors Carel Bertram, Rochelle Davis, Rachel Goshgarian, Maia Carter Hallward, Asli Ilgit, Mahmood Monshipouri, Hootan Shambayati, Nadine Sinno, Keith Walters, Nicole F. Watts, Russell Zanca.
    pages cm. — (Foundations in global studies: the regional landscape)
Includes bibliographical references and index.
ISBN 978-0-7656-3976-9 (pbk. : alk. paper) — ISBN 978-0-7656-3975-2 (cloth : alk. paper)
1. Middle East.   2. Middle East—Civilization.   3. World politics.   I. Volk, Lucia.
II. Bertram, Carel, 1943–
DS62.M57 2014
956—dc23 2013043260

—Maps by Richard Garratt, MTM Publishing—

ISBN: 978-0-7656-3975-2 (hbk)
ISBN: 978-0-7656-3976-9 (pbk)
ISBN: 978-1-3157-1468-4 (ebk)

Typeset by Apex CoVantage, LLC in Times.

Printed and bound in Great Britain by
CPI Group (UK) Ltd, Croydon, CR0 4YY

Contents

About This Book

The Middle East in the World: An Introduction—the second book in Foundations in Global Studies: The Regional Landscape series—provides a fresh, systematic, and comprehensive overview of the Middle East. Including coverage of three subregions—the Middle East, North Africa, and parts of Central Asia and the Caucasus—the Middle East considered here is cogent and diverse at the same time: the vast areas under this formulation share patterns of history and culture, but also diverge in dramatic ways across the broad reach of its geography. For instance, Central Asia and the Caucasus, often considered under a separate rubric in the traditional area studies approach, are considered critical here in understanding how the "Middle East" developed across the centuries and how it is defined today. And while more focus is given to the more typical "core" Middle East countries, such as those in Southwest Asia (including Lebanon, Israel, Iraq, Syria, Saudi Arabia, the United Arab Emirates, etc.)—as well as Egypt and Tunisia, for instance, in North Africa—the globalized complexion of the Middle East is made clear in our broader reach.

The exploration of globalizing processes is indeed the focus of *The Middle East in the World*, and the series as a whole. As we examine a host of global patterns that are reflected in and that shape the region—money flows, diasporic movements, hybridity in language, political movements affected by worldwide media and movement of ideas—the "in the World" part of the title gets a full hearing. Indeed, the variations in this wide region's social, cultural, economic, and political life are explored within the context of the globalizing forces affecting *all* regions of the world.

In a simple strategy that all books in the series employ, this volume begins with an overview and foundational material (including chapters on history, language, and, in the case of the Middle East, religion), moves to a discussion of globalization, and then focuses the investigation more specifically through the use of case studies. The set of case studies exposes readers to various disciplinary lenses that bring the region to life through subjects of high interest and importance to today's readers. Among others, these topics include the Green Movement in Iran; concerns about oil and water resources in the Persian Gulf countries; the Palestine-Israel peace process; linguistic diversity and hybridity in Tunisia; and the social, political, and economic context of the cotton industry in Uzbekistan.

A deliberate attempt has been made to show the connections between peoples and countries that make up the Middle East, and to counter the contemporary media focus on turmoil in the region. For instance, the chapters in Part Two—on history, language, and religion—illustrate clearly that the region is much more than the sum of its civil and regional conflicts.

In addition to her own contributions as author of the overview and fundamentals chapters, the editor, Lucia Volk, codirector of Middle East and Islamic studies at San Francisco State University (SFSU), has assembled a team of specialists—both from SFSU and beyond—to contribute case studies to this volume. The team represents a broad range of disciplines involved in the study of the Middle East, including, among others, anthropology, art history, geography and the environment, geopolitics and international affairs, history, linguistics, and political economy.

Resource boxes, an important feature of the volumes in this series, are included to preserve currency and add utility. They offer the readers links to excellent sources— mostly online—on the topics discussed. The links—which include connections to timely data, reports on recent events, official sites, local and country-based media, and visual material—establish a rich archive of additional material for readers to draw on. The URLs included are known to be current as of September 1, 2013, and in the case of expired URLs, enough information has been provided for the reader to locate the same, or similarly useful, resources.

Part One

Overview

1

Introducing the Middle East

Lucia Volk

In January 2011, audiences across the globe were glued to their television screens. The world was closely following the uprisings that erupted in almost every state of the Arab Middle East following the death of a Tunisian street vendor by the name of Mohamed Bouazizi, who had set himself on fire to protest the humiliating treatment he received from the local police and the subsequent dismissal of his complaints by the municipal authorities. News media were teeming with images of peaceful protesters flocking to major squares in their cities and towns, demanding that governments and government institutions be accountable to their citizens. They chanted, "The people want the fall of the regime!" and defied police and security forces, as well as army detachments. The protests sometimes ended in violent clashes; other times they ended peacefully. The faces of the protesters were young and old, male and female, urban and provincial, and multi-denominational. In other words, the images of the popular uprisings were very different from previous newscasts of a Middle East populated with insurgents and terrorists. The uprisings, both peaceful and violent, were organized and executed by broad coalitions of students, labor unions, political parties, religious movements, and civic institutions, and facilitated by personal networks as well as social media.

On January 14, 2011, the Tunisian president of twenty-three years, Zine al-Abidine Ben Ali, stepped down and flew to exile in Saudi Arabia. On February 11, Hosni Mubarak, Egypt's president of thirty years, resigned from office. He was later tried and sentenced to life imprisonment. On November 23, Yemeni leader Ali Abdullah Saleh resigned after thirty-three years in office after receiving assurances of immunity, while in Libya, only a month earlier, rebels had captured and killed Muammar Qaddafi, who had ruled with an iron fist since 1969. That these "presidents-for-life" had to yield to popular (and secular) pressure in the Middle East surprised many analysts. They had theorized that change in the region would come via political Islam. In other words, the uprisings presented a challenge for scholars and students of the Middle East. Arguably, the level of popular discontent had been high for many years, so why did the uprisings happen when they did? Why were they successful in some countries, but not in others? How did protests in one country affect those in others?

Across the region, protesters wanted to change the status quo, because they wanted to live with respect and dignity, and provide for their families. Many of the protesters were—and still are—unemployed or underemployed, whereas a small group of busi-nessmen and government officials at the top of the hierarchy had amassed spectacular

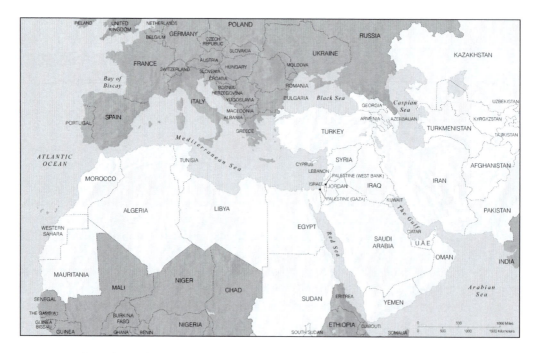

amounts of wealth. Similar to the participants of the Occupy Wall Street movement that erupted in September 2011 in New York and across the United States, the protesters in the Middle East demanded a more just distribution of wealth and power. The Arab uprisings occurred in the aftermath of one of the most severe global economic crises in history, set off by risky and unregulated debt deals made by investment and commercial banks. Domestic economies contracted around the world, stifling growth and opportunity. Young people in the Middle East, as elsewhere, were particularly affected. Protesters in Egypt held up signs displaying solidarity with protesters in the United States, or vice versa. Student activists connected globally via Facebook, Twitter, and YouTube, circumventing traditional, state or privately owned news media that often under- or misreported events.

Young women, in particular, emerged as protagonists during the demonstrations. Via a YouTube video that went viral, the Egyptian student, Asmaa Mahfouz, asked her fellow Egyptians to come meet her in Cairo's Tahrir Square to demonstrate against the government: "If we still have honor and want to live in dignity, we will go down on January 25, we'll go down and demand our rights, our fundamental human rights." Her voice carried great urgency and conviction. First thousands, then hundreds of thousands of protesters congregated on Tahrir Square on and after January 25, in a movement that would topple the president. In Yemen, another woman became the public face of the uprising by speaking out against the corruption and dysfunction of the government of President Ali Abdullah Saleh. Tawakkul Karman, the creator of Women Journalists Without Chains, led protesters in chanting "The Yemeni people have had enough." Karman was one of three awardees of the 2011 Nobel Peace Prize. Both Mahfouz and Karman are articulate, compelling speakers, and they see their role as taking an active part in politics and shaping a better future for themselves and the societies they live in.

A collage of images from the 2011 uprisings in the Middle East and North Africa, often referred to as the "Arab Spring." Clockwise from top left: Egypt, Tunisia, Yemen, and Syria. *(Wikimedia Commons, http://commons.wikimedia.org/wiki/File:Infobox_collage_for_MENA_protests.PNG.)*

A video of Asmaa Mahfouz asking fellow Egyptians to protest against the government can be found online (http://www.youtube.com/watch?v=1JW3m8uwcL4).

Watch an interview with Tawakkul Karman, the founder of Women Journalists Without Chains (http://www.youtube.com/watch?v=lsZ6kHamRfQ).

Events in the decade preceding the uprisings painted a very different picture of the Middle East. In the aftermath of the tragic events of September 11, 2001, when four commercial planes were hijacked and turned into assault weapons that killed almost 3,000 civilians in New York, Pennsylvania, and Washington, DC, the United States led coalition forces into decade-long wars in Afghanistan in 2001 and Iraq in 2003. Both wars turned out to be immensely costly in terms of human lives and expenditures on the side of the coalition forces, but even more so for Afghans and Iraqis. In 2008 global grain shortages caused bread riots in many countries of the Middle East—all of them net food importers—proving that daily subsistence was precarious, and that the governments had few solutions to the basic problems of their people. In Iran in 2009, people took to the streets to protest what they considered fraudulent elections—only to be brutally repressed by the Iranian police and security forces. In other words, Western audiences had come to understand the Middle East through a very particular lens, one that emphasized violence, both international and domestic.

From a Western perspective, the events of 9/11 changed the terms of engagement with the Middle East. From the perspective of many in the Middle East, the attack on civilians in the United States was a continuation of ongoing wars and invasions that had killed many civilians in their countries, with direct or indirect support of the West. The perpetrators of the September 11 attacks were members of a radical terror organization called al-Qaeda. Some of al-Qaeda's leaders once had been participants in the resistance efforts that had repelled the Soviet occupation of Afghanistan over the span of a bloody, decade-long war (1979–1989). These so-called mujahideen were acclaimed by President Reagan as courageous freedom fighters. The film *Rambo III* (1988) featured John J. Rambo (Sylvester Stallone) taking up the good fight alongside the Afghan resistance on horseback against Soviet helicopters. The film ended with a special credit "to the brave Mujahideen fighters of Afghanistan." At the time, the United States was so intent on winning the Cold War against the Soviet Union that it did not consider the possibility that the men who were able to defeat one superpower might imagine they could bring down the other as well.

Charlie Wilson's War (2007) is a feature-length film starring Tom Hanks and Julia Roberts that deals critically with the American involvement in the Afghanistan war. Information about it can be found easily online by searching the film's title. The following links provide a good starting point:

- Trailer for the film (http://www.youtube.com/watch?v=UHl-6uH8MUQ).
- GlobalResearch.com's criticism of the film's handling of the historical record (http://www.globalresearch.ca/hollywoods-dangerous-afghan-illusion-charlie-wilsons-war/5331107).

Both the United States and European colonial powers have a long history of alliances with governments and nongovernmental forces in the Middle East, depending on their own definitions of national security and national interest. Who is "with us" or "against us" depends on the historical context and is not set in stone. Whether political change comes about through violence or through peaceful protests is also not set in stone. Yet much too often, especially in the context of Middle East politics, pundits argue that what we see unfold is just a replay of the same violent history that has plagued the region for centuries and that nothing will change. It was that kind of thinking that prevented the experts from anticipating the uprisings of 2011.

It is fair to say that the political and social order of most countries in the Middle East has been profoundly challenged, and in some cases overthrown, whether by forces from without or within, since the mid-1990s. These are unsettling times for many Middle Eastern citizens who live in war zones or countries that are politically or economically unstable or rent by sectarian strife. Many travelers of Middle Eastern descent will not remember a time when they were not "randomly" pulled out of line for additional questioning at the airport. A new generation of plane passengers does not remember the time when it was possible to embark on a flight without elaborate security screenings. In waiting rooms in any transit station, we are now used to seeing signs that warn us not to leave our baggage unattended, or to inform the authorities of any suspicious activity. Ironically, as people across the world have become increasingly interconnected, they also have become more fearful of one other, and security related businesses are booming.

Within this larger framework of political uncertainty, war, fear, and suspicion, this book seeks to look at the Middle East as a region with religious, ethnic, and political complexity. While emphasizing the differences across the region, it also points out that ordinary families in the Middle East still seek opportunities to better themselves, hope for a good life for themselves and their children, and participate in modern life while also celebrating their traditions. Their ambitions, in other words, are not markedly different from those of other people across the world. As global citizens, it behooves us to learn to appreciate the cultural and political differences, while not losing sight of what we share.

Important Linkages Between the West and the Middle East

One of the main reasons to study the Middle East is to gain a better understanding of long-standing linkages between the Middle East and the West. These linkages manifest not only on the level of politics and economics, but also in everyday life. Centrally, the politics of oil (and increasingly other hydrocarbons) tie the West to the Middle East. Oil provides fuel for heating systems and cars, asphalt for our streets, as well as lubricants, glues, greases, cosmetics, polyesters, acrylic fibers, and anything else plastic in our lives. Check your home and count the items that oil made possible. If you bought them, you are part of the larger oil economy that ties you to the Middle East.

Other crucial links that tie the West to the Middle East are the values and practices shaped by Judaism, Christianity, and Islam—three world religions that have their origins in the geographic Middle East. In fact, it is historically inaccurate to speak of a "Judeo-Christian West" versus a "Muslim Middle East," since the three monotheistic religions are branches of the same tree and promote similar values and practices. For instance, Judaism, Christianity, and Islam share the centrality of a God who speaks through angels and prophets, as recorded in a holy book; weekly meetings in houses of worship and the practice of prayers; the belief in a Judgment Day; and the mandate to help the less fortunate—to name but a few. All three religious communities developed powerful organizations and hierarchies of clergymen, at times in direct competition with each other, and all of these hierarchies excluded women for the most part. Across all religions, adherents practice various degrees of piety, from relatively secular to traditional and sometimes literal interpretations of the respective scriptures.

Box 1.1

Edward Said's *Orientalism*

Edward Said (pronounced Sa-*eed*), a former professor of comparative literature at Columbia University, conducted an analysis of European paintings and
novels of the seventeenth and eighteenth centuries. He published his findings
in his widely read 1978 book *Orientalism*. "Orientalism" describes a way
of looking at an entire region of people in a stereotyping manner that makes
"them" profoundly different from "us." Jack Shaheen, a former professor of
mass communications, later used Said's ideas in his critique of Hollywood
movies in the book *Reel Bad Arabs: How Hollywood Vilifies a People*.

    That Westerners often ignore the shared values and practices that bind the West to the
Middle East can be partially explained by a long history of depicting the region and its
inhabitants as inherently different in art, literature, and media. Early European travelers
painted a Middle East filled with veiled beauties, as well as turbaned, sword-wielding
men on horseback in flowing robes, conjuring a society filled with magic and mystery.
Hollywood has continued the tradition of rendering the Middle East as a place where
people dress, speak, and behave very differently. Increasingly, Hollywood has reproduced
a stock image of the Middle Eastern villain who wantonly abducts Western women or
attacks Western men, and who only yields to the excessive use of force. Chuck Norris in
The Delta Force (1986), Arnold Schwarzenegger in *True Lies* (1994), and Demi Moore
in *G.I. Jane* (1997) depict valiant Western individuals who single-handedly defeat entire
groups of such armed villains. Popular Western culture—with its global reach—has
turned Middle Easterners into persons that amuse or, increasingly, scare us. Neither
scenario creates the possibility for a fair or unbiased encounter between the West and
the Middle East.

    Links to the Media Education Foundation's videos concerning Edward Said's
    Orientalism, including interviews with Said, can be found at:

        Part 1: http://www.youtube.com/watch?v=xwCOSkXR_Cw.
        Part 2: http://www.youtube.com/watch?v=n0HYX9JVH8o&feature=relmfu.
        Part 3: http://www.youtube.com/watch?v=tlF5ED-gE5Y&feature=relmfu.
        Part 4: http://www.youtube.com/watch?v=tZLA-mwOdSs&feature=relmfu.

    Another film produced by Media Education Foundation is *Reel Bad Arabs: How
    Hollywood Vilifies a People*, which includes interviews with Jack Shaheen, whose
    book of the same name inspired the film. Information about the video can be
    found online (http://www.reelbadarabs.com/mef.html).

It can certainly be argued that no one is free of the tendency to stereotype: some Middle Easterners still call Westerners *franks*, in reference to the crusaders of the Middle Ages, which is not a flattering designation. During my own travels in the Middle East, I have heard locals describe Westerners as persons devoid of morals or family values, and therefore of a lesser kind. I think it is important to be aware that stereotyping is a practice that occurs in all places. Yet it also bears pointing out that some stereotypes are backed by bigger guns than others. At the end of the day, the political and economic realities of the twentieth and twenty-first centuries allow the West to do to the Middle East what the Middle East cannot do to the West. This fundamental inequality has profound implications for the relationship between individuals, communities, and states in both world regions.

Importance of Language and Terminology

One challenge for students of the Middle East derives from the fact that in discussing subjects related to the Middle East, we use names of people, places, or concepts derived from languages that are written in a different script. So we have to transliterate these foreign words (i.e., spell them phonetically in our Latin alphabet). Since European scholars began reading and translating texts that used Arabic scripts at various times and places, the same word would be transliterated differently. Over time, we have ended up with a confusing array of spellings for various places and names (e.g., Mecca, Mekka, Makkah, etc.; or Muhammad, Mohamed, Mohammed, etc.). Academics eventually did come up with a standardized transliteration table, but that particular form of writing is unfamiliar to the lay audience wishing to learn about the Middle East.

Not only is the script different, but Arabic, Armenian, Hebrew, Persian, and Urdu alphabets contain letters that have no direct equivalent in Western alphabets. In instances when we have a letter that has no equivalent in English, we must transcribe it, or render the sound so that we can pronounce it. For instance, [ع] "ayn," [ج] "dj," [غ] "gh," and [خ] "kh" are letters in Arabic without direct equivalents in English. In English, the letter [ع] "ayn," is depicted by a reverse apostrophe (') in words such as Shi'a or Shari'a; however, this is not always done consistently. Shi'a is also spelled Shia, or Shiites; Shari'a is also spelled Sharia or Shariah. To absorb foreign names and terms, while learning about unfamiliar places, times, and contexts, is already quite challenging. To face different spellings of the same (unfamiliar) word in different readings on the same topic makes matters even worse.

What follows is a list of vocabulary items that will accompany us throughout the rest of the book. Some are terms that have more than one definition, which can be confusing during discussions. Terms are sometimes used interchangeably, even though they should not be. For instance, *Arab* and *Muslim* are often considered one and the same, which can result in misrepresentations of communities or events. The definitions that accompany each term aim to make you aware of nuances of meaning of individual terms, so as to allow us to use them more accurately.

Box 1.2

Arabic Calligraphy as an Art Form

Despite the complexity of considerations surrounding the Arabic script and its transliterations, the decorative script—with its calligraphic styling—has been a source of wide-ranging artistic expression. Below is an example of zoomorphic calligraphy, where Arabic letters are arranged to depict a bird. The letters spell out the sentence *bismallah al-rahman al-rahim* (in the name of God, the benevolent and the merciful).

Arabic calligraphy exists in many different styles, and it is highly valued, since it was the means by which the Quran (also spelled Koran) was preserved and handed down through generations. Calligraphy is used to decorate mosques and palaces, as well as pottery and tiles. Most Muslim artists avoid figurative depictions, since the Quran forbids the worship of idols (i.e., images of God). *(Yassine Mrabet, 2008. Wikimedia Commons.)*

Arab

The English word *Arab* is transliterated from the Arabic noun *'arab*, which translates to "Bedouin." Arabs in this original sense were pastoral people that lived in the desert in the geographic area known as the Arabian Peninsula. However, the term *Arab* is also applied to persons who speak Arabic, whether they are nomadic or not. In other words, *Arab* refers to a person's geographic *and* linguistic origins, although those two labels do not necessarily overlap. Not every Arabic speaker today is from the Arabian Peninsula.

Additionally, the English word *Arab* is used as an adjective, as in the "Arab League," or the "Pan-Arab movement." The Arab League was created in 1945 to give Arab states a unified voice on the world stage. Around the same time, the Pan-Arab movement sought to unify persons who spoke Arabic in one large Arab state. *Arab*, in this particular context, emphasizes linguistic and cultural solidarities that transcend the boundaries of individual nation-states. For instance, citizens of Syria, Tunisia, or Iraq who call themselves Arabs may subscribe to this Pan-Arab political project, while citizens in the same countries who call themselves Syrians, Tunisians, or Iraqis are likely to adhere to nationalist identities and ideologies.

Another political use of *Arab* is the term *Israeli Arab*, promoted by the Israeli government to designate Palestinian citizens of Israel, arguably for the purpose of undermining the claim to Palestinian identity and statehood.

Arabian

This is another adjective derived from *Arab*. It is never used to describe a person or the language. Instead, the word is used for Arabian horses, a collection of stories called *Arabian Nights*, the Arabian Peninsula, and so on.

Arabic

This adjective derived from *Arab* refers primarily to the language, as in "Arabic-speaking populations of the Middle East," or "she used Arabic sources to write her research paper."

Muslim

Muslim is an English word transliterated from the original Arabic noun *muslim*, which translates to "someone who submits [to God's will]." An older spelling, "Moslem," can still be seen in writing, but it is falling out of use. Muslims are adherents of Islam, which has its historical origins in the Arabian Peninsula. Arabs were therefore the first Muslims. Today, however, more Muslims live outside the Arab world than inside it, including in Indonesia, India, Bangladesh, and China. Most residents in the Middle East are Muslims, but significant minorities are Baha'i, Christian, Jewish, Zoroastrian, or some other religion, and some prefer to identify as nonreligious. The terms *Muslim* and *Arab* should therefore not be used interchangeably.

When reporters equate residents in the Middle East with Muslims, they do not only gloss over the fact of regional religious diversity, but also they emphasize that citizens of the Middle East value their religious identities more than gender, class, age, or ethnic identities. By way of comparison, we do not usually refer to "Christians" in news reports about the United States or Europe, although the majority of citizens in these countries practice a version of the Christian faith.

Similar to *Arab*, the word *Muslim* is both a noun and an adjective in English.

Islam Versus Islamism

Islam is the transliteration of the Arabic noun *islaam*, meaning "submission to [God's will]." The word describes a religion, one that sees itself as a direct successor to Judaism and Christianity. *Islamism* combines the name of the religion, Islam, with *–ism*, a suffix that signals an ideology or belief system, as in commun*ism* or capital*ism*. Islamism promotes religious ideas for political ends.

Islamic

An adjective derived from *Islam*, *Islamic* appears in phrases such as "Islamic art and architecture," "(pre-)Islamic history," "Islamic cultural centers," and "programs of Middle East and Islamic studies," as well as in names of organizations, such as the Organization of Islamic Cooperation. The adjective does not usually describe a person. Muslim is used instead.

Islamist

An adjective derived from Islamism, *Islamist* describes a person with a political agenda that they identify with the Muslim faith. Not all Muslims are Islamists. Islamists fall on a spectrum from moderate to extreme. Many Islamist parties or movements today seek out reforms through official political channels, while others call for change by any means necessary. Prominent Islamist political actors include the Justice and Development Party in Morocco and in Turkey, the Ennahda Party in Tunisia, Hamas in the Palestinian Territories, and Hezbollah in Lebanon.

Jew

Jew is an English noun derived from the Hebrew word *yehudim*. A Jew is a member of a particular ethnic *and* religious group, although ethnicity and religion need not overlap. The dual definition and application of the word *Jew* can lead to confusion, since a person might identify as an ethnic Jew but not be very religious, or identify as a member of the Jewish faith but belong to some other ethnicity. In Orthodox Judaism, one is a Jew if born of a Jewish mother.

Semitic and Anti-Semitic

An adjective, believed to derive from the name *Shem*, a son of Noah in the book of Genesis, *Semitic* is primarily a linguistic term, referring to a language family that includes Arabic, Aramaic, Hebrew, and Maltese. In this sense, a Semite is a person who speaks any one of these languages, and whose culture is influenced by beliefs and practices created in and conveyed through these languages.

The word *anti-Semitic* came into circulation in Germany at the turn of the twentieth century, when Jewish citizens experienced discrimination and finally near-extermination by the Nazi government. Anti-Semitism today refers specifically to ethnic hatred of and discrimination against members of the Jewish community, although, technically, they are not the only Semites.

Defining the Middle East

In his much cited 1960 article "Where Is the Middle East?" the history professor Roderic H. Davidson explains why there is no agreement on the exact boundaries of the region. To begin with, *Middle East* is not a label that the inhabitants in the region chose for themselves. According to Davidson's research, the term appeared for the first time in the writings of an American naval officer and strategist, Alfred Thayer Mahan. In 1902 Mahan wrote a short article in the *National Review* about the need for Great Britain to secure the sea routes from the Suez Canal to India and China, in light of the growing Russian influence in the "Middle East." At the time, the terms *Near East* and *Far East* already existed, the former loosely defining the Mediterranean territories of the Ottoman Empire, and the latter describing China. The "Middle" East was now wedged between the two. The discussions at the time were not concerned with precise boundaries, but with questions of naval versus land power, as European empires expanded and consolidated their influence beyond Europe. In 1907 the Russian and British Empires signed a document to respect "the integrity and independence of Persia." In 1916 French and British diplomats sat down to draw up the map that still defines the region. In other words, the "Middle East" emerged as a concept as European powers fought among themselves to control it.

It was British politicians and military personnel who gave the term its currency, and, via World War I reporting, it was picked up by American journalists and academics. Previously, it had been standard practice to use *Near East*, a term that remains in limited use at a few American universities with Departments of Near Eastern Studies, as well as in the U.S. State Department, where regional experts work for the Bureau of Near Eastern Affairs. Whether we use *Middle East* or *Near East*, however, we run into the same problem: *middle* and *near* are relative terms that beg the question, in the middle of or near *what* exactly? The reference point is, of course, Great Britain, which controlled a vast colonial empire across Asia (or the Orient, as the British called it then).

Today, the particular historical origin of the term *Middle East* has led to demands to abandon the term altogether. Since the label defines a particular territory from the point of view of European colonizers, it is certainly problematic. Alternative labels have been proposed and put into circulation, but none has replaced the "Middle East" so far in terms of popularity and usage. For example, in the 1970s, the world historian Marshall Hodgson wrote a three-volume work titled *The Venture of Islam* about the rise and spread of the religion. In his books, he introduced the term *Islamicate*, meaning "pertaining to the cultural world of Islam." In Hodgson's sense, North Africa, the Middle East, Central Asia, Turkey, Iran, Afghanistan, Pakistan, and Israel are Islamicate, since they all bear historical and cultural imprints of Islam, even if not all residents are Muslims. The term, however, never caught on beyond academic circles. Moreover, over the past 100 years, the term *Middle East* has gained currency among residents of the region itself: *ash-sharq al-awsat* in Arabic, *khavare miyaneh* in Persian, and *orta dogu* in Turkish. Should Westerners avoid a term that locals use themselves? Other alternative designations created new problems.

Arab world is a term that refers to countries in which Arabic is the official, or majority, language. The term *Arab* also has the connotations of "from the Arab Peninsula" which narrows the frame of reference. The term excludes Turkey, Iran, Afghanistan, and Israel, as well as countries in Central Asia and the Caucasus, because residents there have other ethnic and linguistic origins. But since the Arab community is the largest single ethnic community in the region, some feel that it should be used to describe the region, rather than the Middle East.

The Arab League is a political organization created in 1945. Its founding members were Egypt, Iraq, Jordan, Lebanon, Saudi Arabia, and Syria. Sixteen more countries joined, among them African countries such as Mauritania, Somalia, Djibouti, and Comoros. The Arab League, similar to the Arab world, excludes Turkey, Iran, Israel, as well as countries from Central Asia and the Caucasus.

Southwest Asia and North Africa (SWANA) is a label used by the United Nations in its official publications. This term focuses on geography and is therefore presumably neutral. It juxtaposes Southwest Asia with Central Asia (Kazakhstan, Kyrgyzstan, Tajikistan, Turkmenistan, Uzbekistan, and Afghanistan), and South Asia (Pakistan, India, and Bangladesh). Yet the term was coined in the West by a U.S.-dominated institution and then applied to the region, which also raises red flags. Moreover, while tectonically part of the Asian land mass, to what extent is the Middle East "Asian"?

Maghreb and *Mashriq* are Arabic terms for "western (lands)" and "eastern (lands)," respectively. The terms loosely correspond to geographic North Africa and Southwest Asia, respectively. They were used by Arabic-speaking historians as they were writing about the spread of Islam. The Maghreb (also spelled Maghrib) had no Arabic name before Arab Muslims conquered and settled the region in the seventh century. Since the terms are Arabic, tied to a particular history of Islam, they appear to exclude non-Arabic and non-Muslim minorities.

Islamic world and *Muslim world* encompass North Africa, Southwest Asia, and Central Asia, as well as South Asia and Southeast Asia, where most of the world's Muslims reside. Through the religion, residents of the Muslim world share important practices and values. Yet the designation suggests a homogeneity that is problematic, since not all Muslims practice their faith in the same way. Moreover, non-Muslim minority communities reside in the region as well.

A recent example of a relabeling away from *Islamic* happened at the Metropolitan Museum of Art in New York. In 2003, curators closed the museum's Islamic Art Galleries for a substantial renovation. Eight years later, the museum reopened the new exhibit space under the banner "New Galleries for the Art of the Arab Lands, Turkey, Iran, Central Asia, and Later South Asia." The curators wanted to emphasize the cultural diversity within the region instead of one single "Islamic" characteristic, which they found misleading. While the new title is certainly more inclusive, it is also unwieldy.

Mapping the Middle East

In light of the preceding discussion, it should not be surprising that the exact boundaries of the Middle East are contested. Scholars generally agree that the region stretches across three continents: Africa, Asia, and Europe; however, they disagree on which countries ought to be included, and on which ones should be excluded. On some maps, the Middle East remains narrowly defined as the region under British colonial influence, starting with Egypt in the west and reaching Iran in the east, and stretching from Turkey in the north to Yemen in the south (see the Library of Congress map of the "Middle East," at http://www.loc.gov/resource/g7420.ct002248/seq-1). On others, North Africa and the Middle East are represented from Mauritania in the west to Afghanistan and Pakistan in the east, and Turkey in the north and Yemen in the south (see the Library of Congress map of "Northern Africa and the Middle East," at http://www.loc.gov/resource/g8220. ct002647/seq-1). The CIA *World Factbook* map (https://www.cia.gov/library/publications/ the-world-factbook/wfbExt/region_mde.html) separates Africa from the Middle East, a region that, on this map, includes fifteen countries, reaching from Turkey, Armenia, Azerbaijan, and Georgia (the Caucasus) to the Arabian Peninsula, and from Israel, the West Bank, and the Gaza Strip to Iran. The United Nations, meanwhile, has a map on which the Middle East reaches from Libya to Afghanistan and Pakistan (http://www. un.org/depts/Cartographic/map/profile/mideastr.pdf). Other organizations present other variations on the map. Each follows its own logic, as well as its own interpretation of history and geography. For students of the Middle East, this presents a dilemma, especially when preparing for a map quiz. What countries do they need to study?

The "Middle East Maps" page on the Perry-Castañeda Library Map Collection site (http://www.lib.utexas.edu/maps/middle_east.html), under the auspices of the University of Texas, assembles maps of the Middle East from a variety of publishers, serving a variety of purposes.

This book presents a map (on page 4) that tries to be as inclusive as possible, while stating clearly that no definitive Middle East exists. It encourages readers to look at the included maps with an appreciation of their contingency and fluency, rather than their finality. Of course, national boundaries remain realities in the sense that travelers need visas to enter and exit countries across the regions. Yet our world has been, and continues to become, more closely interconnected via migration, international trade, and technology, so that national boundaries become just one reality in a multilayered and intertwined world. The map included in this book emphasizes historical connections between communities that were once ruled by successive empires: Persian, Greek, Roman, Umayyad and Abbasid, Seljuk and Ottoman Turkish, to name but the most prominent among them. Over the course of several thousand years, communities from the northwest coast of Africa to northern South Asia, and from the Caucasus and Central Asia to the Arabian Gulf, shared the influences of monotheistic religions, patriarchal societies, and important trade routes that linked regions around the Mediterranean with China. In modern history, these communities experienced European, Soviet, and American political domination. With these interconnections in mind, the Middle East presented in this book comprises three geographic subregions: North Africa (the northern tip of the African continent along the Mediterranean from Mauritania to Egypt), Southwest Asia (the territory east of the Mediterranean, including the Arabian Peninsula), and the Caucasus and Central Asia (from Armenia and Azerbaijan via former Soviet Central Asia, to Iran, Afghanistan, and Pakistan).

Each of these subregions and individual countries within them will be introduced briefly, including tables providing historic, demographic, and economic data as presented in the CIA *World Factbook*. As with all census data, aggregates can hide as much as they allegedly tell. The numbers are included here to highlight some of the historical, demographic, and economic differences between countries in the same region, rather than making absolute statements about the countries themselves.

North Africa

North Africa stretches from the Atlantic Ocean to the Red Sea along the Mediterranean coast. On the far western side are Morocco, Western Sahara, and Mauritania. Mauritania is an Islamic republic in geographic West Africa, and there is disagreement over whether its political system or cultural ties with Africa should prevail when classifying Mauritania as part of the international order. Morocco can look back on its own 400-year-old monarchy, yet the country experienced both Spanish and French colonial influence. In turn, Morocco has claimed the territory of Western Sahara as historically Moroccan, while Western Saharan residents have been fighting for independence, and the United Nations has been so far unsuccessful at ending the conflict. Like Morocco, Algeria has a large Amazigh (Berber) minority population, whose members have been fighting for the recognition of their language and culture. Algeria was the first Arab territory to become a European colony, when French forces landed on its soil in 1830 and French citizens moved to Algeria to settle permanently. Tunisia experienced less extensive French colonization, and is geographically the smallest of all North African countries, made famous most recently by providing the spark that set off the 2011 Arab uprisings. Libya was ruled by Italy during the colonial period, while Egypt was ruled by the British. The Sudan was ruled jointly by Egypt and the British until it gained independence. In 2011, after a Southern Sudanese vote to secede from the North, South Sudan became an independent nation.

Historical trade routes through the Sahara into Central Africa established cultural and political links, which influenced North Africa in very different ways from Southwest Asia. For instance, North African food includes African spices (especially hot peppers) and grains (especially couscous) that are not commonly used in other countries of the Middle East. Contemporary political and economic interests connect North Africa closely

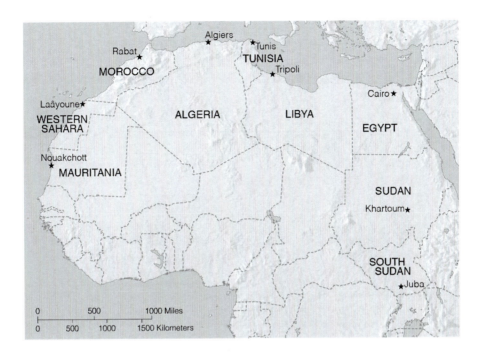

to Europe, and large migrant populations from North Africa live in France, Spain, and Scandinavia. The economies of poorer North African countries (especially Mauritania and the Sudan) depend on agriculture. Morocco, Tunisia, and Egypt have relied greatly on tourism. Libya, and to a lesser extent Algeria and Egypt, has oil and natural gas reserves, and Morocco is one of the largest exporters of phosphate. Few of the countries of North Africa have a diversified economy, and unemployment figures across the region are high, especially among the youth. Tunisian, Egyptian, and Libyan protests toppled long-standing authoritarian regimes. Subsequent elections brought new parties to power, but they have struggled to create stable political systems. In 2013 in Egypt, an army coup replaced the elected, Muslim Brotherhood–led government after only one year in office. Libya has been plagued by regional rivalries and militia violence.

Much of the terrain of North Africa is either desert or semidesert. The most significant fresh water tributary in the region is the river Nile in Egypt. Thanks to canals and elaborate irrigation systems, the Nile has sustained extensive agriculture and large populations. Egypt is the most populous country of North Africa; its population clusters along the Nile, leaving vast regions of the country virtually uninhabited. Only Morocco and parts of northern Algeria get sufficient rainfall to sustain rain-fed agriculture, thanks to the Atlas mountain range (with the highest elevation of Mount Toubkal at 13,600 feet). The vast majority of North Africa's population lives in urban centers along the Mediterranean coast.

Southwest Asia

Southwest Asia is the new designation for territories that Admiral Mahan had designated as the "Middle East" in 1902. Southwest Asia is primarily Arabic-speaking, with the

Table 1.1

North Africa

Country	Capital	Influenced and/ or colonized by	Population, in millions (2012)	GDP per capita in US$ (2011)
Morocco	Rabat	France and Spain	32.30	5,100
Western Sahara	Al-Ayoune*	Spain	0.52	2,500
Mauritania	Nouakchott	France	3.40	2,200
Algeria	Algiers	France	37.40	7,400
Tunisia	Tunis	France	10.70	9,600
Libya	Tripoli	Italy	5.60	14,100
Egypt	Cairo	Britain	83.70	6,600
Sudan**	Khartoum	Britain and Egypt	34.20	2,800
South Sudan	Juba	Britain and Egypt	10.60	—

*Western Sahara is currently under Moroccan control and has no recognized capital. Al-Ayoune is the largest city in Western Sahara. The GDP per capita figures are estimates from 2007.
**Since 2011, divided into Sudan (capital: Khartoum) and South Sudan (capital: Juba).
Source: Compiled from the CIA *World Factbook*, https://www.cia.gov/library/publications/the-world-factbook, accessed July 31, 2013.

exception of Turkey and Israel, and it can be further subdivided into two areas: the so-called Fertile Crescent along the eastern shores of the Mediterranean, and the Arabian Peninsula. With the exception of Turkey, Syria, and Lebanon, all countries in the region were under British colonial influence after the fall of the Ottoman Empire. Countries that are part of the Fertile Crescent are Turkey, Cyprus, Syria, Lebanon, Israel/Palestine, Iraq, and Jordan. The countries of the Arabian Peninsula are Saudi Arabia, Bahrain, Kuwait, Qatar, the United Arab Emirates (UAE), Oman and Yemen. They are often called the Gulf states, and it is these countries that, combined, own most of the known oil reserves in the world. The Mediterranean and the Indian Ocean are the waterways that historically facilitated trade routes, and hence cultural and political contact with different parts of the world. As a result, countries on the Arabian Peninsula display evidence of Indian and Persian cultural influences, whereas countries along the Mediterranean were more influenced by Europe and, via the Silk Road, Central Asia.

The Fertile Crescent

The Fertile Crescent contains those areas of the Middle East that receive the most annual rainfall, and it is here that rivers and rich alluvial soils provide a solid basis for a variety of agricultural crops. The Crescent starts in present-day Israel-Palestine and Lebanon, along the Jordan River, continues along the Lebanon mountain range that produces several rivers, and curves through south and southeast Turkey along the Anatolian plateau, into Iraq, following both the Euphrates and Tigris Rivers. It was along these rivers and in the valleys next to the snow-capped mountains that most of the ancient civilizations

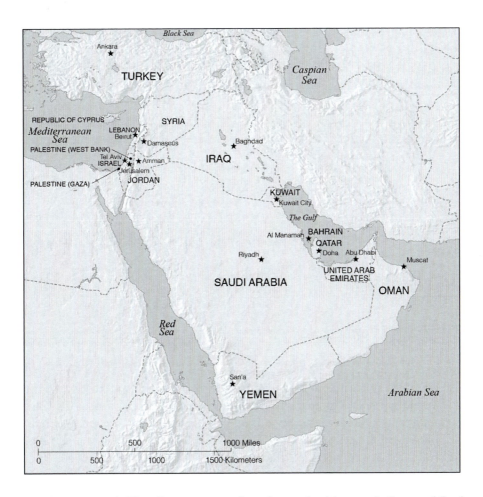

of the region emerged. The climate ranges from hot and arid zones in Iraq and Jordan to wet and cold weather in the mountains of Lebanon, along the eastern Black Sea coast, and the Anatolian plateau in Turkey. Occasionally, there is snowfall in Jerusalem. The Mediterranean coastline has mild temperatures during most of the year.

Turkey is the modern successor state to the Ottoman Empire, with its new capital in Ankara. Turkey straddles two continental plates, Asia and Europe, and therefore often presents itself as the bridge between the two. Turkey has a majority Muslim population, and it has aspired to become a member of the European Union. Cyprus, an island in the Mediterranean, is currently divided into the Republic of Cyprus and the Turkish Republic of Northern Cyprus as a result of conflict between Greek and Turkish Cypriots, allied with Greece and Turkey, respectively. Syria and Lebanon were under French colonial control after the fall of the Ottoman Empire, alone among their British-controlled neighbors (Palestine, Iraq, and Jordan). After the British left Palestine, the state of Israel was proclaimed in 1948, followed by a war that turned approximately 750,000 Palestinians into refugees, and that started the ongoing conflict over who has legitimate rights to the land one group calls Israel and the other group calls Palestine. After the end of Ottoman

Table 1.2

Fertile Crescent

Country	Capital	Influenced and/or colonized by	Population, in millions (2012)	GDP per capita in US$
Turkey	Ankara		79.7	14,700
Republic of Cyprus	Nicosia/ Lefkosia	Britain	1.2	29,400
Syria	Damascus	France	23.0	5,100
Lebanon	Beirut	France	4.1	15,700
Palestine: West Bank	East Jerusalem (contested)	Britain	2.6	2,900
Palestine: Gaza		Britain	1.7	no data
Israel	Tel Aviv/ Jerusalem (contested)	Britain	7.6	31,400
Iraq	Baghdad	Britain	31.0	3,900
Jordan	Amman	Britain	6.5	6,000

Source: Compiled from the CIA *World Factbook,* https://www.cia.gov/library/publications/the-world-factbook, accessed July 31, 2013.

rule, Iraq and Jordan became monarchies, with kings selected from the Hashemite clan of Saudi Arabia by British colonial powers. Jordan became independent as the Hashemite Kingdom of Transjordan in 1946, while Iraq, with its heritage of ancient Mesopotamia, became independent in 1932. Between 1948 and 1967, Jordan ruled the Palestinian West Bank; even today, Palestinians in Jordan are believed to outnumber the local Jordanian population.

The economies of Turkey, Cyprus, Israel-Palestine, Lebanon, and Syria depend heavily on agriculture and tourism, while Iraq is among the top five countries with the largest known oil reserves. Lebanon, parts of Syria, Turkey, Israel, Iraq, and the West Bank and Gaza still have about one-quarter to one-fifth of their labor force in agriculture. Citrus fruit and olives are the main export crops, mainly to markets in Europe. Lebanon markets itself as the "Paris of the Middle East," with casinos, restaurants, theaters, and fashion shows. Israel and the Palestinian Territories offer "Holy Land Tours" to visitors who want to see the places where Jesus lived and preached. Turkey is also a destination for tourists interested in Turkey's Byzantine and Ottoman pasts, as well as tourists interested in New Testament sites such as Ephesus reconfigured into large archeological parks. Syria, Jordan, and Iraq are each home to important archeological sites that showcase the multicultural past of the region. As valuable as the tourism sector can be, it is also quite vulnerable to political instability and war. Because of repeated conflicts in the Fertile Crescent, in particular, many of them related to the Israel-Palestine conflict and, more recently, the U.S. "war on terror," civil strife, and sectarian violence, the region has seen repeated economic setbacks and out-migrations to other parts of the world.

Table 1.3

Arabian Peninsula

Country	Capital	Influenced and/ or colonized by	Population, in millions (2012)	GDP per capita in US$
Saudi Arabia	Riyadh		26.5	24,500
Bahrain	Manama	Portugal and later Britain	1.2	27,900
Kuwait	Kuwait	Britain	2.6	42,200
Qatar	Qatar	Britain	2.0	104,300
United Arab Emirates	Abu Dhabi	Britain	5.3	48,800
Oman	Muscat	Britain	3.1	26,900
Yemen	Sanaa	Britain	24.8	2,300

Source: Compiled from the CIA *World Factbook*, https://www.cia.gov/library/publications/the-world-factbook, accessed July 31, 2013.

The Arabian Peninsula

The arid and semiarid Arabian Peninsula stands in sharp contrast to the Fertile Crescent. With the exception of the mountain regions in parts of Yemen, there is little annual rainfall, and limited opportunity for agriculture. Populations in the Gulf region have traditionally lived off herding and trading. Before oil was discovered in the early 1930s, an important revenue source for leaders who controlled Mecca and Medina—the places that gave birth to Islam—were pilgrims who visited the sites. With the oil industry, significant numbers of migrant workers have come to the Gulf. More than 80 percent of the labor force in Saudi Arabia and the United Arab Emirates are currently non-nationals.

In the late nineteenth century, the British were interested in the ports of Arabia in order to ensure the sea route from Britain to India. Therefore, they entered into "protectorate agreements" with local rulers: in return for using their ports, the British would give certain rulers military protection. The British thus used, among others, the ports at Aden (Yemen), Muscat (Oman), and Dubai (UAE). These "protected" Gulf emirates and kingdoms were some of the last countries in the region to obtain their independence. Bahrain, Kuwait, Qatar, and the UAE have small populations and large oil reserves, which give them some of the highest per capita GDP figures in the world. The UAE is currently home to the tallest building of the world, the Burj Khalifa, at more than 2,700 feet. Qatar is home to the popular, and at times controversial, cable network Al-Jazeera, and it has one of the world's largest proven natural gas reserves. In contrast, Yemen is one of the poorest countries in the world, ravaged by a long civil war in the late twentieth century, in the aftermath of political divisions between the northern and the southern regions of the country. A significant portion of its adult, male population works in oil-producing Gulf states or overseas. The ruler of Oman, Sultan Qaboos, is an absolute monarch who has ruled his country since 1970, which makes him the longest-lasting ruler of the Middle East.

The economies of the countries in the Arabian Peninsula depend largely on oil and natural gas production and refining. The countries that own these natural resources are called rentier states. Rentier states derive a substantial percentage of their national income from one main resource—in this case, oil—which they sell on the international market. The government collects the income and decides how to distribute it among the population. Oil states often offer free education, health care, and housing to their citizens, yet they have limited democratic rights or freedoms.

The Caucasus and Central Asia

The Caucasus and Central Asia are two regions that have historically connected Europe with Asia, in large part via the Silk Road. The area is landlocked, located on both sides of the large freshwater lake of the Caspian Sea. For many centuries, the mountainous Caucasus and Central Asia was an area where other empires—Persian, Greek, Roman, Arab, Ottoman, Russian, or Chinese—ended, and where local dynasties ruled. It was from this territory that new populations migrated to those empires, and at times destabilized or overthrew them. The inhabitants of these regions were among the earliest converts to Islam, and some of the most important contemporary branches of Sufi Islam originated here, which is why the Caucasus and Central Asia are frequently discussed under the rubric "Middle East." Around the same time that Britain and France expanded into North Africa and Southwest Asia, the Russian Empire began to conquer territory in the Caucasus and Central Asia. From 1813 until the early 1900s, Britain and Russia jockeyed over dominance in the region, in what Rudyard Kipling called the "Great Game." After World War I, the communist Red Army defeated Caucasian and Central Asian nationalists and integrated their territories into what became the Soviet Union. The Caucasus and Central Asia were cut off from their traditional trading and migration routes (and from the field of Middle East studies; see Chapter 2) when the Iron Curtain descended after 1945. After the dissolution of the Soviet Union in 1991, newly independent countries emerged, comprising Russian minority populations, mostly Russian Orthodox Christian or secular, and indigenous ethnic communities that adhere either to other branches of Orthodox Christianity (such as Armenians) or to different forms of Islam (the rest of Central Asia).

The Caucasus is named for the Caucasus mountain range, with the highest elevation at Mount Elbrus at 18,500 feet. The region between the Black Sea and the Caspian Sea is currently divided into North Caucasus—part of the Russian Federation—and South Caucasus, the three independent countries of Azerbaijan, Armenia, and Georgia, which the CIA *World Factbook* includes on its map of the "Middle East." The area is mountainous and has historically been home to a variety of ethnic, linguistic, and religious communities. Azerbaijan is predominantly Turkic-speaking (Azeri) and Muslim. Armenian is a language unrelated to any other in the region—legend says that God revealed it to an Armenian monk. Most Georgians are Orthodox Christians or secular, but Georgia also harbors minority communities of Azeris and Armenians. Since achieving national inde-

pendence, Armenia and Azerbaijan have had territorial disputes over Nagorno Karabakh, an area inhabited by Armenians inside Azerbaijan. As a result, Armenia's borders with Azerbaijan and its ally Turkey have been closed, severely limiting Armenian trade.

During the Soviet period, all three countries were economically integrated within the Soviet bloc, but in independence they have established links to Europe and, in the case of Azerbaijan and Georgia, to Turkey. Azerbaijan has significant gas reserves, and it is mineral rich. Azerbaijan's capital, Baku, was home to the oldest and largest oil field in the world at the turn of the nineteenth century. The famous World War II Battle of Stalingrad between Germany and the Soviet Union was fought over control of the Baku oil fields. Almost half of Armenia's labor force is in agriculture, and it remains heavily dependent on Russian investments and the remittances from Armenians abroad. More than half of Georgia's labor force works in agriculture. Georgia's neighbors to the north are Russia's North Caucasian republics of Chechnya and Dagestan, among others, which have been fighting for their independence from Russia. A dispute over South Ossetia led to armed conflict between Georgia and Russia in 2008.

Central Asia includes five former Soviet republics—Kazakhstan, Kyrgyzstan, Tajikistan, Turkmenistan, and Uzbekistan—in addition to Afghanistan and Iran. Its geography is varied, from mountainous regions with snow and rain to dry steppes and severe desert climates. Over the course of the year, but also during the course of a day, temperatures tend to fluctuate significantly. From the Tien Shan, the Pamir Plateau, and the Hindu Kush (from Kyrgyzstan, Tajikistan, Afghanistan to parts of Pakistan) to the Zagros and Elburz Mountains in Iran, Central Asia is part of the great Himalayan mountain range, the largest in the world. Kazakhstan, the largest Central Asian republic, is home to desert and steppe, but also has access to the large water reservoirs of the Caspian and Aral Seas and Lake Balkhash. The two main rivers in Central Asia are the Amu Darya (formerly called the Oxus) and the Syr Darya. Because of irrigation schemes to support agricultural projects along the way, the river levels have been dropping, and due to fertilizers and pesticides, water pollution is on the rise. Kyrgyz and Tajik control of water upstream via a series of hydroelectric dams has led to water conflicts with downstream countries.

Historically, the residents of the region's former Soviet republics are descendants of diverse Iranian and Turkic populations that were converted to Islam over the course of the seventh to tenth centuries CE. Central Asia was home to the relatively short-lived empires of Genghis Khan (1162–1227 CE) and Tamerlane (1336–1405 CE), as well as several important centers of Islamic learning, such as Osh (in present-day Kyrgyzstan), Bukhara, and Samarkand (in present-day Uzbekistan). The area received much of its wealth from trade along the Silk Road until the early seventeenth century, when ships replaced caravans. The Central Asian republics received their names under Soviet rule, based on majority ethnic groups in each territory, and they became independent countries for the first time in 1991. Central Asian countries have been strategic allies in the United States and NATO war efforts in Afghanistan, providing military bases and supply lines.

Persia (name changed to Iran in 1935) and Afghanistan were important stops along the Silk Road, and Central Asian populations migrated for centuries back and forth. Sizable minority Turkic-speaking populations still live in the northern border regions of Iran and Afghanistan today. Persian is Iran's official language, while Afghanistan's two official languages, Pashtun and Dari, are related to Persian. The Qajar Dynasty ruled Iran from 1796 until 1925—although with much British and Russian interference. It was overthrown and replaced by the Pahlavi Dynasty, which lasted until 1979, when Iran became the Islamic Republic of Iran after a popular revolution. Afghanistan obtained its independence from Britain after the Anglo-Afghan war of 1919, first as a monarchy, and, after 1964, as a republic. Government changed often. In this context of political as well as economic instability, the Soviet Union invaded the country in 1979 and installed a pro-Soviet government. In response, the United States, as well as some of Afghanistan's neighbors, armed and financed Muslim fighters, called the mujahideen, to counter the Soviet occupation. In 1989, Soviet forces withdrew, plunging Afghanistan into civil war. The victorious Muslim fundamentalist Taliban sheltered al-Qaeda, leading to a U.S.-led invasion after the 9/11 attacks. Still embattled, Afghanistan is one of the poorest nations in the world today.

Additionally, Pakistan has been included on some maps of the Middle East because of its majority Muslim population. Pakistan obtained its independence from Great Britain in 1947. Clearly part of geographic South Asia, Pakistan has nevertheless had strong ties to its Middle Eastern Muslim neighbors, especially Afghanistan. Afghanistan and Pakistan

Table 1.4

Caucasus and Central Asia

Country	Capital	Influenced and/or colonized by	Population, in millions (2012)	GDP per capita in US$
Azerbaijan	Baku	Russia	9.5	10,300
Armenia	Yerevan	Russia	3.0	5,500
Georgia	Tbilisi	Russia	4.6	5,600
Kazakhstan	Astana	Russia	17.5	13,200
Kyrgyzstan	Bishkek	Russia	5.5	2,400
Tajikistan	Dushanbe	Russia	7.8	2,100
Turkmenistan	Ashgabat	Russia	5.1	7,900
Uzbekistan	Tashkent	Russia	28.4	3,300
Iran	Tehran	Britain and Russia	79.0	13,200
Afghanistan	Kabul	Britain and Russia	30.4	1,000
Pakistan	Islamabad	Britain	190.3	2,800

Source: Compiled from the CIA *World Factbook*, https://www.cia.gov/library/publications/the-world-factbook, accessed July 31, 2013.

are both centers of Taliban insurgencies and targets of ongoing U.S. efforts to dismantle al-Qaeda. In 2011, Osama bin Laden, the leader of al-Qaeda, was tracked down and killed in Pakistan.

The economy of Central Asia is tied to its significant oil and gas reserves, which will become increasingly important in the future, as Gulf oil production approaches its peak. According to the U.S. Energy Information Administration, Kazakhstan is aiming to become a top oil exporter within the next decade, with an estimated 30 billion barrels of proven oil reserves. Azerbaijan, Turkmenistan, and Uzbekistan have substantial natural gas reserves, but they currently lack the infrastructure to capture and export their resources efficiently. Central Asian republics also rely on their agricultural sector for export revenues. Iran has some of the largest oil reserves in the world, while neighboring Afghanistan is claimed to have rich unmined mineral deposits. In the early twenty-first century, Iran has been subjected to severe economic sanctions by the world community because of its unsupervised nuclear program. Pakistan owns nuclear weapons, and it has both industry and agriculture, but its large population remains mostly poor. Pakistan is a recipient of significant U.S. and European foreign aid.

To conclude, no agreement exists among scholars about the precise boundaries around the region called the Middle East. Should the northern border be Turkey or the Central Asian republic of Kazakhstan? Do we include or exclude Iran, Afghanistan, and Pakistan? In the west, does the map end with Morocco, Western Sahara, or Mauritania? Cyprus is a divided island, with half claimed by Greece and half claimed by Turkey in an unsettled dispute. Should only Turkish Cyprus be part of the region? Turkey has applied for membership of the European Union, but does that mean it would no longer be part of the Middle East? Finally, we may ask who has the authority to draw the boundaries under discussion? Academics or politicians? Colonial powers or local residents? If the inhabitants get to decide, what if they disagree among themselves? Feeling confused? Welcome to Middle East studies!

Looking closely at the terms we use and boundaries we draw in discussions on the Middle East is not a trivial exercise. Each geographic designation has a history, and each comes with its own political baggage. At stake in these border discussions are questions and claims of inclusion or exclusion. Including or excluding Cyprus, Israel, Palestine, or Western Sahara on maps of the Middle East makes a political statement that endorses or denies claims to national identity and self-determination. Maps recognize communities by including them, and delegitimize them by excluding them. There are maps on the Internet that show Israel but not Palestine, as well as maps that show the opposite—a very real reflection of the ongoing conflict over contested territory. The act of drawing a map of Kurdistan in Turkey or of Amazigh territories in North Africa can be considered an act of treason, as those borders challenge existing national boundaries.

In contemporary discussions of the Middle East, we therefore need to remain mindful of the historical origins of existing boundaries and terms. As you read on, keep in mind that what we call the "Middle East" is first and foremost an idea, and only second a reality. Ideas have significant power to move people to action, and ideas can change, as can realities—which brings us right back to the beginning of this chapter and the Arab uprisings. There are new generations growing up in the region that seek to shape new realities and new opportunities. It is to them that this book is dedicated.

References and Further Research

Beckwith, Christopher I. 2009. *Empires of the Silk Road: A History of Central Eurasia from the Bronze Age to the Present*. Princeton, NJ: Princeton University Press.

Bonine, Michael E., Abbas Amanat, and Michael E. Gasper, eds. 2012. *Is There a Middle East? The Evolution of a Geopolitical Concept*. Stanford, CA: Stanford University Press.

Cleveland, William L., and Martin Bunton. 2009. *A History of the Modern Middle East*. 4th ed. Boulder, CO: Westview Press.

Davidson, Roderic H. 1960. "Where Is the Middle East?" *Foreign Affairs* 38, no. 4: 665–675.

Gelvin, James L. 2012. *The Arab Uprisings: What Everyone Needs to Know*. New York: Oxford University Press.

Goodson, Larry P. 2001. *Afghanistan's Endless War: State Failure, Regional Politics, and the Rise of the Taliban*. Seattle: University of Washington Press.

Haas, Mark, and David Lesch, eds. 2013. *The Arab Spring: Change and Resistance in the Middle East*. Boulder, CO: Westview Press.

Hodgson, Marshall. 1974. *The Venture of Islam: Conscience and History in a World Civilization*. 3 vols. Chicago: University of Chicago Press.

Leland, William, and Martin Bunton. 2012. *A History of the Modern Middle East*. 5th ed. Boulder, CO: Westview Press.

Mandel Khan, Gabriel. 2001. *Arabic Script: Styles, Variants, and Calligraphic Adaptations*. Translated from Italian. New York: Abbeville Press.

Said, Edward. 1978. *Orientalism*. New York: Pantheon.

Shaheen, Jack. 2001. *Reel Bad Arabs: How Hollywood Vilifies a People*. New York: Olive Branch Press.

2

History and Politics of Middle East Studies

LUCIA VOLK

Global studies, as an academic program and pedagogy, has in many ways replaced an older paradigm called "area studies." Dividing the world into areas based on language and cultures, these older programs of study were created as part of an effort to preempt the spread of communism in the so-called Third World. Knowing about the world during the Cold War was predicated on questions of national security and balance of power. In 1958 the U.S. Congress passed the National Defense Education Act (NDEA), which made federal funds available so that colleges and universities could enhance their science, math, and foreign language courses. The Soviet Union had launched the Sputnik satellite into orbit the previous year, which created a deep sense of urgency among U.S. politicians that the United States had to catch up. Under the auspices of the Higher Education Act of 1965 (HEA), which expanded the provisions of NDEA Title VI, government-funded area studies programs began to produce regional specialists, with a particular interest in regions (potentially) under influence of communism. Area studies were conceived as intrinsically interdisciplinary: students would become proficient in the language, history, politics, and culture of any particular region. In order to understand an area in depth, it was therefore necessary to transcend the boundaries of traditional academic departments.

At the same time that the political ideology of the Cold War divided the world into allies and enemies, the politics of the Israeli-Palestinian conflict added a further complexity in Middle East studies. Not only did the Israeli-Palestinian conflict become one of the most heavily studied conflicts in the region—eclipsing the much bloodier Turkish-Kurdish conflict nearby, for instance—but Israeli-Palestinian scholarship was often driven by justifying one or the other side in the conflict. Indeed, even if an article did not justify either side, the scholar was evaluated by the question "Whose side are you on?" For instance, the work of the Princeton historian Bernard Lewis (b. 1916) has been read as supportive of Israel's policies of Palestinian occupation, whereas the Columbia comparative literature professor Edward Said (1935–2003) was often accused of defending Palestinian aggression against Israel. London-born Bernard Lewis is Jewish and has played a role as foreign policy adviser for U.S. presidents, whereas Edward Said, whose parents were Arab Christians, was Palestinian and did not have similar access to Washington circles. These associations have been used to elevate (or denigrate) each man's academic work, whether or not a particular book or body of research deals directly with Israel or Palestine.

Both Lewis's and Said's respective universities have been home to influential centers of Middle Eastern or Near Eastern studies, which are among about twenty National

Resource Centers (NRCs) focusing on the Middle East that are located across the United States and receive federal support under Title VI. Since the NRCs were created after the start of the Cold War, and after the Soviet Union had taken control of Central Asia, the study of that region, also called "Eurasia" or "Inner Asia," has traditionally been part of the Russia/Eastern Europe NRCs in the United States. In order to be eligible to apply for federal support, existing academic programs in any area studies specialty need to provide evidence of a wide variety of courses in the social sciences, humanities, and the major languages of the region, in order to prove that they can transmit both general and specific case study knowledge of the region. NRCs are under continued supervision and outside evaluation, and they need to reapply for funding every four years.

Information on the National Resource Centers (NRCs) for Foreign Language, Area & International Studies, funded by the U.S. Department of Education, can be found at the NRC website (http://www.nrcweb.org/index.aspx).

A full listing of all the NRCs devoted to Middle East studies can be generated on the "List of NRCs" page (http://www.nrcweb.org/nrcList.aspx) by using the "World Area" menu.

Since the National Resource Centers' funding enabled universities to make resources available to faculty and students, as well as to local communities and constituencies via outreach programs, the interest in the study of less commonly taught languages, such as Arabic, Hebrew, Turkish, and Persian (and others) grew, and more students as well as faculty traveled to the Middle East in order to improve their language skills or conduct field studies. As a matter of course, the topics of research became more contemporary, and fieldwork- and interview-based, in addition to the more traditional archival, text-based work of earlier scholars, many of them in Departments of Near Eastern Languages. At some universities, centers of Middle East studies were opened in addition to departments of Near Eastern languages, with the former focusing on late Ottoman, colonial, and national periods, and the latter on ancient and medieval histories.

In 1966, a group of fifty scholars, including Bernard Lewis, decided to create the Middle East Studies Association (MESA), a private, nonprofit organization that supports and promotes studies of the Middle East. MESA conducts annual national conferences and publishes scholarly journals, such as the *International Journal of Middle East Studies* (*IJMES*), which is considered the flagship publication in the field of Middle East studies. An eight-member board of directors is elected by the membership, comprised of students and faculty from around the world. The membership has grown from the initial fifty to about 3,000. In addition to fostering the study of the region, MESA is also concerned with improving teaching tools and curricula. Its Committee of Academic Freedom monitors incidents of intimidation and harassment of faculty members who study the Middle East.

Box 2.1

Programs of Study in the United States and Abroad

Among the oldest programs, centers, or institutes of Middle East studies, Near East studies, or Central Asian (or Eurasian) studies in the United States are the following:

Harvard University, Center for Middle Eastern Studies	http://cmes.hmdc.harvard.edu/
Indiana University, Inner Asian and Uralic NRC at the School of Global and International Studies	http://www.indiana.edu/~iaunrc/
Princeton University, Department of Near Eastern Studies	http://www.princeton.edu/nes/
University of California at Berkeley, Center for Middle Eastern Studies	http://cmes.berkeley.edu/
University of California, Los Angeles, Center for Near Eastern Studies	http://www.international.ucla.edu/cnes
University of Chicago, Center for Middle Eastern Studies	http://cmes.uchicago.edu/
University of Kansas, Center for Russian, East European and Eurasian Studies	http://www.crees.ku.edu/
University of Michigan, Ann Arbor, Center for Middle Eastern and North African Studies	http://www.ii.umich.edu/cmenas/
University of Texas at Austin, Center for Middle Eastern Studies	https://www.utexas.edu/cola/depts/ mes/center/cmes.php
University of Illinois at Urbana-Champaign, Russian, East European, and Eurasian Center	http://www.reeec.illinois.edu/

Other renowned English-language regional studies centers are at universities in the Middle East and in Europe:

American University of Beirut, Lebanon, Center for Arab and Middle Eastern Studies	http://www.aub.edu.lb/fas/cames/ Pages/index.aspx
American University in Cairo, Egypt, Middle East Studies Center	http://www.aucegypt.edu/gapp/mesc/ Pages/default.aspx

(continued)

Box 2.1 *(continued)*

Central Asia-Caucasus Institute and Silk Road Studies Program, run jointly by Johns Hopkins University and the Institute for Security and Development Policy in Stockholm	http://www.silkroadstudies.org/new/index.htm
School of Oriental and African Studies (SOAS), London, Department of the Languages and Cultures of the Near and Middle East and Centre of Contemporary Central Asia and the Caucasus	http://www.soas.ac.uk/nme/ http://www.soas.ac.uk/cccac/
St. Antony's College, Oxford University, UK, Middle East Centre and Russian and Eurasian Studies	http://www.sant.ox.ac.uk/mec/ http://www.sant.ox.ac.uk/russian/index.html
Cambridge University, UK, Asian and Middle Eastern Studies	http://www.ames.cam.ac.uk
University of Bergen, Norway, Centre for Middle Eastern and Islamic Studies	http://www.smi.uib.no/smi.html
University of Leiden, the Netherlands, Middle Eastern Studies	http://hum.leiden.edu/middle-eastern-studies

For more information about the Middle East Studies Association (MESA), consult its website (http://www.mesa.arizona.edu/about/index.html).

The increasing politicization of Middle East scholars after the start of the two U.S.-led wars in Afghanistan and Iraq in the early 2000s led to the founding of a rival organization for the study of the Middle East, the Association for the Study of the Middle East and Africa (ASMEA). Bernard Lewis was, again, one of the founding members (along with the late Professor Fouad Ajami, former director of Middle East Studies at Johns Hopkins University), as he considered MESA to be too reflexively critical of America's role in the Middle East, as well as too hostile to Israel. MESA members, in turn, tend to consider ASMEA beholden to (and funded by) those forces in Washington that promote U.S. intervention in the region.

For more information about Association for the Study of the Middle East and Africa (ASMEA), consult its website (http://www.asmeascholars.org/).

During the 1960s and 1970s, many of the seminal works of Middle East studies were published. Among them are *Arabic Thought in the Liberal Age, 1789–1939* (1962), by Albert Hourani, and *The Middle East and the West* (1964), by Bernard Lewis. Both books attempted to describe the Middle East's engagement with or rejection of the West, based on the author's evaluation of cultural similarities or differences. Hourani emphasized points of intersection, while Lewis focused on points of conflict. The economic interdependence between the Middle East and the West was illustrated in *Cotton and the Egyptian Economy, 1820–1914: A Study in Trade and Development* (1969), by Roger Owen. By looking at a single commodity, cotton, Owen was able to show that Egypt's economy grew tremendously in the nineteenth and early twentieth centuries, yet this did not translate into development for Egypt, because of foreign control over exports and foreign ownership of the best available lands. The book *Muhammad* (1971), by Maxime Rodinson, similarly looked at economic and social conditions as explanations for the growth and spread of Islam in the Middle Ages. With *The Venture of Islam: Conscience and History in a World Civilization* (1974), Marshall Hodgson presented a three-volume opus on the emergence and spread of Islam, contextualized in a framework of broader world history. Hodgson described the ways that far-flung Islamic societies drew from surrounding cultures and civilizations. What all of these scholars tried to emphasize were the long-standing and mutual connections between the Middle East and the West, or between the Middle East and the world more broadly.

These prominent early scholarly works focused on the history of the region, from the emergence of Islam through the time of the Ottoman Empire. Yet, as Western colonialism drew to a close, more and more scholars focused on its effects on the region. Frantz Fanon's *The Wretched of the Earth* (1963), which he wrote in response to his own observations during the Algerian struggle for independence against France, is considered one of the core works in this canon. Trained in psychology and psychiatry, Fanon argued that colonization left deep mental scars on the colonized as well as the colonizer, and that the colonized needed the catharsis of violent rebellion against their oppressors in order to free both mind and body from their subjugation. Colonialism of Muslim societies by the Soviet Union became the subject of Gregory Massell's widely read and cited *The Surrogate Proletariat* (1974). He showed how "the liberation of women" became a central thrust of Soviet efforts to promote global revolution. Class struggle and gender struggle, in other words, were closely linked, and women who left their homes to become laborers, and who took off their veils while doing so, became the "surrogate proletariat." Whether capitalist or communist, modernizing ideologies of the West had a profound impact on the Middle East and Central Asia.

Western colonialism of the Middle East and its effects on Western scholarship of the region were the central point of study in Edward Said's *Orientalism* (1978). Said stipulated that the existing unequal power relations between the West and the Middle East had an impact on "knowledge" produced about the Middle East. He was emphatic that the colonial interests of Western powers made necessary a view of the Middle East as submissive, backwards, and uncivilized. In other word, the Middle East "needed" the West as a civilizing power. The quotation marks around "knowledge" and "needed"

Box 2.2

Applying Said's Framework

Columbia University anthropology professor Lila Abu-Lughod, a student of Edward Said's, later applied his method of analysis to Western military involvements in Iraq and Afghanistan. In a 2002 essay, which was later published as a book (*Do Muslim Women Need Saving?*), she traced the discussions in Western media about the "need to save Muslim women (from Muslim men, from Islam)," and showed that the concern for women in the Middle East rises and falls with Western strategic interests. In other words, according to Abu-Lughod, what Muslims in the Middle East are alleged to need stands in direct correlation with what Western policymakers want at any given point in time.

indicate that the assessment of what the region required was contingent on the view of a particular kind of Westerner, one that thought about how best to colonize the Middle East. With this critique of past and present Western scholarship about the "Orient," Said called on all students and scholars of the Middle East to begin by acknowledging their own biases before they start to discuss the Middle East.

Since the collapse of the Soviet Union, the premise that long shaped area studies has shifted. Moreover, national boundaries are thought to matter much less, due to significant transborder flows of information, money, and migrant laborers and refugees. Berlin is currently home to the third-largest Turkish community after Istanbul and Ankara; large North African neighborhoods define the urban landscapes of Paris and Marseille; and a firm in Los Angeles publishes an Iranian-American telephone directory. Diaspora communities often remain closely linked to their countries of origin, providing a point of entry for relatives who want to migrate, and sending back significant sums in remittance money. These kinds of transnational, cross-border linkages establish new kinds of geographic units that challenge national sovereignty and regional order. In response to these new trends, the field of global studies gained popularity.

Rather than looking at governments' allegiances to communism or capitalism, the prime motivation was now to assess "possible trajectories for transitions to democracy and free markets in the Middle East" (Khosrowjah 2011, 137). Government and private funders turned to "democracy projects." This new turn of scholarship opened a great divide between some scholars who considered the Middle East's failure to democratize a direct outcome of an Arab, Muslim, or Middle Eastern "mindset" that could not comprehend the way of Western democracies, and other scholars who looked to colonialism and neoliberalism (i.e., systems set up by the West) to explain the same failures. Examples of the first school of thought include the political scientist Samuel Huntington (1984) and historian Bernard Lewis (1996), and examples of the second included Augustus Richard Norton (1995) and Raymond Hinnebusch (2006). Scholars in the first camp can point to groups like the Taliban to make their case. Others can point to the Arab uprisings of 2011 and equally emphatically declare that democratic forces are alive and well in the Middle East. Of course, not all scholars can be neatly categorized as being part of the one or the other side of the debate. Yet they will likely position themselves along a continuum between the two, thereby implicitly reinforcing them.

Another shift in academic thinking on the Middle East occurred after the attacks on the World Trade Center in New York and the Pentagon in Washington, DC, on September 11, 2001. Academic research projects on political Islam and Islamic fundamentalism proliferated. However, very few Middle East experts expected the Green Movement to emerge in Iran in 2009 or the Arab Spring to break out across the Middle East in 2011. The main actors in these events were generally not Islamists. They were youths, student organizations, labor movements, and women's and other civic organizations, who turned out in public squares to demand a change of leadership, economic opportunities, and civil liberties. The two most prominent slogans that were used in these uprisings were "Bread, Freedom, Justice," and "The people want the fall of the regime." Islamist voices were part of the larger movements, but not the driving force. They emerged into the political limelight in the subsequent elections in Tunisia and Egypt because they could rely on organizational structures in their communities that brought out the vote. Once in power, Islamist parties remained under close scrutiny from the people who had taken to the streets. One year into Mohammed Morsi's presidency in Egypt, protesters again filled Tahrir Square to demand that he leave his post. The military took control and clamped down on the Muslim Brotherhood. In 2014, former general Abdel Fattah el-Sisi was elected president of Egypt. At the end of 2013, Tunisia's ruling Islamist party agreed to hand over power to a civilian caretaker government. New elections are to take place in late 2014. Clearly, secular forces remain important in the Middle East. Striving to better understand the ways in which the secular and religious interact with and accommodate each other will lead to a better understanding of Middle East politics.

For scholars of and in the Middle East, these are challenging new times. The first decade of the twenty-first century might have been a decade of wars of intervention and political change imposed from the outside. The second decade of the century opened with compelling stories of claims for change from within. Change never comes easy, especially in economically trying times, which limits what politicians are willing or able to do. High expectations for change after so many years of political status quo are unlikely to be met. Scholars are searching to remake old theories or invent new ones, and citizens of the Middle East are striving to remake their realities. Pointing out global links between social movements, the increasing importance of a discourse of human and civil rights, the deep gap between generations, and a general disenchantment with economic realities will be part of the challenge for those who study the Middle East.

Despite the sense of new beginnings in academic ventures, it is important to state that one factor will remain constant: the Middle East and the West continue to be linked in unequal ways. The United States dominates the region militarily, even if reluctantly. While plans exist to pull U.S. troops out of Afghanistan, perhaps entirely, the strategic importance of the region is unlikely to diminish. The U.S. Fifth Fleet will likely remain in Bahrain, and it will continue to patrol the waters of the Indian Ocean and the Gulf, the hub

---

Box 2.3

Popular Uprisings Across the World

The Green Movement in Iran and the Arab uprisings (or Arab Spring) were ideologically linked to the "color revolutions" in former Soviet-run republics of Georgia (2003), Ukraine (2004), and Kyrgyzstan (2005). These revolutions—using the language of human rights, freedom of speech, civil liberties, and social justice—were mainly nonviolent protests that aimed to bring down unpopular regimes.

---

of most of the world's oil trade. The damage caused by the decade-long wars in Iraq and Afghanistan will take a long time to fix. Residents will continue to mourn friends and relatives they have lost. Despite firm plans to reduce Western economies' reliance on Middle East oil, by finding energy alternatives or turning to local sources, they will not be able to do entirely without Saudi oil supplies, as well as the Saudi government's power to stabilize oil supply and prices due to its vast reserves.

Concern about the rising influence of political (and radical) Islam will ensure that Islamism remains a staple topic within Middle East studies. It stands to reason that Western governments will continue to create funding opportunities for those who want to study and teach in countries of "strategic interest." Moreover, the West is likely to continue its special relationship with Israel, and to be involved in efforts to broker a peace between Israelis and Palestinians to settle the long-standing conflict, which has led to multiple wars and crises between Israel, Palestinians, and surrounding Middle Eastern states. It is therefore probable that academic Middle East programs will remain politicized. Those who want to learn about the region need to be mindful of the influence of politics on ongoing scholarship, by investigating the sources of funding and the institutions that support the scholarship that they read.

In 2002, Daniel Pipes, director of the conservative think tank Middle East Forum, created a website called Campus Watch. On the site, he asked college students to report their instructors online, for all Internet readers to see, if they criticized Israel or made anti-American statements. In April 2003, former senator Rick Santorum (R-PA) drafted legislation that would cut federal funding from U.S. colleges or universities if they permitted faculty or students to criticize Israel openly. In October 2003, while voting to renew federal funding for National Resource Centers, the U.S. House of Representatives created a supervisory board to ensure that the scholarship in the funded universities reflected U.S. national interests, and mandated that Centers of Middle East Studies made student data available to government agencies for recruitment purposes. Meanwhile, since 2005, a Palestinian-led Boycott, Divestment, and Sanctions (BDS) movement has attempted to mobilize for the global isolation of Israel, including the dissolution of ties with Israeli academic institutions. At issue in all these cases are questions of academic freedom and the right to fair and free academic inquiry and exchange.

Recent wars and uprisings have unsettled not just governmental elites in the Middle East, but also academics across universities. The idea that the "Middle East" as a region can be understood through a few opposing lenses, such as the spread of "democracy" versus the spread of "radical Islamism," has been discredited. Increasingly, we see the limitations of asking questions that reduce conversations to either/or, and "us" versus "them." Instead of asking, "Is the Middle East capable of democracy (or human rights, or women's rights, etc.)?" why not ask, "What conditions facilitate democratic governance, here and there?" Most important, perhaps, we need to put more seats at the tables where these debates take place.

The production of knowledge about the Middle East will remain a contentious field in the foreseeable future. The wars in Iraq and Afghanistan, the ongoing Israeli-Palestinian conflict, the recent uprisings that have toppled autocratic governments, sectarian conflicts, and the confrontations between secular and religious forces present enormous challenges for residents of the region as well as those inside and outside the Middle East who want to understand what is happening and to forecast what will happen next.

References and Further Research

Abu-Lughod, Lila. 2013. *Do Muslim Women Need Saving?* Cambridge, MA: Harvard University Press.

Fanon, Frantz. 1963. *The Wretched of the Earth.* Translated from the French by Constance Farrington. New York: Grove Press.

Fawcett, Louise, ed. 2013. *International Relations of the Middle East.* 3rd ed. Oxford: Oxford University Press.

Gause, F. Gregory, III. 2002. "Who Lost Middle Eastern Studies?" *Foreign Affairs* 81 (March/April): 164–168.

Hinnebusch, Raymond. 2006. "Authoritarian Persistence, Democratization Theory and the Middle East: An Overview and Critique." *Democratization* 13, no. 3 (June): 373–395.

Hodgson, Marshall. 1974. *The Venture of Islam: Conscience and History in a World Civilization.* Chicago: Chicago University Press.

Hourani, Albert. 1962. *Arabic Thought in the Liberal Age, 1789–1939.* Cambridge: Cambridge University Press.

Huntington, Samuel P. 1984. "Will More Countries Become Democratic?" *Political Science Quarterly* 99, no. 2 (Summer): 193–218.

Khosrowjah, Hossein. 2011. "A Brief History of Area Studies and International Studies." *Arab Studies Quarterly* 33, no. 3–4: 131–142.

Lewis, Bernard. 1964. *The Middle East and the West.* Bloomington: Indiana University Press.

———. 1996. "A Historical Overview: Islam and Liberal Democracy." *Journal of Democracy* 7, no. 2: 52–63.

Lockman, Zachary. 2004. *Contending Visions of the Middle East: The History and Politics of Orientalism.* Cambridge: Cambridge University Press.

Mamdani, Mahmood. 2004. *Good Muslim, Bad Muslim: America, the Cold War, and the Roots of Terror.* New York: Pantheon Books.

Massell, Gregory. 1974. *The Surrogate Proletariat: Moslem Women and Revolutionary Strategies in Soviet Central Asia, 1919–1929.* Princeton, NJ: Princeton University Press.

Nader, Laura. 2013. *Culture and Dignity: Dialogues Between the Middle East and the West*. Hoboken, NJ: Wiley-Blackwell.

Norton, Augustus Richard, ed. 1995. *Civil Society in the Middle East*. Leiden: Brill.

Owen, Roger. 1969. *Cotton and the Egyptian Economy, 1820–1914: A Study in Trade and Development*. Oxford: Oxford University Press.

Rodinson, Maxime. 1971. *Muhammad*. Translated from the French by Anne Carter. New York: Pantheon Books.

Said, Edward. 1978. *Orientalism*. New York: Pantheon.

Tessler, Mark, ed. 1999. *Area Studies and Social Science: Strategies for Understanding Middle East Politics*. Bloomington: Indiana University Press.

Part Two

Fundamentals

3

Introduction to Middle East History

LUCIA VOLK

Most Western school children today are introduced to the Middle East through lessons on ancient Egypt. That is in part a result of a long-standing Western fascination with ancient Middle Eastern history. During the nineteenth and early twentieth centuries, European archeological excavation teams headed to the Middle East in order to find the remains of ancient empires of Mesopotamia, Egypt, and Persia. Biblical archeologists excavated sites mentioned in the scriptures, in order to prove the historical truth of faith narratives. About the same time this research into antiquity began, Western governments established colonial rule over the region. The military and the scholarly exploration of the region often went hand in hand. When the French emperor Napoleon I led an expedition to Egypt in 1798, he took with him an "army of scholars" to document ancient and modern Egypt—a multiyear endeavor that resulted in the academic field of Egyptology in Paris, as well as a multivolume set of publications under the title *Descriptions of Egypt* (1809–1829). The first American scholarly expeditions to go and claim parts of ancient history were organized in the late nineteenth century. Phoebe Apperson Hearst, mother of the newspaper mogul William Randolph Hearst, sponsored a University of California, Berkeley, excavation in Egypt, and the University of Pennsylvania mounted an expedition to Iraq in search of the famed city-state of Babylon.

This Western focus on ancient history created a deeply rooted image of the Middle East as a place of the past. Western archeologists at the turn of the century did not go on their expeditions to encounter their contemporaries—they wanted to go back in time. Similarly, most Western tourists today go to the Middle East to encounter its past, not its present. Pyramids and mummies are prominent in the Western imagination about the Middle East, whether through television documentaries or popular science fiction movies. The sarcophagus of the "Golden King" Tutankhamen, fondly referred to as King Tut, is probably the most visited archeological artifact on earth. In order to generate tourism, the countries of the Middle East have had to market their past. Moreover, the ancient past has served politicians across the Middle East who invoke historic ancestors in order to legitimize their rule. For example, when Egypt achieved independence in the 1920s, political elites extolled the great achievements of the pharaohs in order to celebrate Egypt's essence and unique identity. In other words, there is no denying that the past has mattered greatly in the Middle East. But it is a dynamic past, driven by changing demands of the present.

The region that came to be known as the Middle East has a very long and complex history, from early antiquity to the present day, that can only be sketched in the following pages. This long history, and this chapter, are divided into six major time periods:

1. Ancient Empires and the Emergence of Judaism
2. The Greco-Roman Empires and the Emergence of Christianity
3. The Middle Ages and the Emergence of Islam
4. The Crusades and the Ottoman, Safavid, and Mughal Empires
5. Colonial Expansion and Anticolonial Movements
6. From the Cold War to the Arab Uprisings

The first three units of this chapter cover the longest period, from antiquity to the Middle Ages. Each of these units presents important historical protagonists, with a focus on empires and their achievements. It is this kind of historical narrative that is used in present-day politics in order to define national identities. Of course, there are other kinds of historical narratives—those that focus on the lives of ordinary people rather than those of rulers and elites, for example—but for this particular project, which aims to show how history continues to be applied in the present, traditional history remains appropriate. In addition, faith narratives are added within their appropriate historical context. In the timeframe from antiquity to the Middle Ages in the same geographic area, the three main monotheistic religions emerged. Judaism, Christianity, and Islam were among the first globalizing forces in this world, since their ideas converted people far beyond the communities where they originated. It may not be difficult to see religion as something that divides us, but religions also have common denominators, especially if they emerged in similar cultural contexts.

The last three units cover the end of the Middle Ages, the transition to the era that historians call *modernity*, and the modern period itself. The term *modernity* describes several important phenomena: the loss of power of religious elites, combined with an end of divinely sanctioned monarchies, and the emergence of secular rule in the form of nation-states; a weakening of the role of religion in people's daily lives, and a new belief in science; the end of a feudal social order that assigned individuals their place in society by virtue of their birth, and the shaping of societies where individuals defined their own place. Modernity is also often equated with the political ascendancy of Europe and North America, and their domination over other regions. Most history textbooks of the modern Middle East begin with the last three centuries of the Ottoman Empire, accompanied by the gradual encroachment and eventually full-scale colonialism by European powers, and end with stories of independence and post-independence. An introduction into the Middle East in the twenty-first century will additionally have to grapple with the Arab uprisings that are transforming the region in profound ways. It is still unclear what long-term impact these popular revolutions will have, but it is clear that the game has changed, and that the Middle East will never look quite the same.

History never stands still; each era has its developments and notable events, its winners and losers. The past continues to be meaningful, because through history we explain our origins and sense of identity. But out of the vastness of time past, we only select certain periods that we deem worthy of remembrance. It would be impossible—or impractical—to remember *everything*. So we need to ask ourselves what kind of history it is that we are told. For each story that is recorded, there are multiple stories that are not. What follows should be read with that proviso in mind. This book can only give you *a history*, but not *the history* of the Middle East.

Ancient Empires and the Emergence of Judaism

Arguably, recorded history started in the Middle East. It was here that the first writing systems developed, making it possible to document and preserve an unchanging record for posterity. It is possible to consider the book of Deuteronomy in the Hebrew Bible the first "history book" that tells of the past so as to give a people, the Jewish people, a distinct origin and group identity.

In the Middle East, small settlements grew to city-states, which became the centers of powerful empires. This political development required administrative and military skills, as well as a solid economic base. Irrigation technology proved crucial in expanding agriculture. Religious belief and public ritual emerged alongside, and often in collaboration with, political power centers. Throughout antiquity, many gods and goddesses were worshipped around the Middle East. As the imperial political structures consolidated, monotheism emerged. Beginning with Zoroastrianism in ancient Persia, the idea took hold that one supreme god ruled the earth. Abraham—the great ancestor of Judaism, Christianity, and Islam—promoted one god who, like a father, loves and expects obedience from his children.

Many of the empires listed below continue to feature in present-day nationalist ideologies in the Middle East. Those who led ancient empires became the "ancestors" of present-day rulers, who needed to legitimize their rule. It is important to remember that when political elites refer to the past, it does not mean that they still live in the past. They may cloak themselves in the mantle of heroic figures of the past when it suits them, but they can take off that mantle any time they please. In politics, this is called "instrumentalism." Politicians often say and do things strategically, in order to obtain approval, or stem opposition, from the people they rule.

Mesopotamia

Often called "the cradle of civilization," Mesopotamia was home to the first large-scale urban societies, dating back to 4,000 BCE. The word *Mesopotamia* comes from the Greek and it means "between rivers"—specifically between the Tigris and the Euphrates Rivers. Able to build elaborate irrigation systems that allowed agriculture on a grand scale, rulers in the region created and sustained city-states with sizable populations, and eventually embarked on imperial conquests throughout the region. Uruk, located on the Euphrates in what today is southern Iraq, might have been the first city in human history. It was here that Sumerians built what was possibly the first civilization. One of our oldest written records, the *Epic of Gilgamesh*, tells of the quest of a king of Uruk to obtain eternal life. Uruk was also an important religious center where people worshipped the powerful fertility goddess Inanna. As time passed, important cities became city-states, and they took control over ever larger pieces of territory. In Mesopotamia, three cities became epicenters of empires: (1) Akkad, (2) Babylon, and (3) Assur.

1. The founder of the Akkadian Dynasty, King Sargon (d. ca. 2280 BCE), has been credited with ruling over the first empire on earth. His daughter, Enheduanna, became an influential priestess in the temple of the moon god. Enheduanna is believed to be the author of two texts about the goddess Inanna of Uruk, and therefore is possibly the first female author in the history of world literature.
2. Babylon has long held a particular fascination for Western scholars, who decoded the first constitution, written by the Babylonian king Hammurabi (d. ca. 1750 BCE). Inscribed on a tall stone surface, the Code of Hammurabi laid down rules to govern trade and property relations, as well as family affairs. It enshrined that the accuser had to bring evidence of guilt to try the accused, rather than have the accused defend his or her innocence. Old Testament scholars believe that Abraham, the great ancestor of the three monotheistic religions, grew up in Mesopotamia in the city of Ur around the time of Hammurabi, before he migrated east to the land that God promised him and his descendants.
3. After 1400 BCE, the Assyrians first asserted their power and became the regional empire of Mesopotamia for about 300 years; they regained power between the ninth and the sixth centuries BCE, expanding into Anatolia, and toward Persia. The historian Marc van de Mieroop (2006, 247) speaks of "Assyria's world domination." While the historical record traditionally emphasizes the military might of the Assyrians—something the Assyrians themselves documented through expansive pictorial reliefs on palace structures—it also shows that they enjoyed poetry and literature, as large volumes of tablets found in various libraries attest. The Assyrians were defeated by the joint forces of their neighbors, the Babylonians and the Medes.

> Many of the archeological remains of Assur are now on exhibit in the Pergamon Museum in Berlin, since it was German excavation teams that conducted most of the exploration in the area. Information about the museum's collection, housed in the Museum of the Ancient Near East, is available on its website (http://www.smb.museum/smb/sammlungen/details.php?objectId=23&lang=en).

Babylon reenters the Mesopotamian limelight during the so-called Neo-Babylonian era (ca. 620–540 BCE). In particular, King Nebuchadnezzar II (ca. 605–562 BCE) takes center stage with his successful military campaigns to the West. He conquered, among other communities, the Kingdom of Judah, taking its Jewish population back to Mesopotamia, and thus into exile. At its height, the Neo-Babylonian Empire stretched from the Mediterranean to northern Arabia and to Persia. In Babylon, exiles from the ancient

Kingdom of Judah began to compile the Pentateuch, or the Five Books of Moses. According to Jewish tradition, God dictated these books to Moses on Mount Sinai. Religious scholars today believe that there were several authors who wrote down the Pentateuch over several centuries, starting during the time of Babylonian exile. Central in the first of the five books, the book of Genesis, is God's creation of the universe and his promise of the land of Canaan to Abraham and his descendants. The second book, Exodus, tells the story of Jewish exile in, and exodus from, Egypt under the leadership of Moses. In other words, the early written records of Judaism prominently feature themes of exile and return, themes that would remain salient in much of modern Jewish history.

Besides military prowess, King Nebuchadnezzar possessed an appreciation of architecture. One of the seven wonders of the ancient world was the Hanging Gardens he commissioned to be built in the city of Babylon. He also took an interest in his past, and is said to have searched for the material remains of King Sargon of Akkad, whom we might call "the Father of Empires." More recently, Iraqi president Saddam Hussein presented himself as a modern-day Nebuchadnezzar. In 1982 Hussein ordered workers to reconstruct the 600-room palace of the Neo-Babylonian king. Each one of the bricks the workers used carried the inscription "In the era of Saddam Hussein, protector of Iraq, who rebuilt civilization and rebuilt Babylon."

See the British Museum's website (http://www.mesopotamia.co.uk) for maps and more information on Mesopotamia.

Ancient Egypt

The dynasties that emerged on the banks of the Nile about 3000 BCE were based on river-fed agriculture that was able to sustain large populations. The ancient Egyptians are probably most known for their funerary architecture, including vast pyramids with lavish tomb chambers. Tourists who land in Cairo in order to discover Egypt's ancient history will likely be taken on a tour of Saqqara, the royal tombs of the ancient capital Memphis, followed by a visit to the pyramids of Giza. Both sites are a comfortable driving distance away from downtown Cairo, and they are the remains of the so-called Old Kingdom of approximately 2600–2100 BCE. After a period of political unrest and decline, Memphis ceased to be the capital of the empire, and new rulers and dynasties moved their capital to Thebes, outside present-day Luxor.

The Egyptian dynasties that elicit the most contemporary recognition, and take up most contemporary museum space, lived through the New Kingdom, which began about 1550 BCE and lasted to about 1050 BCE. Queen Hatshepsut (ca. 1508–1458 BCE) was one of the first pharaohs of this period, and she was a great-ancestor of King Tutankhamen (ca. 1332–1323 BCE). The era of the New Kingdom was reportedly a time of great wealth and prosperity, as the lavish tomb chambers, elaborate palaces, and funerary cities from this time attest. Ramses II, or Ramses the Great (ca. 1300–1213 BCE), led the last, great military drive for expansion of the Egyptian Empire. His expansive tomb complex in the Valley of the Kings near Luxor is probably the most famous Pharaonic tourist site in contemporary Egypt. The biblical Moses would have led the Israelites out of Egypt shortly after the end of Ramses II's rule. The Egyptian Empire began to decline around 1100 BCE, after sustained attacks by what Egyptian records call "the sea people." Archeologists do not have a solid explanation for the events that transpired at that time, nor is there certainty about the exact origin of these invaders. Subsequently, Egypt came under the rule of the Persian, Greek, Roman, and Ottoman Empires.

The discovery of King Tut's tomb chamber in 1922 coincided with the formation of the modern Egyptian state. The Egyptians who celebrated their independence from British colonial rule proudly looked back to, and identified with, their great ancestors. Nationalist poetry extolled the accomplishments of ancient Egyptians, and it celebrated the fact that modern Egyptians finally ruled themselves again. The period of Pharaonic nationalism came to an end in the 1950s under President Gamal Abdel Nasser, who championed Egypt's Arab identity instead. Nasser wanted to unite all Arabic-speaking residents of the region into one unified political body under the banner of Pan-Arabism. Egypt's unique Pharaonic traits and heritage detracted from this political project. However, members of Egypt's minority Coptic Christian community continue to emphasize their Pharaonic roots. Copts are one of the largest denominations among the Eastern Orthodox churches, and they claim to be one of the oldest Christian communities in the world. In the Coptic narrative, the Pharaonic heritage helps to distinguish them from Arab Muslims, who, from the Coptic point of view, brought a foreign culture and belief system to the Nile with the expansion of Islam. So in a conversation about Pharaohs in contemporary Egypt, it is possible not to be talking about the pyramids at all, but about who has the right to call themselves an Egyptian today.

Hittites of Anatolia

From approximately 1800 to 1100 BCE, the Hittite Empire ruled over much of what is today Turkey and northern Syria. The Hittites were contemporaries of the Babylonians, Assyrians, and ancient Egyptians, and they went to war against them. The capital of the Hittite people was in the city of Hattusha in central Anatolia, where some of the archeological evidence of this civilization was recovered as early as 1834 CE. Hattusha contains a large temple complex and many smaller temple structures indicating the worship of many different kinds of deities at the time. The mysterious "sea people" who defeated the Egyptian Empire are also cited in connection with the demise of the Hittite Empire.

The ancient Hittite civilization became a crucial component in the development of a new national identity of modern republican Turkey. Eager to set themselves apart from the old imperial Ottomans and their Islamic traditions, modern Turks sought a different kind of heritage. One might have expected a Turkish leader to embrace the heritage of famous generals or kings. The great ancestors of the Turks were Genghis Khan and Tamerlane, both successful leaders who created empires. However, instead of a history that would have created ties with Central Asia, where both of these generals lived, the new republic of Turkey wanted to connect to Europe and the Mediterranean. Therefore, Turkey's first president,

Mustafa Kemal Atatürk (1881–1938), promoted his country's unique Hittite past. He dispatched local students to European universities to train in archeology, and he hired European professors to occupy chairs in the first archeology programs at Turkish universities. From here, excavation teams headed out to Anatolia in order to unearth Turkey's unique past. In this context, it is also important to mention that Atatürk moved the Turkish capital from the former Ottoman capital of Istanbul on the Bosphorus to Ankara in central Anatolia, and therefore closer to the country's historical and cultural roots, as he envisioned them.

This selective promotion of one past over other equally available pasts is what makes archaeology such a politically charged discipline. As one scholar called it, archaeology creates "facts on the ground" that, because they are material and tangible, have a lot of credibility (Abu El Haj 2001). Archaeologists create facts by deciding which layer of the historical record is worth preserving, and which layers can be destroyed or never unearthed. (Think of sequential civilizations adding their material remains on top of each other, like the layers of a cake.) Archaeologists therefore are very important in nation-states eager to create a unique national identity.

Rulers Along the Mediterranean

Phoenicia is a name that Greek historians gave to the coastal region of present-day Lebanon. Phoenicia comprised several ports along the eastern shores of the Mediterranean, including the city-states of Byblos, Sidon, and Tyre, which are mentioned in the Old Testament. Between roughly 1200 BCE and Alexander the Great's conquest in 333 BCE, the Phoenicians were primarily traders and seafarers. They sold, among other things, purple dye coveted by aristocrats and royalty all over Europe. Phoenicians also invented a letter-based alphabet, which is the ancestor of the writing system in most Western languages. It is debated if the Phoenicians were an independent civilization or a regional alliance ruled by larger empires to the north (Hittites), east (Assyrians), or south (ancient Egypt).

> For examples of Phoenicia's archaeological record, see the "Iron Age" page on the website of the National Museum of Beirut (http://www.beirutnationalmuseum.com/e-collection-fer.htm).

Contemporaries of the Phoenicians, the Israelite tribes—descendants of Abraham, Isaac, and Jacob—began to form a political unit that solidified into a monarchy under King David about 1000 BCE. His son Solomon (ca. 970–930 BCE) continued to rule this Kingdom of Israel and is credited with having built the first Jewish temple. For this project, as well as for his royal palace, he turned to the Phoenician king Hiram of Tyre to buy durable cedar timber. A struggle of succession began after Solomon's death. The southern Kingdom of Judah split off from the northern Kingdom of Israel (also called Samaria), and several decades of war ensued. Eventually, the kingdoms made peace, but they remained separate entities. The northern Kingdom of Israel succumbed to the mighty armies of the Assyrians in 720 BCE, and the southern Kingdom of Judah surrendered to the armies of the Babylonians in 586 BCE. The Babylonian army destroyed the Kingdom of Judah, as well as the first Jewish temple. A large part of the Jewish population was taken captive and resettled in Babylon.

> Images of the early and late Israelite periods are available on the website of the Hecht Museum in Tel Aviv (http://mushecht.haifa.ac.il/archeology/cronological_eng.aspx).

In contemporary history, both Phoenicia and the ancient Kingdom of Israel matter, as they have given legitimacy to national identity projects in Lebanon and Israel, respectively. When Lebanon became independent after centuries of being a part of the larger Ottoman Empire, some Lebanese Maronites looked for a way to distinguish themselves from the Arab Muslim communities around them. They turned to the ancient inhabitants of the port cities of Phoenicia as their "ancestors." Similarly, the historical narrative of the Kingdom of David and Solomon, as well as the two successor territories of Judah and Samaria, was later used to establish the link of Jewish diaspora communities to what would become the modern state of Israel in 1948. Archaeological evidence was invoked to legitimate present-day claims to particular territories. Of course, pious Jews in Israel did not need the affirmation of the archaeological or historical records, because they could read in the book of Genesis of God's promise to Abraham: "To your descendants I give this land, from the river of Egypt to the great river, the Euphrates" (Genesis 15:18).

The Persian Empire

As the Neo-Babylonian era came to an end, a new imperial power emerged that stretched from the Mediterranean into Central Asia. A leader with significant military skill, Cyrus the Great—as history books would later call him—defeated the Medes and Babylonians, and became the ruler over the ancient Middle East. Cyrus released Jewish captives in Babylon, and many returned to the shores of the Mediterranean, while others stayed in the land they had come to call their home. After Cyrus's death in 530 BCE, his successor, Cambyses II, conquered and ruled Egypt. Cambyses's successor, Darius (521–486 BCE), began the construction of the capital city of Parsa in the historical region of Fars (today the Fars Province in southern Iran), a project involving laborers from across his empire. Darius's successor, Xerxes, completed the construction thirty years later. Greek historians would call the city *Persepolis* (city of Persians), and they described it as "the richest city under the sun," where "private houses had been furnished with every sort of wealth over the years" (Mousavi 2012, 58). Darius also famously attacked Greek forces at the Battle of Marathon in 490 BCE. Legend has it that a Greek soldier, Pheidippides, ran twenty-six miles from Marathon to Athens to announce the Greek victory over the Persian forces, after which he is said to have collapsed and died. Little did Pheidippides know that he would inspire a popular sport, the modern marathon.

The Persian Empire ruled over a vast territory. In order to govern the diverse populations, Persian kings left significant autonomy to the provinces, and they did not impose their own beliefs, which, as we know from inscriptions on their tombs, included Zoroastrianism. The precise origin of this ancient belief system is debated, but scholars now date it to about 1200 BCE. A man by the name of Zoroaster (also called Zarathustra) began to preach the message of a supreme god, Ahura Mazda, from whom all other gods emanated. The creator god, Ahura Mazda, was locked in a struggle with the Evil Spirit, a negative life force. The world was created as a stage for their struggle. Each person had a role to play during her or his lifetime, siding with the forces of good or evil. People would be held accountable for their deeds when they died, with the promise of eternal life in heaven or hell. Zoroastrianism can be considered a prototype of monotheism. Although many gods were worshipped, one supreme deity stood above all. Zoroaster's sayings were recorded long after his death in a book called the *Gathas*. Zoroastrianism was practiced in various communities throughout the realm—as remnants of fire temples attest—but it was not enforced as a state religion. It continues to be practiced in various forms, including among the Parsi community in India.

Greek forces, under Alexander the Great, attacked and defeated the Persian forces of Darius III in 333 BCE in Issus, Syria. The Sasanian Empire, also called the Neo-Persian Empire, would emerge later (224–651 CE) and become an important player in the pre-Islamic Middle East (see below). In 1971, Mohammad Reza Pahlavi, the Shah of Iran, spent an estimated US$ 100 million to celebrate "2,500 Years of Persian Empire" in the remains of the ancient city of Persepolis, which was restored for the occasion (a slide show marking the occasion, titled "2,500 year celebration of Iran's monarchy," is available on YouTube at http://www.youtube.com/watch?v=P1xSdH2PbJ4). The expensive celebrations did not stop the decline of the monarch's popularity, however. The Shah would be overthrown in the 1979 Iranian Revolution.

The Iranian-French author Marjane Satrapi chose *Persepolis* as the title for a memoir, published in the style of a graphic novel, about her coming of age during the Iranian Revolution. Satrapi later made a feature-length film, based on her memoir, with the same title. The Movieweb.com page about the film (http://www.movieweb.com/movie/persepolis) includes a link to an interview with Satrapi. The interview, entitled "Persepolis - Exclusive: Marjane Satrapi," can also be accessed through Movieweb.com's YouTube channel (http://www.youtube.com/watch?v=v9onZpQix_w).

Greco-Roman Empires and the Emergence of Christianity

Many Western history books describe the time of Greek and Roman world dominance as the time European culture was formed. Greek city-states are said to be the cradle of democratic government. The ancient Romans introduced the senate, a consultative body of elders. In the Roman Senate, prominent citizens could make their voices heard, thereby transforming the monarchy into a republic. Neither Greek nor Roman political systems were democratic in the sense of including all citizens equally in decision making, and true equality is arguably an ideal that many contemporary democracies still work to achieve. But a republic was a very new form of governing that defined politics as a "public matter" (from the Latin *res publica*), rather than a matter of royalty or aristocrats, who maintained their status by virtue of their birth.

Neither the Greek nor the Roman Empire emerged out of a vacuum, but both incorporated cultural and political elements from their imperial predecessors, especially the ancient Egyptians. Both empires extended their rule and influence around the Mediterranean and to the East, where they defeated and built on the ruins of the ancient empires mentioned above. The Sasanian Persians, a successor empire to the Persia of Cyrus and Darius, stopped their expansion. As new empires took over the reins of power, the cultures and traditions of the subject populations mixed with those of the new rulers. Greek became the language of many elites, and it remained so, even during Roman times, but locals continued to speak their own languages. For instance, Jesus of Nazareth is believed to have lived and preached during the time of Roman rule in his native language, Aramaic. When the Gospels were first written down, however, they were written in Greek.

The life and death of Jesus would change the way we count time. The Gregorian calendar starts with Year 1 at the time Jesus is presumed to have been born. The old designation BC (Before Christ) and AD (from the Latin *Anno Domini*, "In the Year of the Lord"), which reference Christian belief, have been changed to the secular BCE (Before the Common Era) and CE (Common Era), respectively.

Greek and Roman Rule and the Life and Death of Jesus Christ

Greek city-states formed a political alliance after their victory over the Persian army in 490 BCE. Competition among themselves and repeated Persian attacks kept the Greeks from expanding their power until the emergence of Alexander the Great, from the northern Greek region of Macedon. His successful military campaigns brought Greek (or Hellenistic) culture to Central Asia and eastern Anatolia, Mesopotamia, and Egypt. From 323 BCE, the year that Alexander the Great died, until about 100 BCE, the Middle East was under the rule of the Hellenistic Empire of Alexander's successors. It was the Roman army that defeated the Greeks in successive battles. Romans adopted many Greek cultural traits and administrative processes, so that historians today speak of a Greco-Roman world or culture.

The most famous Roman ruler in the historical record is Julius Cesar (100–44 BCE), subsequently rendered immortal in novels, plays, and films. Emperor Augustus (63 BCE–14 CE) features prominently in the history of the New Testament, as it was his census decree that sent Mary and Joseph from their native Nazareth to the town of Bethlehem, where, according to scriptures, Jesus was born in a manger. Jesus grew up during a time of Jewish unrest and discontent with the Roman overlords. Since he was from the line of

King David, Jesus raised hopes in some of his Jewish followers of rebuilding a Jewish kingdom and defeating Roman imperial rule. The anticipated overthrow did not occur, however. When Jesus spoke of a new kingdom, he meant the kingdom of heaven. Instead of insurrection against the Romans or retribution for the suffering caused by Roman rule, Jesus admonished his followers in one of his most famous sermons, the Sermon on the Mount, to turn the other cheek. This message did not sit well with those among Jesus's contemporaries who wanted to see an uprising. Jesus was also suspect among Jewish religious leaders, who saw their own authority threatened. In the end, they turned Jesus over to Roman authorities, who crucified him as "King of the Jews." According to the New Testament, Jesus rose from the dead after three days in the grave and ascended to heaven from where he will return once more on Judgment Day. Christians believe that Jesus died to atone for their sins, and therefore make possible eternal life.

The Roman Empire was at the height of its power at the turn of the millennium. It stretched from Britain to Egypt and Mesopotamia. Revolts in subject territories were put down by force. In 70 CE, Rome asserted its power over the restive Jewish population with the destruction of the Second Temple in Jerusalem. With the symbolic center of Jewish worship in ashes, this date marked the beginning of the Jewish diaspora, with communities migrating to all parts of the globe, where new branches and practices of Judaism evolved. Over the centuries, members of Jewish communities had to decide if they wanted to become part of the majority cultures that surrounded them, or maintain their own, separate lifeways and traditions. There were at times sharp divisions between those Jews who defended the orthodoxy of their faith and those who became more open to ideas and practices of their host cultures. Some branches of Judaism advocated a spiritual connection to the divine rather than a more legalistic, orthodox practice. The debates over what exactly constitutes Jewishness remain quite lively today.

Early Christianity and the Byzantine Empire

Early Christian communities were severely persecuted under Roman rule, as the worship of a divinity other than the Roman emperor was seen as treasonous. Early Christians survived in small base communities. The Gospels were not yet written down, so the converts to the new faith looked to the Hebrew Bible and to letters from apostles or community leaders for guidance. The new faith spread widely and consolidated after Emperor Constantine (272–337 CE) converted to Christianity in response to a military victory he credited to divine intervention. Constantine began to build himself a new capital, which he designated as the "Second Rome," in the Eastern town of Byzantium, which would later be renamed Constantinople (and still later, Istanbul). Constantine, however, does not bear the title of first Christian ruler. That title goes to King Tiridates III (250–330 CE), who is said to have converted all of Armenia to Christianity in the year 301, upon his own conversion and baptism. Many Armenians today proudly point to their ancestors as "the first Christian nation."

The Roman emperor Theodosius (347–395 CE) made Christianity the official religion throughout his empire. After Theodosius's death, the Roman Empire split into two: the Western Roman Empire, with its seat in Rome; and the Eastern Roman Empire, with its seat in Constantinople. The Western half of the empire did not survive the onslaught of Germanic tribes—the Visigoths, Franks, Ostrogoths, and Vandals—who established their own successor kingdoms in southern Europe and northern Africa. However, the Eastern Empire, which Western historians call the Byzantine Empire, existed until the fifteenth century. Muslim historians call the Byzantines "Romans" (in Arabic *Rum*), and some members of Eastern Orthodox churches today call themselves Rum Orthodox. So, depending on whose history book you read today, when Seljuk Turks conquered Constantinople in 1453, they had defeated either the Byzantine Empire or the Roman Empire.

The most prominent ruler of the Byzantine Empire was Justinian the Great (482–565 CE). His armies set out to reconquer some of the lost territories of the Western Roman Empire, especially in North Africa and Italy. He is remembered for rewriting Roman law in the Code of Justinian, which defined citizens of the empire as Christians, and for commissioning the construction of the Hagia Sophia (Greek for "holy wisdom"), a basilica in Constantinople. Christian monasticism, the rejection of worldly goods and powers, flourished as a separate manifestation of religion under Byzantine rule. Opposed to the official church, with its trappings of wealth and power (and its close relationship to the emperor), some believers formed small communities and dedicated their lives to prayer, fasting, and serving the poor.

As official Christianity spread with the support of the emperor, it split into various denominations. Believers began to disagree about the exact nature of Jesus Christ: Was he divine or human? If he was divine, how could he die? If he was human, how could he rise from the dead? Could he be both? If so, how? If God was supposed to be one, how could he have a son? Different church leaders gave different answers to these questions, and independent Christian communities emerged: the Oriental Orthodox churches (predominantly in Egypt, Ethiopia, Eritrea, etc.); the Eastern Orthodox churches (in the core of the Byzantine Empire and later in Slavic countries and Eastern Europe); and the Church of the East (predominantly in Iran and Iraq, as well as in India and China). These Orthodox or Eastern churches continued to practice their faith using different liturgical languages, such as Syriac, Coptic, or Greek, each community relying on its own theological writings and interpretations. These early Christians communities would later be among the first to witness the emergence of Islam, and they have lived among Muslim communities until the present.

The Byzantine Empire's most important neighbor (and enemy) to the east was the Sasanian (Neo-Persian) Empire with its capital city of Ctesiphon, near modern-day Baghdad. The Sasanian influence stretched from Mesopotamia to Afghanistan and Central Asia to the northeast. Like the Byzantines, the Sasanians ruled over a polyglot and multicultural population. Since the Byzantine and Sasanian Empires were each other's most immediate rivals, they attacked each other frequently. The last great military campaign (603–629 CE) almost led to the Sasanian conquest of the Byzantines. Persian troops conquered Jerusalem, the Syrian town of Antioch, and Egypt, but a palace revolt in Ctesiphon interrupted the Persian campaign and both powers agreed to a truce. The populations in both realms suffered greatly from the effects of the repeated wars, and historians have argued that there was a great sense of disaffection just at the time when new political and religious forces gathered in the Arabian Peninsula.

Box 3.1

Hagia Sophia: A Long-Lived but Ever-Changing Symbol

The Hagia Sophia was, at the time, the largest enclosed man-made structure on earth. Although the building was repeatedly damaged and partially destroyed by earthquakes, fires, and wars, rulers kept restoring it as an important symbol of their power. Mehmed the Conqueror, who defeated the Byzantine/Roman Empire in 1453, protected the cathedral building and turned it into a mosque. Today the building houses the Ayasofya (Hagia Sophia) Museum; its website (http://www.ayasofyamuzesi.gov.tr/en/) is a good source of information on the history of the structure.

Box 3.2

The "Original Christians"

Accurate numbers of the contemporary populations of Christians in the Middle East are difficult to ascertain, due to a lack of census data and recent population displacements, especially of religious minorities. Historically, their cultural, economic, and political influence on the region has been substantial. They call themselves the "original Christians," as their rituals and practices date back to the time of Jesus Christ. The BBC's "Guide: Christians in the Middle East" (http://www.bbc.co.uk/news/world-middle-east-15239529) is a good source of information on these populations.

The Middle Ages and the Emergence of Islam

The Middle Ages lasted roughly from the fourth to the fourteenth century. This period of about 1,000 years is thus named in Western history books because it is considered the period between an illustrious Greco-Roman antiquity and the exciting era of the Renaissance (French for "rebirth") in fifteenth-century Europe. Of course, many significant developments took place during this time, but they did not occur in Europe. As Eurocentric and problematic as the designation "Middle East," the "Middle Ages" witnessed a complete transformation of the social order, which was to a large extent initiated by the advent of Islam.

Islam emerged in Mecca, in what became the Kingdom of Saudi Arabia, and spread across the regions previously under the control of the Roman Empire and further east. Central to the faith narrative of Islam is the life of the Prophet Muhammad and his successors. Similar to Christianity and Judaism, Islam would split into competing denominations or branches, as well as into official (or orthodox) Islam, which often aligned itself with ruling powers, and countercurrents—for instance, Sufism—that insisted on personal, spiritual practice and the denunciation of wealth and power.

History books call the first two Islamic empires by the name of the ruling families: the Umayyads and the Abbasids. Under the Umayyad and Abbasid Empires, Muslim influence extended from the Iberian Peninsula to the Caucasus and Central Asia. Muslim rulers absorbed administrative structures and royal court etiquette from their Byzantine and Sasanian predecessors. Artistic and scientific achievements under Umayyad and Abbasid rule are said to have created the body of knowledge that made the European Renaissance possible. During that time, Jewish, Christian, and Muslim scholars engaged in lively debates, as each looked to their traditions for instruction on how to live a good life. A third early Islamic empire emerged in 969 along the Nile. This was called the Fatimid Empire, with reference to Muhammad's daughter Fatimah. The Fatimids were the most important medieval Shiite dynasty in the region.

Emergence of Islam

In sixth-century Mecca, the prominent Quraysh tribe controlled the market and the sacred site of the Kaaba, a shrine filled with statues and images of the various gods worshipped on the peninsula at the time. Both the market and shrine were sources of revenue for the Quraysh. One branch within the Quraysh tribe was the Banu Hashim clan, to which belonged the three brothers Abu Talib, Abbas, and Abdullah. About 570 CE, Abdullah's wife gave birth to a son they called Muhammad. Muhammad's father died before his son's birth, and his mother died when he was a young boy. As a result, Muhammad was raised first by his grandfather and then by his paternal uncle Abu Talib, a trader. Muhammad became a trader himself, and through his work he acquired the honorific Arabic title *al-amin*, "the trustworthy one." Khadija, a widow who ran a caravan business in Mecca, hired him, and about 595 they married. Fifteen years Muhammad's senior, Khadija was both a successful businesswoman and the first convert to Islam. They remained married until Khadija's death in 619 and raised four daughters: Fatimah, Zaynab, Kulthum, and Ruqayyah. Two sons died in infancy. All four daughters became respected members of the early Islamic community, and three of them became wives of subsequent Muslim leaders.

Muhammad worked as a respected businessman in the Meccan community until he was about forty years old. At that time, he began to receive what he considered divine revelations from God through the angel Gabriel. The revelations came in the form of Arabic verse, which Muhammad memorized. His followers later wrote them down in what would become the Quran (from the Arabic *qara'a*, which means "to recite" or "to read"). The early revelations condemned greed, arrogance, and selfishness, and praised kindness and generosity. They spoke of God's mercy, yet also of his punishment for those who disobeyed. One early revelation spelled out that there was only one God and no other. This single, all-seeing, all-knowing deity was going to take everyone to account on Judgment Day. With his revelations, Muhammad soon made enemies in his own Quraysh tribe, whose members feared the loss of revenue from their pilgrimage shrine, which housed a wide variety of deities. The more revelations he recited to the public, the more hostility Muhammad experienced in Mecca. In the year 622, fearing for his life, Muhammad moved to the oasis town of Yathrib. That year is called the year of the *hijra* (Arabic for "migration") and eventually became Year 1 in the Islamic calendar.

In Yathrib, he continued to receive revelations, and it was there that he established the institutional foundations of Islam, including the first mosque structure, the Quba Mosque. Yathrib eventually changed its name to Medina (short for the Arabic *medinat al-nabi*, "City of the Prophet"). Clashes between Muhammad's Meccan opponents and his new Medinan defendants continued until 630, when Mecca surrendered. The Meccan shrine of the Kaaba was cleansed of its idols and rededicated to the worship of one God. Subsequently, it became Islam's holiest shrine. Today, the cube-shaped structure stands draped in valuable cloth in the middle of the Grand Mosque of Mecca, where millions of Muslims gather annually to perform the ritual of pilgrimage (in Arabic *hajj*).

You can convert dates from the Gregorian to the Islamic calendar on Islamicity's website (http://www.islamicity.com/PrayerTimes/hijriconverter1aPartner.htm).

Because of their sacred status, Medina and Mecca are open only to Muslim visitors, yet computer technology enables non-Muslims to take virtual tours. An image of the Grand Mosque, for example, can be found online (http://www.gigapan.com/mobile/iOS/1.0/?id=109851).

Muhammad's Succession

Muhammad died in 632, and the young Muslim community had to find a new leader. A son would have been named the successor following patriarchal practice at the time. But since Muhammad had no surviving son, the elders of the community met and elected Abu Bakr, who had been both the father-in-law and longtime companion of the Prophet. Abu Bakr lived only two more years, at which point the community elected Umar al Khattab, also Muhammad's father-in-law. After Umar died, Uthman ibn Affan led the Muslim community. Finally, Mohammad's cousin Ali ibn Abi Talib, who was married to Mohammad's daughter Fatimah, became the leader of the Muslim community. These four men—Abu Bakr, Umar, Uthman, and Ali—received the honorific title of "the Rightly Guided Caliphs" (in Arabic, the *rashidun*). During the time of the four caliphs, Islam expanded from the Arabian Peninsula into the territories of contemporary Syria, Iraq, and North Africa to the west, and Iraq, Iran, and Central Asia to the east. Muslim armies defeated the forces of both the Byzantine and Sasanian Empires in a very short time.

However, the succession described above did not occur without dispute. There was a group of believers who considered Ali, as a blood relative of the Prophet (their fathers had been brothers), to be the most worthy successor. The "followers of Ali" (in Arabic

---

Box 3.3

Muhammad's Wives

After Khadija died in 619, Muhammad remarried several more times. Many of his wives were widows, but he also married nine-year-old Aisha, the daughter of Abu Bakr. It is impossible to ascertain if these marriages were marriages of the heart, acts of compassion, or part of strategic alliance building. For instance, when Muhammad wed Ramla (the daughter of his fiercest Meccan rival, Abu Sufyan) or Safiyya (the daughter of an Arab Jewish tribal leader subsequent to his military defeat), it is plausible that he was making strategic choices. It is also possible that Muhammad married widows to act as their protector. In the end, however, it is impossible to say why Muhammad took so many wives after his monogamous, and, by all reports, happy marriage to Khadija.

In contemporary society, polygamy has been a subject of much debate. Muhammad practiced it in the latter part of his life, and the Quran allows it, if the wives are treated equally. But many women today argue that their husbands no longer treat them equally after they marry a new wife. Across the Muslim world, polygamy has become less and less common.

---

shi'at Ali, from which we derive the English word "Shiite") promoted Ali's leadership from the beginning, and did not recognize Abu Bakr, Umar, and Uthman. They believed that Muhammad had designated Ali as his successor before his death, and that therefore no leadership decision had to be made by his friends and companions. Shiites recognize only descendants of Ali as legitimate successors of Muhammad. The successors are called *imams*, and believers hold them in particular reverence. Certain imams are considered visible manifestations of the spirit of God. Those who believed in the legitimacy of the four "Rightly Guided Caliphs" would come to be called Sunnis (from Arabic *sunna*, "habitual practice" or "norm," in reference to the way of life of the Prophet Muhammad).

The disagreement over succession erupted into war among various factions after the death of the third caliph, Uthman. A close relative of Uthman, Muawiya, who had won respect in the community after his successful military campaigns against the Byzantine Empire in Syria, decided he had better credentials than Ali to lead the community. Ali's and Muawiya's troops met in the Battle of Siffin (657) in present-day Syria. The battle was inconclusive. The leaders went into arbitration, at which point many of Ali's men defected, because they wanted a military and not a negotiated solution. That group of disaffected men became known as the Kharijites (from Arabic *kharaja*, "to leave"). They looked at Ali's arbitration decision as misguided, and concluded that his bloodline was not enough to make him a good Muslim ruler.

The Kharijites went on to conduct fairly radical politics for the time: piousness was the only prerequisite for a leader, rather than noble lineages or closeness to the Prophet—or patriarchal rules for that matter. Kharijites would never consolidate their power to establish an empire, but their ideas kept their currency, especially in border regions of the later

Islamic empires among Amazigh in North Africa or Arabs in Oman. *Kharijite* became a label contemporary Middle East rulers have used derogatorily for any group that opposed them. For instance, both Anwar Sadat and Hosni Mubarak, former presidents of modern Egypt, dismissively referred to anti-regime groups as Kharijites.

Early Islamic Dynasties: Umayyads, Abbasids, and Fatimids

After the death of Ali in 661 in Kufa—he was assassinated while praying by a member of the Kharijite community—Muawiya claimed leadership of the Islamic community and established what would become known as the Umayyad Dynasty. Through his sister Ramla, Muawiya had become Muhammad's brother-in-law. Muawiya reasserted the political control his clan had exercised in Mecca, yet now he ruled under the banner of Islam in Damascus. Ali's oldest son, Hassan, acquiesced to Muawiya's taking over the reins of the Muslim community. Muawiya's son Yazid, however, faced a new challenge from Ali's second son, Hussein, in a battle in 680 in Karbala. In this battle, Hussein, many members of his family, and many supporters lost their lives. The Umayyad Dynasty subsequently expanded through North Africa and into Spain.

In the contemporary Shiite community, Hussein's defeat in Karbala is remembered annually during the ten-day religious holiday called Ashura (from Arabic *ashara*, "ten"). During Ashura, the story of the Battle of Karbala and the death of Hussein and his family are retold, a practice not unlike the public retelling of the Passion of Christ before Easter. For Shiite believers, Hussein's death teaches that you have to stand up for what is right, even if the (military) odds are stacked against you. Hussein chose to die rather than submit to what he considered corrupt and misguided leadership. For Shiites, the name Yazid has come to stand for corruption and evil. In Lebanon, for instance, members of the Shiite political group Hezbollah use the name Yazid to refer to the United States and Israel.

The generals of the Abbasid Dynasty overthrew the last Umayyad ruler, Marwan, in Damascus in 750. However, the Umayyad rulers of Spain continued the Umayyad lineage for six more centuries. By the tenth and eleventh centuries, Cordoba was one of the world's great centers of commerce, culture, and learning. The period of Muslim rule over Spain and Portugal (the exact territorial boundaries kept changing) lasted until the defeat of the last Muslim ruler by the Catholic Spanish crown in 1492. Historians refer to this European Muslim empire as *al-Andalus*, and they celebrate it as a site and a time of religious tolerance. In al-Andalus, Muslim, Jewish, and Christian scholars translated, studied, and debated Arabic-language writings on disciplines such as medicine, mathematics, and philosophy. As they translated from Arabic, they realized that Muslim scholarship had further developed ideas of ancient Greek philosophers. Treatises by the Muslim scholar Ibn Sina (980–1037) were translated and subsequently taught in European universities. The Cordoba-born scholar Ibn Rushd (1126–1198) produced works that advanced new ideas in science, religion, and metaphysics, which influenced later medieval Christian philosophers, scientists, and theologians. One ninth-century Christian scholar in Cordoba lamented, "The Christians love to read the poems and romances of the Arabs; they study the Arab theologians and philosophers . . . all talented young Christians read and study

---

Box 3.4

The Dome of the Rock

Probably the best-known surviving example of Umayyad architectural genius
of that time is the Dome of the Rock in Jerusalem. It was the Umayyad ruler
Abd al-Malik (646–705) who decided to build the domed structure at the
site of the destroyed Jewish temple, an area that had become a municipal
garbage dump during Byzantine rule. The rock sheltered by the dome has
deep religious significance: Abraham, the ancestor of all three monotheistic
religions, is believed to have prepared his son in sacrifice to God at this
location (Genesis 24: 4–13). The rock is also believed to be the site from
which Muhammad went on a "night journey" that brought him face-to-face
with God. The Dome of the Rock has also become an important Palestinian
nationalist symbol, and the image can be found on posters, images, and the
walls of buildings next to slogans asking for the liberation of Palestine.

---

with enthusiasm Arab books; they gather immense libraries at great expense; they despise
the Christian literature as unworthy of attention" (cited in Lockman 2004, 26).

Voices on all sides may argue today that "Muslim civilization" and "Judeo-Christian civilization" are inherently incompatible, but al-Andalus scholars are among those who beg to
differ. They point to several hundred years of Muslim rule during which members of Muslim,
Christian, and Jewish communities seemed, for the most part, to be getting along.

During that same time, the Abbasid Empire expanded Muslim rule eastward into
Central Asia. In the region of Khorasan (present-day Afghanistan), Arabs had settled
and intermarried with local Iranian communities. Increasingly, the population came to
resent Damascus-based Umayyad rule, and armed opposition spread throughout the
empire, which was overwhelmingly non-Arab. Abu Muslim al-Khorasani, the general
who defeated the last Umayyad ruler, went on to claim descent from the family of the
Prophet himself: from Muhammad's uncle Abbas. The Abbasids built their new capital,
Baghdad, in between the Tigris and Euphrates Rivers, along an important trade route
that connected Iran and Central Asia with Syria and Egypt. The Abbasid ruler Harun
al-Rashid (763–809) established the House of Wisdom (in Arabic *bayt al-hikma*), which
became the biggest center of scholarship and learning of its time. Harun al-Rashid's
successors added observatories, laboratories, and an unparalleled library, where Greek,
Persian, and Indian texts were translated, studied, and developed. During Abbasid rule,
the first collection of stories for what Westerners would come to know as the *Thousand
and One Nights* (or *Arabian Nights*) was assembled. It was also during Abbasid times
that Persian scholars and writers adopted the Arabic script for their language. The poet
Firdawsi completed the *Shahnahmeh*, an epic recording the history of Iran, under early
eleventh-century Abbasid rule.

From Baghdad it was quite difficult to control the territories of North Africa, which
became increasingly independent during the Islamic Middle Ages, when a series of

kingdoms and dynasties rose and fell between Morocco and Egypt. In Morocco, a great-grandson of Ali by the name of Idris established the Idrisid Dynasty in the city of Fes, after which followed several more independent dynasties. As a result, the present-day ruler of Morocco, King Muhammad VI, calls himself a direct descendant of the family of the Prophet Muhammad. First in Tunisia, and then in Egypt, members of the Ismaili Shiite community established the Fatimid Dynasty in the tenth century. The Ismaili Shiite held Ismail, the seventh imam after Ali, in particular reverence. From their base in the region of contemporary Tunisia, the Fatimids attacked Egypt, where they founded the city of Cairo in 969. The Fatimids claimed to be descendants of Ali and Fatimah, and they established their caliphate as a direct challenge to that of the Abbasid rulers in Baghdad. The Fatimids ruled Egypt until 1171. The contemporary Druze in Lebanon, Syria, and Israel trace their heritage to Fatimid Egypt. Contemporary Ismailis under the leadership of the Agha Khan similarly see themselves as descendants of the Fatimid line.

In Baghdad, meanwhile, the Abbasid rulers, not trusting their own military, began recruiting mercenaries from across ethnic and tribal communities that they hoped would be more loyal. Among people they recruited were Turks, originally a nomadic people that had come via Central Asia to the Middle East, and converted to Islam in the process. The Abbasid plan backfired, however, and eventually their hired guns took over running the affairs of the state. Late Abbasid rulers fronted regimes that other people ran for them. In 1258, Abbasid rule came to a dramatic end after a siege and attack by Mongol troops led by a grandson of Genghis Khan. The House of Wisdom was completely destroyed, and many of the manuscripts and discoveries lost.

> The historical narrative from 1258 resurfaced in Arab popular culture with the publication of the comic book series titled *The 99*. "The 99" are a group of Muslim superheroes, whose powers are based on recovered gemstones that preserved the knowledge of the House of Wisdom. A website is devoted to *The 99* (http://www.the99.org/).

The Crusades and the Ottoman, Safavid, and Mughal Empires

This section outlines the transition from the Middle Ages to modernity. It describes the emergence (and decline) of three Islamic empires after the end of Abbasid rule: the Ottoman, Safavid, and Mughal empires. In all three cases, the builders of these political entities had Turkic origins. Some had arrived in the Middle East from Central Asia, settled, and taken on many of the local customs and traditions. Others arrived via military conquest—for instance, as part of the Mongol invasion that destroyed Baghdad. The Mongols established their own competing empires that stretched from China to Eastern Europe until their defeat in the fourteenth century. One of them was the Ilkhanate, which controlled territories from Turkey to Afghanistan. The Ottoman Empire was subsequently established by leaders of a Seljuk Turkish tribe, and it became one of the longest-lasting political entities in the Middle East. Other Muslim empires were established in Central Asia and northern India, respectively.

It was the arrival of the Seljuk Turks and their attacks on different parts of the Byzantine Empire that spurred the Western military response we now call "the Crusades." Importantly, the Crusades took place while the Catholic Church based in Rome and the Eastern Orthodox Church based in Constantinople were battling for control of Christianity. Western history books traditionally focus on the fact that the Crusades were the first extended hostile encounter between "the Christian West" and "the Muslim East." But some Western crusaders also attacked Constantinople, the seat of Eastern Christianity, rather than meeting Muslim armies in Jerusalem. In other words, neither "the crusaders" nor "the Muslims" were unified groups; instead, battle lines ran between and across the two groups.

Seljuk Turks and the Crusades

As some Seljuk Turks took control of the Abbasid Empire, more and more Turkish tribesmen migrated and settled in Anatolia. Increasingly, they would clash with troops of the declining Byzantine Empire. Byzantine and Seljuk troops met in 1071 in what would turn out to be a catastrophic defeat for the Byzantine rulers. Some of the Seljuk troops moved on to capture Jerusalem, which set off the Crusades.

Upon receiving the Byzantine emperor's plea for help, Pope Urban II responded in 1096 with a call to "rid the sanctuary of God of the unbelievers, expel the thieves and lead back the faithful" (cited in Lockman 2004, 28). In 1099, European crusaders captured Jerusalem and established several fortifications/kingdoms along the Mediterranean coast. The Muslim forces regrouped soon thereafter and attacked the crusaders' positions. So, in 1145, a Second Crusade was organized. It ended up as a military failure for the Europeans: in the Battle of Hattin in 1187, Muslim forces defeated most of the crusader forces. The Muslim military commander who led his troops to victory, Saladin, became the stuff of legend.

In 1192, Saladin met with the leader of the Third Crusade, King Richard the Lionheart. The two men agreed on a three-year truce and access to the city's holy sites for Christian pilgrims. Saladin would become an icon of Muslim chivalry among the nobility in Europe. He would also go on to govern Egypt, replacing Fatimid Shiite rule with a Sunni dynasty. Similar to what happened to the Abbasids in Baghdad, Saladin's dynasty would eventually be overthrown and replaced by the Mamluks, well-trained and high-ranking slave soldiers that had originally been hired to protect the ruler. In Egypt they established the Mamluk Dynasty, which would rule from 1250 to 1517, when it was defeated by the Ottoman Empire.

A Fourth Crusade was called in 1202, but it never reached Jerusalem. Instead, the Venetians who provided the ships for the Crusades persuaded the Latin Christian forces to attack Constantinople, Venice's great trading rival at the time. It is important to recall the year 1054, when the so-called Great Schism occurred, which divided the Christian

---

Box 3.5

Crusades as a Powerful Symbol

Saladin was a Kurdish general in the Seljuk army. Born in Tikrit in present-day Iraq, he had worked his way up through military ranks and established himself as ruler of Egypt. Saladin died in Damascus in 1193, and was buried in the garden outside the Umayyad Mosque. Eight hundred years later, Saddam Hussein would lay claim to this lineage by virtue of a shared birthplace, Tikrit, though they obviously did not share the same ethnicity. Hussein commissioned murals and postage stamps that showed him side by side with Saladin, the crusader-defeating general. Also, in many of his speeches, Osama bin Laden called on his fellow Muslims to fight against "the crusaders," evoking images of Europeans of the Middle Ages invading sacred Muslim sites. This rhetoric was mirrored in the United States, when President George W. Bush publicly referred to "the war on terror" as a crusade. In both cases, conflict was framed as part of a larger battle between good and evil.

---

world into the Eastern (Orthodox) churches and the Western Roman Catholic Church. The main centers of Eastern Christianity were the cities of Jerusalem, Alexandria, and Constantinople, whereas the Roman Catholic Church settled in Rome. Each side accused the other of causing the East-West split, and of preventing reconciliation. The leaders of both communities excommunicated each other. Over the next centuries, further splits occurred, as some parts of the Eastern community sought to reestablish relations with Rome, and therefore created hybrid "Greek Catholic," "Armenian Catholic," and "Coptic Catholic" communities. The Reformation movement of sixteenth-century Europe further split the Christian world, leading to the emergence of Protestant Christianity, with its own branches and sub-branches. Christianity might be the largest religious denomination in the world today, but it is a community with deep rifts and disagreements.

The Early Ottoman Empire

One Seljuk general by the name of Osman had come to control an area in Anatolia that was close to the Byzantine border. In the early 1300s he began a series of military campaigns to defeat the once powerful Eastern Christian Empire and replace it with his own: the Ottoman Empire. Due to their solid agricultural base on the Anatolian plateau, and their early embrace of gunpowder technology, descendants of Osman were able to conquer much of south-eastern Europe—the Balkans—and eventually all of Anatolia. An interim capital was established in the European town of Edirne. From there, the Ottomans mobilized to attack what remained of the Byzantine Empire: the capital city of Constantinople. The city fell to Ottoman ruler Mehmed the Conqueror in 1453.

Mehmed the Conqueror went on to consolidate his rule in Anatolia, then turned around and pushed further into Europe, laying siege to Belgrade in 1456 CE. He also invaded Italy and headed to Rome to attack the Vatican, but he was unsuccessful in that attempt. He died in 1481, one of the most celebrated Ottoman rulers. In 1516 the grandson of Mehmed, Sultan Selim, marched the Ottoman army toward Syria and Egypt, where he defeated the ruling Mamluk Dynasty. He was able to integrate the "bread basket" of Egypt, and subsequently took control of Mecca and Medina in the Arabian Peninsula. Sultans now used "Custodian of the Two Noble Sanctuaries" as part of their elaborate royal title. They also helped organize and participated in the annual pilgrimages to Mecca and Medina. Both Selim and his son Suleiman (or Süleyman) used their capable navy to take control over many strategic ports around the entire Mediterranean, including Algiers, Tunis, and Tripoli, as well as Nice, Corsica, and Rhodes.

Suleiman would go on to rule the Ottoman Empire for forty-six years, from 1520 to 1566. Many remember Suleiman primarily for his military expeditions into Europe, in particular his two attempts to conquer Vienna in 1529 and 1532. He was unsuccessful both times, due in part to overextended supply lines and bad weather. For the next 100 years, relations between Ottoman and European royalty were tense, with repeated military engagements culminating in the famous Battle of Vienna on September 12, 1683, during which the large Ottoman forces were defeated by an alliance of European powers. The epic battle is rendered in a large number of European paintings, and the date is often taken as a turning point in history. After centuries of Middle Eastern dominance, Europe now was on the ascendant.

Suleiman did not only have military credentials, he was also a patron of the arts and architecture. He employed painters, poets, bookbinders, and goldsmiths at his court. Under his rule, the famous architect Sinan built Suleiman's Mosque (or the Süleymaniye Mosque) in Istanbul. He also renovated the Dome of the Rock in Jerusalem. After the study of edicts of previous sultans and the opinion of Islamic legal scholars, Suleiman issued a codified book of law, which was used to administer justice for the remainder of Ottoman rule. History books today refer to him as either "Suleiman the Magnificent" or "Suleiman the Lawgiver."

By the end of the sixteenth century, Istanbul had about 700,000 inhabitants, which made it considerably larger than Paris or London at the time. While reliable census data is hard to come by, the Ottoman Empire at the turn of the seventeenth century might have ruled about 30 million people, more or less evenly divided among the European, Asian, and African parts of the empire. Ottoman Turkish, the language of the royal court, was heavily influenced by Arabic and Persian, and, like the Persians before them, the Ottomans adopted the Arabic script. Court Turkish differed from Turkish spoken in the streets, while Arabic remained the language of religion.

Safavid Empire

The Safavid Empire was founded in the early 1500s by a group of men who belonged to the so-called Safaviyya Sufi order, which had emerged in present-day Azerbaijan among a group of Turkmen and Kurds. The Safavids would slowly expand their influence over neighboring territories, in particular into what is present-day Iran. Their military was famously known as the "red heads" (*kizilbash* in Turkish) on account of their red headdress. This Sufi order embraced Shiite Islam, and therefore came in conflict with an increasingly orthodox Sunni Ottoman sultan.

The most famous Safavid ruler was Shah Abbas (1587–1629), who, following the Ottoman model, reorganized his army into a paid, standing army, equipped with rifles and gunpowder. This enabled him to repel the Ottomans and take over some of their territories. He took Baghdad from the Ottomans in 1622, and moved into the Caucasus and Central Asia. Safavids converted their predominantly Sunni subject populations to Shiism, and made Shiism the official state religion. Since that time, Shiism has been more of a Persian, and less of an Arab religious practice. Under the Safavids, an important center of Shiite theological learning emerged in the city of Qom, south of Tehran. This is where, much later, Ayatollah Khomeini would obtain his education.

> Examples of Safavid art are available at the Metropolitan Museum of Art's webpage, "The Art of the Safavids before 1600" (http://www.metmuseum.org/toah/hd/safa/hd_safa.htm).

Mughal Empire

About 1500, a descendant of Genghis Khan and Tamerlane by the name of Babur (1483–1530) emerged to build the Mughal Empire. Babur had established a small kingdom with its seat in Kabul, the capital of present-day Afghanistan, and eventually moved his troops southward. In 1526 Babur moved into Agra and Delhi, the cities that became the centers of the Mughal Dynasty. It was in Agra that the great-great-grandson of Babur, Shah Jahan, built the famous Taj Mahal mausoleum as a tribute to his late wife Mumtaz Mahal. Shah Jahan also had the Red Fort constructed in Delhi, the palace from which the emperors ruled. Muslim influence in India spread from Delhi to Hyderabad through conquests and political alliances. Islam had already come to southern Indian shores via merchants from the Arabian Peninsula, as India was one of the main stops on the sea route between the Middle East and China.

Historical accounts of early Mughal rule emphasize the multilingual and multiethnic character of the population under Mughal control. For instance, it is reported that the Mughal emperor Akbar, Shah Jahan's grandfather, gathered Hindu, Christian, Zoroastrian, and Muslim scholars for debates at his court. In the twentieth century, under the influence of the British colonial "divide and conquer" rule and local nationalist politics, the population of the Indian subcontinent was sharply divided, particularly between Hindus and Muslims. This division led to the violent partition of colonial British India into predominantly Muslim Pakistan and predominantly Hindu India, through war and population transfer. In retrospect, commentators nostalgically remembered the Mughals as rulers who had been able to accommodate religious differences.

The PBS website for "Treasures of the World" (http://www.pbs.org/treasuresoftheworld/taj_mahal/tlevel_1/t1_mughal.html) contains more information on the Mughal Dynasty.

The Late Ottoman Empire

From 1492 onward, as a result of their expanding naval prowess, European states began to build far-reaching colonial empires. Raw materials from the colonies fueled the Industrial Revolution and the creation of wealth in the West. For instance, British merchants acquired cotton relatively inexpensively in Ottoman Egypt, then sold expensive European textiles to the Egyptians. Local textile industries in the Middle East, such as silk spinning factories in Lebanon, were put out of business by European steam-powered spinning machines. Selling local goods cheaply, while acquiring expensive European tastes, Ottoman emperors soon found themselves deeply in debt to European banks and lenders. Not only did Ottoman sultans lose their financial footing, Ottoman-appointed rulers in the provinces increasingly fought for, and obtained, quasi-independence from Istanbul.

One of the most prominent and independent Ottoman rulers was Muhammad Ali of Egypt. Considered a reformer in most history books, he came to power in 1805 amid the disarray left behind by Napoleon's scholarly and military expedition to Egypt. He firmly established his power in Cairo, and then launched military campaigns into the Arabian Peninsula, Syria, Libya, and the Sudan. Egypt would come to rule the Sudan in a shared colonial arrangement with the British, importing Sudan's raw materials, as well as slave labor. Muhammad Ali is both credited and blamed for promoting Egypt's cotton agriculture. During times of high cotton prices, Egypt earned substantial amounts of foreign currency. Yet once the global cotton market collapsed, Egypt's economy collapsed. At this point, most of Muhammad Ali's modernization and reform projects came to a halt.

While Muhammad Ali was working to modernize Egypt by making it adapt to Western markets, the Ottoman sultan in Istanbul attempted various economic and legal reforms during the latter half of the nineteenth century in what we now call the Tanzimat period. The sultan gave up some of his power by granting the various ethnic and religious subject populations across the empire legal autonomy. A new school system was instituted, as well as a constitution that granted individuals certain rights. Yet the Ottoman reforms could not stem the mounting tide of nationalism, which had already galvanized communities across Europe. Under the influence of nationalism, Ottoman subjects came to identify as Turkish, Kurdish, Armenian, or Arab, with each community developing its own aspirations for self-rule based on shared language, ethnicity, and culture. In 1908, the Young Turk movement mobilized and tried to overthrow the Ottoman sultan, but this effort did not succeed. Internally weakened, the Ottoman Empire entered World War I in 1914 on the side of the German monarchy.

During the course of the war, the Ottoman military attacked, displaced, and killed an estimated 800,000 to 1.5 million members of the Armenian, Assyrian, and Greek communi-

---

Box 3.6

The Armenian Question

Despite consistent efforts of members of the Armenian American community to make it so, the United States government does not recognize the Ottoman military's targeting of Armenians during World War I as genocide, while most members of the European Union, Russia, Chile, and Argentina do. The most recent Armenian Genocide Bill was submitted to Congress in July 2013. Similar efforts in 2010 failed. It is a politically very sensitive matter that pits the government of Turkey against the government of present-day Armenia and the worldwide Armenian diaspora. The text of the 2013 Armenian Genocide Bill is on the webpage of the Armenian National Committee of America (http://www.anca.org/action_alerts/action_docs.php?docsid=15).

---

ties. Armenians call these events a genocide or Holocaust, claiming they were targeted for extermination as a non-Turkish, non-Muslim minority. Armenians have demanded some form of recognition and apology from the Turkish government. The Turkish government so far has refused to give either, arguing that the events happened in the context of a war, that members of the Armenian community had welcomed the invading Russian army, and that there were deaths on both sides.

By 1918, the allied British and French forces had defeated the Ottoman armies, bringing an end to the Ottoman Empire. In 1917, the Russian Revolution brought an end to the Russian monarchy, and after a period of civil war, which the Bolshevik forces won, the Union of Soviet Socialist Republics (USSR) was established in 1922. British, French, and Soviet forces went on to shape the Middle East for a significant part of the twentieth century.

Colonial Expansion and Anticolonial Movements

The beginning of European colonial rule in the Middle East is variously dated to Napoleon's landing in Egypt in 1798, or to the installation of a French colonial government in Algeria in 1830. The Russian Empire had taken control over what it called "Turkestan" (present-day Turkmenistan, Uzbekistan, and Tajikistan) by 1876, and Russian forces kept pushing into Iran and Afghanistan. Yet Western influences had been in the Middle East for much longer. European merchants had set up trading ventures throughout the Ottoman Empire, enjoying special rights and privileges through the Ottoman system of "capitulations." Christian missionaries, both Catholic and Protestant, had established churches and schools in or near the "Holy Land" and among Eastern Christian communities, which they sought to convert "back" to what the Europeans considered the true faith. European travelers came to visit biblical sites or marvel at the remnants of ancient empires, while painters and writers illustrated and described them. In his 1978 book *Orientalism*, Edward Said argues that these seventeenth- and eighteenth-century European encounters with the Middle East set the stage for the military occupation and colonial control of the nineteenth century.

Across North Africa, the Middle East, and Central Asia, local resistance mounted as soon as Europeans arrived to establish colonial rule. Resistance encompassed not only popular protests and military action, but also the resistance to perceived Western values and ideas. For instance, when Western powers wanted to "emancipate Muslim women" as part of their modernizing plans, the veil became a symbol Muslim women proudly wore as a sign of their rejection of Western influence. In Algeria, women decided to veil to show their solidarity with the anticolonial movement. As portrayed in the 1966 film *The Battle of Algiers*, they would conceal weapons under their full-body veils. Alternatively, they would unveil and dress in Western clothing in order to infiltrate Western neighborhoods of the capital without arousing suspicion. The veil became both symbol and weapon.

The independence struggles in the Middle East were fought by secular political groups, such as the Algerian National Liberation Front (Front de Libération Nationale, or FLN), or the Palestinian Liberation Organization (PLO). Political Islamism did not emerge as a potent force in Middle East politics until citizens became disenchanted with their secular postcolonial regimes in the latter part of the twentieth century. If Islamist organizations were part of anticolonial struggles, the secular regimes that assumed power after independence suppressed them. It was not uncommon for Islamists to be imprisoned and tortured in Egypt, attacked in Syria, and silenced in Iran and Turkey. It is in large part because of their opposition to secular regimes, which became increasingly corrupt and incompetent, that Islamist parties have enjoyed such widespread popularity since the late twentieth century. Like the popularity of secular independence parties before them, these Islamist movements will wane if they do not deliver what they promise. Strong challenges to Islamist rule were already mounted in Egypt and Turkey in the summer of 2013, when secular social movements took to the streets to demand more democratic, inclusive rule. In the case of Egypt, secular social movements in unison with the country's army unseated the Islamist president Mohammed Morsi after only one year in office.

French, British, and Soviet Colonial Rule

A key year in the discussion of European colonial designs in North Africa and the Middle East is 1916. That year, a British and a French diplomat, Sir Mark Sykes and François Georges-Picot, signed what would come to be known as the Sykes-Picot Agreement. In the document, the two European superpowers agreed to divide the territories of the Ottoman Empire into British and French spheres of influence. They were planning ahead for their victory in World War I. At the same time, British politicians also made promises of control over Ottoman territories to both Arab and Jewish leaders in order to obtain the communities' support for their war effort. Obviously, the Sykes-Picot Agreement and the promises to community leaders were incompatible. In the end, the Sykes-Picot Agreement prevailed, and the victorious powers created the current map of the Middle East via negotiations at various peace conferences after 1918. One could argue that the postwar map realized in print what had already been happening on the ground. The British had long established informal relations with Middle Eastern leaders along the sea route to India, while the French had a long history of expanding their influence along the Mediterranean coast of North Africa to Algeria, Tunisia, and Morocco. Spain and Italy had smaller zones of influence in North Africa—the former in Morocco, the latter in Libya. With the end of World War I, formal colonial rule of the "Middle East" began.

Soviet reconquest of the Russian Empire's territories in the Caucasus and Muslim Central Asia was not completed until the late 1920s, when local nationalist uprisings had been defeated. At that time, the Soviets began to reorganize farm lands into collectives and forcibly settle nomadic populations. Some of the residents attempted to escape the violence and the reorganization by fleeing to China and other neighboring countries in Europe and the Middle East. The borders of the Central Asian republics, were drawn to divide ethnic communities in order to dilute anti-Soviet nationalist sentiments. Stalin-era borders, like the ones drawn by French and British diplomats, still define the region today.

Colonial styles of rule varied considerably. To the degree that they could, colonizers would take advantage of existing cleavages between communities, or create new ones, and give one group significant privileges over others. For the most part, the Europeans moved into capital cities and took control over governments and the military, while leaving the countryside under the control of rural notables. In exceptional cases, however, the entire country was to be reformed in the Western image. In Algeria, for instance, the French pursued a strategy of "settler colonialism," which meant that they encouraged native French citizens, often impoverished, to settle on affordable land in Algeria. These French settlers raised their children in Algeria, and over generations they lost their connection to the mainland. French urbanites derogatorily called them *pieds-noirs*, meaning "black feet." By 1960, the *pieds-noirs* numbered over 1 million. When Algeria's independence struggle began, this group of people was caught between the two sides, not identifying as Algerian or French. They organized their own armed resistance and attacked both Algerian and French forces.

In contrast, in Syria, the French did not settle any of their mainland population, but instead influenced and coopted local elites, mainly recruited from religious minority communities. While the French held ultimate control in all important matters, there were degrees of collaboration and power sharing between French and local elites. Applying the principle of "divide and rule," the French divided the territory of the former Ottoman province of Syria into several administrative units along ethno-religious lines, including separate states for the Druze, the Alawites, and the Maronites. Only the latter became an independent country, when the Lebanese Republic was established in 1926; the others became part of the Republic of Syria.

British colonial rule also differed according to country. In the Arabian Peninsula, the British ruled by "protectorate," which meant that they entered into treaties with local rulers, promising them military protection in exchange for use of port facilities and favorable terms of trade. In Egypt, Jordan, and Iraq, the British ruled by "mandate," meaning they ostensibly tried to teach the locals the ins and outs of self-rule, while making most of the important decisions themselves. They established constitutional monarchies in each country after their own British model, and they encouraged the creation of political parties, provided they did not openly oppose British rule. The local populations, for their part, considered the newly created kings to be colonial puppets with little legitimacy. King Farouk of Egypt was exiled in 1952, while King Faisal II and several members of his family were killed in Iraq in 1958. Both Egypt and Iraq became republics, while in Jordan, despite several serious challenges, the British-instituted monarchy survived.

Soviet colonial rule was aimed at reorganizing traditional societies along communist principles. Private property was abolished and religion was outlawed. Collective production planned by the state, be it in agriculture or industry, created a new work environment. Everybody had to learn Russian in schools. Cultural, linguistic, and religious differences were suppressed. Due to war or state planning, entire communities were uprooted. Both the countryside and urban centers were affected, but the countryside probably experienced a more dramatic change under the modernizing force of the state.

It also bears mention that some Middle Eastern countries engaged in colonial schemes of their own. Most prominently, the Egyptian ruler Muhammad Ali (mentioned above under "The Late Ottoman Empire") invaded the Sudan several times in order to control the spice, gold, and slave trade. From 1899 to 1956, Egypt and Britain together ruled the Sudan as a "condominium" (Latin for "co-rule"). It was during that time that a Sudanese Muslim elite emerged and took control of the government in Khartoum. Southern Sudan would rise up against northern dominance after independence, leading to decades of civil war, which was only resolved in 2005. In 2011, after a referendum, a new country of South Sudan, with Juba the capital city, emerged. A much less known ongoing independence struggle is taking place in the region of Western Sahara, currently under Moroccan control. In 1991, after a ceasefire agreement between warring factions, the United Nations Mission for the Referendum in Western Sahara (MINURSO) was created. A referendum about possible independence of Western Sahara has yet to take place.

Anticolonial Movements

One of the fiercest anticolonial struggles emerged in British-controlled Palestine shortly after World War I. As stated earlier, during World War I, British diplomats and politicians had given conflicting promises to both Arab allies in the Middle East and Jewish interest groups in London. They had told Arab leaders that they would be able to rule an Arab state after the imminent collapse of the Ottoman Empire, but at the same time they promised Baron Walter Rothschild, a prominent leader in the Jewish community in Britain, that Palestine was to become a national home for the Jewish community. After World War I, the British did not fulfill either promise, but instead divided Ottoman territorial spoils with France. However, Arab, Palestinian, and Jewish communities continued to project their national ambitions onto the same piece of land. Palestinians made claims of land ownership, pointing to olive groves their families had tended for generations, as well as their long-standing Christian and

Muslim traditions. Jewish immigrants and refugees, who began to arrive in the region as a result of persecution in Europe, pointed to their historical and religious links to the land once ruled by King David. The native minority Jewish communities that existed predominantly in and around Jerusalem did not get involved in the nationalist project initially.

At the turn of the twentieth century, emerging European nationalist ideologies prescribed states where people shared the same language, culture, and ethnicity. Minority communities often experienced stereotyping, harassment, and legal disenfranchisement. Jewish communities across Europe, many of whom had led relatively assimilated lives, became targets of anti-Semitic hate. As a consequence, Jewish leaders organized rescue efforts. They argued that Jews had their own legitimate national claim for a state—not unlike the Germans, Poles, French, and others. The political movement for the establishment of a Jewish state in Palestine was called Zionism. Theodor Herzl, an Austrian journalist, wrote an influential book called *The Jewish State* in 1896. The idea for a separate Jewish state did not immediately find a warm reception, as Jewish communities had by then lived for two millennia in other countries, which they considered their homes. Yet, as European anti-Semitism grew, more and more Jewish leaders were convinced that a Jewish state was the only way to protect their community.

Meanwhile, the local population in Palestine saw the influx of European Jews with a mixture of hostility and fear. They organized resistance against the British colonial regime as well as against Jewish settlers. From their perspective, Jewish communities did to Palestine what *pieds-noirs* had done to Algeria: dispossess the native population. When the British tried to restrict immigration numbers to Palestine in order to reassure and calm the anxious Arab population, Jewish groups organized an underground militia and attacked the British. From their perspective, every Jewish life that escaped the slaughterhouses of Europe needed to find safety in a Jewish state.

Realizing that they were in the middle of a conflict they could not win, the British proposed the idea of partition of the territory into Jewish and Arab sectors in the late 1930s. The partition proposal was revisited by the United Nations after World War II. Local Arabs strongly rejected the proposed partition, seeing themselves as the legitimate inhabitants of the region, where they constituted the majority of the population at the time. It made no sense to them that these European immigrants should be entitled to half of their territory. The United Nations, however, fully cognizant of the horrendous loss of Jewish life during the Holocaust, saw it as its moral duty to create a Jewish state. In 1947, UN Resolution 181 partitioned the territory, which almost immediately led to civil war. One year later, after the official end of British control over Palestine, the State of Israel was established, which turned the ongoing civil conflict into an international war.

Both sides in the Palestine-Israel conflict continue to remember the 1948 struggle very differently. An Israeli narrative of the war can be found at the website of the Israeli Ministry of Foreign Affairs (http://www.mfa.gov.il/MFA/History/Modern+History/Israel+wars/Israels+War+of+Independence+-+1947+-+1949.htm).

A Palestinian narrative is available at the website "1948" (http://www.1948.org.uk/un-resolution-181).

Box 3.7

The Battle of Algiers

Gillo Pontecorvo's 1966 film *The Battle of Algiers* is probably the most compelling visual rendering of an Arab independence movement. In one scene French soldiers cordon off the entire Arab "old city" (in Arabic the *casbah*) in Algiers with barbed wire, restricting the movement of the residents within. In another scene of the film, French policemen detonate bombs in the *casbah* to punish an alleged suspect for killing a policeman. In response, Algerian women place bombs in popular bars and in an Air France travel agency in the "modern city" of Algiers, home to most of the expatriate French community. The film shows how the conflict became increasingly brutal as each side reacted to the other's increasing use of violence. The film is available on YouTube (http://www.youtube.com/watch?v=7bOr_U_92xE).

The fiercest anticolonial struggle against French rule happened in Algeria. What Algerians call "the War of Independence" and the French simply "the Algerian War" lasted from 1954 to 1962. It pitted Algeria's National Liberation Front (in French, Front de Libération Nationale, or FLN) against French police, military, and paramilitary units, resulting in large numbers of civilian casualties.

The French had the stronger military and security apparatus, with which they battled locals who knew the terrain and the culture. It was an unequal war, with vastly more Algerian casualties than French casualties. It has been argued that the Algerian struggle for independence was so bloody because of large numbers of French settlers, who, after several generations, felt at home in Algeria and did not want to leave. When Algerians demanded that all French go home, *pieds-noirs* organized their own resistance that targeted Algerian as well as any French forces that supported the end of colonial rule in Algeria. After the war ended in 1962, the French government evacuated 800,000 *pieds-noirs* back to France.

The FLN turned itself into a political party, and its guerrillas became the new country's army. Deriving their legitimacy from their willingness to sacrifice their lives in the fight against the French, the FLN initially did not have, and later did not tolerate, domestic opposition. Challenge to the FLN's one-party rule would eventually emerge in the form of the Islamic Salvation Front. After the Front won municipal elections, and stood to win national elections, the military staged a coup and took over power. A ten-year civil war ensued (1991–2001) that shattered the country's social and economic fabric. Algeria remains a state run by the military and security apparatus, rather than elected officials.

In other Middle Eastern countries, departing European colonial powers left local, pro-Western elites in charge, most of them urbanites, who did not necessarily have the interests of the larger national community in mind. These elites would come to face challenges from their military, which became the recruiting ground for a new generation of nationalist leaders. Most of the military men came from modest backgrounds and rose to power through the

---

Box 3.8

Rule by Martial Law

Many independent states in the Middle East used to govern their populations via "martial law," often under a declaration of a "state of emergency." In a state of emergency, civic rights and liberties are severely restricted, allowing governments to detain government opponents without granting them due process, to shut down the press if it becomes too critical, and to limit participation in the electoral political process. For instance, Egypt's state of emergency lasted from 1967 to 2012; Algeria's went from 1965 to 1976, 1988 to 1989, and 1992 to 2011; and Turkey's was in place from 1980 to 1987, and from 1990 to 2002 in predominantly Kurdish regions of Turkey. Several governments declared a state of emergency in the wake of the Arab uprisings in 2011, including Tunisia, Bahrain, and Yemen.

---

ranks. For instance, a "Free Officers' Coup" brought General Gamal Abdel Nasser to power in Egypt in 1952. Nasser abolished the British-instituted constitutional monarchy, created a republic, and made sure to remain its president until he died in 1970. Colonel Muammar Qaddafi took power in Libya in a military coup in 1969. In Syria, similarly, Hafez al-Assad used the military to rise to power and ruled the country from 1970 until 2000, when he was succeeded by his son Bashar al-Assad. Saddam Hussein took the same path in Iraq in 1979, and remained in power until 2003. In Turkey, Mustafa Kemal Atatürk rose from humble origins through the Turkish army to become president, a post he held until his death in 1938. Mohammad Reza, a brigadier in the army, managed to overthrow the Qajar Dynasty of Iran to establish his own, the Pahlavi Dynasty, instead. In the post-independence era, the military and internal security forces remained important political players in most Middle Eastern countries.

The states on the Arabian Peninsula followed a different anti- and postcolonial trajectory. The local emirs and sheikhs had entered into protectorate agreements with the British in order to solidify their own rule against that of rival elite families or popular uprisings. These elites did not, on the whole, object to foreign presence, but rather found ways to prolong it. Because the states that developed in the Gulf discovered oil, the leaders had a steady and ample stream of income with which they could, if necessary, buy off opposition to their regime. In fact, many of the Gulf states struck a so-called "ruling bargain" with their citizens, whereby the state offered a wide array of benefits to individuals, including free education, health care, and housing, in return for their political acquiescence to the regime.

One Gulf country that claims to have escaped colonial influence altogether is Saudi Arabia. Abd al-Aziz ibn Saud (1881–1953) was a tribal leader from the eastern region of Najd. He was a charismatic figure with remarkable military and diplomatic skills, and he derived part of his political legitimacy from a conservative interpretation of Islam,

---

Box 3.9

Islam in Saudi Arabia

The Saudis follow the teaching of a charismatic preacher by the name of Muhammad ibn Abd al-Wahhab (1703–1792), who struck an important political alliance with rulers of the al-Saud clan in central Arabia at the time. He urged believers to return to the fundamentals of the faith, and to shun later interpretations of sacred texts. Article 1 of the Saudi constitution enshrines the Quran and the sayings and deeds of the Prophet Muhammad in the hadith literature as the foundational legal texts of the country.

Saudis do not call themselves Wahhabis but Muslims. Yet their religious practice differs significantly from that of their coreligionists in other parts of the region. Saudi society is more strictly gender-segregated than most other Muslim countries; as of the printing of this book, Saudi women still cannot vote or drive cars. A "religious police" ensures that shopkeepers close their businesses to pray during daily prayer times. Religious difference is not tolerated in Saudi Arabia, although noncitizens who work in Saudi Arabia are allowed to worship in specifically designated areas.

Contemporary opposition to the rule of the king of Saudi Arabia has come from both secular and ultraconservative religious camps. The most prominent member in the latter camp was Osama bin Laden, who accused Saudi Arabia's leadership of selling out to the West and abandoning the true principles of Islam. Fifteen of the nineteen hijackers that perpetrated the terror attacks of September 11, 2001, were citizens of Saudi Arabia.

---

called Wahhabism. Ibn Saud established the Kingdom of Saudi Arabia in 1932, after successfully defeating or outmaneuvering all local rivals. Once Ibn Saud controlled the holy cities of Mecca and Medina, his rule had added religious legitimacy. In 1938, prospectors discovered oil in the Arabian desert. With oil money in Ibn Saud's coffers, he was able to consolidate his regime and present himself as a true defender of Islam, at a time when the other Arab states embraced secular ideologies of nationalism or socialism. American oil companies seized their opportunities in Saudi Arabia, just at the time that U.S. oil wells were running dry, and a special relationship was born.

From the Cold War to the Arab Uprisings

Many countries in the Middle East obtained their independence during the time of the Cold War. In pragmatic terms, this meant that each country had to find a patron and ally in either the United States or the Soviet Union. As part of their political strategy, each superpower sought to limit the other's influence in other countries via alliances. The United States sent economic and military aid to countries that felt threatened by the Soviet Union, which, in turn, sent aid to its own allies. In this binary global power game, some Middle Eastern states enlisted on the side of the United States (e.g., Iran, Israel, Jordan, Lebanon, Turkey, and most of the Gulf states), others on the side of the USSR (e.g., Tunisia, Egypt, South Yemen, and Syria). The Soviet Union also incorporated the Muslim-majority regions of Central Asia, which became the countries of Kazakhstan, Kyrgyzstan, Uzbekistan, Tajikistan, and Turkmenistan after the Soviet Union's dissolution. Gamal Abdel Nasser of Egypt briefly championed nonalignment, and became the president of the Non-Aligned Movement (NAM) in 1964. But the countries involved never unified to become a legitimate third power on the world stage.

The Cold War created a situation where countries that had fought so hard to escape colonial control now had to seek out one of two foreign patrons, and thus continue foreign interference in their domestic affairs. In return for financial aid, Middle East governments had to open up their countries to U.S. or Soviet markets, welcome U.S. or Soviet military bases and advisers, or sign treaties of mutual cooperation. Overall, the period of the Cold War was not conducive to the development of strong democratic institutions in the Middle East. Yet Cold War trajectories by no means followed identical patterns. The Iranian monarchy, for example, began as an ally of the United States and later became an enemy, whereas Egypt, a country with a state-run economy and anti-Western ideology, became a champion of capitalist market principles and an initiator of peace with Israel. Over time, superpower support for Middle East regimes friendly to their cause—whether or not those regimes had been democratically elected—created a groundswell of resentment among the local populations.

The growing discontent of average people who had limited opportunities for political participation fueled opposition movements in many countries, which were generally violently suppressed by increasingly authoritarian governments. Since the ruling ideologies across the Middle East, with the exception of the Gulf states, were secular and "modern" following a Western model, the opposition movements often mobilized around religious ideologies.

Iran

During the Cold War, Iran became an early ally of the United States, mainly because it saw itself threatened by communist influence. The United States helped Mohammad Reza Pahlavi, the Shah of Iran, to build up his army and internal security apparatus. In 1951, Prime Minister Mohammad Mosaddeq led a populist movement to nationalize Iran's oil, confirming the Shah's fears of communist infiltration. Once the parliament passed the oil nationalization law, the British called for a boycott of Iranian oil sales across the globe. The United States, propelled by its own oil interests in other regions of the Middle East, supported the boycott, leading to a collapse of the Iranian economy. Rising domestic resentment against Mosaddeq propelled the Iranian military, financed by the United States and still loyal to the Shah, to depose Mosaddeq and reinstate the Pahlavi regime. Once back in power, the Shah created the SAVAK, an internal security apparatus that would become well known for its repressive practices. Both the United States and Israel aided the Shah in running extensive surveillance operations, and as the regime cracked down, internal opposition grew.

Box 3.10

The Iranian Hostage Crisis

On November 4, 1979, soon after the Iranian Revolution, a group of radical students took fifty-two hostages in the U.S. Embassy of Tehran, putting the Islamic Republic on an immediate collision course with the United States. The students, most of them secular, demanded the return of the Shah from the United States so he could stand trial in Iran. The United States did not extradite the Shah, who was undergoing medical treatment. The Shah died in exile in Egypt in July 1980.

A botched, secret military rescue attempt of the hostages in August 1980 cost President Jimmy Carter his chance for re-election. The hostages were released on January 20, 1981, the day after President Ronald Reagan had been sworn into office. They had been in captivity for 444 days. Diplomatic relations between the two countries have since remained strained, with Ayatollah Khomeini famously calling the United States "the Great Satan," and President George W. Bush referring to Iran as part of a larger "Axis of Evil." Barack Obama's phone call to Iranian president Hassan Rouhani in late September 2013 was the first direct conversation between leaders of the two countries since 1979.

As left-wing parties struggled to mount their opposition in Iran, a new voice of dissent emerged, the voice of radical Shiite cleric Ayatollah Khomeini. Previously an unknown member of the Iranian religious establishment, Khomeini emerged into the public with openly antigovernment and anti-Western sermons. In 1963 the SAVAK arrested Khomeini, which led to massive street protests. Khomeini was exiled to Turkey, then Iraq, and finally to France. His taped political sermons secretly made it into Iran, however, where his popularity spread. When the 1973 OPEC oil embargo quadrupled world oil prices, Iran's revenues rose dramatically and the Shah began purchasing billions of dollars' worth of U.S. weapons. With the weapons came U.S. defense contractors, military advisers, and Western personnel, exacerbating anti-American sentiments. Opposition organized both on the political Left and among members of the conservative religious establishment, culminating in the 1979 Iranian Revolution. The revolution ultimately deposed the Shah and turned Iran's monarchy into an Islamic republic. Secular and other opposition forces as well as religious minorities were suppressed, Before any election, candidate lists are vetted by the Council of Guardians, made up of religious authorities. Political decisions are similarly scrutinized to assure they are in accordance with Islamic law.

The new leaders of the Islamic Republic undertook many social reforms that benefitted previously marginalized communities, especially in the provinces of Iran. While many Western observers did not expect the new religious leadership to last very long, thinking it ill equipped for political office, the Islamists proved adept at using the country's large oil incomes to subsidize welfare programs, education, and health care. Large-scale, organized, anti-regime forces would not emerge until the 2009 Green Movement.

Egypt

Although Egypt had nominally achieved independence from Great Britain in 1922, the British continued to exert significant political influence and extended their military presence on Egyptian soil, protecting their trade routes to India. Egypt's King Farouk proved to be a rather unpopular ruler, and the parliamentary elites did little to meet the needs of the Egyptian masses. Opposition against local elites, as well as the British, began to mobilize in 1928. Led by a schoolteacher, Hasan al-Banna, a group emerged that called itself the Muslim Brotherhood. Islam, rather than Western-style modernization, was believed to be the solution for the challenges facing Egyptian society. Foreigners and foreign ideology could not be trusted. Militant members of the Brotherhood began to attack foreigners, as well as pro-Western Egyptian politicians. They killed, for instance, Prime Minister Mahmud al-Nuqrashi, who wanted to outlaw the Muslim Brotherhood, in 1948. In response, Hasan al-Banna was killed in 1949.

In the early 1950s, attacks on British army units in Egypt increased, and after a particularly bloody British retaliation, riots and demonstrations shut down central Cairo. In the midst of this chaos, a group of young military officers under the leadership of Gamal Abdel Nasser staged a coup in July 1952. Nasser would rule Egypt for the next twenty-nine years. He became a widely popular proponent of Arab socialism, secularism, and anticolonialism. He also banned the Muslim Brotherhood in Egypt. Nasser promoted secular, socialist ideologies that championed Arab language and culture, but not Islam. In 1958, Nasser attempted to have Arab leaders join a United Arab Republic, in order to build a strong, unified Arab political voice. Only Syria and Yemen joined, however, and the alliance broke apart in 1961.

Nasser was a particularly charismatic leader, and his radio broadcasts would bring traffic to a standstill not only in Cairo, but in other Arab capitals as well. He was popular with Egyptian peasants due to his land reforms. He expanded public education and built up a national healthcare system. In 1956, he nationalized the British-controlled Suez Canal, as a direct challenge to the former colonial power. The seizure of the Suez Canal led to retaliatory action by the combined forces of Great Britain, France, and Israel. The United States and the Soviet Union reprimanded Great Britain, France, and Israel for the attack, fearing destabilization in the region. Thousands of Egyptian Jews were expelled from Egypt over the Israeli attack, as were British and French nationals who resided in Egypt. Egypt moved further into the Soviet sphere of influence, asking for and receiving significant financial and military aid.

Nasser was discredited by the defeat of the Egyptian army in the Arab-Israeli War of 1967. During that war, Israel again defeated all Arab armies, and it seized the West Bank (including East Jerusalem), the Gaza Strip, the Syrian Golan Heights, and the Egyptian Sinai Peninsula. No longer a credible champion of Arab unity, Nasser and his Pan-Arab ideology lost influence. He died in 1970. Nasser's successor, Anwar Sadat, had been one of the officers who had staged the 1952 coup. Rather than following Nasser's political lead, however, Sadat cut Egypt's relations with the Soviet Union and aligned Egypt with the United States. The United States and Egypt established regular diplomatic relations in 1974.

In 1979, Sadat signed a peace treaty with Israel at Camp David in the United States, a deal that President Jimmy Carter helped to broker. Subsequently, Egypt became the second largest foreign aid recipient of the United States, after Israel. Sadat opened Egypt to global markets, cut domestic subsidies, and reduced public employment. His policies followed structural adjustment directives of the International Monetary Fund (IMF). The measures created significant hardships among the Egyptian population, but they benefitted a small circle of elites. The system that evolved has been described as "crony capitalism," meaning that businessmen with close ties to the government were able to purchase former state-owned enterprises or licenses at below market value, and in return they paid kickbacks to members of the government. In this game, people always lost. The West rewarded Anwar Sadat with the Nobel Peace Prize for his peacemaking efforts, but his pro-Western policies were deeply resented by Egyptians at large. Sadat was assassinated by a member of a radical Islamist group during a military parade in 1981.

Sadat's successor, Hosni Mubarak, continued Sadat's pro-Western policies. Egypt remained the second largest aid recipient of the United States for the next three decades. Mubarak continued to court foreign investments as long as they benefitted his inner circle, while at the same time restricting the press and political opposition; in particular, his security apparatus monitored and jailed increasing numbers of Muslim Brotherhood members. As Mubarak began to groom his son Gamal to succeed him as Egypt's next president, the Tunisian uprising erupted and spilled into Egypt. After weeks of popular protest in Cairo and other urban centers, with the army refusing to use excessive force, Mubarak resigned.

Popular Uprisings Across the Middle East

After 1990, when the Cold War had ended, the global political order was restructured. Countries that emerged from under Soviet control, such as the majority-Muslim republics of Central Asia, began to express their ethnic heritage and traditions freely, and they rejected Russian TV and radio channels, the Cyrillic script, and mandatory Russian classes in their schools. Yet soon, they saw conflict erupt between the old, governing elites, and new parties and movements that were emerging. Government corruption, high unemployment, and restrictions on the press and civil liberties made the region ripe for protest moments. The so-called Rose Revolution of 2003 toppled President Eduard Shevardnadze in the Republic of Georgia. Kyrgyzstan saw popular revolts that ousted governments in 2005 and 2010. In Uzbekistan, protesters went out on the streets in the aftermath of the Kyrgyz 2005 uprising, but they were met with a violent response by security forces. Throughout early 2000, popular protests challenged Central Asian governments to be accountable to their people.

Yet, with the U.S.-led war in neighboring Afghanistan and the rise of radical Islamists who crossed borders to join the fighting, Central Asian countries became strategically important, and stable authoritarian governments that cooperated in the "war against terror" were preferable to democratic, but unstable ones. Moreover, with significant oil and gas reserves, many of the Central Asian regimes have the option to buy the consent of their citizens, rather than offer political reforms. It is the same line of reasoning that made Western powers financially and militarily support leaders in the Arab world, despite an obvious record of undemocratic governance. For its part, the Russian government, too, prized stability in the region, including the suppression of Islamist insurgencies as well as pro–Western democracy movements that could gain influence and even spread into the Russian Federation.

Then, in 2008 the world experienced the largest economic crash since the Great Depression in the late 1920s. Financial markets had become so closely intertwined globally that a debt crisis, initially the result of reckless mortgage lending and securitizing in the United States, had a domino effect everywhere else. In the Middle East, where some of the richest citizens had invested in what turned out to be toxic assets, economies collapsed. North African and Levant countries that rely heavily on European markets for their exports saw European buyers disappear. European tourists stopped coming to North African and eastern Mediterranean beaches. Remittance money stopped flowing from the rich Gulf countries to the poorer neighboring countries that relied on them. Middle Eastern governments had less money to subsidize food or other daily necessities, just as global food prices began to go up in response to droughts. As prices and unemployment rose and incomes dropped, average citizens across the Middle East felt the squeeze. Young people, who make up more than half of the populations across the Middle East, were particularly affected by the economic downturn. Forced to take odd jobs, often in the informal economy, they had few realistic prospects. But they had aspirations.

Then, on December 17, 2010, in the little known town of Sidi Bouzid in Tunisia, 160 miles south of the capital Tunis, a twenty-six-year-old street vendor by the name of Mohamed Bouazizi set himself on fire in front of a local government office. Days before, police had come to confiscate the produce he was selling, and while doing it, they had publicly humiliated him. He had tried to complain to local officials in person, but had not been heard. In an act of desperation, he killed himself in public, sparking first local, then national protests against police corruption and mistreatment of civilians, and ultimately against the government that permitted such abuses to happen. The popular demands for human rights and dignity were accompanied by a public indictment of political elites that pilfered public coffers and abused their powers. President Zine al-Abidine Ben Ali, who had ruled Tunisia for twenty-three years, stepped down on January 14, after his military refused to follow his orders and shoot the protesters. In other words, in less than one month, people in the street—students, unions, civic organizations—brought down a seemingly untouchable government. The news made headlines across the world, and in other Arab countries citizens began to ask themselves, "If Ben Ali can be made to leave, can we change our government, too?"

Massive demonstrations took place in Tahrir Square, Cairo, on January 25, 2011. That day was National Police Day in Egypt, a holiday President Mubarak had instituted in 2009. The Egyptian police, not unlike the security forces in Tunisia that had harassed Mohamed Bouazizi, had a longstanding reputation for bribery and corruption. Egypt also had a tragic victim of police abuse: the twenty-eight-year-old Khaled Said, who had been beaten to death by police in Alexandria, allegedly for drug possession. A holiday in honor of the Egyptian police was therefore not a day many Egyptians wanted to celebrate. A

Box 3.11

Khaled Said and Public Protest

In response to Khaled Said's death at the hand of Egyptian police, Egyptian Google employee Wael Ghonim created a Facebook page called "We are all Khaled Said" (in colloquial Egyptian Arabic, *Kullena Khaled Said*). Other anti-regime protest groups joined forces, such as the Egyptian Movement for Change, commonly known as *Kefaya* (in English, "Enough") created in 2004, and the April 6 Youth Movement, created in 2008. Using the event feature on Facebook, they asked swelling numbers of followers to show up at public protests. A first protest in Alexandria to commemorate the death of Khaled Said brought out several thousand people. Subsequently, protests grew larger in scope and numbers.

Wael Ghonim's memoir of the events is titled *Revolution 2.0: The Power of the People is Greater than the People in Power*. The "We are all Khaled Said" Facebook pages are available in Arabic and English (http://www.facebook.com/ElShaheeed and https://www.facebook.com/elshaheeed.co.uk).

---

protest action was organized via social media and through personal networks, bringing at first thousands, then tens and hundreds of thousands of citizens out into Tahrir Square, determined to stay until there was change.

Mubarak stepped down on February 11, 2011. In January 2012, an Egyptian court sentenced Mubarak to life in prison for his role in the killings of protesters during the uprising. Egypt's Supreme Council of the Armed Forces (SCAF) formed an interim government. During subsequent parliamentary elections, the Islamist Freedom and Justice Party, which is affiliated with the Muslim Brotherhood, was elected to power by a large margin (38 percent), alongside the socially and religiously even more conservative al-Nour Party (28 percent). In the final presidential run-off elections, the Muslim Brotherhood candidate Mohammed Morsi narrowly defeated Ahmed Shafik, a candidate with close ties to the Mubarak regime. Morsi claimed victory in part because he obtained the votes of secular opponents of the old regime. Only a few weeks into the new political order, these same secular voices became openly critical of controversial decisions of the Morsi-led government, and they began returning to the streets for more anti-regime protests.

During the time of this dramatic political change in Egypt, longtime Yemeni president Ali Abdullah Saleh tried to leverage his ability to fight al-Qaeda terrorists with the United States, and he struck backroom deals with various local elites, hoping to stay in power. However, street protests continued in many different cities, especially university cities, and the Yemeni army began to disintegrate into opposing factions. After months of mediation from neighboring Gulf states that did not want revolution to spread to their countries, Saleh finally abdicated his rule. An interim government was put in place with the mandate to prepare for national elections in 2014, but the political situation remained unsettled.

In other countries across the Middle East, presidents were not deposed as easily. Having witnessed the events in Tunisia and Egypt, other rulers made sure they had the allegiance of their armies. In Libya and Syria, well-trained and well-equipped military units continued to follow their orders to shoot protesters. Libya's Muammar Qaddafi had elite units under the command of his four sons, as well as a mercenary army of soldiers recruited from neighboring countries. He ordered them to crush the uprising against his regime without any compunction for loss of lives. It was the threat of widespread killings of civilians that led NATO—with the support of the Arab League—to institute first a no-fly zone over Libya, and later to provide air support for anti-Qaddafi forces. Qaddafi himself was captured and killed close to his hometown of Sirte on October 20, 2011. Elections to a new parliament took place in 2012, with a broad coalition of liberals and moderate Islamists running and winning under the umbrella of the National Forces Alliance. Radical Islamist parties did not obtain a large share of votes. Nevertheless, Islamist forces took up resistance to the new government. Meanwhile, ethnic and regional militias with a variety of allegiances compete for control of territory and resources, making the country ungovernable.

The Syrian uprising continues as of the writing of this book. As happened in Tunisia, it started in a remote provincial town. In March 2011, a group of teenagers spray-painted anti-regime graffiti on the walls of buildings in Daraa, a predominantly Sunni town in southern Syria. State security forces promptly arrested the teenagers. When parents demanded their release, clashes with the police resulted. Anti-regime protests erupted across Syria, and they grew in size and organization. The Syrian president, Bashar al-Assad, used his military to crush the uprising. A member of a Shiite minority group, the Alawites, al-Assad could rely on most of the officer corps recruited from his community. In a reorganized Syria, it was clear that the Alawites would lose power, so they were fighting both for the regime and for their own survival. As more protesters—"terrorists" in the eyes of the government—were killed, funerals became sites for even larger protests. Members of the opposition organized an interim transitional government council in Turkey. In order to counter the regime's firepower, the opposition got armed, and they welcomed increasing numbers of defectors from the Syrian army, as well as armed Islamist groups from Iraq and other parts of the Middle East.

As efforts of various international bodies—the Arab League, the European Union, the United Nations—failed to mediate the conflict, the country descended into civil war and Syrian citizens began fleeing the violence to neighboring Turkey, Jordan, and Lebanon, and beyond.

Antigovernment sentiment in Algeria, Morocco, Jordan, and the Gulf states was either quickly and violently subdued, or it did not gain popular traction. In the case of the monarchies in Morocco and Jordan, reforms were promised and put into practice, which stifled the spread of public protests. In Algeria, citizens did not turn out in large numbers when called to protest in public squares, possibly because of vivid memories of their civil war during the 1990s. Algeria was also able to employ oil revenues for public subsidies. Similarly, Gulf monarchies used their oil money to fend off popular discontent. The rulers of Kuwait and Saudi Arabia made gestures at political reform. In the case of

Bahrain, however, home to the U.S. Fifth Fleet, Saudi troops were called in to disperse anti-regime protesters. Bahrain's ruling al-Khalifa family is Sunni, whereas the majority of the population is Shiite, so the popular protests raised the specter of a Sunni-Shiite sectarian crisis in the Gulf.

Looking Beyond the Protests: Ideological Divides, Economic Challenges

Since secular regimes took the brunt of the wave of protests across the Middle East, and saw their governments overturned (e.g., in Egypt, Tunisia, Libya, and Yemen), it appeared that the political wave that was sweeping over the region might be anti-secular and pro-Islamist, which greatly concerned Western observers. Yet, as evidenced by the 2009 Green Movement in Iran, and the 2013 protest movements in Turkey as well as in Egypt, it is clear that such lines cannot be drawn so simply. A relatively small protest against commercial development of one of the last parks in Istanbul turned into massive street protests against the Islamist government of Prime Minister Recep Tayyip Erdoğan. The protesters were met by a violent police response, which, in turn, brought more protesters into the streets in cities across Turkey. In Egypt, a new protest movement called Tamarod (Arabic for "rebellion"), made up of some of the social organizations that had brought down the Mubarak regime, collected over 22 million signatures that demanded an end to Morsi's regime. The same organization brought thousands into Cairo's streets on June 30, 2013, exactly one year after Morsi had been sworn into office, and within days, the Egyptian military staged a coup that removed Morsi. While anti-Morsi protesters celebrated in Tahrir Square as army helicopters flew overhead, Morsi supporters gathered in similar numbers in Rabia al-Adawiya Square in another part of Cairo and demanded that their elected president return. In the Islamic Republic of Iran, a reformist president was popularly elected in June 2013, triggering a fierce backlash from regime hardliners.

The fault line between Islamist and anti-Islamist political forces in the Middle East runs deep. Each side is deeply suspicious of the motives of the other. Islamist parties fear a loss of cultural identity due to secular Westernization, while anti-Islamist parties and movements fear that Islamists want to impose religious laws that will limit their individual freedoms and oppress religious and other minorities. Islamist parties, meanwhile, have a vivid memory of surveillance, incarceration, and intimidation during the time of authoritarian, secular rule. In other words, they experienced in the past the very government action the other side fears.

The economic troubles that beset the Middle East, from North Africa to Central Asia, will take a long time to fix. New governments will not be able to offer quick solutions. The elites that have profited from the old regimes will fight to retain their power and privileges, perpetuating the vast gap between the rich and the poor. With growing populations, and mounting unemployment among the youth, governments face increasingly impatient citizens. But stark economic inequalities are challenges societies face on a global scale. Global solidarity manifested itself during the Arab uprisings, when young people in Tahrir Square raised posters that showed support with the Occupy movement in the United States, and vice versa. There are signs that young and old are demanding a more equitable distribution of wealth and a more sustainable economy. Those who protest against their government's abuses of fundamental civil and human rights will be able to count on the support of a global audience via social networks, blogs, and alternative media. Methods of nonviolent protest can be learned and shared. While the role of militaries and police forces across the region cannot be underestimated, they will have to contend with increasingly sophisticated, nonviolent social movements, which have already begun to reshape the Middle East.

References and Further Research

Abu El-Haj, Nadia. 2001. *Facts on the Ground: Archaeological Practice and Territorial Self-Fashioning in Israeli Society*. Chicago: University of Chicago Press.

Atabaki, Touraj, and John O'Kane, eds. 1998. *Post-Soviet Central Asia*. London: Tauris.

Boyce, Mary. 2001. *Zoroastrians: Their Religious Beliefs and Practices*. New York: Routledge.

Cleveland, William L. 2004. *A History of the Modern Middle East*. 3rd ed. Boulder, CO: Westview Press.

Donner, Fred M. 2010. *Muhammad and the Believers: At the Origins of Islam*. Cambridge, MA: Harvard University Press.

Gelvin, James L. 2012. *The Arab Uprisings: What Everyone Needs to Know*. New York: Oxford University Press.

Ghonim, Wael. 2012. *Revolution 2.0: The Power of the People Is Greater Than the People in Power*. Boston: Houghton Mifflin Harcourt.

Haas, Mark L., and David W. Lesch, eds. 2013. *The Arab Spring: Change and Resistance in the Middle East*. Boulder, CO: Westview Press.

Haddad, Bassam, Rosie Bsheer, and Ziad Abu-Rish, eds. 2012. *The Dawn of the Arab Uprisings: End of an Old Order?* London: Pluto Press.

Hourani, Albert. 1991. *A History of the Arab Peoples*. Cambridge, MA: Harvard University Press.

Lockman, Zachary. 2004. *Contending Visions of the Middle East: The History and Politics of Orientalism*. Cambridge: Cambridge University Press.

Meskell, Lynn. 1998. *Archaeology Under Fire: Nationalism, Politics and Heritage in the Eastern Mediterranean and Middle East*. New York: Routledge.

Mousavi, Ali. 2012. *Persepolis: Discovery and Afterlife of a World Wonder*. Boston: Walter de Gruyter.

Van de Mieroop, Marc. 2006. *A History of the Ancient Near East, ca. 3000–323 BC*. 2nd ed. Malden, MA: Blackwell.

4

Language in the Middle East

LUCIA VOLK

Language defines the culture and identity of a person. We are what we speak. Children learn their mother tongue by picking up cues in the environment around them. Most linguistic processes happen at an unconscious level. Speakers do not intentionally look for a noun, verb, and object when formulating a sentence in their mother tongue. What we speak connects us to our family, neighborhood, and community. Language enables us to be social beings, but also it can become a barrier that divides us from people who do not speak our language. Learning foreign languages has therefore been one of the most fundamental humanist projects in the history of education, and it belongs to the core mission of most liberal arts curricula. In many colleges and universities, students cannot graduate without fulfilling a foreign language requirement.

Prior to nation-states, multiethnic and multilinguistic monarchies were the political norm, and political elites often spoke a different language than many of their subjects. With the advent of the nation-state in the nineteenth century, political units became smaller, and they were increasingly defined by one dominant language, suppressing minority languages and dialects. Official languages were standardized (via the publication of lexica and grammar books), and they were taught and tested in schools. Individuals who grew up in nonstandard language communities often ended up politically and economically disenfranchised. Language is therefore not just a matter of cultural difference and diversity, but also a matter of social justice.

Language Diversity in the Middle East

Preceding chapters have emphasized the fact that the so-called Middle East is historically, politically, religiously, and economically plural. So it should come as no surprise to hear that the languages of the region belong to various branches of larger language families. Arabic, Hebrew, and Aramaic belong to the family of Semitic languages; Persian, Kurdish, and Urdu are Indo-European languages; and Turkish belongs to the larger Turkic language family. Armenian and Tamazight—the language formerly known as Berber—have unique histories unrelated to those of their neighbors. Each one of these main languages can be divided into regional dialects, with some linguists arguing that these should be considered separate languages entirely. Kurdish communities speak Kurmanji (also spelled Kurmanci), Sorani, and Zaza-Gorani; Persian can be divided into

Box 4.1

"Coffee, Please"

Asking politely for a coffee in each one of these languages would sound quite different (in approximate English transliteration for languages with different script), although in most cases the word for coffee is recognizable.

Table 4.1

Coffee in Middle Eastern Languages

Language	"I would like a coffee, please!"
Darija Arabic (for instance, in Morocco)	bghit qahwa, ila kan mumken!
Masri Arabic (in Egypt)	ʻayez (male speaker)/ʻayza (female speaker) ahwa, lau samaht!
Shami Arabic (for instance, in Lebanon)	baddi ahwe, lau samaht!
Khaliji Arabic (for instance, in Oman)	baghi qahwa, lau samaht!
Hebrew	Ani rotze (male speaker)/rotza (female speaker) kafe, bevakasha!
Kurmanji Kurdish	Ez qehwekê dixwazim, ji kerema xwe re!
Persian	Man qahveh meekhoram, lotfan!
Tajik	Man kahbe taghaaza daarem!
Turkish	Bir kahve istiyorum, lütfen!
Azeri	Bir qehve isteyirem, zehmet olmasa!
Western Armenian (for instance, in Turkey)	Yes sourdj gouzem, hadjeess!

Source: Compiled by Lucia Volk.

After you order your coffee, your host, regardless of linguistic affiliation, will likely ask you if you want your coffee sweet, medium, or bitter. If you indicate sweet, do not be surprised if the host heaps several scoops of sugar into the traditional small coffee cups. Sharing small cups of coffee—or tea—throughout the day used to be a very common practice across the region, although with the increasingly fast pace of life in urban centers, it is a practice that is falling out of use.

A cup of coffee, a piece of sweet called Turkish Delight, and a glass of water, served in a coffee shop in Istanbul. *(Tema, 2010. Wikimedia Commons.)*

Parsi, Dari, and Tajik branches; Armenian comes in Eastern and Western dialects; Turkic languages include Azeri, Kazakh, Kyrgyz, Turkmen, and Uzbek, as well as Turkish; spoken Arabic differs from country to country, and even city to city, with major dialects in North Africa (Darija); Egypt (Masri); Jordan, Palestine, Syria, and Lebanon (Shami); and the Gulf states (Khaliji).

When Arab citizens from North Africa, the Fertile Crescent, and the Gulf get together, they cannot assume that their version of the vernacular (Darija, Masri, Shami, Khaliji, etc.) will be understood by their interlocutors, who are native speakers of other vernaculars. However, due to the widespread cultural influences of Egyptian movies and Lebanese television, Masri and Shami vernaculars have more currency across the region. Consequently, speakers of other vernaculars will try to accommodate themselves to the grammatical structures and words of these "prestige vernaculars," or even adopt them wholesale. Depending on their background, education, and the topic of conversation, the speakers also may draw on Modern Standard Arabic or a foreign language for clarification.

Modern Standard Arabic (MSA) is a standardized version of Arabic used in literature and newspapers, on radio and television, in religious settings, during official meetings of heads of state at the Arab League, or on other official occasions. MSA has a different grammar, lexicon, and pronunciation from the regional vernaculars. It derives its rules from Classical Arabic, the form of the language that appears in the Quran. It is taught in every country across the Arab world, but no child grows up speaking it, as it is not part of everyday use. Thus, it would be strange to hear a person order coffee in MSA: *Uridu qahwatan, lau samahta.*

Currently, many Arab elementary, middle, and high school students learn not only MSA (especially in grammar, literature, or religion classes), but also Western languages (mostly English or French), which means that they are multilingual by the time they graduate from school. Throughout the day in any given Arab home, at work, or on the street, it is not uncommon to hear simultaneously MSA from a radio or TV set and vernacular and foreign languages in spoken conversation. In other words, code switching—the linguistic term for changing from one language to another within one speech act—is part of the contemporary Arab experience. For instance, during a visit with a family in Rabat, the capital of Morocco, I sat at a dinner table with the TV tuned to a news channel (and MSA) in the background, listening to four languages spoken at once: the family's oldest daughter was married in Spain and spoke in Spanish to her children, while also speaking Moroccan Arabic to her mother and English to me and another German exchange student. The son of the family switched between Moroccan Arabic, when addressing his mother; French, when addressing his sister (both of them had been educated in French in their Moroccan schools); and English, when addressing his European guests. Nobody but me seemed to find the linguistic diversity in any way peculiar.

Nonnative speakers used to focus mainly on MSA in college or university, adding one of the vernacular Arabics to their repertoire after a foundation in MSA. Increasingly, though, Arabic departments are integrating vernaculars in their language instruction from the beginning, given the role that these vernaculars play as everyday languages throughout the Arab world. Yet in order to read Arabic newspapers or novels, nonnative speakers

Box 4.2

Pleasantries

Among the endearing features of Arabic, Persian, and Turkish are short sayings of gratitude or praise to acknowledge a service or kindness received, many of which place emphasis on good health. In some Arabic vernaculars, people say *Ya'teek al-afiyeh!* (May [God] give you health) when they want to express appreciation for someone exerting effort at or completing a task, such as washing your car, carrying your groceries, sweeping the street, or doing other forms of work. The Turkish equivalent is *Kolay gelsin!*, and in Persian you might say *Khaste nabashid!* (which translates, roughly, to "May the work come easy!" or "May you not get tired"). If someone has cooked a meal for you, it is appropriate to thank the host with the phrase "May your hands be healthy!" (*Yislamu idayk* in Levantine Arabic; *Elinize sağlık!* in Turkish) or "May your hands not hurt!" (*Daste shoma dard nakonad!* in Persian). To which the host is likely to reply, "Enjoy your meal!" (*Sahtayn!* in Arabic; *Afiyet olsun!* in Turkish; *Nooshe jan!* in Persian—literally, "Twice health [to you]" or "Let health be," or "Let your soul be nourished," respectively). In both Arabic and Turkish, you compliment a person who has just received a haircut, shave, or taken a shower with *Naeeman!* or *Sıhatler olsun!*, respectively.

Additionally, in Persian, there is the practice of *ta'arof*, for which there is not a good translation in English. If you (a) host someone, or (b) are a guest in someone's house, it is expected that you (a) express delight about the visit, regardless of how inconvenient it might be, and (b) give apologies for inconveniencing the host, and refuse repeatedly to eat or drink what the host offers, since it is impolite to appear hungry.

need to acquire linguistic competence in MSA. Advanced students might eventually add classes in Classical or Quranic Arabic. In sum, Arabic is a language that requires adding layers, which is both the challenge and the beauty of it.

You may enjoy reading Zohreh Khazai Ghahremani's humorous short essay "A Lie Is No Longer Considered a Sin, When Hospitality Is the Intention," in the Archives section of the Iranian.com website (http://iranian.com/Ghahremani/2005/March/Taarof/).

Language Mixers Versus Language Purists

Because of the geographic proximity of various linguistic communities in the Middle East, many loan words and expressions have crossed linguistic boundaries. One important explanation for language mixing is the long history of trade that connected the communities across the Middle East. Merchants have incentives to learn and use each other's vocabulary, as this helps them buy and sell their products. It explains, for instance, why coffee or sugar sound so similar across most Middle East languages, as seen in the "coffee table" above. Cities along trade routes became major centers of commerce, and it was at such sites that languages changed and evolved.

Another example of language mixing comes from religion. In all monotheistic religions, sacred texts have played an important role. To be a learned religious person (such as the *ulama* in Islam) meant to be able to read and write. In addition, those who could read and write were also hired as administrators throughout the various empires in the region. At institutions of religious learning and at royal courts, there were lively exchanges among scholars from multiple linguistic backgrounds.

Finally, military conquest is another way in which languages and vocabulary have been spread and shared. Indeed, Urdu, the official language in Pakistan, derives its very name from the Turkish word for "army" (*ordu*). Once foreign armies conquered and settled in a new region, they shared their own language and absorbed the local language. For instance, Arabic was not a native language in North Africa, but rather arrived with Arab armies and the expansion of Islam in the seventh century, and it then mixed with local Coptic-Greek or Amazight languages. Turkish arrived in Anatolia from Central Asia via Turkic settlers and conquerors from the tenth century onward. Spanish, French, British, Italian, and Russian armies and administrations also brought their languages into the Middle East.

In many cases, the local elites in each region adopted the foreign languages, since they interacted most with the new rulers, whereas rural populations, most of them without access to schooling, retained their native languages. Local elites, in this sense, were the ultimate language mixers: they translated the will of the foreign ruler to the native population, and vice versa. One good example, again, is Urdu, which has its roots in Sanskrit. In daily use, Urdu and Hindi are very similar, yet the literary form of Urdu is heavily infused with Arabic and Persian. Interestingly, these linguistically and culturally hybrid elites also eventually developed ideologies of language purity as a way to protect local cultures against foreign influences.

Language purity became very important during the time of nation-state creation in the Middle East after World War I and World War II. Political leaders of new states set out to purify their national language by removing foreign vocabulary and substituting newly created words derived from word stems in their own language. In the 1920s and 1930s, Turkish and Persian leaders eliminated Arabic words from their vocabulary as part of their nationalization campaigns. Turkish also dropped the Arabic script the Ottomans had used and switched to the Latin script instead. This was an important symbolic move of the new republic toward a more European identity. The Turkish government outlawed the public speaking of Kurdish, as well as Kurdish language education. (Kurdish, in turn, saw its own set of reforms, including the adoption of the Latin script in the place of Arabic in Kurmanji-speaking regions.) Modern Hebrew became the first official language of the State of Israel, and an important tool to fuse Jewish immigrants from different parts of the world together into a new society. Language was to be a homogenizing force within nation-states, allowing all citizens to communicate with each other. Conversely, linguistic difference was seen as a threat to the nation-state.

Box 4.3

Creating Modern Hebrew

Eliezer Ben-Yehuda (1858–1922) is considered the "father of Modern Hebrew." An early immigrant from Lithuania who arrived in Palestine under Ottoman rule in the late nineteenth century, Ben-Yehuda compiled the first Hebrew-language dictionary and published the first newspaper articles in Hebrew. Biblical Hebrew was mainly a liturgical language at the time. Ben-Yehuda created new words based on related word stems from biblical Hebrew and borrowed words from European or neighboring Semitic languages. For Ben-Yehuda, speaking Hebrew became a way to create a secular Jewish identity, since he was not an observant Jew. The United Nations Educational, Scientific and Cultural Organization (UNESCO) honored Ben-Yehuda in 2007 with a special commemoration for his efforts in preserving linguistic heritage.

To read more about Eliezer Ben-Yehuda's life, his work, and Modern Hebrew, see the website of the Academy of the Hebrew Language (http://hebrew-academy. huji.ac.il/English/BenYehuda/Pages/default.aspx).

In today's global era, it is no longer possible (if it ever was) to draw tight boundaries around language communities. Migration flows have subverted nation-state boundaries, creating transnational spheres that connect migrants in host countries more closely to their relatives in the countries of origin than to their neighbors next door. New Internet technologies now offer blog spaces and chat rooms where people can connect from any part of the world and speak in languages of their choosing. More and more writing about the Middle East happens outside sanctioned (and often censored) media. Via blogs, Internet diaries, or social media, new voices reach a global audience. New technologies will continue to affect how communication occurs within and across language communities around the world.

Language Origins

The English alphabet, sometimes called the Latin alphabet, is said to have its origins along the Mediterranean coast in present-day Syria and Lebanon. A people called the Phoenicians, whom the Old Testament calls the Canaanites, lived in this area around 1500–500 BCE. They were famed traders, who sailed to ports around the entire Mediterranean to trade grains and spices, dyes (especially purple dyes extracted from a particular sea snail), and metals and pottery, among other goods. Written languages at that time were logographic, meaning they employed symbols that captured a word. For instance, Assyrian, Hittite, or ancient Egyptian scripts employed such symbols. The Phoenicians

---

Box 4.4

Illegal Letters

In 2009 in Turkey a Kurdish political leader, Mahmut Alinak, was indicted on criminal charges for a letter he wrote to Prime Minister Recep Tayyip Erdoğan. His offense was not the content of the letter, but the fact that he used illegal letters to write it: Q, W, and X. These letters belong to the Kurdish alphabet. Based on Article 222 in the Turkish penal code, the use of letters that are not part of the Turkish alphabet undermines the Turkish nation-state, which is based on Turkish language and identity. Alinak received an eighteen-month prison sentence.

---

devised a new system of phonetic spelling, which allowed people to recombine a fixed number of letters, rather than learning a new sign, for each new word. This new phonetic system spread around the Mediterranean and gave rise to the phonetic systems in Aramaic and Syriac, and later to Arabic, Cyrillic, Coptic, Greek, Latin, and so forth. Indeed, most writing systems in today's world operate by way of alphabets.

Languages across the Middle East adopted various scripts. In the case of Kurdish, Latin, Arabic, Cyrillic, and Armenian, scripts were used throughout history, of which only the first two, Latin and Arabic, have currency today. During the time of the Ottoman Empire, Turkish (what is now called Ottoman Turkish) used to be written in Arabic script, but with the emergence of the state of modern Turkey, Turkish changed to the Latin script, as did most other Turkic languages in Soviet Central Asia. Then, in 1940, Soviet authorities changed the script of Kazakh, Kyrgyz, Tajik, Turkmen, and Uzbek to Cyrillic, which is used for Russian. Once those nations obtained their independence after 1991, some of the leaders devised plans to return their languages to the Latin script, but not all of those plans were implemented.

The script used by a language, in other words, has little to do with its grammar or structure, nor does it indicate which languages are related. Arabic and Persian writing may look alike, but they belong to different language families. Kurmanji and Sorani Kurdish scripts look different, but both belong to the Indo-European language family. Modern Turkish might look like a European language, but it is not related to any of them; instead, Turkish is grammatically related to Mongolian and Korean. Aramaic, Syriac, Arabic, Persian, Hebrew, and Sorani are written from right to left, whereas Armenian, Kurmanji, Turkish, and Uzbek are written from left to right.

If you want to teach yourself a few words of Turkish, you can do so online for free at the Turkish Language Class website (http://www.turkishclass.com/).

Table 4.2

Comparison of Letters in Select Middle Eastern Alphabets

Aramaic	𐡀 [alaph]	𐡁 [beth]	𐡂 [gamal]	𐡃 [dalath]
Syriac	ܐ [alap]	ܒ [bet]	ܓ [gamal]	ܕ [dalat]
Arabic	ا [alif]	ب [ba]	ج [jim/gim]	د [dal]
Western Armenian	Ա [ayp]	Բ [pen]	Գ [kim]	Դ [ta]
Hebrew	א [alef]	ב [bet]	ג [gimel]	ד [dalet]
Kurmanji Kurdish	A [a]	B [be]	C [dje]	Ç [tshe]
Sorani Kurdish	ا [a]	ب [ba]	ج [dje]	چ [tshe]
Persian	ا [alef]	ب [be]	پ [pe]	ت [te]
Urdu	ا [alif]	ب [be]	پ [pe]	ت [te]
Turkish	A [a]	B [be]	C [dje]	Ç [tshe]
Uzbek	A [a]	Б [be]	Г [ge]	Д [de]

Source: Compiled by Lucia Volk.

Language and Religion

Another way of looking at languages in the Middle East is through the lens of its mono-theistic religions—Judaism, Christianity, and Islam—and their sacred texts—the Bible, the New Testament, and the Quran. All emphasize language as an important instrument of religious meaning and practice. The Gospel according to John the Evangelist begins, "In the beginning was the Word, and the Word was with God, and the Word was God." Through text, we come to know God and God's divine will. The first verse that was re-vealed to the Prophet Muhammad begins, "Read, in the name of your Lord who created (all that exists)." In both Orthodox Judaism and Islam, the memorization and recitation of sacred texts and prayers is an important part of a young person's religious education.

Language also becomes a means by which God teaches humans lessons. The story of the Tower of Babel begins with people disobeying God's will and building a tower that will reach heaven. God's punishment is to separate humankind into different language commu-nities: "Let us go down and confuse their language so they will not understand each other" (Genesis 11:7). The New Testament picks up the issue of language plurality in the story of the Pentecost, which Christians celebrate fifty days after Easter Sunday. According to scriptures, Jesus's followers gathered in a room and received the Holy Spirit in the shape of "tongues like fire" that descended on the individuals. The Holy Spirit enabled the dis-ciples to transcend the language boundaries that had been imposed on them. When curious neighbors came to check what was going on, they were all amazed and marveled, saying

Box 4.5

Consonants and Vowels

Arabic, Hebrew, and Persian are consonantal writing systems, which means short vowels are not included as part of the word. Instead, these vowels are added as diacritics, or marks above or below the consonants they modify. For instance, to write the name Muhammad in Arabic, you start with the consonants *M-h-m-d* (remember, the script is written right to left):

Then, you place a diacritical mark called *shadda*, which looks like a small *w*, above the second *m* to double that letter, -*mm*. Finally, you write the short vowel *u* (shaped like a 9) and the short vowel *a* (shaped like a slanted minus) above the *M-h-m* respectively to create *Mu-ha-mma*. The circle-shaped diacritic (°) on the -*d* in the end is called a *sukun*, indicating that the letter *d* is without a vowel (or silent). Now you have *Mu-ha-mma-d*, or Muhammad. The diacritical marks are not usually included in newspapers or in literature, which means the reader has to be able to add them in her or his mind, in order to pronounce each word and understand its meaning.

(Morgan Phoenix. Wikimedia Commons, http://commons.wikimedia.org/wiki/File%3A Muhammad_Salat.svg.)

In the writing sample above, you also see the added Arabic annotation, *sall allahu alayhi wa sallam*, nestled into the final letter -*d*. This translates to "May God send blessings and peace upon him," which is a standard expression of respect that practicing Muslims use when they mention the Prophet's name.

The name Muhammad itself is derived from the Arabic word for praise, *hamd*. Muhammad therefore translates to "one who is praised" or "praiseworthy." Other popular male names derived from *hamd* are Mahmoud, Ahmad, and Hamid, which carry similar meanings.

Box 4.6

Gender in Turkish

Turkish is a gender-neutral language. Instead of *he, she,* or *it,* Turkish uses the pronoun *o*. Some Turkish names are also gender-neutral, so it may not be immediately obvious, if you join a conversation about a person you have not met, if you are talking about a man or a woman.

Compound Words in Turkish

Agglutination describes a process of adding up word parts into one long word or concept, so that one sentence might be rendered in one long word. For instance, the English phrase "They say he should not be forced to run" would look this way in Turkish: *Koşturulmamalıymış*. One of the longer examples of Turkish agglutination, which is mostly cited in order to impress foreigners, is the following construction: "Hearsay has it that you are one of those whom we were not able to turn into a Czechoslovakian." In Turkish this reads: *Çekoslovakyalılaştıramadıklarımızdanmışsınız*.

Besides the various branches of Turkic languages, Finnish, Hungarian, Japanese, and Korean are also agglutinative languages.

---

to one another, "Behold, aren't all these who speak Galileans? How do we hear everyone in our own native language? Parthians, Medes, Elamites, and people from Mesopotamia, Judea, Cappadocia, Pontus, Asia, Phrygia, Pamphylia, Egypt, the parts of Libya around Cyrene, visitors from Rome, both Jews and proselytes, Cretans and Arabians: we hear them speaking in our languages the mighty works of God!" (Acts 2:7–11).

From a historical perspective, this passage illustrates that Jerusalem under Roman rule was cosmopolitan, with residents from all parts of the empire. In the context of this New Testament story, these ethnic and linguistic differences no longer matter and the message of the New Testament is that Jesus died for all, thereby uniting what used to be a (linguistically) divided humankind.

Language also plays a central role in the Quran. Some believers consider the verses of the Quran as an extraordinary, miraculous example of Arabic poetry—indeed, for some they are proof that the Quran is of divine origin. Because of this, as well as the intrinsic difficulty to render the rhyme and sound of poetry in foreign languages, the Quran is considered to be untranslatable. Quran scholars such as Michael Sells have argued that it is crucial that the Quran be heard, rather than quietly read, so that its poetic quality can be appreciated. During the holy month of Ramadan, Muslims around the globe read the entire Quran out loud in nightly installments. Muslims worldwide recite verses during their daily prayers in Arabic. Because the Arabic of the Quran is considered untranslatable, the linguistic unity of the religious community is preserved. For Muslims whose native tongue is not Arabic, reciting sections of the Quran requires an extraordinary feat of aural memorization.

Language and Literature

Early Writings

Arabic, Persian, and Turkish have a long and proud history of poetic achievement. In the Arabian Peninsula before the emergence of Islam, Bedouin tribes would hold poetry competitions, where poets would perform, and at the end of the evening the listening public would decide which poem deserved the prize for best literary achievement. Within this historical context, it is no surprise that the Quran was revealed in the form of poetry. Each section (or *sura*) of the book has a particular rhyme and meter, which not only makes the text sound beautiful, but also helps a person memorize it.

During the Middle Ages, literary excellence was tied closely to poetry. Poets, who composed accolades of the accomplishments of the king, became important persons in a royal court. Tribal poets crafted compositions that reflected the joys and tribulations of desert life. *Qays and Leila* (also called *Leila and Majnun*) is the title of a famous tragic love poem that has been likened to Shakespeare's *Romeo and Juliet*. Qays sees and falls deeply in love with Leila, but their parents forbid them to marry, which drives Qays to madness. This particular poem—famous in Persian, Azeri, Arabic, and Turkish—is part of a multicultural canon of stories about young love that is thwarted by rules of the elders. Poems have, of course, a long tradition in Judaism, in the form of psalms and songs. Additionally, Hebrew religious poetry was composed and recited in synagogue services in al-Andalus, or Andalusia, in medieval Spain. For instance, the poet and philosopher Moses Ibn Ezra, who lived in eleventh-century Granada, composed poems that became part of an important *siddur*, or traditional Jewish prayer book.

Also in the Middle Ages, nonpoetic forms of writing emerged, most famously *A Thousand and One Nights*, a compilation of folk tales that were collected and written down in Arabic during the time of the Abbasid Empire in Baghdad (750–1258). The stories have origins not only in Arabic, but also in the traditions of neighboring Persian, Turkic, and Indian communities. The main protagonists of the story are Persian: on her wedding night, the new wife, Scheherazade, begins to tell her royal husband, Shahryar, stories before they go to sleep. Each night, she ends a story on the cusp of an exciting new development, which she will only reveal on the following night. The king, who had previously killed his wives after the wedding night out of fear of unfaithfulness, is so enthralled by the stories that he does not execute Scheherazade. After the passing of 1,001 nights listening to her stories, he falls in love with her and they live happily ever after. Stories from this collection that have become part of the Western literary tradition are the tales of Aladdin, Ali Baba and the Forty Thieves, and Sinbad.

An early work of Persian literature with continuing contemporary relevance is *The Divan of Hafez* by Shams al-Din Mohammad of Shiraz (1315–1390), who wrote under the name Hafez (or Hafiz). Hafez's poetry is considered the pinnacle of the Persian lyric tradition, and modern Persian households are likely to have a copy on their bookshelves.

The ambiguous nature of many of the poems makes them especially intriguing for divination or fortune telling. Most Persian speakers argue that Hafez's poems speak directly and profoundly about human nature generally, but also that they capture the essence of what it means to be Persian.

> Information about the life of Hafez, and some of his poetry in translation, is available online on the Internet Sacred Text Archive (http://www.sacred-texts.com/isl/pdh/pdh02.htm).

Ottoman poetry, highly influenced by the Persian tradition, was an equally acclaimed mode of Turkish literary expression throughout the Middle Ages. Turkish prose writing, however, did not develop into a substantial body of writing until the nineteenth century. Rather, from the fifteenth century onward, lyric, and to a lesser degree narrative, poetry was the predominant literary art form in the Ottoman courts and in the houses of political elites. Ottoman poets—such as Fuzuli (1483–1556), Baki (1526–1600), and Ahmet Nedim (1681–1830)—drew heavily on metaphors based in Sufi thought and Turkish folk poetry to speak on topics ranging from the Ottoman bureaucracy, to the nature of love, to depictions of the city of Istanbul. Images of the nightingale and the rose, symbolic of lovers, abound throughout.

> Information about the life of Fuzuli and excerpts of his poetry in translation are available online on the Turkish Cultural Foundation website (http://www.turkish-culture.org/literature/literature/poetry/fuzuli-work-english-634.htm?type=1).

Modern Writings

Modern Arabic prose is often associated with the Egyptian novelist and Nobel Prize-winner Naguib Mahfouz (1911–2006). His long and illustrious literary career left a legacy too extensive to mention here, but his *Midaq Alley* and *Cairo Trilogy* are probably his most widely read works. He famously broke with classical Arabic literary conventions and focused on the lives and sentiments of ordinary Egyptians. Mahfouz's realist novels inspired the contemporary Egyptian writer Alaa al-Aswany (b. 1957) to write similarly revealing stories about a close-knit Cairo neighborhood. In his best-selling book *The Yacoubian Building*, he tells the history of members of different social classes whose lives come to intersect in a slowly disintegrating apartment building in Cairo, a metaphor for Egyptian society at large. A similarly critical look at an unravelling social order was expressed in the five-volume novel *Cities of Salt* by Abdelrahman Munif (1933–2004). Exiled from his native Saudi Arabia, Munif tells an indicting tale of oil profits and commercialization and their impact on what once was an egalitarian Bedouin society.

Aziz Nesin (1915–1995) was a prolific Turkish writer. Born in the last days of the Ottoman Empire, he grew up during the early days of the Turkish Republic and became a frequent critic and a champion of free speech. He opposed the military junta that came to power in 1980, as well as political Islam, which subsequently emerged. He was frequently jailed by the authorities and also attacked by Islamists. Probably his best-known work in English is his multivolume autobiography *Istanbul Boy*. Turkey's most famous contemporary writer, and the recipient of the Nobel Prize for Literature in 2006, is Orhan Pamuk (b. 1952). His novels often address tensions between cultures and ideologies, such as secularism and religion, tradition and modernity, and the material and the spiritual. He has spoken publicly on the issue of Kurdish oppression by the Turkish military, as well as the Armenian genocide, which resulted in criminal charges for his alleged insult of the Turkish Republic.

The best-known contemporary Hebrew-language author is Amos Oz (b. 1939), whose literary work consists of fiction and nonfiction, including essays and short stories. He describes the gaps and fissures inside Israeli society with both apprehension and empathy, and his writing is deeply personal as well as political. Oz lived most of his life on an Israeli kibbutz, concerned with building an egalitarian society. He cofounded the Israeli Peace Now organization, championing a two-state solution to end the Israel-Palestine conflict. Since the publication of his memoirs, titled *A Tale of Love and Darkness*, he has been considered a contender for the Nobel Prize for Literature.

Modern Middle East poets have been writing both against the conventions of classical poetry as well as against political and social injustice. One of the most famous modern Arabic poets is the Syrian author Adonis (b. 1930), who has lived most of his life in exile in Lebanon and France. Adonis sees himself as a revolutionary and a secularist, equally critical of the East and the West. His poem "Concerto for Jerusalem" deplores the ugliness and inhumanity of a city holy to three monotheistic religions. Next to Adonis (a perennial Nobel Prize nominee), the Palestinian Mahmoud Darwish (1941–2008) is probably the most recognized contemporary Arab poet. Darwish wrote about displacement, loss of home, and life under occupation. Much of his poetry can be read or heard in Arabic and English translation online (see, in particular, the website "Mahmoud Darwish . . . in the Presence of Absence," at http://www.mahmouddarwish.com/english/introduction.htm).

You can read a section of "Concerto for Jerusalem," a poem by Syrian poet Adonis, at the website of the journal *Banipal: Magazine of Modern Arab Literature* (http://www.banipal.co.uk/selections/79/232/adonis/).

A list of other authors published in *Banipal* can be found on the magazine's "Issue Index" page on its website (http://www.banipal.co.uk/contributors/issue_index.cfm).

Nazım Hikmet (1902–1963) stands out as one of the giants of modern Turkish literature, specifically in the realm of poetry. Blending literary aesthetics with politically engaged writing, Hikmet was both revered and persecuted for his communist views. The "Romantik komünist," as he is often called today, was imprisoned in Turkey for years, and ultimately died in exile in Moscow. His legacy lives on in Turkey today; for instance, cultural centers bear his name, and it is quite possible to hear one of his passionate, nationalist statements, *Bu memleket bizim* (This country is ours), quoted in contemporary speeches.

The modern Persian poet Ahmad Shamlu (or Shamlou, 1925–2000) is similarly famous for his politically engaged, anti-tyranny, pro-liberation poems in Persian. His love poems are also considered some of the finest in modern Persian. Unaffiliated politically—except for a very brief stint in the Communist Party—Shamlu spoke and wrote against abuses in both the monarchy and the Islamic Republic of Iran. Forugh Farrokhzad (1935–1967) is another noteworthy Persian poet. She is celebrated as a pioneer of modern Persian poetry and an avant-garde artist and feminist figure. Farrokhzad also directed and narrated the critically acclaimed film *The House Is Black*, about a leper colony in Iran in the 1960s.

> Poems by Ahmad Shamlu can be found in Persian and in translation online on the website "Ahmad Shamlu" (http://shamlu.com/trama.htm).
>
> The website "Forugh Farrokhzad" (http://www.forughfarrokhzad.org/) offers information on the poet's life and work.

The Pakistani poet Faiz Ahmad Faiz (1911–1984) was another left-leaning intellectual who used poetry for political commentary. He also wrote romantic poetry, drawing heavily on Arabic and Persian poetic traditions. Writing in Urdu, his work was widely translated and read from India to Turkey. (He is also a translator of Nazım Hikmet's poetry.) Faiz was imprisoned and exiled for his work, but also he served as the chair of Pakistan's National Council of the Arts, depending on the government at the time. One of his often-cited works, expressing the dashed hopes among citizens of the newly independent Pakistan, begins,

> Bury me, oh my country, under your pavements,
> Where no man now dare walk with head held high . . .
> (Aslan 2011, 440)

It is in the literature of the region that we can see the clearest examples of the mixing of neighboring cultures. From the Mediterranean to the Indian Ocean, first poetic and later prosaic sensibilities that were mutually intelligible emerged and flourished. Symbolism in Ottoman Turkish poetry would have been recognizable to Urdu, Persian, and Arabic

---

Box 4.7

Hip-Hop and Poetry

Some popular modern-day poets who promote political awareness and social criticism are hip-hop and rap artists who fuse their own poetic heritage and local instrumentation with U.S. performance style and culture. As shown, for instance, in the 2007 documentary *I Love Hip Hop in Morocco*, young local musicians draw large crowds to concerts and festivals (see the trailer at http://www.youtube.com/watch?v=OnGt2n-eDQU). Moroccan hip-hop artists, such as H-Kayne (*ech kayne?* is Darija for "what's going on?"), rap about unemployment, censorship, class differences, the spread of consumerism, and so on (see a short documentary on LinkTV at http://www.linktv.org/newmuslimmusic/hkayne). The Palestinian rap group DAM brings the gritty reality of living under Israeli occupation to world audiences (see DAM perform "Born Here" in both Arabic and Hebrew on YouTube at http://www.youtube.com/watch?v=zIo6lyP9tTE). Iran's best-known hip-hop artist, Hichkas (translates to "Nobody"), raps about the limited opportunities for Iran's youth (see his video at http://www.youtube.com/watch?v=QU1NNAH6b_g). In all these cases, online videos have helped spread the popularity of the artists across and beyond the Middle East.

---

speakers at the time. Moreover, literature has been an important tool not only for personal self-expression, but also for political commentary, and authors across the Middle East have taken considerable risk to express their views. At times, their work escaped official censorship or indictment, due to their use of metaphors and symbolism. (The local audiences, fully aware of official censorship criteria, were able to read between the lines.) In other instances, the authors were imprisoned, or escaped and lived in exile for extended parts of their lives.

References and Further Research

Adonis. 2012. *Adonis: Selected Poems*. Translated by Khaled Mattawa. New Haven, CT: Yale University Press.

al-Aswany, Alaa. 2004. *The Yacoubian Building: A Novel*. Cairo: American University in Cairo Press.

Ali, Agha Shahid. 2000. "The Middle East and Central Asia." In *The Poetry of Our World: An International Anthology of Contemporary Poetry*, edited by Jeffery Paine, 407–417. New York: HarperCollins.

Aslan, Reza, ed. 2011. *Tablet and Pen: Literary Landscapes from the Modern Middle East*. New York: W.W. Norton.

Brunwasser, Martin. "Illegal Letters in Turkey." *The World*, November 25, 2009. http://www.theworld.org/2009/11/illegal-letters-in-turkey/.

Carmi, T., ed. 2006. *The Penguin Book of Hebrew Verse*. London: Penguin.

Hafez, Shamseddin. 2006. *The Poems of Hafez*. Translated by Reza Ordoubadian. Bethesda, MD: Ibex.

Hikmet, Nazim. 1986. *Selected Poetry*. Translated by Randy Blasing and Mutlu Konuk. New York: Persea Books.

Jaggi, Maya. "Adonis: A Life in Writing." *The Guardian Online*, January 27, 2012. http://www.guardian.co.uk/culture/2012/jan/27/adonis-syrian-poet-life-in-writing.

Levine, Mark. 2008. *Heavy Metal Islam: Rock, Resistance, and the Struggle for the Soul of Islam*. New York: Three Rivers Press.

Mahfouz, Naguib. 1992. *Midaq Alley*. Translated by Trevor Le Gassick. New York: Anchor Books.

———. 2001. *The Cairo Trilogy*. Translated by William M. Hutchins, Olive Kenny, Lorne Kenny, and Angele Botros Samaan. New York: Alfred Knopf.

Munif, Abdelrahman. 1987. *Cities of Salt*. Translated by Peter Theroux. New York: Random House.

Nesin, Aziz. 1977–1990. *Istanbul Boy: The Autobiography of Aziz Nesin*. Parts 1–3. Translated by Joseph S. Jacobson. Austin: University of Texas Press.

Oz, Amos. 2004. *A Tale of Love and Darkness*. Translated by Nicholas de Lange. Orlando, FL: Harcourt.

Pamuk, Orhan. 2001. *My Name is Red*. Translated by Erdag Goknar. New York: Alfred Knopf.

———. 2004. *Snow*. Translated by Maureen Freely. New York: Random House.

Sells, Michael. 1999. *Approaching the Qur'an: The Early Revelations*. Ashland, OR: White Cloud Press.

5

Religion in the Middle East

LUCIA VOLK

Religion is one of the oldest globalizing forces, creating communities of believers that provide support for each other locally as well as across the world. Since the Middle East is the geographic origin of Judaism, Christianity, and Islam, it can rightly be called the world center of monotheism. All three belief systems contain within them multiple branches and subdivisions, as adherents have debated the meaning and significance of sacred texts, and differed on some of the prescribed sets of practices mandated by each.

Members of early faith communities lived as neighbors in large cities and towns. Through efforts of conversion, as well as historical and contemporary processes of migration, adherents of monotheism can now be found in all regions of the world. As a matter of fact, the majority of the adherents of Judaism, Christianity, and Islam now live in regions outside the Middle East. Conversely, other religious believers have migrated into the Middle East, most prominently adherents of Hinduism, since many South Asian workers now staff oil rigs and do domestic work in oil-rich countries of the region. (Immigrant workers outnumber natives in most Arab Gulf states.)

While religion can build and strengthen community, it also segregates believers from each other. Religion is often considered to be a major cause of conflict and war. In the case of the Israel-Palestine conflict, commentators make much of the fact that Jews, Muslims, and Christians fight over access to holy sites in Jerusalem and beyond, while in Iraq, religious gatherings have been a frequent target of sectarian violence. Religion, however, is not usually the underlying cause of conflict. More often than not, power struggles, territorial disputes, economic disparities, and political oppression are the primary factors that lead to war. With other conditions underlying grievances, political leaders then resort to religious rhetoric in order to mobilize their base. "Let us liberate Jerusalem!" has remained a potent rallying cry during conflicts, from the time of the Crusades until the present-day conflict over Israel and Palestine, even though the root causes of each conflict differ.

The political use of religion must be strictly separated from personal and communal practices of faith. When studying the region's monotheisms, it is striking how many similarities exist across the core values and practices, including the centrality of sacred texts, the emergence of a class of scholars whose role is to educate the communities at large, and various countercurrents and debates within each of the religions. There is also, of course, the overlap between religious values and the social values of patriarchy. Patriarchal societies were the backdrop for the emergence of monotheisms, and societal and religious values continue to reinforce each other. The beginning of this chapter will explore these similarities.

The second part of the chapter will focus on differences between religions, especially from the point of view of politics. Contemporary nation-states in the Middle East and elsewhere govern religiously diverse societies. Liberal constitutions protect religious pluralism, yet what constitutional texts mean in practice varies a great deal from country to country. In most countries of the Middle East, a form of Islam is the religion of the vast majority of the population. Should other religions be treated equally or have a separate legal status? Should people have the choice not to be religious? If minorities experience discrimination, or even persecution, what legal recourse does their state provide? If minorities come to positions of power, what protects the interests of the majority? These questions have relevance not only in the Middle East, but also across the globe. Diversity in all its dimensions is and will continue to be a political challenge.

Shared Religious Values and Practices

As mentioned above, Judaism, Christianity, and Islam share important tenets of faith (such as the belief in God, angels, and prophets); rituals (such as praying, fasting, and giving to the poor); places and practices of worship (such as temples, synagogues, churches, mosques, or shrines); and belief in an afterlife. These faiths profess a fundamental relationship of reciprocity between humans and the divine, where humans promise obedience and good deeds, and God, in turn, promises eternal life. God communicates his wishes and plans for humanity through rules and laws, transmitted to and through prophets to the rest of the community. These divine revelations are then written down in sacred texts.

Judaism is based on two main texts: the Bible and the Talmud. The Bible consists of the Five Books of Moses, or the Pentateuch, which explain how the world came to be, and how God entered into a covenant with his people. Through Moses, God gave his people Ten Commandments to instruct them to worship only one God, and to guide their life as a community with commandments against lying, stealing, killing, adultery, and disrespect toward one's parents. Additionally, the Bible contains the books of Prophets, Psalms, and Songs, which describe the history and struggles of the Jewish people and give instructions on how to worship God. The writings of the Talmud, begun during Jewish exile in Babylon in the sixth century BCE, provide commentary and interpretation on the Bible. Throughout the centuries many more books of interpretation were compiled, as well as books of prayer and worship. In the late 1940s and 1950s, hundreds of religious texts in ancient Hebrew and older Semitic writing were discovered in caves at Qumran, south of Jericho. Known as the Dead Sea Scrolls, some of these texts are, in part, copies of the Hebrew Bible, while others are classified as "nonbiblical," including the book of Tobit and the book of Enoch, or as additional interpretations of Biblical texts or historical texts. These archaeological finds raise the question of how the Bible was compiled, and who decided what texts to include and exclude.

For more information on the Dead Sea Scrolls, see the online Leon Levy Dead Sea Scrolls Digital Library (http://www.deadseascrolls.org.il/learn-about-the-scrolls/introduction).

The content of the Hebrew-language Bible is roughly equivalent to the content of the Christian Old Testament. Christians additionally (or primarily) refer to the New Testament, which is based on Greek and Aramaic sources. It contains the story of Jesus Christ, who is believed to have come to this earth to fulfill words of the earlier prophets, die for the sins of humankind, and be resurrected. The New Testament contains four overlapping versions of Jesus's life written by different evangelists: Matthew, Mark, Luke, and John. Throughout his ministry, Jesus taught lessons about forgiveness and compassion, and he healed the sick. He emphasized the importance of the laws of Moses, yet he also exhorted believers to love their neighbors. His often cited so-called Golden Rule was: "Do to others what you would have them do to you, for this sums up the Law of the Prophets" (from the gospel of Matthew 7:12).

In addition to the four Gospels written by Matthew, Mark, Luke, and John, a fifth book, the Gospel of Thomas, which contains additional sayings and deeds of Jesus, has been found and translated. Believed to have been written in the second or third century after Jesus Christ's birth, the Gospel of Thomas gives Bible scholars a new perspective on Jesus. Not all scholars agree that these are authoritative scriptures, however, and they are not part of the New Testament canon.

> Additional information on the Gospel of Thomas is available at the Gnostic Society Library's website (http://gnosis.org/naghamm/nhl_thomas.htm).

Islam's holy book is the Quran, which consists of chapters of revelations that place Muhammad next in the line of prophets from Abraham to Jesus. The Quran gives instructions for building a just society, as well as visions of heaven and hell. The Quran is written in Arabic verse, considered so perfect that it cannot be translated (non-Arabic versions are considered interpretations). Across the world, Muslims whose native tongue is not Arabic learn to recite passages of the Quran in the original. In addition, Muslims refer to sayings and deeds of Muhammad collected by scholars in the early centuries after his death.

> The opening of the Quran, called *al-fatiha*, is a prayer every Muslim learns to recite. You can hear a recitation of the al-fatiha, and an English interpretation of it, in a YouTube video (http://www.youtube.com/watch?v=i-MD3beQPwM).

The sayings and deeds of Muhammad are collected in so-called *hadith* (pronounced ha-deeth) literature. Hadith is the Arabic word for "talk" or "story." There are several collections of hadith, and in each case, the author of the deeds or sayings must provide a chain of people reporting the event, in order to establish the credibility of what is written. Not all hadith authors and scholars agree with the hadiths of others.

You can find a collection of various hadiths at the website, The Hadith of the Prophet Muhammad at Your Fingertips (http://www.sunnah.com). The "About" section of the website, accessed at the bottom of the homepage, explains the site's objectives, the purpose and importance of hadiths in the practice of Islam, and how the hadiths on the site have been collected.

The official texts in each religion instruct believers on how to relate to God and each other, as well as how to conduct business, settle disputes, deal with strangers, and so forth. Some of the texts are believed to be divine revelations, meaning that they are God's original words. For instance, Orthodox Jews consider the Pentateuch to be God's words as spoken directly to Moses. Some Christians take the Bible to be God's literal word, and Muslims consider the Quran to have been transmitted from God to Muhammad via the archangel Gabriel. For those who believe in the divine origin of the texts, the books become sacred objects. Any mishandling, or even threat of defacement, is taken as an affront. Other believers consider sacred scriptures to come from the pen of religious scholars who compiled the narratives based on a variety of sources over several centuries. Whether believers see sacred texts as divine words or as divinely inspired words can influence their interpretation of them.

Entire bodies of scholarship have emerged surrounding the holy books of the monotheistic traditions, debating the exact meanings and the precise parameters of given rules and laws. What did God mean when he said the Sabbath was holy and therefore a day of rest? What activities are permitted on a Sabbath, and which are clearly forbidden? When Jesus shared bread and wine with his disciples during what is called the "Last Supper," and declared the bread to be his body and the wine his blood, was this a symbolic or literal pronouncement? When Muhammad allowed Muslim men to take four wives, followed by the condition that every wife is treated equally, did he thereby disallow polygamy in most cases, since equal treatment of wives is nearly impossible to realize? Believers have different answers to these questions, which then result in different personal and communal practices.

There have been many disagreements between believers of the same religion, leading to internal divisions. For instance, Jews disagree about the proper honoring of the Sabbath, the extent of kosher food rules, and the acceptable forms of dress for Jewish men and women, among other things. Catholic and Protestant religious observances vary considerably, and a Communion service—the ritual reenactment of the Last Supper—has a different role and significance in each. There are disagreements over allowing one Christian to participate in the sacrament of the Eucharist in another Christian community. Within Islam, certain orthodox believers designate others as "unbelievers" (in Arabic *kuffar*) for having different interpretations of the concept of divinity. For instance, considering both Muhammad and his cousin and son-in-law Ali as manifestations of the divine, as some Shiite Muslims do, is considered heresy by orthodox Sunni Muslims.

The question of who gets to interpret the meaning of divine texts, therefore, is important. Across all monotheistic religions, scholars or experts emerged, almost exclusively male,

The Sunni–Shia Divide is a multimedia presentation available on the website of the Council on Foreign Relations (http://www.cfr.org/peace-conflict-and-human-rights/sunni-shia-divide/p33176#!).

who took it upon themselves to read and interpret scriptures for laymen and laywomen. Rabbis took on leadership positions in the Jewish communities, reading the Bible and providing their own commentaries on the divine will. Priests and pastors transmitted the Old and New Testaments to their respective Christian communities, in some cases building hierarchies of knowledge from priests to bishops, cardinals, and up to the pope. In the Catholic Church, the pope is assumed to be infallible, meaning that on matters of faith he is beyond error. Muslim clergy are called the *ulama*, the learned (from the Arabic *alama*, "to learn"). *Ulama* study in religious schools to become authorities in religious texts. They usually lead congregations in prayer or serve as judges in religious courts. Throughout history, some *ulama* decided to remain as close as possible to the original wording of the Quran, while others included independent reasoning in their interpretations of scriptures. Out of this history came four different legal schools in Sunni Islam, and thus different sets of rules for Muslim piety that explain why Islam is practiced differently in, for instance, Morocco, Turkey, Saudi Arabia, and Malaysia.

Over time, and across all religions, the judgment of these learned religious men would repeatedly be called into question by followers who sought other interpretations or other ways of knowing. An early anti-Rabbinical movement in Judaism was the Karaite movement that emerged in the ninth to the eleventh century in the Byzantine Empire. Karaites questioned the authority of rabbis, and the authority of the Talmud, a compilation by rabbis of laws and legal debates (called Mishnah and Gemara). According to religious scholar Nicholas de Lange (2000, 68), "so acute was the rift between Karaites and their Talmudically oriented opponents, the Rabbanites, that they formed separate communities in the same towns, which sometimes had to be separated by a wall." Karaites held that it was each person's individual responsibility to study the Torah and discover its meaning. In the Middle Ages in Europe, Jewish mysticism became an important counter-Rabbinical force, claiming that Jewish scriptures contained hidden meanings that were not part of the official canon. Mysticism stipulates a more intuitive and less scriptural relationship to God. Out of this tradition emerged the Hasidic movement in eighteenth-century Poland. Hasidic Jews opposed not only Rabbinical authority but also the encroachments of modernity and the increasing secularization they saw around them in Europe.

A similar line of reasoning—about an individual relationship to the divine without mediating scholars or priests—was used in Europe by Martin Luther (1483–1546), who stood up against the authority of the Catholic Church. Luther's work led to the Protestant Reformation, and the further split of the Christian community, already divided along Catholic and Orthodox lines. Luther was incensed that Catholic priests kept knowledge of the Catholic Holy Scriptures to the circle of learned, since reading the Bible required knowledge of Latin. After Martin Luther, the Old and New Testaments would be printed in vernacular languages, making them more accessible to a wider audience. Protestant Christianity itself developed a variety of different branches. The evangelical communities emphasized the personal relationship of the believer with the savior Jesus Christ. Revivalist movements from the eighteenth through the twentieth centuries posed challenges to established, more traditional Protestant church communities that were seen as following texts but lacking in spirit. Referring to the original texts of the New Testament, in which Jesus healed the sick and drove out demons, Pentecostal churches emphasize the power of the Holy Spirit.

In Islam, those who advocated for a more personal, direct relationship to God became known as Sufis. Sufism (from the Arabic *suf*, meaning "wool," in reference to the inexpensive cloth many Sufis wore as outward sign of their rejection of material comforts) insisted that faith cannot only be studied and understood by scholars, but has to be experienced on a more personal level. Sufi communities practice *zikr*, meditative prayer, repeating the ninety-nine names of God. Some Sufis practice *sema*, or turning in place. The mind thereby reaches another stage of consciousness, opening up to the divine. For Sufis, such practices are more important than legal arguments of the *ulama*. The mere recitation and study of religious texts, even by the most learned scholar of a prestigious religious institution, cannot match the immediacy of experiencing the divine. There are some debates within some Sufi communities concerning the extent to which a person must be a Muslim in order to be a Sufi, or if Sufism is a belief system that transcends theology entirely. This very radical position has led orthodox Muslims to doubt that Sufis are Muslims at all.

Finally, within Judaism, Christianity, and Islam, we can draw distinctions between traditionalists and reformers. What characterizes traditionalists is their wish to practice religion as closely as possible to what they consider its original form. To that end, they turn to scriptures in their original language, and are critical of subsequent translations, additions, or reinterpretations. They are critical of fellow religionists who have adapted meanings to modern times, and who have become increasingly secular or cultural in their practice, who attend houses of worship on holidays only, or pick and choose the rules they want to obey and those they want to dismiss. Traditionalists tend to take scriptures literally.

Reformers (or modernizers) reinterpret scripture in light of societal and cultural changes. For instance, all monotheistic religions emerged in communities that clearly privileged men. As the religious hierarchies formed, it was mostly men that staffed the positions of authority. In the twenty-first century, different social norms apply in many societies. While men still hold most positions of political and financial power, societal attitudes about the public role of women are shifting. Reformers in all three religions have pushed for the opening of the positions of rabbi, priest, or sheikh to women. Conversely, in response to the Orthodox Jewish tradition which holds that only a Jewish mother can bestow Jewish identity on a child, Reform Judaism now considers children of a Jewish father and non-Jewish mother to be Jewish. Also, if one has no Jewish relatives, it is possible to convert and become Jewish. In the most liberal religious communities, openly gay men and lesbians are welcomed as members, and they may become leaders. Some modernizers

---

Box 5.1

Sufism's Contemporary Appeal

Sufism obtained new levels of popularity in the West once scholars started translating poems and writings of Jalal ad-Din Muhammad Rumi, a thirteenth-century Persian scholar and teacher who settled in Anatolia. He began to explain God's loving essence to a group of devotees, who went on to create the Mevlevi order. Many of Rumi's poems can be found in translation, either in books or online. A brief documentary about Rumi is on YouTube (http://www.youtube.com/watch?v=pSyDmh0q8wA).

---

question if we should even refer to God with the pronoun *he*, or if we should use *she* or gender-neutral language to describe divinity.

Belief in God used to be something that suffused one's family and community life, with a set of shared rituals and practices that bestowed a sense of shared identity from birth. But in our globalizing world, exposure to all sorts of religious beliefs is much greater than ever before. Within a consumerist worldview, individuals now get to choose what religion they want, or if they want no religion at all. Significant numbers of Jews, Christians, and Muslims today regard their religion as a form of cultural identity rather than a belief system and a practice of everyday piety. While numbers of agnostics or atheists on official record in the Middle East are relatively small—some countries in the Middle East do not allow citizens to identify as atheist on public records—it stands to reason that these numbers could rise, as they have across the world.

Monotheistic Religions and Patriarchal Societies

A link exists between the patriarchal societies typical in the Middle East (and in other regions of the world) and religious practices that emerged in the region. In patriarchy, men take leadership roles in families and, by extension, social groups outside of familial bonds. And while family practices rooted in patriarchy are changing, religious life in the Middle East continues to rely on male hierarchies that encourage separate religious and social spheres for men and women.

Anthropologists distinguish two basic forms of social organization: unilineal and bilineal descent groups. Unilineal societies, in which one inherits one's name, identity, and property from either the father or the mother, are the most widespread in the world (approximately 60 percent). They come in two forms: patriarchies (inheritance from the father's line, approximately 45 percent) and matriarchies (inheritance from the mother's line, approximately 15 percent). Bilineal descent groups exist in the remaining 40 percent of the world's societies, where one's name, identity, and property are inherited from both the father and mother. Evolutionarily speaking, patriarchies emerged predominantly among pastoralists, whose wealth depended on herding. Matriarchies typically emerged in agricultural societies where women had crucial economic roles, such as in maize cultivation among the Iroquois, or wet rice cultivation in southern India. Bilineal descent groups are most often associated with foraging and industrial societies, where wealth is either owned collectively by the group, or by either men or women (or by both jointly). In bilineal societies, either the group or any individual possessing wealth can pass it on to their offspring (usually evenly divided). In unilineal societies, uncles, aunts, and cousins on the father's side are usually called by a different name from kin on the mother's side.

The word *patriarchy* has its roots in the Greek language and literally means "rule of the father." Men—usually the oldest male in any given household—hold decision-making power, and women—mothers, sisters, daughters, wives—depend on the men. Men inherit property or wealth from their fathers, while women may inherit a smaller percentage than their brothers, or none at all. While patriarchy is first and foremost a strategy to organize a society's economic resources and distribute wealth, it is also a system of values. Middle Eastern communities, whether Jewish, Christian, or Muslim, along with most of South Asian, Southeast Asian, and Chinese societies, belong under the larger umbrella of patriarchal societies. Culturally speaking, each form of social organization brings along with it a set of values and norms that aim to shape the individual as member of the larger group.

In traditional Middle Eastern societies, men are valued if they provide financially for their family and protect their interests. A man who does not fulfill his financial obligations stands to lose his honor in the eyes of other members of the community. At the same time, women are valued particularly as mothers and nurturers, and they are expected to look after children and after the in-laws in their old age. As a result of their diverging roles, women and men are seen as important and complementary to each other (but not necessarily as equals). In present-day societies across the Middle East, especially in urban settings, more and more women are joining men in taking paid work outside the house in order to contribute to household expenses. Yet women also remain the primary caretakers of children and are responsible for housework.

This gender distinction is reflected in monotheistic religions, where men and women often move in separate physical spaces, and where women assume different roles than men. For instance, in religious texts we find exhortations for women to subordinate to and obey their husbands (see Ephesians 5:22–24 in the New Testament, and the Quran 4:24), or for women to segregate themselves from their husbands during the time of menstruation, which is considered a time of impurity. Women are considered biologically and ritually unclean during and after their menstruation, which requires monthly offerings to atone for their uncleanness (see Leviticus 15:19–32 in the Old Testament). Synagogues and mosques separate women's spaces from men's, placing women behind a barrier or on a different floor of the building. The reason for this is the belief that women's bodies will inspire impure thoughts in men and therefore distract them in prayer. The Quran exhorts both men and women to be modest, but women receive much more elaborate instructions on how to exercise their modesty than men (as in the Quran 24:30–31). Similar modesty concerns prevailed in early Christian communities, as in the following quote from Paul's First Letter to Timothy in the New Testament:

Box 5.2

The Patriarchal Bargain

Deniz Kandiyoti, a professor of development and gender studies in the school of Oriental and African Studies at the University of London, has looked closely at patriarchy and asked why it has remained such a pervasive and relatively stable organizing principle in so many societies across the world, and why women have generally continued to embrace it, given that it clearly privileges men in the political, economic, and ideological domains. In a much-cited (and much-debated) 1988 article, she theorized that young women strike a "patriarchal bargain," whereby they will pay their dues as daughters-in-law in households that may or may not treat them kindly, because as they age they will be taken care of by their sons, over whom they will wield considerable influence at times. In other words, women do obtain concrete benefits of economic security and status, provided the men (i.e., their sons) hold up their part of the bargain. Of course, there are instances when that does not occur. A woman who no longer has the support of her son or her husband risks falling into poverty and social isolation.

In the Middle East, as elsewhere, men own more wealth and command higher incomes on average, which leaves many women economically disenfranchised. As long as the majority of the world's women do not have equal access to the world's wealth, many of them will have to strategize and either strike the patriarchal bargain (in the hopes of marrying someone who will provide for them, and giving birth to sons who will take care of them) or strike out on their own (despite the prevailing labor conditions that values women's work less than men's). And it is this larger economic inequality that Western women share with the women in the Middle East.

"I also want women to dress modestly, with decency and propriety, not with braided hair or gold or pearls or expensive clothes, but with good deeds appropriate for women who profess to worship God. A woman should learn quietness and full submission. I do not permit a woman to teach or to have authority over a man: she must be silent." (1 Timothy 2:9–14)

In other words, all monotheistic religions have rules that distinguish men from women in terms of their moral and mental capabilities, and in their likelihood of transgressing against God's will. These religious values complement and reinforce those that exist in patriarchal societies.

Religion and Politics

How Middle Eastern states manage religious differences in the societies they govern differs from country to country. Some designate one religion as the state religion, while affording other religions various degrees of protection. Some countries define themselves as primarily secular and guarantee the freedom of religion in their constitution. Enshrining such freedoms in the constitution does not automatically guarantee that they are enforced, and some countries in the Middle East do not have a constitution. Across these configurations, whether or not individuals can practice their religions openly without fear of stigmatization and harassment can change over time, depending on the interests of those who rule, the level of cohesion of each religious group, and the overall well-being of the society.

Across the Middle East and Central Asia, the record for the guarantee of religious freedom by the government is mixed. The Association of Religion Data Archives (ARDA) measures and compares religious freedoms by region and country across the world, based on U.S. State Department International Religious Freedom Reports. ARDA uses the designations of Northern Africa, Western Asia, and South-Central Asia (ranging from former Soviet Central Asian states to Bangladesh) in the presentation of its data from this region. Looking at the aggregates, on a scale of 0 to 10, with 0 indicating no government interference in religion, the regions in the Middle East compare negatively to world averages, as seen in Table 5.1. If broken down into select country comparisons, more differences are evident, as seen in Table 5.2.

As these tables show, most governments in the region, with a few exceptions, heavily regulate religions and favor one religion over others. These tendencies reflect constitutional, as well as other institutional, factors. Afghanistan, Iran, Morocco, Saudi Arabia, and Yemen define themselves as Islamic states. Afghanistan's constitution does not provide for freedom of religion. Saudi Arabia does not have a constitution, relying on the Quran and the words and deeds of the Prophet Muhammad as the foundational documents of the monarchy. The Islamic Republic of Iran's constitution defines the aim of the government as a struggle to realize Islamic principles and values and to spread its revolutionary ideas at home and abroad. Yemen is an Islamic state that relies on Islamic law as the source of all legislation. Morocco is an Islamic and sovereign state, with Islam as the state religion and freedom of worship for all. The Moroccan king carries the title "Commander of the Faithful" (in Arabic *amir al-mumineen*), a title used by the early leaders of the Muslim community.

Israel does not have a formal written constitution, but rather a set of Basic Laws that define the state as both Jewish and democratic. Nobody can stand for Israeli elections if they negate the existence of the State of Israel as the state of the Jewish people.

In contrast, Turkey's constitution is based on secularism (although President Recep Tayyip Erdoğan and his party have sought to tip the balance back toward Islam in Turkey). In the words of the constitution, it is the role of the state to safeguard "the everlasting existence, prosperity, and material and spiritual well-being of the Republic of Turkey." Similarly, Turkmenistan and Uzbekistan are defined as secular, democratic states that guarantee religious freedom. In all three countries, religious institutions are separated from state institutions.

Lebanon, a multidenominational state, guarantees the right to freedom of opinion, religion, and conscience. At the same time, it guarantees that religious communities can run their own schools, based on general guidelines by the state, and it stipulates the equal representation of Christians and Muslims in parliament and proportional representation of each religious community within each branch of government. Cyprus defines its citizens as

Table 5.1

Measures of Religious Freedom

	Northern Africa	Western Asia	South-Central Asia	World Average
Religious composition	90 percent Muslim, 8 percent Christian*	89 percent Muslim, 6 percent Christian, 3 percent Jewish*	53 percent Hindu, 36 percent Muslim, 4 percent Christian*	
Government Regulation of Religion Index	7.1	5.9	7.3	3.0
Government Favoritism of Religion Index**	7.5	7.1	6.3	4.6

*Other religions make up less than 1 percent each of each region's population, adding up to 100 percent total.

**Government Favoritism Index is a measure that indicates special privileges or subsidies awarded to one or select religions in each state. A score of zero would indicate no interference.

Source: Association of Religion Data Archives, www.thearda.com, accessed August 1, 2013.

Table 5.2

Religious Freedom by Country

	Religious groups (over 1 percent of the population)	Government Regulation of Religion Index	Government Favoritism of Religion Index
Afghanistan	99.7 percent Muslim	7.7	8.3
Algeria	98.5 percent Muslim, 1.2 percent agnostic	7.5	8.9
Bahrain	85 percent Muslim, 7.5 percent Christian, 6.5 percent Hindu	6.2	7.8
Cyprus	75 percent Christian, 22 percent Muslim	3.6	7.4
Egypt	90 percent Muslim, 10 percent Christian	8.1	8.3
Iran	99 percent Muslim	9.0	8.8
Iraq	97 percent Muslim, 2 percent Christian	6.0	8.0
Israel	73 percent Jewish, 20 percent Muslim, 4 percent agnostic, 2.5 percent Christian	4.1	7.9
Lebanon	58 percent Muslim, 36 percent Christian, 3 percent agnostic	4.9	7.0
Morocco	99.6 percent Muslim	6.0	7.0
Saudi Arabia	92 percent Muslim, 4 percent Christian, 2 percent Hindu	9.8	9.2
Tunisia	99.5 percent Muslim	6.2	8.2
Turkey	98 percent Muslim, 1 percent agnostic	5.1	6.8
Turkmenistan	95 percent Muslim, 3 percent agnostic, 2 percent Christian	8.5	8.7
Uzbekistan	94 percent Muslim, 3 percent agnostic, 1 percent Christian	8.8	7.6
Yemen	99 percent Muslim	6.4	5.6

Source: Association of Religion Data Archives, www.thearda.com, accessed August 1, 2013.

either Greek-speaking and members of the Greek Orthodox Church, or Turkish-speaking and Muslims. Primary education is compulsory and under the control of each one of the religious communities. Iraq defines itself as a country of multiple nationalities, religions, and sects, as well as part of the larger Islamic world. Islam is the official state religion, but the constitution guarantees full religious rights to other religious communities. Accusations of others for being unbelievers are outlawed.

The Islamic Republic of Iran and the Kingdom of Saudi Arabia, which take the Quran as their constitution, have the highest index for government regulation and favoritism of religion, followed by Turkmenistan and Uzbekistan, states that define themselves as secular and democratic. In other words, the fundamental religious or secular nature of the state in itself is not a clear predictor of actual religious freedoms.

According to the ARDA, neither Lebanon nor Israel regulates religions very heavily, but both prefer one religion over others. In Lebanon, only a Christian can become president of the country, and Christians fill many important positions in the military and security apparatus, as well as the ministries of education and culture. In Israel, new non-Jewish citizens must swear a loyalty oath to Israel as a Jewish and democratic state. (A proposed measure to require this loyalty oath of all current Arab Palestinian citizens of Israel did not pass.) Only in 2007 did a non-Jewish politician become a member of Israel's cabinet.

Turkey has a medium score on government regulation of religion. Until recent times, the military forcefully upheld the Kemalist tradition of secularism; it stepped in on multiple occasions during Turkey's history to remove what it saw as Islamist political influences. In Egypt in the summer of 2013, the Egyptian military similarly removed the Islamist president Mohammed Morsi. Turkey currently has a secular constitution, whereas Egypt's 2011 constitution confirmed Islam as the religion of the state, and Islamic law as the principal source of legislation. Christian communities in both Turkey and Egypt regularly launch complaints that requests for church buildings or restoration permits are denied. Church buildings are also at times targets of attacks and defacement. For instance, during the 2011 Egyptian uprisings, a Coptic church was set on fire, and when members of the Coptic community protested in front of the state TV station, the security forces shot at them, killing at least twenty-five people.

On the level of international politics, a fundamentalist Islamic monarchy, such as Saudi Arabia, as well as a secular republic, such as Turkey, are both allies of Western countries. Although the U.S. State Department houses the Office of International Religious Freedom (OIRF), which tracks violations of religious freedoms around the world, the OIRF's annual reports have yet to influence U.S. foreign policies in a noticeable and consistent way.

The annual reports, as well as country reports and fact sheets, of the U.S. State Department's Office of International Religious Freedom are available on its website (http://www.state.gov/j/drl/irf).

An example of a U.S. State Department Report on Religious Freedom on Syria (2012) can be found at http://www.refworld.org/cgi-bin/texis/vtx/rwmain?page=search&docid=519dd485b7&skip.

Religious Minorities

It is impossible to define the many different subdivisions within each of the major mono-theistic religions accurately, although brief explanations of the various religious sects important in the Middle East are included at the end of this section. On the one hand, religious communities are constantly changing and evolving, making precise definitions impossible. On the other hand, members of religious communities often disagree over their principles and priorities. The conditions in which minorities, religious and otherwise, live in the Middle East are too complex to fully explain here; but it is possible to explore a few simple points. Religious minorities, as well as ethnic minorities, have lived in the Middle East under predominantly (Byzantine) Christian or various kinds of Muslim rule for many centuries. In some cases, the minorities were actively persecuted; in others, they were able to live peacefully, and even prosper.

Toward the end of the Sunni Ottoman Empire (especially during the late nineteenth and early twentieth centuries) and between World War I and World War II (1918–1939), members of Christian, Jewish, and various Shiite Muslim communities emigrated to the West in larger numbers than Sunni Muslims. It is documented that before and after the turn of the twentieth century, up until World War II, the majority of emigrants from the Middle East to the Americas were Christians. During subsequent wars and ongoing economic instability in the region, more Christians chose to join relatives already abroad, further diminishing the Christian presence in the Middle East. At the same time, and especially after the creation of the State of Israel, members of the worldwide Jewish diaspora migrated to the Middle East. Proportionately, more minority Alevi Turks migrated to Germany to find work in the 1960s than Sunni Turks. Many secular Shiites, Baha'i, and Manicheans left Iran after the monarchy was toppled and the Islamic Republic of Iran was instituted. Many Chaldean Christians became humanitarian refugees in Europe and the United States during the recent U.S. wars in Iraq in the 1990s and 2000s. In many cases, members of religious minorities have access to global social networks that facilitate their immigration.

Below is a sample of minority groups in the Middle East, who have occupied either precarious or quite powerful positions in society, along with links to reference sites of religious or heritage organizations that represent them.

Alawites

Located primarily in Syria, Alawites look to Muhammad's cousin and son-in-law Ali and his descendants for guidance, and are therefore part of the Shiite Muslim community. They go back to the ideas of Ibn Nusayr (d. 868), who combined ideas from Christianity, Zoroastrianism, Greek philosophy, and Islam. (Some scholars refer to Alawites as Nusay-ris.) Alawites believe in reincarnation of the souls of men, according to their good or bad deeds in their current lives. Alawites are gradually initiated into the religious concepts and ideas of their community. Alawites were hoping to obtain their own state after the fall of the Ottoman Empire, but French colonial powers combined Alawites, Christians, and the majority Sunni population into the Republic of Syria. Despite comprising roughly

10 percent of Syria's population, Alawites rose to political power through the ranks of the military under the leadership of Hafez al-Assad (1930–2000), and remained in power when his son Bashar (b. 1965) replaced him. Bashar al-Assad's rule has been challenged by a popular uprising that started in 2011, and some of those who mobilized against him used his Alawite identity to argue that he did not represent the majority of Syrians.

> For more information on the Alawites in Syria, see Robert Mackey's "Syria's Ruling Alawite Sect," in the *The New York Times* blog "The Lede" (http://thelede. blogs.nytimes.com/2011/06/14/syrias-ruling-alawite-sect/).

Alevis

A community of believers primarily located in Turkey, southern Europe, Cyprus, and Greece, Alevis hold that both the Prophet Muhammad and Ali, his cousin and son-in-law, are manifestations of the divine. Similar to *Alawite*, the term *Alevi* is a derivative of the name Ali. Alevis have historical connections to the Safavid Empire that emerged out of a religious and political movement in Azerbaijan. Alevism is a syncretic religious tradition, combining elements from pre-Islamic Central Asia with Islam. Alevis do not pray in mosques but assembly houses, and their practices include Sufi elements, such as repeating the name of God as a form of meditation (called *zikr*), or using music or dance in their ceremonies. In contemporary Turkey, they have been both suppressed as a minority and elevated as model Muslims by different Turkish governments. Alevi communities exist among both Turkish and Kurdish communities in Turkey.

> For more information on Alevis, see "Turkey: The Alevi Faith, Principles, Beliefs, Rituals and Practices (1995–2005)," on this website of the Immigration and Refugee Board of Canada (http://www.refworld.org/docid/42df61b320.html).

Armenians

Armenians call themselves the first Christian nation, since King Tiridates III (250–330 CE) is said to have converted all of Armenia to Christianity in the year 301. Originally residents of the mountainous regions of present-day eastern Turkey and western Iran, they proudly consider Mount Ararat, where Noah's ark is believed to have hit dry land after the great flood, as part of their heritage. The Armenians fused their national and religious identity very closely, and defended it against Persian and Arab rulers of the region. Some Armenians came to political prominence under the Ottoman Empire, and the community enjoyed a protected status, along with other religious minority groups. In 1915, during World War I, the Armenians were considered collaborators with Russia, which led to systematic killings of Armenian communities across the empire. Between

800,000 and 1.5 million Armenians died, and many more became refugees. These survivors now live in the Armenian Republic in the Caucasus, as well as in diaspora across the world.

> For information on the heritage and religion of Armenians, see the Armenian Heritage web page, on the website of the Armenian Church (http://www.armenianchurch-ed.net/armenian-heritage/).

Baha'is

The Baha'is are followers of Baha'ullah (1817–1892), who saw himself in the line of the monotheistic traditions that came before him, recognizing the message of Zoroaster, Abraham, Buddha, Jesus, and Muhammad. Baha'ullah embraced the concept of oneness of God and sought to unify believers in one global society. He lived in Iran and, similar to Muhammad, claimed to have received divine revelations over several decades. Similar to the Buddha, he had a privileged upbringing, but he gave up his privileges. After he began to receive revelations, he was exiled from Tehran to Baghdad, Constantinople, Edirne, Alexandria, Haifa, and Acre. He spent the last twenty-four years of his life in Acre, in present-day Israel, where he wrote down his Most Holy Book. Acre is a sacred destination for Baha'is worldwide today. Most Sunni and Shiite Muslims do not recognize Baha'ullah's revelations, and in many countries, such as the Islamic Republic of Iran, Baha'is face persecution. According to the Baha'i International Community website, there are about 5 million Baha'is worldwide today.

> For information on the Baha'i faith, go to the religion's official website (http://www.bahai.org/).

Chaldeans (or Assyrians)

One of the earliest Christian communities, the Chaldeans (or Assyrians) trace their ethnic and historical origins to the ancient Assyrian Empire in Mesopotamia. They split off from other Eastern (Orthodox) Christian communities over a disagreement about the nature of Jesus Christ: Was he human or divine, or was he both? Chaldeans use Syriac, a language closely related to Aramaic (the language Jesus spoke), in their church liturgies. Similar to the Armenians, the Chaldeans developed a sense of ethnic, geographic, and religious identity that set them apart from their predominantly Muslim neighbors. Historically residing in the region around the town of Mosul in northern Iraq, Chaldeans migrated to Baghdad after Iraq's independence. Some Chaldeans were targeted by Saddam Hussein's Arabization and resettlement program (which mainly targeted Iraq's Kurdish population), while other Chaldeans rose to positions of political prominence under Saddam Hussein, such as Tariq Aziz, who served as deputy prime minister from 1979 to 2003. Due to the dislocations of war and repeated outbreaks of communal violence—including attacks on churches and kidnappings of priests—many Chaldeans have emigrated. Large Chaldean (or Assyrian) diaspora populations live in the United States and Australia.

For information about current events in the Chaldean-Assyrian Church, visit the official news site of the Chaldean-Assyrian Church (http://www.news.as-syrianchurch.org/).

Background information on the Chaldean-Assyrian community in Iraq is provided online by the U.S. Bureau of Citizenship and Immigration Services (http://www.refworld.org/cgi-bin/texis/vtx/rwmain?page=search&docid=3dee0b564&skip=0&query=chaldeans).

Druze

The Druze emerged as a religious community at the time of the Fatimid Empire in Egypt in the early 1000s CE. The Druze call themselves *Unitarians*, because one of the central goals of the faith is for the believer to experience oneness with God. The Druze faith, containing elements of mysticism, Sufism, and Islam, spread from Egypt to the mountain regions of present-day Lebanon, Syria, and northern Israel. The full extent of the faith is known to only a few initiates. The Druze, similar to the Alawites, believe in the reincarnation of souls. During Ottoman times, the Druze became wealthy and powerful landlords in the Mount Lebanon and Jabal Druze regions, and subsequently held cabinet positions in all Lebanese and Syrian governments. The numerically smaller Druze community in Israel today serves in the Israeli Defense Forces (IDF), alongside Jewish Israelis (while Palestinian Israelis are not allowed to serve).

For information on the Druze, see the website of the Druze Heritage Foundation (http://www.druzeheritage.org/dhf/The_Druze_Faith.asp).

Manichaeans

The Manichaean faith is based on the writings and teachings of the prophet Mani, born in third-century Iraq, which was ruled at the time by the Persian Parthian Empire. Manichaeans consider the world to be in a struggle between the forces (or Gods) of good and evil, or light and darkness. The human soul is influenced by and participates in those struggles. Material desires lead to darkness, spiritual ambitions to the good. Mani placed himself in the lineage of Zoroaster, Buddha, and Jesus, and saw himself as a prophet who received divine revelations. Manichaeism spread from Mesopotamia into Central Asia and China,

Europe, and Egypt. During the time of the Roman Empire, Manichaeism was the main rival to Christianity. Augustine of Hippo (354–430 CE) was a prominent Manichaean who later converted to Christianity, and is now known as St. Augustine. Today, Manichaean communities exist between Egypt and China, with the main religious center in Iran.

Information on the Manichaean community today can be found on the website of the United Manichaean Assembly (http://www.manichaean.org/).

Maronites

Originally an Eastern Orthodox Christian community, the Maronites accepted the supremacy of the pope in Rome in 1180 CE. The Maronites derive their name from Saint Maron, a monk and missionary who lived in the region of present-day Lebanon and Syria in the fifth century. Both Maronite and Druze minorities came to live next to each other in Mount Lebanon under Ottoman rule, and from the sixteenth century onward, both Druze and Maronite leaders fought the Ottomans repeatedly, obtaining, temporarily, autonomy from the empire. After 1918 the French colonial powers carved Lebanon out of the larger Syrian territory they had come to control in order to provide a majority Christian state in the Muslim-majority Levant region. The constitution mandates that the president of Lebanon must be a Maronite Christian, and Maronites have guaranteed access to other political offices and administrative positions according to constitutionally mandated quotas. Over the past two centuries, many Maronites (and other Christians) emigrated from the region to Latin America, the United States, France, and Australia in order to find better economic opportunities, so that the current demographic balance in Lebanon favors Muslims. Nevertheless, Christians and Muslims in Lebanon share power according to a 50/50 quota agreement.

For more information about the Maronite religion, see the Maronite Heritage website (http://www.maronite-heritage.com/).

Conclusion

In the early twenty-first century, we live in an increasingly globalizing world that brings people of ethnic, cultural, and religious differences into close proximity with each other, and states must find ways to manage and negotiate those differences among their citizens. Religious leaders and communities play a role in setting examples in their interactions with members of other faiths. Interfaith dialogue initiatives exist across the Middle East, working not only toward tolerance of religious difference, but also for an acceptance of each faith as a valid path toward God. As an exercise in overcoming exclusive claims of salvation, interfaith dialogue offers a framework to dismantle exclusive claims to territory or power.

Across the Middle East, there are many examples of peaceful and supportive interactions between members of different religious communities. As neighbors, they have shared resources, celebrated each other's holidays, and commemorated each other's dead. Throughout the region's history, which includes many instances of conflict and violence, instances of reconciliation and acts of solidarity did occur. When Iraqi Jews were persecuted by an ultranationalist Iraqi government during World War II, many found safe havens in homes of Christian and Muslim friends. Throughout Lebanon's national history, in history books and on national holidays, members of Muslim and Christian communities have been jointly remembered as martyrs for the national good. Interfaith marriages have become increasingly common across the Middle East. When Coptic churches became targets during the 2011 Egyptian uprisings, Egyptian Muslims came to stand alongside Copts against the Muslims who attacked them. Religious affiliation does not automatically determine on which side of a conflict a person might stand, so other, accompanying factors must be examined to gain an understanding of how religion might exacerbate or ameliorate any given crisis.

References and Further Research

Abu-Nimer, Mohammed, Amal Khoury, and Emily Welty. 2007. *Unity in Diversity: Interfaith Dialogue in the Middle East*. Washington, DC: U.S. Institute of Peace.

Armstrong, Karen. 1993. *A History of God: The 4000-year Quest of Judaism, Christianity, and Islam*. New York: Random House.

Baskin, Judith R., and Kenneth Seeskin, eds. 2010. *The Cambridge Guide to Jewish History, Religion, and Culture*. Cambridge: Cambridge University Press.

De Lange, Nicholas. 2000. *An Introduction to Judaism*. Cambridge: Cambridge University Press.

Droeber, Julia. 2013. *The Dynamics of Coexistence in the Middle East: Negotiating Boundaries Between Christians, Muslims, Jews and Samaritans in Palestine*. London: I.B. Tauris.

Kandiyoti, Deniz. 1988. "Bargaining with Patriarchy." *Gender & Society* 2, no. 3: 274–290.

Lapidus, Ira. 2002. *A History of Islamic Societies*. 2nd ed. Cambridge: Cambridge University Press.

McManners, John, ed. 2002. *The Oxford History of Christianity*. 2nd ed. Oxford: Oxford University Press.

Rumi, Jalal ad-Din. 2004. *The Essential Rumi*. Translated by Coleman Barks and John Moyne. Reprint edition. San Francisco: HarperOne.

Sennott, Charles M. 2001. *The Body and the Blood: The Middle East's Vanishing Christians and the Possibilities for Peace*. New York: Public Affairs.

Films

These films deal with interfaith relations or similarities between religious communities.

Arranged. 2007. Directed by Diane Crespo and Stefan Schaefer. New York: Cicala Filmworks. Tells the story of a Jewish and a Muslim school teacher who become friends as their families try and arrange marriages for them.

Forbidden Marriages in the Holy Land. 1995. Directed by Michel Khleifi. Seattle: Arab Film Distribution. Khleifi interviews eight couples in Israel-Palestine about the joys and challenges of their interfaith marriages.

Hassan and Marcus. 2008. Directed by Ramy Imam. Cairo: Good News Group. Tells the fictional story of a Muslim sheikh and a Coptic theologian who each have to take on a new identity as part of a witness protection program. The Muslim takes on a Coptic identity, the Copt a Muslim identity; then both men meet.

I Named Her Angel. 2005. Directed by Nefin Dinc. New York: Filmmakers Library. Introduces Mevlevi Sufism through the eyes of a twelve-year-old Turkish girl, who learns to do the *sema* prayer.

Jerusalem: Sacred & Profane. 1996. Directed by Rick Ray. Santa Barbara, CA: Rick Ray Films. Takes viewers on a tour of religious sites in Jerusalem, emphasizing the residents' diversity of beliefs.

Monsieur Ibrahim. 2003. Directed by Francois Dupeyron. New York: Sony Pictures Classics. Tells the story of a friendship between a Jewish boy from a broken home and an introverted Muslim shop owner in a poor neighborhood of Paris.

Salata Baladi (An Egyptian Salad). 2008. Directed by Nadia Kamel. New York: Women Make Movies. Tells the filmmaker's family's multicultural and multireligious story through photos and reminiscences, as well as travels to members of the extended family in Italy and Israel.

The Return of Sarah's Daughters. 1997. Directed by Marcia Jarmel. San Francisco: Patch-Works. Tells the spiritual journey of two Jewish women, Rus and Mariyam, who explore different branches of Judaism.

Ways of Faith. 1982. Directed by Ali el-Mek. Seattle: Arab Film Distribution. Portrays various Muslim communities in the central Sudanese town of Umduban. The film shows parents discussing whether or not to send their children to religious schools, whether to take a sick child to a hospital or a shrine, and whether to adhere to Sufi or orthodox interpretations of the Quran.

Part Three

The Global Context

6

Globalization in the Middle East

Lucia Volk

Globalization is an umbrella term for a host of phenomena that involve people, products, ideas, and money crossing national boundaries in ways that challenge the sovereignty of individual nation-states. An example of a global agent is the transnational corporation (TNC) with headquarters and offshore accounts in various countries. Such corporations subcontract labor and supplies from other corporations that are equally far-flung across the globe. Car parts, for example, are now produced in multiple countries and sourced to a central location for final assembly. TNCs make production decisions based on the availability of a skilled labor pool, low labor costs, and favorable tax conditions, which require the cooperation of governments. Governments, for their part, need to help generate employment for their own citizens. In this situation, elected officials of governments deal with unelected heads of TNCs, with the latter at times exercising significantly more power than the former. Nation-states, therefore, are no longer sovereign, at least not in ways they once were.

If the twentieth century was the century of nation-state actors, the early twenty-first century is characterized by the increasing interdependence of nations, international agencies and organizations (such as the United Nations, the World Bank, the International Criminal Court, and environmental and human rights nongovernmental organizations [NGOs]), and transnational corporations. Around the globe, "flows" and "webs" have replaced boundaries around distinct territories. Of course, humans have created connections with others throughout history. People interacted and traded with each other long before nation-states were created: think of the Silk Road, or of caravan trade across North Africa or the Arabian Peninsula. However, the scale and speed with which people connect in the twenty-first century is unparalleled. More affordable air and sea transportation make it possible for more people to travel farther than ever before, and they can expect to find Coca Cola and McDonald's logos wherever they land. While they are traveling, new phone and computer technologies allow them to stay connected with their relatives back home. Millions of investment dollars can be transferred instantaneously from New York to Dubai, or vice versa, at the push of a computer button. Satellite television and Internet connections bring programming from every conceivable corner of the world right into our living rooms and onto our computer screens. Information about political unrest, environmental disasters, or economic collapse is available anywhere in the world in real time.

At the same time that increasing flows of money, people, information, images, and ideas travel around the globe, a trend to shore up resistance against those currents is also on the rise. For example, consumers in the Western world are turning to local products that are grown or manufactured in a sustainable way. Slow food movements encourage people to cook and share meals with each other, rather than partake in fast food from a global franchise. Similarly, citizens in countries formerly colonized by the West mobilize around their ethnic or religious heritage and community, protecting their own values and traditions endangered by global consumer culture. Resistance takes the form of anticapitalist, environmental, and human rights movements that tend to connect globally via online technology.

Opponents of globalization say it creates vast economic inequalities and benefits a select few, while imposing costs of environmental (soil, air, or water) degradation and resource depletion on everyone. Proponents of globalization, meanwhile, emphasize its potential to bring economic growth to every part of the globe and to end poverty by integrating communities into a global market based on everyone's competitive advantage. Corporations relocate factories to countries that offer favorable conditions for production, regardless of cultural differences, and thus generate income and opportunity for development, and raise standards of living, in all regions of the globe. Depending on whose side of the debate you are on, the world looks either increasingly equitable and promising, or increasingly unequal and on the brink of the abyss.

Does Globalization Equal Westernization?

As the Nobel Prize-winning economist Amartya Sen has argued, globalization is a phenomenon with a long history that has, for the most part, produced progress for everyone. According to Sen (2002), "Over thousands of years, globalization has contributed to the progress of the world through travel, trade, migration, spread of cultural influences, and dissemination of knowledge and understanding (including that of science and technology)." Technological innovations—such as moveable-type printing, the crossbow, gunpowder, the magnetic compass, the kite, and the rotary fan—spread from China to the rest of the world around 1000 CE. Arab mathematicians developed algebra and geometry and exported these concepts to Europe, where they helped launch the Renaissance, which took Europe out of the so-called Dark Ages. Although the West drives much of today's technological and scientific innovation, Sen dismisses globalization's equation with, and condemnation as, Westernization. In his words, resistance is "a serious and costly error, in the same way that any European resistance to Eastern influences would have been at the beginning of the last millennium."

Many globalization scholars would concur that the phenomenon itself has a long history. What scholars disagree about is its precise origin. Not everyone considers Chinese traders and Arab mathematicians as prototypes of the global. Figures such as the British merchant of the East India Company or the Spanish missionary who converted New World peoples to Christianity are the prototypes more commonly cited. In other words, in the view of critical scholars, agents of globalization were Europeans, and they started to globalize through the process of colonization. Raw materials were extracted and exported at low cost to home countries, while the colonized were educated to become consumers of finished and more expensive products, creating relationships of debt and dependence. The sociologist and social historian Immanuel Wallerstein (2004) has argued that the world can be divided into "centers" and "peripheries" (as well as "semi-peripheries") that depend on them. In this line of thinking, the "centers" happen to be located in the Global North—the United States and Europe—whereas "peripheries" are the poorest countries of Africa, Asia, and Latin America. "Semi-peripheries" are in between these extremes, showing some evidence of economic development, but not the same level of wealth that can be found in the "centers." A profoundly unequal world-system, globalization benefits the West at the expense of the rest.

For those who support globalization, the operative words are *liberalization* and *development*. For instance, during the 1980s and 1990s, the four "Asian Tigers"—South Korea, Taiwan, Hong Kong, and Singapore—were able to generate significant economic growth in their respective countries by liberalizing their economic systems and opening up to the global market. Since the early 2000s, economic analysts have pointed to the economic growth in the so-called BRIC countries (Brazil, Russia, India, and China), which they say are challenging, and will eventually overtake, North American and European global dominance. Investors are told to put their money into "emerging markets" rather than businesses in the United States or Europe, both of which have struggled since the 2008 financial crisis.

So was Amartya Sen right when he argued that different regions of the world take turns as leaders of globalization? Or are the Asian Tigers and the BRIC countries merely rising from the status of "periphery" to "semi-periphery," and ultimately still dependent on the West? How you answer these questions will determine if you equate globalization with Westernization or not.

Hegemony Versus Hybridity

A different kind of globalization discussion takes place between scholars who debate the emergence of a global consumer culture that has come to dominate (or threaten) cultures everywhere else. On one side of the debate are those who see globalization as a hegemonic, Western-controlled process that encourages mass consumption of culture and consumer goods. In a globally converging world, shopping districts in any capital of the world offer the same Western brands (i.e., Nike, Gap, and Apple), and those with the financial means strive to attain them. In mass media, Hollywood sets global cultural standards, disseminating its ideas about heroism, beauty, and moral values. In short, Western ideas and products dominate consumer tastes around the world.

The opposing camp argues that, far from globalization being controlled by the West in a top-down, hegemonic way, culture operates in more complex ways. American corporations are mindful of local tastes and preferences. For instance, McDonald's needs to offer teriyaki burgers in Asia, pork burgers with paprika garnish in Eastern Europe, and beer with its fries in Germany, instead of simply imposing its U.S. menu on other societies. Soft drink producers adjust the formula of their drinks to local tastes and ingredients, so that while a brand's soda can might look similar across the globe, the actual product is

Drinking Seven Up in Jordan, 2012. Arabic letters in the red circle spell out "S-v-n," and the Arabic letters "u" and "p," in white, form the shape of a 7 on top of the lime and lemon slices. *(Photo by Nora Elmeligy. Used by permission.)*

different in different localities. Print and television media conglomerates produce different versions of their magazines, newspapers, and shows for their African, Asian, European, or Latin markets. In other words, globalization is best understood as a mixing of ideas from corporate headquarters with ideas on the ground, which creates new, hybrid products. Instead of globalization, some scholars propose the term *glocalization*, to better express the fusion of the global and local. This process of glocalization operates not only outside the West (with McDonald's being the most frequently cited example), but in the United States and Europe as well: consumers in the West now eat sushi in the form of "California rolls," listen to and imitate K-Pop from Korea, or practice "power yoga," a fitness-based version of the Indian spiritual tradition.

Whether you see an increasingly hegemonic or hybrid world depends on your definition and understanding of culture. On a fundamental level, cultures around the world are constantly changing. It is problematic to think they are not, because that can lead to the practice of essentializing, or stereotyping, other people. As discussed in the introductory chapter of this book, thinking of the Middle East as a place where Bedouins live in tents, as they have for thousands of years, freezes the image of "the Orient" in a zone of timelessness that does not reflect contemporary life in the region, and it defines residents of the Middle East as very different from citizens in the West. This process of essentializing creates the impression of irreconcilable divisions between members of different cultures. Cultures are intrinsically hybrid, however, each capable of absorbing new ideas, and adapting to change—a fact demonstrated when new generations challenge the norms and rules of their elders, which often they do. Yet cultures do not change at equal rates. Many of the global ideas circulating today have their origin in the Global North, and especially in the United States. These ideas are absorbed and adapted elsewhere at a faster rate than that at which citizens of the United States absorb and adapt foreign ideas. Should we be worried about this lopsidedness? Or should we place faith in the resilience of local ideas?

Globalization—and Westernization—in the Middle East

The reactions to globalization among residents and political leaders in the Middle East have been varied, which should not come as a surprise. Those who believe that globalization is a hegemonic force bent on changing local lifeways mobilize to resist it, wholesale or in part; those who believe it is a system that can enable or enhance people's lives find ways to adapt to it or embrace it fully. Where a person is in the social order in the Middle East—in particular, their educational and income levels—will have something to do with whether they belong to the group of resisters or adapters. A leather dyer in Morocco who has online skills might find more customers for his leather products via online marketing. Other colleagues might feel threatened by industrial leather production in China under-cutting Moroccan prices, thereby endangering the traditional dyeing processes and the livelihood of dyers in Morocco.

The Arabic word for globalization, *awlama*, derives from the same root as the Arabic word for "world" or "globe." Grammatically, the neologism, or newly created word, turns "globe" into a verb "to make something global." In its most common usage, globalization is equated with technological innovation, with the Internet, satellite TV, and cell phones. Thanks to globalization, Lebanese mothers can speak or Skype with their children who are working in Saudi Arabia and Canada; they can watch Mexican or Egyptian soap operas; they can vote for their Arab Idol or root for contestants on the Arabic version of *Who Wants to Be a Millionaire?* The Turkish word for globalization, *kuresellesme*, literally means "taking the shape of a globe." For most Turks, it carries positive connotations, as they see Turkey as a part of the global family, both of the West and the East. The Persian neologism *jahani-shodan* (literally, "globe-oriented") similarly evokes innovations in global information technology. Even the most conservative Iranian politician will want a cell phone, satellite TV, and access to the Internet. In other words, in everyday usage, the word *globalization* does not evoke images of Western hegemony; rather, it is seen as the process (or the tool) of spreading information and allowing communication around the globe.

Westernization, however, is a concept that focuses more specifically on aspects of cultural change, and here the meanings are more ambiguous. Among citizens of the Middle East, having a Westernized look or taste can be considered a sign of status or distinction, as well as a sign of selling out, or of hating your own. The Lebanese have a proverb that says, in the Shami Arabic vernacular, *kil franji brinji*, which loosely translates

Old City of Fez, Morocco, 2010. Below, vats of colored and neutral dyes are applied by hand, with cow-hides drying in the sun; above, modern apartment buildings with satellite dishes. *(Photo by Lucia Volk)*

to "everything Western is more desirable." (In Persian, the word *gharbzadegi*—literally "West-struck"—carries similar connotations and value judgments.) I have heard the expression in Beirut in the context of discussions about buying foreign rather than local products, of spending vacations in France rather than Egypt, and of sending children to private English- or French-language universities rather than public Arabic universities. Students who go to the American University of Beirut, for instance, are often labeled *muta'amrikeen*, or "Americanized," which is not usually meant as a compliment. Yet those same students also are considered to be more ambitious and successful than fellow students at Lebanon's Arabic-language universities.

The degree to which a citizen of the Middle East displays alleged Western tastes or preferences is a subject that is discussed—and judged—among family members, friends,

---

Box 6.1

Young Students in Beirut

People in the Middle East, especially young people, engage in often lively debates about foreign influences in their lives, and about the exact definition of their local, ethnic identities. Within the context of two English-language private schools in Beirut, the International College and the American Community School, where I worked as a teacher in the 1990s, I had many conversations with students who were keenly aware that a foreign language was being used to teach a foreign curriculum. Yet this education was considered one of the best in Beirut. During that time, I observed many instances of self-stereotyping, which I discuss in my 2009 journal article "Crossing the East-West Divide." In essence, students firmly embraced two very different sets of values: on the one hand, they saw themselves as open-minded and tolerant (values they equated with the West), as well as fiercely loyal to their families and family values (values they equated with their own culture). Yet at the same time, they also acknowledged that too much pride in their community could lead to sectarianism, or disrespect for members of other communities, and that too much tolerance could lead to the overstepping of cultural or moral boundaries. This "moral map" of two sets of interconnected and opposing values—open-mindedness and a lack of morals versus rootedness and intolerance—was represented by ideological markers of "the West" for the first set and "the East" for the second, regardless of actual links between these values and the geographies in question (Volk 2009, 205).

---

and acquaintances. Those who judge negatively see the person engaged in such behavior as selling out their local culture, while those who judge positively see the person as taking new opportunities to better herself. Westernization, particularly in regions of the Middle East that were formerly colonized by Western powers, is a double-edged sword.

But what of the spread of a global consumer culture, promoted by transnational corporations, across the Middle East? Are these influences hegemonic, or are they hybrid? Especially in regions of the Middle East that were formerly colonized by Western powers, foreign influences are looked upon with some degree of anxiety and suspicion. Should shopping malls in the Middle East carry the same brands they carry in the United States and Europe, threatening local industry? Should Hollywood movies define new fashion trends and beauty ideals in areas where dress codes remain relatively modest and body types differ? Should people in other countries be enticed to eat French fries, drink sodas, or smoke Marlboro cigarettes at the same time that consumers in the West are being taught about potentially damaging effects of such products on their health? Answering no to these questions leads to another: Should citizens in the Middle East be allowed to make their own choices in the matter?

Meanwhile, young people across the region text and tweet using a "chat alphabet" called Arabizi to render their national Arabic languages; for a discussion of this see Chapter 18). They also listen to U.S. musicians and then produce their own hip-hop and heavy metal. People, not just of the younger generations, bring a specific cultural twist to fast-food consumption by sitting in a McDonald's over coffee for hours, or by calling in their burger and fries order for home delivery. In other words, people appropriate foreign ideas, tools, or products in order to create their own cultural vocabulary. The massive demonstrations that took place across the region at the end of the first decade of the twenty-first century showed how tech-savvy young people could use these innovations to challenge the rules of their own parents and of their governments.

The question about the hegemonic power of European and North American ideas and values is further complicated if one takes the longer, historical view. Following the logic of Amartya Sen's argument mentioned above, one can see that the Middle East, prior to Western colonialism, was controlled by a series of rulers who themselves adopted new ideas and values, and who imposed those on their subject populations. Rulers in the Roman Empire, as well as the Kingdom of Armenia, for instance, converted local populations to Christianity after their own conversion experiences, prior to which their subjects practiced a variety of faiths. Similarly, Islam spread to areas where Judaism and Christianity, as well as polytheistic religions, were practiced, as happened under Umayyad, Abbasid, and Safavid rule, among others. The very idea of monotheism traveled with Abraham from Mesopotamia to the Mediterranean, where it mixed with and displaced other religions. So while it is quite common in academic literature to consider the spread of secular nationalism in the twentieth century as a hegemonic force, we might equally consider the propagation of new religious ideas by political elites at other times in history as instances of hegemony.

Is there any agreement on what constitutes cultural authenticity in any region of the globe? When taking the long view from the time of ancient empires until the present, we see how cultures, languages, and beliefs in the Middle East have diverged, mixed, and changed. Judaism, Christianity, and Islam are not homogeneous religions; nor are Turkish, Persian, and Arabic homogeneous languages. Subject populations under new rulers learned a new language, but also retained their own. Scholars and poets across cultures and regions exchanged their ideas, adapting metaphors or rhyme schemes, or abandoning them in favor of new forms or expression. So who gets to be the arbiter of "authenticity"? If someone in North Africa code-switches from Arabic to French, or if students in Lebanon or Iraq write in English in online blogs, does that make them any less authentic as Arabs? Posing a similar question in a different context: Are only veiled women authentic Muslims? Or might women from North Africa to Central Asia who do not veil for whatever reason be just as authentic?

Across the Middle East, elements of foreign cultures exist side by side with local ideas, and individuals are ready to adopt innovations that make their lives easier or more secure. The region, indeed, would be a much simpler place to study today if hegemonic forces had in fact won the day. So readers are encouraged to look at the Middle East as a place where hybridity and hegemony coexist, and to appreciate how, when, and why one or the other becomes the framework people in the Middle East (or scholars in the West) use to make sense of the world around them.

Globalization, as discussed above, is an umbrella term for a wide variety of phenomena and developments, from Internet technology to Hollywood films, from immigrant lives to stock markets, from fast foods and carbonated soft drinks to farming technologies, and

Box 6.2

Shopping in (Hybrid) Style

Dubai, a city in the United Arab Emirates, is home to many large, modern shopping malls. Among them is the Ibn Battuta Mall, which combines elements of a theme park with those of a shopping mall. Ibn Battuta was a fourteenth-century Moroccan scholar and traveler who documented his thirty-year journey from Morocco to China in detail. Each section of the mall is decorated according to the world regions Ibn Battuta traversed. An overview of the mall, as well as information about various store locations, is available at its website (http://www.ibnbattutamall.com/Directory/Directoryone.html).

A YouTube search for "Ibn Battuta Mall" yields shoppers' videos of the various "courts" inside the mall, including the one available at http://www.youtube.com/watch?v=0I95Qx3jy-w.

Crosswalk sign in front of an Ikea store in Abu Dhabi, United Arab Emirates. *(Photo by Lucia Volk)*

from water levels to air quality. In other words, there are few topics today that do not fall under the rubric of "the global." This is because so many have come to realize that what people do in one region of the world has repercussions for people in others.

References and Further Research

Peterson, Mark Allen. 2011. *Connected in Cairo: Growing Up Cosmopolitan in the Modern Middle East.* Bloomington: Indiana University Press.

Ritzer, George. 2011. *Globalization: The Essentials.* Malden, MA: Wiley-Blackwell.

Schaebler, Birgit, and Leif Stenberg, eds. 2004. *Globalization and the Muslim World: Culture, Religion, Modernity.* Syracuse, NY: Syracuse University Press.

Sen, Amartya. 2002. "How to Judge Globalism." *The American Prospect* 13 (January 4). http://prospect.org/article/how-judge-globalism.

Straubhaar, Joseph D. 2007. *World Television: From Global to Local.* Thousand Oaks, CA: Sage.

Volk, Lucia. 2009. "Crossing the East-West Divide: Lebanese Returnee Youth Confront 'Eastern' Sectarianism and 'Western' Vice." *Harvard Middle Eastern and Islamic Review* 8: 200–226. http://cmes.hmdc.harvard.edu/files/u1/HMEIR08_pp200–226.pdf.

Wallerstein, Immanuel. 2004. *World-Systems Analysis: An Introduction.* Durham, NC: Duke University Press.

Watson, James L. 1997. *Golden Arches East: McDonald's in East Asia.* Stanford, CA: Stanford University Press.

7

Key Issues of Globalization in the Middle East

LUCIA VOLK

As discussed in the previous chapter, the term *globalization* connotes a wide range of economic, social, and historical forces and "flows" that interact with each other. Taking many forms, it enables some and threatens others, sometimes both at once. Since these developments are ongoing, it is difficult to assess where this journey might ultimately lead. Social scientists are busy collecting data that show the extent and intensity of global flows, along with the effects these flows have on individuals and communities in various localities. Unfortunately, experts differ in their assessments of the impact of globalization on people's well-being and on the health of the planet. They differ even more on their proposed solutions to the perceived impacts, from building a radically new economic system that emphasizes sustainability over profits to a complete realization of the free market, which would require the dismantling of governmental regulations. They also differ in their assessment of consumer choice as a force that has either surrendered to the market or that will be able to regulate the market. Most of them will agree, however, that governments have lost much of their decision-making power to individual agents, institutions, and other forces that operate transnationally.

Three sites of global flows are presented and discussed as they pertain to the Middle East: migration, money, and ideas. With every topic, the flows go in both directions—from and to the Middle East—and often they are overlapping. For instance, the movement of people results in the movement of money (remittances), while the flow of ideas might coincide with or cause migration flows. Because of significant wealth and income differentials within the Middle East, global flows hold different challenges and promises for different groups in the region.

Migrant Flows

Migration to, from, and within the Middle East is multifaceted. Its causes and features vary across time, specific area, and geopolitical context.

Migrations to the Americas, Europe, and Beyond

Before the region was called the Middle East, which first occurred in 1902, residents from lands under the Ottoman Empire began to emigrate to various parts of the globe to escape conflict and to search for better economic opportunities. One of the most extensively documented groups of migrants came from present-day Lebanon and Syria, who left for North and South America, as well as Europe and Australia, in the late nineteenth century. Because they left their villages and towns under Ottoman Turkish rule before the creation of independent states, they were registered as "Turks" (or Turcos in Latin America) upon their arrival. Most of these "Turks" were actually of Arab descent, and they began life abroad as peddlers or owners of small stores. Once they had established themselves, they encouraged relatives back home to join them, and their family businesses grew.

The majority of the early immigrants to the Americas, and to Europe and Australia, were Christian Arabs, many of whom brought with them extraordinary entrepreneurial skills, and they therefore often became quite successful, as described in Albert Hourani and Nadim Shehadi's *The Lebanese in the World: A Century of Emigration* (1992). Currently, the richest man in Mexico, Carlos Slim, is of Lebanese descent, as are the Colombian pop icon Shakira and Paulo Salim Maluf, the mayor of São Paulo and a presidential candidate in Brazil. Darrell Issa, George Mitchell, and John Sununu are three prominent U.S. political figures with family connections to Lebanon. While reliable figures are difficult to come by, it is estimated that about 16 to 20 million persons of Lebanese descent currently live abroad, compared to 4 million in Lebanon itself (Nabti 2004). Why more Christians than Muslims migrated from the Middle East in this early period, has been the subject of some debate. To some, persecution by the Muslim majority induced Christian residents of the Ottoman Empire to leave. Others argue that Christian families in the Middle East traded more successfully with Christian Europe, thereby creating the wealth necessary to pay the initial cost of migration.

Palestinians are the other regional group with a well-documented history of migration during the late Ottoman Empire, especially to the Americas. Additionally, as a result of the 1948 and 1967 wars with Israel, hundreds of thousands of Palestinians lost their homes and became refugees in neighboring countries, Europe, the United States, and elsewhere. The creation of the State of Israel in 1948 also triggered a refugee stream from the large Jewish communities of North Africa, Iraq, and Iran. Blamed for the policies of the government of Israel that had made Palestinians homeless, these Jews faced hostility and discrimination from their old neighbors. Hundreds of thousands of them fled to Israel or, if they could, to the United States. Most of them lost their citizenship rights in the countries they left. What makes Palestinian and Jewish migrant groups different from others in the region is the fact that neither one can, under present political conditions, return to reclaim their lost homes. Those Jews who migrated to Israel have been able to secure their citizenship and create new roots there, but many became second-class citizens compared to Jews who migrated to Israel from Europe. Palestinian refugees, meanwhile, have had to look for financial and logistical support from their receiving countries, as well as from the United Nations Relief and Works Agency for Palestine Refugees in the Near East (UNRWA), a UN organization created in 1949 to deal specifically with Palestinian refugees worldwide. Depending on the host country, some Palestinians were able to obtain new citizenship papers, but others remain, to this day, without identity cards or passports.

The website of the United Nations Relief and Works Agency for Palestine Refugees in the Near East contains information on its history and ongoing work (http://www.unrwa.org/).

For a discussion of the relationship between European and Arab Jewish immigrants to Israel, see an article by Professor Ruth Tsoffar from the University of Michigan, along with relevant film recommendations, online at My Jewish Learning (http://www.myjewishlearning.com/culture/2/Film/Israeli_Film/Sephardic_Films.shtml).

From the 1960s onward, accelerated economic growth resulted in a large labor migration to Europe, involving predominantly residents from around the Mediterranean. Turkish, Moroccan, Algerian, and Tunisian citizens, as well as citizens of Italy, Greece, Spain, and Portugal, went to work as laborers in factories and mines in Germany and France, where post–World War II labor shortages provided work opportunities. Treaties between the German government and the governments of sending countries stipulated that workers remain in Germany temporarily—hence the term "guest worker"—but the demand for inexpensive, foreign labor remained high, and so the migrants stayed. Similar to the migrants who moved to Germany, Moroccans and Algerians began to head to France after World War II, based on political and economic links established during colonial rule. While these migrants responded mainly to economic "pull" factors, the communities that sent migrants often lived on the margins in their own countries. North African migrants were disproportionately of Amazigh backgrounds, coming from the Atlas Mountains region, while many Kurds sought to escape political oppression and outbreaks of armed violence in southeastern Turkey. In 1973 an oil embargo was imposed on the West in response to its support for Israel in the 1973 Arab-Israeli War, creating an economic crisis in most Western countries. As a result, legal migration routes to Europe were cut, and work permits were rescinded. European governments tried to pay immigrants to go back home, but with limited success.

According to 2011 statistics from the European Commission (http://epp.eurostat.ec.europa.eu/), Turks and Moroccans are the two largest non-European immigrant groups in the European Union today, accounting for over 4 million people. In terms of the number of residents of Turkish descent, Berlin today is the third-largest Turkish city in the world, after Istanbul and Ankara. An estimated 10 percent of France's current population is of North African origin. In Germany, sociologists and urban planners have begun to speak of *Parallelgesellschaften*, or "parallel societies," a term that encapsulates the deep social divisions between Middle Eastern work migrants and European natives. The divisions are based on religious and cultural differences, but also on educational and class differences. Entire neighborhoods on the outskirts of Paris have turned into immigrant ghettos, with significantly higher levels of poverty and crime than in the more central areas of Paris. Conversely, it is the neighborhoods

Box 7.1

Headscarf Legislation in France

The cultural clashes between native Europeans and Muslim Turkish and Arab migrants have escalated over the past decades. Right-wing politicians in Europe routinely run on anti-immigrant platforms. In France, laws enforce secularism in public (not unlike laws that exist in Turkey), while allowing religious practice at home, which has led to conflicts over North African Muslim women wearing headscarves to school, university, or public employment.

In 2004 the French government adopted laws against headscarves (as well as any other religious symbol) in schools and universities in order to protect France's secular identity. In 2010 the French government went further and outlawed the wearing of a face veil or full-body burqa, while permitting regular veils that cover a woman's hair. The argument was that clothing which hid a woman's face entirely from view posed a hindrance to communication and social interaction in a secular society.

at the center of Berlin that are home to the highest concentration of Turkish and Arab migrants, and those areas are considered zones of urban blight.

An NBC report from February 2, 2004, entitled "Debate Over Religious Symbols Divides France," explores the 2004 headscarf debate in France (http://www.nbcnews.com/id/4106422/ns/world_news/t/debate-over-religious-symbols-divides-france/).

The BBC report on the 2010 debates—"French Senate Votes to Ban Islamic Full Veil in Public"—which led up to the face veil ban includes images of various Muslim veiling styles (http://www.bbc.co.uk/news/world-europe-11305033).

Large second- and third-generation immigrant populations with limited contact to their countries of origin, but with various degrees of integration in or interaction with their host societies, pose a challenge to European policymakers. Because of declining birth rates across most European societies, immigrants and their descendants are needed to meet labor demands, yet many of them still do not feel welcome.

Migrants to and Within the Middle East

Across the Middle East and North Africa, the discovery and exploitation of oil led to massive labor migrations, starting in the 1960s. This trend increased even more after 1973, when higher oil prices led to an economic boom in the oil-rich Gulf states. In resource-poor countries across the Middle East, young people looked for employment opportunities abroad. The increase in oil revenue led to a building boom in the Gulf, which required contractors, builders, architects, engineers, and so forth. Egyptians, Lebanese, Syrians, Yemenis, and Palestinians, as well as Europeans and Americans, flocked to the region. Subsequently, South Asian workers, who accept lower wages than Arab or Western workers, also arrived in the Gulf to do both domestic and construction work.

Migrant workers send much of their earnings back home to their families. Twelve percent of global remittances in 2012, or US$61 billion, came from six Gulf countries alone (McGinley 2013). Yet oil prices are volatile. For instance, Saudi Arabia's oil export revenues plummeted from US$119 billion in 1981 to US$21 billion in 1988 (Henry and Springborg 2010, 43). Remittances revenues dropped correspondingly.

The oil exporters and the Middle East countries that have sent workers to the oil-producing countries are dependent on oil income and remittance income, respectively. Oil prices are set in the global market, which does not necessarily follow the law of supply and demand: while oil demands have been increasing steadily around the globe, political or economic developments elsewhere tend to affect the price of oil. For instance, in response to war, or the threat of a war, oil prices may rise for consumers worldwide. At the same time, diplomatic channels between the United States and Saudi Arabia, the largest petroleum exporter in the world, as well as other oil-rich nations, can lead to an increase in oil supply, resulting in a price drop. Also, the worldwide economic crisis of 2008 led to a sudden drop in demand for oil, which immediately reduced the price of oil. In other words, the earning potential that oil affords is often decided outside oil-producing regions, and this circumstance opens up both Gulf economies and remittance economies to high levels of instability. Migration flows trail oil price developments.

Other migration flows inside and to the Middle East include war refugees and economic migrants from conflict zones and from countries of the former Soviet Union. When the Soviet Union collapsed in 1991, almost 1 million Soviet Jews and their families migrated to Israel (Tolts 2007). In some cases, the migrants fled ethnic conflicts that erupted as new nation-states consolidated; in other cases, migrants sought better opportunities for themselves and their children. More recently, in the early 2000s, the wars in Iraq and Afghanistan, as well as civil war in Syria, produced both internally displaced and international refugees, especially in neighboring countries. Due to the repeated wars with Israel, Palestinian refugees and their descendants now number an estimated 5 million in neighboring Jordan, Syria, Lebanon, Egypt, and beyond. Hundreds of thousands of war refugees and migrants from the Sudan reside and work in Egypt, and tens of thousands live as legal and illegal immigrants in Israel. Additionally, refugees and migrants from unstable Caucasus and Central Asian countries have gone to neighboring Turkey.

The legal status for refugees from military conflict zones and economic refugees varies in countries across the Middle East. Rarely do they obtain full citizenship rights, and many end up at the margins of their host society. The migrants can hope to find work, even illegally, if the host economy is doing well, but they will lose their jobs at the first sign of an economic

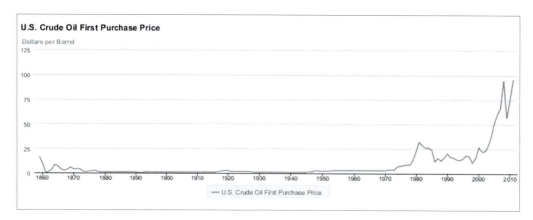

Crude oil price development, 1860–2010. The graph shows the price hike after 1973, a drop and volatility after 1980, and two price spikes after 2001. *(U.S. Energy Information Administration (EIA), http://www.eia.gov/.)*

downturn. Legal migration routes to countries of the European Union and the United States have become increasingly difficult in the wake of the terror attacks of September 11, 2001, and the global economic downturn of 2008 only added to this problem. As a result, forced or voluntary migration within the Middle East will continue to rise.

Money Flows

The world's largest proven oil reserves are in the Middle East, with Saudi Arabia, Iran, Iraq, Kuwait, and the United Arab Emirates at the top of the list of oil-exporting nations. Qatar and Iran, after Russia, the United States and Canada, hold the world's largest known natural gas reserves. Central Asia also holds rich oil and gas reserves, and the region is beginning to build the infrastructure to export them. Some of the money earned from oil or gas is transferred into investment vehicles, the largest of which are state-owned sovereign wealth funds, which fuel economic growth both inside and outside the region. However, despite substantial revenues in oil-producing countries (with correlated remittance revenue for migrant workers), the Middle East is one of the world's largest recipients of foreign aid.

Although John D. Rockefeller's Standard Oil was the world's largest oil company at the end of the nineteenth century, Azerbaijan in the Caucasus is usually credited with being the birthplace of the oil industry, dating back 100 years earlier. Major oil prospecting and extracting began in the Middle East, first in Iran and then in the Arabian Peninsula before World War II, but it became commercially viable only after the war ended, at a time when U.S. oil wells had begun to run dry. The predecessors of present-day Exxon Mobil and Chevron, two of today's most important U.S.-based energy transnational corporations, made an agreement with Saudi Arabia's King Ibn Saud in 1944 that created Aramco, one of the most successful oil ventures in history. (The company was renamed Saudi Aramco in 1988.) After World War II, global oil consumption rose precipitously in the United States, but especially in Europe and Japan, which turned the Middle East from a relatively neglected region of the world into one of major strategic importance. Oil became the engine of the region's development.

Oil began to define how the West related to the Middle East during World War II, linking economic interests closely with matters of national security. An iconic moment in oil history was the meeting of President Franklin D. Roosevelt of the United States with King Ibn Saud of Saudi Arabia on the USS *Quincy* to "discuss mutual problems of trade and relations," as reported in a 1945 newsreel.

The first three minutes of the 1945 newsreel footage from YouTube, "President Roosevelt Meets Middle East Leaders—1945," show Roosevelt's visit with Ibn Saud (http://www.youtube.com/watch?v=mZNwVgvqU_w).

Despite the fact that the price volatility of oil (and gas) is a constant, revenue streams for hydrocarbons have grown in absolute terms, as well as a percentage of total export revenue. Table 7.1 presents comparative data for several Gulf countries and Algeria.

These revenue streams are substantial, particularly for some of the Gulf countries with small native populations. The oil revenue has fueled residential building booms, as well as the building of schools and universities, hospitals, and commercial enterprises. The United Arab Emirates is currently home to the tallest building in the world, Burj Khalifa, which is over 2,700 feet (830 meters) in height, as well as the Burj al Arab, a six-star luxury hotel built in the shape of a sail on a man-made island. Qatar won the bid to host the 2022 World Cup, an event that draws football (soccer) audiences globally, promising to build more than ten air-conditioned, enclosed stadiums for the occasion. Saudi Arabia is currently working on the development of the King Abdullah Economic City in the desert, a walled city with residential units, commercials zones, an industrial

Table 7.1

Oil and Gas Revenue of Selected Middle East Countries

Country	Export revenues in billion US$			Percentage of export revenue of national GDP	
	1975	1997	2007	1997	2007
Saudi Arabia	29.5	45.5	210.2	90	90
United Arab Emirates	no data	13.7	90.6	38	62
Iran	7.7	15.7	64.1	79	83
Algeria	4.3	7.5	59.2	96	98
Qatar	1.8	4.0	38.2	60	91
Kuwait	8.4	11.8	14.9	85	no data

Source: Adapted from Henry and Springborg 2010, 45. Used with permission.

park, and the world's largest port facilities (Ouroussoff 2010). That oil economies should have this kind of spending money should not surprise anyone.

However, the Gulf countries, and the Middle East countries in general, have a bad record at attracting foreign direct investment (FDI) from abroad. Because of the region's perceived political volatility, private capital accumulated as a result of globalization has been going to other regions in the world. Baghat Korany (2009, 72), a professor of political economy, writes that "whereas in 1998 FDI flows as a percentage of GDP were 3.9 percent for East Asia and 3.5 percent for Latin America, they were only 0.7 percent for MENA [the Middle East and North Africa]." Export revenues of countries across the Middle East (aggregate figures of oil- and non-oil-exporting countries) are substantially lower than those in Latin America, South Asia, or East Asia. With rapidly growing populations across the Middle East, the overall economic (under)performance worries political analysts and politicians in the region, who anticipate more political instability, which in turn limits prospects for economic growth.

Proportional to its geographic and demographic size, the Middle East has received much more U.S. foreign aid than any other region in the world. According to U.S. Census Bureau figures in 2001, only two countries received more than US$1 billion in U.S. aid: Egypt and Israel, with the latter receiving more than US$1 billion more than the former. In 2009, seven countries received more than US$1 billion in aid. In addition to Egypt and Israel, these countries were Afghanistan, Iraq, Pakistan, the Sudan, and the West Bank/Gaza.

These sums include military aid, which can be substantial. According to an August 8, 2013, National Public Radio (NPR) report on military aid to Egypt, the United States has been sending more tanks and F-16 fighter jets to Egypt than it needs. Of more than 1,000 tanks sent since the late 1980s, more than 200 have never been used, and one source from George Washington University cited in the radio broadcast opined, "There is no conceivable scenario in which they'd need all those tanks short of an alien invasion" (Simon 2013). So why so much military aid? According to the NPR report, the answer is that it helps weapons manufacturing companies in the United States.

While oil purchases transfer money from the United States, Europe, Japan, and, increasingly, China to the Middle East, weapons sales to oil-producing states—some paid for with foreign aid money (i.e., tax money), some by governments directly—transfer some of that money back to the oil-purchasing nations. Highly sophisticated weapons technology is needed, so the argument goes, for oil producers to defend their natural resources. Weapons manufacturers in the United States, as well as in Britain, France, Germany, and China, have benefitted from sales to the region that, some estimate, absorb about 40 percent of the global arms trade (Henry and Springborg 2010, 33). For instance, according to Al Jazeera, in October 2010, the United States concluded a US$60 billion agreement with Saudi Arabia to deliver eighty-four F-15 fighter jets, a variety of helicopters, and upgrades on its existing fleet of seventy F-15s. Moreover, the United Arab Emirates will pay the United States US$7 billion for a new missile defense system. France, Britain, and Germany are also important arms suppliers to the Gulf. Of course, the militarization of the Gulf leads to increased security concerns in the region and beyond, which then

Table 7.2

Countries Receiving More than US$1 Billion in U.S. Aid, 2001 and 2009

	2001	2009
Total U.S. aid budget (in US$ millions)	16,836	44,957
Afghanistan	106	8,764
Egypt	1,716	1,785
Iraq	0	2,256
Israel	2,839	2,432
Pakistan	188	1,783
Sudan	96	1,213
West Bank/Gaza	240	1,039
Total aid to Middle East (in US$ millions)	5,185	17,072
Middle East aid as percent of total aid budget	30	43

Source: U.S. Census Bureau, Statistical Abstract of the United States, 2012.

requires additional weapons purchases. In response to a perceived increased threat from Iran, the United States authorized an additional US$20 billion in arms to Israel, Saudi Arabia, and the United Arab Emirates in April 2013.

While energy and defense businesses have been able to reap profits from relations with the Middle East, especially with the Gulf countries and Israel, the U.S. government and U.S. military have shouldered enormous costs to pay for military operations, especially for the recent wars in Iraq and Afghanistan. According to an analysis by the economists Linda Bilmes and Joseph Stiglitz, the Iraq war would cost American taxpayers nearly $3 trillion, including payments for ongoing medical care (Bilmes and Stiglitz 2008). The war in Afghanistan cost taxpayers close to $500 billion between 2001 and 2011 (Bingham 2012). The human costs on all sides have been equally staggering. According to a March 19, 2013, *New York Times* editorial titled "Ten Years After," the Iraq war cost 4,500 American soldiers' lives, while more than 30,000 were wounded, and over 100,000 Iraqi civilians were killed during that time (some estimates go to 150,000). By 2013, over 2,000 American soldiers had died in Afghanistan (Dao and Lehren 2012), and nearly 20,000 had been wounded (Bingham 2012). The infrastructure in Afghanistan was already in shambles after ten years of war against the Soviets, followed by four years of civil war and the subsequent Taliban rule that ended in late 2001. While Afghan casualty figures are difficult to verify—the UN only started to count casualty figures in 2007—the official number of about 20,000 is considered to be an underestimate by most observers (Bingham 2012).

Flow of Ideas

Two well-known observers of globalization, Thomas Friedman and Benjamin Barber, wrote influential books about the subject at the turn of the millennium. Friedman's *The Lexus and the Olive Tree* (1999) and Barber's *Jihad vs. McWorld* (2001) presented globalization as a competition between two sets of ideas: Western forces of leisure and consumption, presented symbolically by a luxury car and fast food, are challenging the (Middle) Eastern forces of unyielding rootedness and ethno-religious identities, presented by the olive tree and the Muslim concept of *jihad* (literally, "struggle"). Barber elaborated that the centrifugal, outward forces of "McWorld" lead to indifference and uniformity, while the centripetal, inward forces of jihad lead to a hardening of identities, with possible conflict and bloodshed. These opposing forces, jihad and "McWorld," pull humanity in two directions. We might physically inhabit one globe, but we might as well live on two separate planets.

The metaphors used in the titles of Friedman's and Barber's books are problematic, since they stereotype both West and East as sites of shallow consumerism and deep-seated fanaticism, respectively. Yet they reflect accurately one notion of globalization: it is accompanied by a fundamental conflict over identities and values. In the era of nation-states, identities were confined to specific territories, with their languages and traditions, whereas the era of contemporary globalization is characterized by movement and innovation (some call it "deterritorialization") and identities that are increasingly in flux. Instead of continuing the professions of their grandparents and living close to their kin in homes built on lands of their fathers, young people today, for example, grow up into a service-sector job, marry later in life, have fewer children (if any), and move into apartments in urban centers. Not only have individuals become unmoored from their traditional homes, but traditional ideas have also changed. Ideals that propel lives of the twenty-first century are, increasingly, self-improvement, individualism, and consumerism. These ideas carry the global economy forward, and they meet resistance in places where communal values and traditions still matter, whether those places are in the geographic (Middle) East or the West.

One of the main conflicts of ideas in the twenty-first century is that between secularism and religion. Many, or even most, people who regard themselves as religious, whether Jewish, Muslim, Christian, or some other faith tradition, look disapprovingly on those who do not profess any religion or are only "temporarily religious" on major holidays. On the other hand, many of those for whom religion is not a big part of their personal identities look at those for whom it is with the same kind of disapproval. The tensions between practitioners and non-practitioners of the faith could be said to be as old as religion itself. In the Old Testament, we learn that God had to send repeated reminders to his chosen people, who had veered off the prescribed path or found idols to worship.

By the nineteenth and twentieth centuries, secularism had become a dominant feature in states across the globe, as nationalism led to the creation of nation-states that replaced divinely ordained monarchies. The nation-states that emerged in the Middle East after colonialism followed secular nationalist principles. Religious movements or parties were strictly controlled, or they were outlawed and disbanded. So it seemed that secular modernizers would be the ones to define globalization. Yet, surprisingly, it was the forces of globalization that led to a revival of religion and tradition. Via the Internet, cable television, and social media, religious leaders have been able to spread their word to ever-growing audiences. As satellite channels became popular in the Middle East, so did TV imams, or Islamic religious leaders and religious scholars who appeared on talk shows to give advice on how to improve one's sex life within marriage or how to be properly charitable. Muslim Internet dating websites made it easier for young Muslims

Box 7.2

Religion via Satellite

After his initial career in accounting, the Egyptian televangelist Amr Khaled (b. 1967) came to prominence in the Arab world in the early 2000s via several different satellite TV shows. Considered an approachable, engaging preacher who wears suits and ties rather than robes and turbans, he appeals predominantly to young viewers across the Arab world. He preaches tolerance of and peaceful coexistence with other religions, yet urges Muslims to embrace their faith in order to build a strong society that honors local traditions.

to find suitable spouses beyond the immediate social network of their families. Religious charities could now collect donations globally via the Internet. Modern technology, in other words, helped bring religion into much wider circulation, and it helped make religion more interesting to members of the younger generation.

Even the ideologically most conservative organizations, such as al-Qaeda, are adept at using satellite technology to spread their message. Politically radical preachers in Yemen can broadcast sermons that their followers can view (and act upon) in the United States. Similar to the growth of organized crime with the expansion of unregulated, global cross-border flows, global terror organizations have benefitted from the ease with which money and ideas can be transferred between countries and information can be shared across great distances. In other words, globalization allows radical religious organizations at the margins of their respective societies to take a much more prominent role on the world stage.

Adherents of secular ideologies in the Middle East have had to adjust to the invigorated presence of religion, from Turkey to Morocco, and from Uzbekistan to Egypt. For instance, in the summer of 2013, secular parties and movements came face-to-face with religious counterparts in Istanbul and Cairo. In Turkey, popular opposition to a plan to demolish the small park next to Taksim Square in central Istanbul—home to a statue of Kemal Atatürk, the father of Turkish secularism—erupted into a full-scale public protest in the summer of 2013, with fierce battles against Turkish security forces. In Cairo, a coalition of secular social movements and parties protested the policies of the Islamist Egyptian president Mohammed Morsi, and the Egyptian army deposed him from office. Both sides in these conflicts used social media and television to garner support for their cause, seeking to build webs of solidarity, largely by blaming and denigrating their opponents. For the foreseeable future, globalization promises to remain the stage on which secular and religious identities and ideologies will compete.

Conclusion

In light of these developments, one might well ask whether globalization is a good thing or a bad thing for the Middle East. To the extent that it brings citizens of the region economic opportunities, as proponents of globalization promise, it might be exactly what the region needs. In order to attract international investment, countries in the Middle East need to reform legal structures, curb corruption, and deliver on promises made in contracts. International pressures might help to reinstitute trust in the political system in places where few citizens bother to go to the police to file a complaint, or expect a judge at a public court to render a just verdict (this explains the appeal of slogans calling for their replacement with Sharia courts). But globalization also poses challenges for the Middle East, where for decades many governments have imposed tariffs on foreign goods, both to protect local industries and to collect reliable tax revenue. Tariffs on foreign goods have allowed local industries to function without regard for competitiveness or productivity, and a sudden opening to global markets would lead to the collapse of much of the region's remaining industry outside the energy sector. Aside from oil and natural gas, it is not clear what the Middle East's comparative advantage on the world market might be, nor is it clear what sectors could promote job growth.

Globalization proponents and opponents across the Middle East each face challenges in their thinking and policymaking options. Global flows have already undermined traditional political, economic, and social structures in the region. Without income from the global energy market, global investment funds, and remittance money, many of the nation-states of the Middle East would no longer be able to function. The benefits of globalization are distributed unevenly, however, and this divides citizens in the Middle East, not unlike the citizens in other world regions, into two groups: the few who possess wealth and can generate opportunities, and vast numbers of people who possess little and have little hope to improve their lives. Overcoming the profound inequalities of today's world will be the challenge of the twenty-first century.

References and Further Research

Al Jazeera. 2010. "US Confirms $60bn Saudi Arms Deal." Al Jazeera Online, October 20. http://www.aljazeera.com/news/middleeast/2010/10/20101020173353178622.html.

Barber, Benjamin R. 2001. *Jihad vs. McWorld*. New York: Ballantine Books.

Bilmes, Linda, and Joseph Stiglitz. 2008. *The Three Trillion Dollar War: The True Cost of the Iraq Conflict*. New York: W.W. Norton.

Bingham, Amy. 2012. "Afghanistan War by the Numbers: Lives Lost, Billions Spent." ABC News Online, May 1. http://abcnews.go.com/Politics/OTUS/billions-dollars-thousands-lives-lost-afghanistan-war/story?id=16256292.

Brand, Laurie A. 2006. *Citizens Abroad: Emigration and the State in the Middle East and North Africa*. Cambridge: Cambridge University Press.

Copland, David. 2013. "Israel Grapples with Wave of North African Migrants." NBC News, May 31. http://worldnews.nbcnews.com/_news/2013/05/31/18660834-israel-grapples-with-wave-of-north-african-migrants?lite.

Dao, James, and Andrew Lehren. 2012. "In Toll of 2000, New Portrait of Afghan War." *New York Times*, August 21. http://www.nytimes.com/2012/08/22/us/war-in-afghanistan-claims-2000th-american-life.html?pagewanted=all.

Foroohar, Manzar. 2011. "Palestinians in Central America: From Temporary Emigrants to a Permanent Diaspora." *Journal of Palestine Studies* 40, no. 3: 6–22.

Friedman, Thomas L. 1999. *The Lexus and the Olive Tree*. New York: Farrar, Straus, Giroux.

Henry, Clement M., and Robert Springborg. 2010. *Globalization and the Politics of Development in the Middle East*. 2nd ed. Cambridge: Cambridge University Press.

Hourani, Albert, and Nadim Shehadi. 1992. *The Lebanese in the World: A Century of Emigration*. London: I.B. Tauris.

Içduygu, Ahmet. 2009. *International Migration and Development in Turkey*. Human Development Reports Research Paper 2009/52. Washingtion, DC: United Nations Development Programme. http://hdr.undp.org/en/reports/global/hdr2009/papers/HDRP_2009_52.pdf.

Korany, Baghat. 2009. "The Middle East Since the Cold War: Still Insecure." In *International Relations of the Middle East*, edited by Louise Fawcett, 61–78. 2nd ed. New York: Oxford University Press.

McGinley, Shane. 2013. "Revealed: Where Gulf Expats Sent Remittances in 2012." *ArabianBusiness.com*, May 13. http://www.arabianbusiness.com/revealed-where-gulf-expats-sent-remittance-in-2012–501232.html.

Nabti, David Munir. 2004. "Family Remittances Vital in Lebanese Economy." *Daily Star*, July 20. http://www.dailystar.com.lb/Special-Coverage/Planet-Lebanon-2004/Jul/20/Family-remittances-vital-in-Lebanese-economy.ashx.

Ouroussoff, Nicolai. 2010. "Saudi Urban Projects Are a Window to Modernity." *New York Times*, December 12. http://www.nytimes.com/2010/12/13/arts/design/13desert.html?pagewanted=all.

Rock, Aaron. 2010. "Amr Khaled: From Da'wa to Political and Religious Leadership." *British Journal of Middle Eastern Studies* 37, no. 1: 15–37.

Shanker, Thom. 2013. "U.S. Arms Deal with Israel and 2 Arab Nations Is Near." *New York Times*, April 18. http://www.nytimes.com/2013/04/19/world/middleeast/us-selling-arms-to-israel-saudi-arabia-and-emirates.html.

Simon, Julia. 2013. "Egypt Might Not Need Fighter Jets, But the U.S. Keeps Sending Them Anyway." National Public Radio, August 8. http://www.npr.org/blogs/money/2013/08/08/209878158/egypt-may-not-need-fighter-jets-but-u-s-keeps-sending-them-anyway?sc=ipad&f=1001.

Tolts, Mark. 2007. "Post-Soviet Jewish Demography, 1989–2004." In *Revolution, Repression, Revival: The Soviet Jewish Experience*, edited by Zvi Gitelman and Yaacov Roi, 283–311. Lanham, MD: Rowman & Littlefield.

Part Four

Case Studies

8

Introduction to the Case Studies

LUCIA VOLK

The preceding chapters emphasized the geographic, historical, linguistic, and religious diversity of the region we have come to call the "Middle East." The chapters that follow present specific case studies from experts across academic disciplines that explore contemporary issues in light of the existing diversity in both local and global contexts.

These chapters span four main themes: history, politics, economics, and culture. Topics include an analysis of the multicultural Middle Ages in Anatolia and Spain; social movements in Iraqi Kurdistan and Iran; the challenges of managing water and oil resources in Saudi Arabia; Lebanese blogging; and Tunisian texting. The authors of the case studies hail from a variety of disciplines; indeed, many of them work in an interdisciplinary fashion, so that thematic overlap exists. In all of the chapters, the authors draw links between their specific cases and larger, global challenges and trends. How will cultural diversity be managed in an increasingly interconnected global society? How will people organize to govern their political and economic affairs in times of hardening ideological divides and ongoing scarcity? These case studies from the Middle East resonate with trends in other regions of the globe, where populations struggle with similar questions.

The first case study, by the historian Rachel Goshgarian, suggests that the Middle Ages were a time of vibrant multiculturalism, with Jewish, Christian, and Muslim communities exchanging ideas and practices within growing and contracting empires that ruled over Anatolia and the Iberian Peninsula. While it is difficult to know with certainty what categories of cultural identity mattered most to the inhabitants of the Mediterranean regions at that time, it is possible to argue that religious identities were neither fixed nor inherently antagonistic. Goshgarian's evidence from the textural and architectural record of the tenth through the thirteenth centuries shows that communities knew of each other's beliefs and shared some of each other's practices in a spirit of coexistence, or *convivencia*. We then have to question why, in the twenty-first century, we divide the world into a "Judeo-Christian West" versus a "Muslim East," rather than map a world where similarities are emphasized.

Hootan Shambayati, a political scientist, analyzes Turkey's modern history, examining whether the country should be considered a "model" of a democratic and moderate Islamic state, as many claim. Examining the shift from a secular, protectionist Turkish Republic founded in the 1920s toward a more conservative, free market-oriented Turkey in the 2000s, Shambayati shows how larger economic trends empowered provincial players, who came to challenge traditional urban elites. In the early 2000s, Turkey's secular, liberal parties lost political power to conservative, Islamist parties in nationwide elections. The mostly secular legislature and military continued to defend Turkey's constitutionally guaranteed secularism in the face of the rising popularity of political Islam. Shambayati explores the challenges that the ideological struggle between secularists and Islamists presents to democracy itself.

Maia Carter Hallward, similarly, investigates the challenges raised by two opposed, and quite different, perspectives in the Middle East. In her case study of the Palestine-Israel conflict, the political scientist and international peace and conflict resolution scholar demonstrates that negotiators on both sides of the Palestine-Israel conflict understand "peace" quite differently, and therefore negotiate past, rather than with, each other. Israelis conceive of peace as an absence of violence, whereas Palestinians take peace to mean a recognition and resolution of the injustice of dispossession and displacement. In other words, one side sees peace through the lens of "security" and the other through the lens of "justice." These two ideologies are not necessarily opposed, but they privilege different conditions that must be met for a peaceful coexistence to become possible. Analyzing the Oslo process of the 1990s, as well as the al-Aqsa uprising of the early 2000s, Hallward explains why official peace negotiations have failed, and also makes a case for interpersonal, civil society initiatives to bridge the current distrust and cynicism between Israelis and Palestinians.

Mahmood Monshipouri, an international relations scholar with expertise in human rights, has studied the 2009 Green Movement in Iran, which happened in response to alleged election fraud that gave President Mahmoud Ahmadinejad a second term. Using the language of rights—the right to vote, to express themselves freely, to assemble in public—the protesters demanded that Ahmadinejad step down, and that the opposition candidate be declared the winner. The government responded with "external enemy narratives," claiming that the protesters were influenced by foreign ideas that Western imperialist powers used to unseat a government they did not like. Again, two ideologies clashed, one that was part of a global human rights discourse and another that depicted Iran under threat from the West, based on a long history of Western intervention in the country. Local values and global ideologies mobilize different segments of the same populations against each other across the Middle East, as we saw, for instance, during the 2011 Arab uprisings.

Nicole Watts, a political scientist, presents an unusual case study of these uprisings in her chapter on the protest movements in Iraqi Kurdistan. In 2011 the Kurdish Regional Government (KRG), which rules semi-autonomously over the northern region of Iraq, became the target of public protests demanding more transparent and responsive governance. After decades of opposing the forces of Saddam Hussein, who was a formidable "external enemy," the Kurdish communities of post-Saddam Iraq now demanded a more inclusive and open political system from their own Kurdish politicians. They questioned the legitimacy of the old resistance fighters who had come to occupy political office. Instead, they sought a variety of civic rights and freedoms. Similar to protesters in Iran in 2009 and protesters across the Arab world after 2010, Kurdish protesters used social media and a global discourse of human rights to stake their claims.

In Asli Ilgit's case study of the management of water and oil resources in Saudi Arabia, we again encounter a national government challenged by global forces; in this case, the Saudi Kingdom faces volatile global energy markets and increasing water scarcity that makes it dependent on agricultural imports from abroad. A political scientist, Ilgit emphasizes the risks faced by governments that must use a significant portion of their oil wealth to produce and distribute water, to invest in agricultural ventures abroad for food at home, and to diversify employment opportunities for their growing populations. While Gulf states were able to subdue political unrest in their countries during the 2011 Arab uprisings, their two main resource challenges, water scarcity and oil price volatility, might create political instability in the future amid a growing and increasingly restive population.

The cultural anthropologist Russell Zanca takes a look at another economic challenge, the changing global cotton economy, and its effects on the rural populations of Uzbekistan. Including a case study from Central Asia in a book on the Middle East reminds us of centuries of cultural and economic exchange between the regions, only to be cut off when the Soviet Union incorporated the Central Asian republics into its fold in the 1920s. Known for their bountiful cotton harvests due to abundant water supplies and fertile soil, Uzbeks have a long history of exporting "white gold." Yet rural populations are increasingly migrating to cities and abroad, while global cotton prices have declined, and profits no longer correlate to the amount of labor required to grow it. A trend seen across the Middle East—the flight from a rural lifestyle, the crowding of cities, and the increasing exodus of migrants—has created the conditions for nationally unsustainable economies. More and more countries have become dependent on remittances from abroad that finance local consumption, but do not create sufficient economic opportunities to stem the tide of out-migration.

Carel Bertram, an Islamic art historian, tackles the ideological divide between traditionalists and modernizers in the Middle East. Her case study centers on the images of the traditional Ottoman house that resurfaced as the modern "Turkish house" during the early decades of the Turkish Republic. Throughout the 1930s, Turkish intellectuals and politicians expended great efforts to modernize Turkish society and eradicate traces of what was considered a conservative, Muslim Ottoman past. Yet tradition did not simply disappear. In her close reading of paintings, novels, and music of 1930s Turkey, Bertram shows how Turks used artistic expression to come to grips with profound social change around them, particularly the trend toward the modern, which was at times unsettling. She also shows how contemporary Armenian-Americans have come to embrace the "Turkish house" as proof of their community's Ottoman heritage after a century of exile and diaspora, thereby showing the potential healing power of cultural symbols in situations of rupture and loss.

In her chapter on counterinsurgency and culture, the anthropologist Rochelle Davis turns the analytical lens back on the West, and in particular on the U.S. military, asking how the introduction of "culture" into military operations manuals during the 2003–2013 war in Iraq helped or hindered how soldiers executed their missions and interacted with the local population. Using interviews with American soldiers and Iraqi civilians, Davis is able to show the limits of cultural sensitivity training and cultural awareness in combat situations, where a militarily superior army battled increasingly sophisticated insurgents. If all civilians are potentially the enemy, understanding Arab or Muslim culture and respecting local traditions also becomes a means to conduct surveillance, capture, and kill, rather than an opportunity to engage "the hearts and minds" of the population. It is therefore important to examine how exactly the West creates and deploys cultural knowledge of populations in the Middle East.

Nadine Sinno, a scholar and translator of Arabic literature, focuses her case study on a new literary genre, Internet blogs, written by Lebanese women during the time of the July 2006 war between Hezbollah and Israel. Aiming to deconstruct the Western image of a passive and silent Arab woman, Sinno shows how middle-class Beirutis took to their keyboards in order to communicate to a global audience the day-to-day ordeals of a war they had to endure but could not control. Complementing, and often contradicting, mainstream media reports that presented casualty figures and an inventory of destruction on the frontlines, these Lebanese bloggers described the "home front." They shared their personal fears of getting killed or losing loved ones, their attempts at maintaining a sense of normalcy and routine in the midst of unpredictability, and their frustrations with political elites on both sides of the war. They also used their blogs to help organize local resistance and recruit international support.

Finally, the linguist Keith Walters gives an example of the contemporary cultural diversity of the Middle East by focusing on the different languages and dialects spoken in Tunisia. He explores the complex mixture of languages used across various segments of Tunisian society—indigenous populations that still speak Amazigh (formerly called Berber); national communities that speak regional varieties of Tunisian Arabic; educated Tunisians who speak Modern Standard Arabic, French, and/or English; and young Tunisians who create "Arabizi," Internet Arabic in English script. In so doing, Walters presents the pride Tunisians take in their multilinguistic competencies. They see themselves as able to preserve and execute various levels of local identities and traditions, while engaging in standard Arabic, French, English, and Internet conversations within and across national boundaries. The plurality of language use in Tunisia illustrates how local, national, and global identities can and do coexist, making the case for the hybrid nature of globalization.

9

Diversity in the Medieval Middle East

Inclusions, Exclusions, Supporters, and Discontents

RACHEL GOSHGARIAN

There was one Adam in Paradise
And one Eve like him
And one international language
Until they ate from the fruit tree

Now, isn't it amazing
And even surprising
That from one Adam and one Eve
So many nations were born to the world?

Each one with its own language
Such that none likes the other
One is Armenian, one Georgian
One is Muslim and one Assyrian.

And is it fair that it is so
And how did you decide that it must be so . . .
That one has children aplenty
And another remains without heir?
–Frik, cited in Sharabkhanyan 1987, 59

In the poem "The Complaint" excerpted above, the early fourteenth-century Anatolian Armenian poet Frik enumerates the injustices of the world and, in a bold move, outright questions God for making the world so unfair. He is perplexed by the number of "nations" inhabiting his world, and he seems frustrated that some are more fertile than others. It should not go unnoticed that one of the most prolific and popular Anatolian Armenian poets of the late medieval period includes in his poem an enumeration of the "nations," religions, and languages of those people surrounding him. In addition to the four nations mentioned in the beginning—Armenian, Georgian, Muslim, and Assyrian—he also brings up Russian, Arab, Jewish, Alan, Kurdish, Tatar, Mongol, Chaghatai, Frank, Venetian, Genoese, Roman, and Greek communities in later stanzas. That "so many nations were born to the world" (as he puts it), and all seemed to be living in his general area, was cause enough for him to write a poem entitled "The Complaint."

It might be surprising to imagine that the societies of the medieval Mediterranean were brimming with diversity. The concepts of diversity and multiculturalism seem, in many respects, to be associated with modernity. However, linguistic and religious diversity were facts of everyday life throughout the medieval world. And—very much like today—diversity had its share of proponents and its discontents. In considering the religious diversity of the medieval Middle East, scholars often praise Islam for inclusive policies toward Christians and Jews, even when aspects of those policies were discriminatory. The concept of *dhimma*—the protection of the "people of the book"—meant that Christians and Jews could continue practicing their own religions even when conquered by Muslims. In fact, the model of dhimma as defined in the Quran and in the *hadith* (the sayings of the Prophet Muhammad) stipulated that while Christians and Jews must pay a supplemental tax in exchange for exemption from military service, they were not to be forcibly converted to Islam. Dhimma policies thus stipulated a separate tax (which can be considered discriminatory), and yet the tax non-Muslims paid granted them privileges and allowed them to practice their faiths. In fact, dhimma as a concept was considered a novelty of tolerance when it was elaborated in the seventh century.

The protection of the "people of the book" was prescribed by the Quran and the hadith, but some descriptive sources from the medieval period (from the seventh through the fifteenth centuries) show that these prescriptions were not always followed. For example, in many cities under Islamic rule, Christians and Jews were compelled to wear specific colors and/or types of clothing in order to physically distinguish themselves from Muslims. Non-Muslims were not allowed to mount horses in certain cities and towns, and making public noise associated with Christian and Jewish religious practices, such as chanting, singing, and bell-ringing, was discouraged and occasionally considered a punishable offense. Forced conversion was legally restricted, but in practice, mechanisms to encourage conversion were occasionally developed and even institutionalized as a means to integrate local non-Muslim populations into the larger Muslim society. For instance, under a practice known as *devshirme* (literally, "collecting"), Christian children were recruited to serve in the Ottoman army and court. Ottoman representatives visited various towns with large Christian populations in order to force boys into service. They were separated from their families, converted to Islam, learned Turkish, and either entered into military service or began working at the palace. While this practice was criticized by some Christians living in the Ottoman Empire, it also meant that some of the most important functionaries of the Ottoman State were, in fact, of Christian origin. And some of them did maintain ties with their families, whether in the Balkans or in Anatolia.

This chapter sheds light on the complex nature of interfaith interactions in medieval Anatolia (Asia Minor), with a comparative look at the Iberian Peninsula at the same time. Anatolia from the late eleventh through the late fifteenth centuries was populated primarily by Armenian and Greek-speaking Christians. However, from the late eleventh century on, Anatolia became home to a number of principalities whose rulers were Muslim. The earliest example of direct Muslim rule in the region is that of the Seljuk Sultanate

This sixteenth-century manuscript is filled with scenes from the life and times of the Ottoman sultan Suleiman the Magnificent, who ruled from 1520 to 1566. This particular scene depicts the Ottoman practice of *devshirme*, the recruiting of boys into the service of the empire. The recruits are in the foreground, wearing red costumes. *(Wikimedia Commons.)*

(1077–1307 CE), which existed at the same time as the Byzantine Empire, the Mongol State (called the "Ilkhanate"), the Cilician Armenian Kingdom, and various Turkish principalities. Based on a general consideration of the political history and an analysis of literary texts composed in the late medieval period, this chapter will show that diversity was a part of everyday life in the late medieval Middle East. It will also show that this diversity was multilayered; it was not uniquely defined by religion, but also by language and lifestyle. On the one hand, diversity seems to have propelled creativity and innovation in architecture, literature, and social patterns of organization. On the other hand, as shown in the poetry of Frik, the multiculturalism that was a part of everyday life was not without its critics. As Frik explains, each "nation" has "its own language/Such that none likes the other." While Christians and Muslims, nomadic, rural, and settled peoples, did live together in Anatolia, the fact that so many of them "spoke different languages" made coexistence a challenge.

Methodology: Understanding Medieval Societies Through Social History

Many scholars have a tendency to explain history through the lens of political entities and borders. This sort of history is called "political history." When studying late medieval Anatolia, however, social history tends to be more useful. "Social history" is the study of the ways in which people lived their everyday lives through analysis of the social structures and processes that are often seen as the background to economic and political history.

While the geography of late medieval Anatolia is overwhelmingly complex, the scholarly narratives about that time that have been constructed, whether in Armenian, English, French, or Turkish, share the tendency to "read history backward." The titles of the two best-known tomes on the time period, Speros Vryonis's *The Decline of Medieval Hellenism in Asia Minor and the Process of Islamization from the Eleventh Through the Fifteenth Century* (1971) and Claude Cahen's *Pre-Ottoman Turkey* (1968), indicate this trend in historical inquiry. While Vryonis considers the time period from the perspective of the decline of the Greek-speaking Byzantine Empire, Cahen sees these centuries as a long preparation for the eventual emergence of the Ottoman Empire. Both tomes consider history through the lens of a linearity that assumes certain inevitabilities; for example, it assumes that the (Christian) Byzantine Empire had to end, or that the (Muslim) Ottoman enterprise had to succeed. This chapter presents a less linear approach to understanding a range of interfaith interactions that took place in a region characterized not by one dominant culture or language (that fails or succeeds), but rather by the predominance of cultural, linguistic, and religious multiplicity.

The lens of social history allows the historian of the late medieval Middle East to clarify the ways in which diversity was experienced. A social historian can use texts, including architecture, art, epics, poetry, and so forth, in order to see patterns of interactions and practice. As should be clear, only a fraction of individuals living in the medieval period participated in the creation of architecture, art, or literature. And only a fraction of all the texts, whether artistic or literary, composed in the medieval period is extant. Thus, while resources for medieval social historians may be limited, the importance of considering various types of sources becomes more important. For example, while a modern historian might consider one specific genre of text, such as newspaper articles or tax documents, a medieval historian generally attempts to consider as many available types of sources as possible in order to create a more comprehensive interpretation and understanding.

This chapter will investigate architectural and literary sources that will help explain the ways in which diversity was considered in the late medieval period. At the same time, special attention will be paid to literature associated with urban brotherhoods. During the late medieval period, both in the Middle East and in Europe, brotherhoods (or confraternities) existed in most cities. These brotherhoods played a range of roles, depending on when and where they existed. Some of them provided spiritual guidance, some organized particular crafts or trades (e.g., guilds), some engaged in violence (similar to modern gangs), and some participated in all of the above.

Mapping Medieval Anatolia and Iberia

Anatolia, also known as Asia Minor, generally comprises much of modern Turkey. In the medieval period, this space was difficult to define, in both geographical and political terms. The inhabitants of the Byzantine Empire (330–1453 CE) called themselves *Romaioi*, or Romans, and thus, geographers (especially Eastern geographers) considered the lands held by them to be Roman (in Arabic, Persian, and Turkish: *Rum*). Known as the Eastern Roman Empire, the Byzantine Empire was divided into a range of administrative provinces, several of which were located in Anatolia, including Anatolikon, Armeniakon, Kappadokia, Paphlagonia, and Thrakesion.

By the eleventh century, however, the provincial system had become relatively obsolete. In the early thirteenth century, after several Byzantine military defeats at the hands of the Seljuk Turks, most authors (both local and foreign) began to use the term *Roman* to refer to the regions ruled by the Seljuks of Konya rather than to the Byzantine Empire, and the remaining regions of Anatolia under Byzantine (or Armenian) control became known as principalities of smaller regions of the larger geographic entity. In the mid-thirteenth century, the Mongols invaded Anatolia, defeating the Seljuks and various other principalities, both Christian and Muslim.

For this reason, the medieval period in Anatolia cannot be studied effectively from the perspective of one principality or one central power. In fact, during this time of geopolitical fluidity and change, medieval geographers, travelers, and historians (foreign and local, Christian and Muslim) had many different ways of referring to Anatolia. This was, in part, because the borders kept changing. It was also because the region was populated by diverse religious and linguistic communities that were in constant contact with each other across porous and changing boundaries. It is possible to argue that the thirteenth and fourteenth centuries in this particular region were, in fact, a time of cultural, geographical, and political "in-betweenness." The interaction among different linguistic and religious communities is reflected in a certain hybridity of style in the architecture, literature, religious establishments, and social institutions that were developed in late medieval Anatolia.

During this same time period, on another shore of the Mediterranean, regions of modern France, Portugal, and Spain experienced a similar kind of cultural coexistence between Christians, Jews, and Muslims, which has been most closely associated with the Muslim-controlled area of al-Andalus (in the southeastern part of Iberia). Arabic-speaking Muslims conquered regions of the Iberian Peninsula as early as 711, and a significant Arabo-Muslim political and cultural presence was maintained in the conquered regions until 1492. As in Anatolia, however, borders in the region were continually changing. And modern historians, such as Jerrilynn D. Dodds and María Rosa Menocal, in *The Arts of Intimacy: Christians, Jews and Muslims in the Making of Castillian Culture* (2008), often consider medieval Iberia (from the eleventh through the fifteenth centuries) through the lens of the loosely defined and fragmented Muslim *taifa* emirates. During the over 700 years that the Iberian Peninsula was home to Christians, Jews, and Muslims, a great degree of cultural intermixing took place, similar to what happened in Anatolia. Because

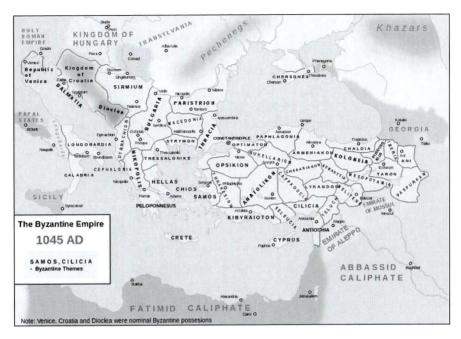

Byzantine Empire, 1045. *(Wikimedia Commons. Map by Andrei Nacu.)*

the region was a bastion of diversity, new architectural, intellectual, and literary forms developed.

Considering medieval Iberia through the lenses of diversity and multiculturalism has been a significant academic course of inquiry. Historians who study Anatolia are just beginning to consider the medieval period via this kind of framework, while historians who study medieval Iberia have engaged with the ways in which religious diversity affected social interactions and cultural production for over sixty years. In 1948, the Spanish historian Américo Castro first used the term *convivencia* (meaning "coexistence") in order to describe the tolerant interactions between Christians, Jews, and Muslims in medieval Spain. Castro saw these interactions as largely positive permutations. An American historian, David Nirenberg (1996), working roughly fifty years after Castro, posits a different interpretation of these relationships, suggesting that the interactions between religious communities in late medieval Europe can best be described as competition, with times of coexistence.

Cultural convivencia is most obvious at the linguistic level: during this time period, approximately 4,000 Arabic words were introduced into the Spanish language. Arabic language influences in Spanish manifest themselves in everyday terms, such as *aceituna* (olive), *almuerzo* (lunch), *azúcar* (sugar), and *cero* (zero); and in philosophical concepts, such as *alquímia* (alchemy), *azar* (chance), and *paraíso* (paradise). Another important and visible area of cultural interaction in Iberia is in the architectural forms that developed in the region. One of the most famous examples is the Grand Cathedral/Mosque

Interior of the Grand Mosque (Mezquita) in Córdoba, originally built as a church in the sixth century. The distinctive and celebrated columns of the interior of the mosque at Córdoba were constructed using material from Roman buildings that had fallen into disrepair. The mosque's design echoes some architectural motifs of the Ummayad Mosque in Damascus, also constructed in a former church. *(Photo by Lucia Volk.)*

at Córdoba, considered one of the finest examples of both Moorish and Renaissance architecture. Originally constructed as a church in the sixth century, it was converted into a mosque and used as such for over three centuries until it was reconverted into a Catholic church in the thirteenth century. (Interestingly, recent immigration to Spain from Morocco has led to an increased Muslim presence in Córdoba, and there have been appeals on the part of the Muslim community in Córdoba to allow Muslims to pray in the structure.)

A medieval lyric epic, the *Poem of El Cid*, offers further evidence of cultural interactions in the region. Most likely crystallized in the twelfth century in Castille, a region in the northern part of modern Spain, the epic tells a romantic story based on the activities of Rodrigo Díaz de Vivar, an eleventh-century Christian who helped make the eventual "reconquest" (or "Reconquista") and unification of Spain, which culminated in 1492, possible. Muslims in Iberia gave him the name "El Sidd," meaning "the sir" in Arabic. While El Cid became a hero of Spain, the fact that he is best known by his Arabic moniker indicates how deeply interpenetrated linguistic cultures in Iberia were.

Other linguistic examples highlight the cultural crosscurrents. Large populations of Christians lived in the Iberian Peninsula from the seventh through fourteenth centuries, and they spoke a language known as Mozarabic, an Arabized Romance language that was generally written with the Arabic alphabet. Many of the poets who composed in Arabic, Hebrew, and Latin used more than one language in their works, and they also shared new styles, subjects, and themes. The amount of poetry composed in Iberia in the late medieval period in Arabic, Hebrew, and Spanish is remarkable, but perhaps even more striking is the similarity of approach and theme that these poetries share.

At the same time, the regulation of daily life in cities populated by various religious communities presented challenges. An important source for our understanding of how Christians, Jews, and Muslims lived together in cities is the "Fuero of Teruel," the Urban Charter of the city of Teruel, in eastern Spain. The charter was granted to the city by Alfonso II of Aragon (1157–1196). This text, composed in the late twelfth century, includes detailed regulations for daily life in a Christian-controlled city that was also home to Jews and Muslims. The text prescribes various regulations of the city's public baths:

> Of the public bath: Following this are provisions about the public bath. The [male] bathers may go to the communal bath on Tuesdays and Thursdays and Saturdays, according to the law. Women may go to the bath on Mondays and Wednesdays. Jews and Moors may go on Fridays, and on no other day by any means. . . . Moreover, if the Jews or Moors bathe on some other day than Fridays, each of the bathers shall pay a fine of 30 *sueldos* to the judge and the *alcaldes* and the *almotacaf* by thirds with the plaintiff, if it should be proven according to law. Moreover, if a man enters the bath or any bathhouse on the women's days, he shall pay a fine of 30 *sueldos*, if it should be proven. If not, he shall swear that he was accused falsely and be believed. Moreover, if a woman enters on the men's days, as was said, she shall pay 30 *sueldos* [as was specified above]. (Klein 1999)

While this text shows that Christians, Jews, and Muslims did use the same public baths, it prescribes that they should not use them on the same days. At the same time, it seems that Christian, Jewish, and Muslim women were permitted to bathe together, suggesting that religious distinction was more significant among men in Teruel than it was among women.

As this and other examples show, both convivencia and competition existed side by side. The dichotomy between the two makes room for the range of simultaneous actions that were taking place as various hierarchies (political, religious, and social) competed for power. These actions included, in the most general terms, peace and violence, and inclusion and exclusion. In the context of our understanding of the medieval Mediterranean, coexistence and competition defined reactions to diversity in both Iberia and in Anatolia.

Conquests and Islamizations

When historians consider the medieval Middle East, one of the most central features studied is the spread of Islam. In addition, Islamic models of societal organization are examined. Scholars focus on the unifying message of Muhammad, and on the Arab nature of the Islamic conquests of the region, from Egypt to Iraq.

The spread of Islam out of the Arabian Peninsula was a surprisingly swift process. Muhammad began preaching the message of Islam in 610 CE, and by 636 CE, four years after his death, Muslim Arabs had conquered Jerusalem, the holiest city in both Christianity and Judaism, from the Byzantines. The rapidity with which the conquest and subsequent conversion took place has long been of interest to scholars. The message of Islam—its focus on monotheism, or the belief in one God—was familiar to the largely Christian and Jewish populations that were exposed to it, making conversion relatively easy. Additionally, the conquering armies had a great capacity for building alliances. Familial and tribal associations formed the basis of social structures in the mainly nomadic Arabian Peninsula in Muhammad's time, an organizational principle that strengthened Islamic forces as they conquered various cities of the Middle East. It enabled close ties within armies, as well as the rapid building of social ties with new populations.

Unlike the early Islamic conquests of the Fertile Crescent and North Africa, the Islamization of late medieval Anatolia was gradual, in part because of the cultural, ethnic, and religious diversity of the peoples living there. In their analysis of the settlement of Turkic-speaking Muslims in Anatolia, scholars place their focus primarily on the "decline" of a Byzantine Empire that had been weakened after decades of war with the neighboring Persian Empire. The ingenuity and uniqueness of the Ottoman Turks (in comparison with other Turkish principalities, or *beyliks*) have also been considered an important element in the establishment of a unified Muslim rule in Anatolia. Still, around 400 years passed between the first Seljuk Turkish incursions into the region in the mid-eleventh century and the Ottoman conquest of Constantinople. Prior to the Seljuk Turks' arrival in the region, Byzantine Anatolia was home to a varied population. The official religion of the empire was Christianity, but within Byzantine borders lived a great number of people who practiced forms of Christianity that were distinct from the official state version of Chalcedonian Orthodoxy. While Greek was the official language of the Eastern Roman Empire, several languages were spoken in Anatolia, including Arabic, Aramaic, and Armenian. The Byzantine Empire was also home to a relatively significant Jewish population.

In the aftermath of the Byzantine defeat by the Seljuk Turks at the Battle of Manzikert in 1071, the landscape of the shrunken Byzantine Empire became even more diverse. With the entrance of Seljuk tribes from Iran, the already diverse peoples living in Anatolia encountered not only new languages (both Turkish and Persian), but also a large nomadic population and a governing Muslim class interested in establishing Islamic institutions in the region. It was, in fact, the arrival of the Seljuks in Anatolia that provided the impetus for the events that have most consistently colored a modern interpretation of the medieval rapport between Christianity and Islam—the Crusades.

The Byzantine emperor Alexios Comnenos, who ruled from 1081 to 1118, as depicted in mosaics in the Hagia Sophia, the main cathedral in the Byzantine capital of Constantinople (now Istanbul). The Hagia Sophia was converted into a mosque after Constantinople was conquered by the Ottomans in 1453. *(Wikimedia Commons.)*

When Pope Urban II called European Christians to crusade in 1095 during the Council of Clermont (in France), he did so after having received a letter from the Byzantine emperor, Alexios Comnenos. The emperor wrote a letter to the pope, imploring him to help the Byzantines fight off the new Turkish Muslim intruders into Anatolia and the Holy Land. Over the course of the next four centuries, European Christians would venture to the Holy Land, many of them on foot through Anatolia. The interactions between the crusaders and the local populations living in Anatolia (whether Arabs, Armenians, Byzantines, or Turks) added another level of complication to the cultural diversity already present in the region. While the crusaders had originally promised to return lands to Byzantine rule that they were able to "take back" from any of the Muslim powers in the region, they never did. In fact, the lands conquered by the crusaders were turned into what became known as "Crusader states," adding another layer of state-level competition among Christians in the Middle East.

Christian Competition in the Middle East

In 1204 the Byzantine capital city of Constantinople (today's Istanbul) was attacked by armed crusaders from Western Europe, who claimed to have stopped in the city en route to the Holy Land in order to collect funds and supplies. However, the crusaders not only violently attacked the Christian capital and robbed it of many of its famed relics, they also conquered it, expelling the Byzantine emperor and making the city the capital of a short-lived Latin empire. These crusaders never proceeded on to the Holy Land.

That the capital of a Christian empire was attacked by crusaders whose primary goal was to support Christian initiatives in the Holy Land in the face of increased Islamic power helps to reveal the ultimate aims of crusading enterprises in the thirteenth century. Rather than fighting in the name of God for the Holy Land, the Crusades soon became an opportunity for certain individuals and powers to increase their wealth and political influence. Thus the Crusades were just as much about power relationships as they were about faith. Christian Byzantium had been militarily engaged with various Muslim powers for centuries, and yet its request for help from Western Europe to push back the Seljuks only *increased* the speed with which the Byzantine Empire fell. Even in the context of the relations between Europe and the Middle East during the Crusades, a simple Christianity versus Islam dichotomy falls short in explaining the real implications of cultural or religious identity during this time period.

This sack of Constantinople illustrates, in fact, the complexities associated with interfaith relations that distinguished the late medieval period. Perhaps the most telling reflection on this moment of Byzantine history is the quotation attributed to Loukas Notaras, the Constantinopolitan adviser to the Byzantine emperor (and a grand admiral), upon the Ottoman conquest of Constantinople in 1453: "Better the turban of the Turk than the tiara of the Pope" (as cited in the fifteenth-century *History of Mikael Doukas*, published in *Bonn Corpus Scriptorum Historiae Byzantinae*, by I. Bekker, 1834, 246.)

Also during the Crusades, coexistence manifested itself in another way. Richard the Lionheart (king of England, 1189–1199) attempted to arrange a marriage between his sister and the brother of Saladin (the most famous hero of the Counter-Crusade and founder of the Ayyubid Dynasty). Intermarriage between Christians and Muslims was commonplace in Anatolia, and it was quite frequent between the Seljuk Turkish and Byzantine elites. At the same time, recent scholarship by Rustam Shukurov (2012), a Byzantine historian who conducts research at Moscow State University, has uncovered information indicating that some Byzantine women who married into the Seljuk Dynasty maintained their Christian religious practices and passed them on to their children (future Seljuk sultans), many of whom were baptized at the Hagia Sophia, the main cathedral in Constantinople. A consciousness of conversion did develop in the medieval period, but a thirteenth-century Cilician Armenian law code suggests that conversions to Islam were reversible:

> If, after converting, a man should return to his faith and his family within seven years' time, then his wife should welcome him into the home. If seven years has passed, then she may do as she chooses. The law is the same if the wife converts. (Galstyan 1958, 92–93)

This suggests, once again, that religious identities in this time period were fluid. In fact, our contemporary understanding of the significance (and permanence) of a person's religious identity might be limiting our attempt to understand the medieval period.

Anatolian Architectural Hybridities

Until the establishment of Ottoman suzerainty over the region in the mid-fifteenth century, Anatolia was a place of cultural "betweenness." The Seljuks were the first Turkic Muslim entity to become established in the region. They were followed by many other similar Turkish and Persian-speaking principalities, which existed either as subservient to the Seljuks or in direct competition with them. At the same time, the Armenians established their own principality and, later, kingdom in the region. And after the First Crusade, a Latin Crusader state was established around Antioch. This was followed by the entrance of the Mongols into the region. Those Mongols who had converted to Islam (and were known as the Ilkhanids) extended their territory into Anatolia in the mid-thirteenth century, forming the largest contiguous land empire in the history of humankind. As all of these political entities established themselves in Anatolia, they supported the construction of churches, mosques, religious schools (*medreses*, or *madrassas*), dervish lodges (*zaviyes*), and caravansaries (inns), completely transforming the physical landscape both of urban areas and the hinterland. These physical structures, in turn, altered the cultural life of the region, by providing spaces within which individuals could gather to pray, study, or participate in the development of mystical religious practices.

The architectural programs funded in Anatolia—by a range of individuals associated with myriad local principalities—altered the urban and rural landscapes of the region. On a purely aesthetic level, these architectural programs are material evidence of the kind of hybridity that was common in late medieval Anatolia. Many of the masons and architects constructing new "Islamic" buildings (e.g., mosques, *madrassas*, and dervish lodges) were members of indigenous Christian populations. As a result, while many of the buildings and their functions were new, the physical appearance of much of the early Islamic architecture of Anatolia looks very similar to what is traditionally considered the Armenian, Byzantine, and Georgian (i.e., Christian) architecture of the region.

Cultural Hybridities in Textual References

Textual sources available to us from this time period include chronicles, hagiographies (glorified recountings of the lives of saints), poetry, and pious endowment deeds. These texts were composed in a range of languages, including Arabic, Armenian, Byzantine Greek, Persian, Syriac, and Turkish. Many of these sources indicate that the Islamic institutions created during this time period were used not only by Muslims, but also by Christians.

The Armenian cathedral at Ani was completed in the early eleventh century. In the aftermath of the Seljuk conquests, the church was turned into a mosque. The building lost its dome in 1319, after a major earthquake. *(Wikimedia Commons.)*

Hovannavank is a thirteenth-century church and monastery dedicated to John the Baptist. It was founded by the Zakarid dynasty, based in Ani. It continues as a working church in the Republic of Armenia. *(Wikimedia Commons.)*

A twelfth-century tomb, located in Divrigi (present-day Turkey), constructed for Sitte Melik, daughter of the Muslim Mengücek ruler Fakhr al-Din Bahram Shah. The geometrical design of the walls and roof construction is similar to that of Armenian churches of the period. *(Wikimedia Commons.)*

The Poetry of Rumi

Jalal ad-Din Muhammad Rumi (1207–1273)—often referred to as either Rumi (meaning, literally, "of Rum") or Mevlana (meaning "our master")—was one of the most important characters in the diverse landscape of late medieval Anatolia. Born in Bakht (in modern-day Afghanistan), he moved into Anatolia with his father, a Muslim judge, in the thirteenth century. He became a significant Muslim mystic in the region, and after his death, his son founded a religious order following the teachings of his father. (This order is today called the Mevlevi Order of Dervishes or, sometimes, the "Whirling Dervishes.") Based in the Seljuk capital of Konya, Rumi was a prolific poet. He composed his work primarily in Persian, but he also spoke and wrote in Turkish, and he knew some Armenian and Greek as well. His writing seemed to encourage diversity. Rumi wrote poetry in which he inserted lines and verses in other languages, including Armenian, Greek, and Turkish. His hagiography, composed in the fourteenth century, suggests that both his poetry and his openness to diversity contributed to his capacity to gain (and convert) followers of diverse backgrounds:

> Come, come, whoever you are.
> Wanderer, worshiper, lover of leaving. It doesn't matter.
> Ours is not a caravan of despair. Come, even if you have broken
>   your vows a thousand times. (cited in Malak 2004, 151)

Chronicles and hagiographies alike indicate that Christians did "come" to Rumi. There is evidence of the participation of Christians and converts in new Islamic institutions, such as madrassas and dervish lodges, in Konya. At the same time, the participation of Christians in Islamic institutions, as shown in the literature by and about Rumi, indicate that conversion was not necessarily a condition for real urban coexistence.

Armenian Priests and Poets in Erzinjan

In the northeast of Anatolia during the thirteenth century, the city of Erzinjan seems to have existed under simultaneous Armenian, Mengücek (Turkic), and Mongol domination. With a large Christian Armenian population, the city was home to many churches and monasteries. At the same time, Armenian priest-poets living in and around the city—like Rumi in Konya—were interested in other languages and cultures and supported tolerance and inclusion.

Born around 1260, Kostandin of Erzinjan (or Erzincan) most likely pursued a religious education in one of the Armenian monasteries around Erzinjan, although it is thought that he was never ordained a priest and left the walls of the monastery to live a more worldly life. Writing in a vernacular style, Kostandin was the first Armenian poet to incorporate what is traditionally considered Islamic imagery of the "Rose and Nightingale" into Armenian poetry. Manuscripts of his poetry were composed in the thirteenth century and copied throughout the medieval period. His poetic works were first published in Venice in the eighteenth century, in an Armenian monastery on the island of San Lazzaro. Later editions come from the former Soviet Union and a 1991 dissertation written at the University of Leiden.

Known for his unique style, Kostandin recited poems while surrounded by members of a *futuwwa*-type brotherhood. *Futuwwa* was an Islamic code of behavior for celibate members of guild-like, faith-based confraternities. The code was developed in and around Baghdad when it was the seat of the Islamic caliphate in the tenth century, but it became an important model of social organization in late medieval Anatolian cities for both Christians and Muslims. We know that some Armenian and Greek-speaking Christians participated in these sorts of urban confraternities, based on epigraphic and textual evidence of Armenians and Greeks bearing titles associated with these brotherhoods. Armenians, who made up the majority of the population in the city of Erzinjan in the medieval period, created their own futuwwa-like organizations, with written codes filled with restrictions and rules very similar to those present in Islamic codes and, yet, focused on the primacy of Jesus Christ.

Apparently, Kostandin's confraternity brothers in the mountains of Erzinjan were not only interested in the Islamic concept of futuwwa, but also they shared an intimate knowledge of Persian literary culture, especially the famous epic, the *Shahnameh*, for one of Kostandin's poems begins with:

A man was seated and recited the *Shahnameh* aloud. The brothers asked me, recite for us a poem in the manner of the *Shahnameh*. I composed this poem. Read it in the meter of the *Shahnameh*. (cited in Van Lint 1996, 68)

This one sentence indicates that some Armenians living in Erzinjan were aware of Persian culture and familiar enough with its literature to know the specific meter of the *Shahnameh*, the Iranian national epic.

Yovhannes (or Hovhannes) of Erzinjan, born in Erzinjan in the thirteenth century, also pursued his religious studies and was ordained a celibate priest. While still a student, he translated the Arabic *Epistles of the Brethren of Purity*, composed in the city of Basra in present-day Iraq in the tenth century. This particular work is a collection of fifty-two chapters composed by a group of individuals that deal with mathematics, music, logic, astronomy, and the physical and natural sciences. The text also explores the nature of the soul and approaches matters related to ethics, revelation, and spirituality. Justifying his translation of the Arabic-language text, he explains, "May our brothers be peace-loving in this world; may they take pleasure in speaking with and listening to men from every nation, such that they become wise from every nation, grow and gain wisdom" (cited in Baghdasaryan 1977, 227).

The philosophy articulated here by Yovhannes speaks to the way in which he thought about the diversity of culture, faith, and language, and it indicates an appreciation for other cultures and religions. This same Yovhannes composed two Armenian futuwwa-like texts, which appear to be largely translations of a Turkish-language futuwwa text composed in the nearby city of Tokat, indicating the likelihood of a good deal of intellectual interaction between Armenian-speaking Christians and Turkish-speaking Muslims in the region.

Aflaki's Hagiography of Rumi

Despite the trends noted above, on the ground, diversity could represent a challenge. The hagiography of Rumi and his family members was composed in Persian in the fourteenth century by Shams ad-Din Ahmad Aflaki. As it is a hagiography, scholars suggest caution when drawing conclusions from the text. Yet, while some of its stories do seem fantastic, the text offers great insight into late medieval Anatolian urban life. In one instance, Aflaki relates an incident that took place when Rumi's grandson, Chelebi Amir Arif, visited Sivas, a city under Mongol control but with a significant Turkish-speaking, Muslim population and a large and old Armenian (Christian) population. The text indicates that Amir Arif became visibly upset when he saw that a disheveled man mumbling in Armenian in the middle of one of the city's streets had acquired a great following of believers.

According to the hagiography, Amir Arif became jealous that this man was referred to as the "pole of the world" (an Islamic mystical appellation for someone who is extremely close to God). Amir Arif proceeded to dismount his horse and cross through the crowd that was surrounding the man. He slapped the Armenian-speaker three times on the neck and ordered him to close up shop. Given the significance of Amir Arif and his family in the development of Anatolian Islam, one would expect little reaction, if any, to his action.

In this fourteenth-century version of the *Shahnameh*, Bahram Gur (a hero of the epic) is depicted fighting a lion. This illumination is taken from what is now known as the Demotte *Shahnameh*, for the French art dealer Georges Demotte. This particular manuscript is also known as the Great Mongol *Shahnameh* as it is considered the most brilliant example of Mongol Ilkhanid painting. *(Wikimedia Commons.)*

However, the "knaves" of Sivas (members of an urban confraternity) responded immediately to Amir Arif's aggression inflicted upon this citizen of Sivas. Even though he was ostensibly considered a guest of honor in Sivas, his attack on a local man inspired an organized defense from the urban confraternity members. As noted above, many of the urban confraternities in Anatolia during this time used constitutions that were based on the Islamic code of chivalry called futuwwa. Further, the hagiography, in calling the Armenian speaker the "pole of the world," elevates an ostensibly non-Muslim (or a convert to Islam) to a "perfect person" in the context of Islamic mysticism.

In relating this story, Aflaki's text exposes confusion or comingling of various identities: an Armenian-speaking (Muslim? Christian?) mystic was defended against the grandson of Rumi by members of an urban confraternity in Sivas who used an Islamic code of chivalry. This passage suggests that linguistic and religious identities did not have clear boundaries, especially in urban centers. Cities provided rich soil for the development of localized, urban-based allegiances, even in opposition to family members of a well-known and respected mystic. And it was within cities that different peoples "speaking their own languages" had the most regular interactions. Ultimately, it seems that these interactions bred something like a new, urban language representative of both coexistence and competition.

A Book of Advice

The fourteenth-century, Kirshehir-based Muslim mystic Ashik Pasha composed a book of advice, the *Gharibnameh*, one of the first Turkish-language works penned in Anatolia. The goal of the *Gharibnameh* is to provide instruction to Muslims who desire to lead a life dedicated to mysticism. At the same time, the text offers insight into the day-to-day complications associated with diversity. Ashik Pasha inserts some Armenian text, composed using the Arabic alphabet, into a section of his work, alongside Arabic, Persian, and Turkish, indicating knowledge of—or, at the very least, familiarity with—all of these languages. That this sort of linguistic knowledge existed in a small city like Kirshehir suggests that cities offered an environment in which people interacted with neighbors of different faiths who spoke different languages. In fact, the anecdote below, narrated by Ashik Pasha in his *Gharibnameh*, can be understood as a straightforward meditation on linguistic difference and human similarity.

The text tells of an Arab, a Persian, a Turk, and an Armenian who were traveling together without knowing each other's languages. While on their journey, they happened to come across a piece of gold and started to fight over it. Locals overheard them yelling and approached the four men, asking them why they were beating each other. They were so caught up in fighting over the gold piece that none of them answered. Finally, individuals arrived who understood all of the languages spoken by the four travelers, and they realized that each one of the men actually wanted to use the gold in order to buy grapes. One of these onlookers took the coin and purchased grapes for the four travelers. All four travelers were pleased, and their fighting stopped. The author thus showed that a temporary misunderstanding due to language barriers was easily resolved, since the underlying desires of the travelers were the same.

That one of the chapters of Ashik Pasha's advice literature deals with misunderstanding between individuals speaking different languages, emphasizing their common human desires, suggests that cities like Kirshehir were home to multilingual, multicultural, and multireligious environments, and that this sort of environment occasionally created the potential for misunderstanding and confusion. At the same time, the text encourages readers (or listeners) to be patient with one another, and it posits that all languages are, in fact, one: that of humanity.

Conclusion

In considering the history of the medieval Mediterranean—and the medieval Middle East—these myriad sources shed light on the ways in which individuals experienced diversity (of faith and language, primarily). While the political histories of both Anatolia and the Iberian Peninsula during the late medieval period are remarkably complex, examining the social history of these two regions allows for a better understanding of diversity as a long-term trend, and as a challenge. While Islam provided a relatively tolerant paradigm for accommodating religious difference, it is clear that interfaith interactions were not always harmonious. At the same time, it would seem that peaceful coexistence was the norm, rather than the exception, on both shores of the Mediterranean. Looking at the historical record through the lens of social history, there is clear evidence of cultural and linguistic mutual influence and interpenetration. Maybe, then, the question of whether individuals living in diverse societies in the Middle Ages were or were not tolerant of each other's differences is not a very productive one to ask. Instead, the better line of inquiry involves how the differences manifested themselves and were negotiated in specific contexts.

References and Further Research

Aflākī, Shams al-Dīn Ahmad. 2002. *Feats of the Knowers of God* (Manaqeb al-ārefin). Translated by John O'Kane. Leiden, the Netherlands: Brill.

Baghdasaryan, Edvart. 1977. *Hovhannēs Erznkacʻi ev nra xratakan arjakə* [Hovhannēs of Erzinjan and his wisdom literature]. Yerevan: Armenia SSR Publications.

Bekker, I., ed. and trans. 1834. *History of Mikael Doukas*. Published in *Bonn Corpus Scriptorum Historiae Byzantinae*, Vol. 20. Bonn: Prussian Academy of Sciences.

Braude, Benjamin, and Bernard Lewis. 1982. *Christians and Jews in the Ottoman Empire: The Functioning of a Pluralistic Society*. New York: Holmes & Meier.

Cahen, Claude. 1968. *Pre-Ottoman Turkey*. London: Sidgwick and Jackson.

Castro, Américo. 1948. *España en Su Historia: Cristianos, Moros y Judíos* [Spain in its history: Christians, Muslims and Jews]. Buenos Aires: Editorial Losada.

Dodds, Jerrilynn D., and María Rosa Menocal. 2008. *The Arts of Intimacy: Christians, Jews and Muslims in the Making of Castillian Culture*. New Haven, CT: Yale University Press.

Erdmann, Kurt. 1961–1976. *Das anatolische Karavansaray des 13. Jahrhunderts* [The Anatolian caravansaries of the thirteenth century]. Berlin: Gebr. Mann.

Galstyan, A.G., ed. 1958. *Datastanagirkʻ* [The Law Code of Smbat Sparapet]. Yerevan: Armenian National Press.

Hamilton, Rita, and Janet Perry, ed. and trans. 1985. *The Poem of the Cid: Dual Language Edition*. London: Penguin.

Klein, Elka, trans. 1999. *El Fuero de Teruel*. Translated from the text edited by Max Gorosch (Stockholm, 1950). Internet Medieval Sourcebook. http://www.fordham.edu/halsall/source/1276teruel.asp.

Malak, Amin. 2004. *Muslim Narratives and the Discourse of English*. Albany: State University of New York Press.

Nirenberg, David. 1996. *Communities of Violence: Persecution of Minorities in the Middle Ages*. Princeton, NJ: Princeton University Press.

Riley-Smith, Jonathan. 2008. *The Crusades, Christianity, and Islam*. New York: Columbia University Press.

Sharabkhanyan, P.E., ed. 1987. *Hayocʻ Lezvi Patmutʻean Kʻrestomatia* [A miscellany of Armenian literature]. Yerevan: Yerevan University Press.

Shukurov, Rustam. 2012. "Harem Christianity: The Byzantine Identity of Seljuk Princes," in *The Seljuks of Anatolia: Court and Society in the Medieval Middle East*, edited by A.C.S. Peacock and S.N. Yildiz, 115–150. London: I.B. Tauris.

van Lint, Theo. 1996. *Kostandin of Erznka: An Armenian Religious Poet of the XIIIth–XIVth Century*. PhD diss. Leiden, the Netherlands.

Vryonis, Speros. 1956. "Isidore Glabas and the Turkish *Devshirme*." *Speculum* 31, no. 3: 433–443.

———. 1971. *The Decline of Medieval Hellenism in Asia Minor and the Process of Islamization from the Eleventh Through the Fifteenth Century*. Berkeley: University of California Press.

Wolper, Ethel Sara. 2003. *Cities and Saints: Sufism and the Transformation of Late Medieval Anatolia*. University Park: Pennsylvania State University Press.

Yavuz, Kemal, ed. and trans. 2000. *Garib-Nāme of Aşık Paşa*. Istanbul: TDK.

10

Democracy, Secularism, and Islam
Examining the "Turkish Model"

HOOTAN SHAMBAYATI

After the Arab uprisings of 2011, many observers looked to Turkey as a possible democratic model for its Arab neighbors. This admiration stems from Turkey's emergence as a major regional political and economic actor under the Justice and Development Party (JDP). The JDP (also known as AKP, for its Turkish name, Adalet ve Kalkinma Partisi) is a party with roots in political Islam that has been in power in Turkey since November 2002. For the liberal advocates of the "Turkish model," JDP's rule represents an example of how democracy can thrive under a political party with roots in political Islam. More religious advocates of the model see Turkey as an example of how Islam can thrive and come to power in a modern democratic setting. At the same time, however, critical voices argue that despite some reforms under the JDP, the Turkish government continues to violate civil liberties and the rule of law, and they warn that under JDP's rule, Turkey is in danger of becoming a theocratic dictatorship.

> The website of the Justice and Development Party offers extensive information concerning its organization, political agenda, and leadership (http://www.akparti. org.tr/english).

Public opinion surveys of overwhelmingly Muslim societies in the Middle East show strong support for democracy at levels comparable to those found in the West (see Table 10.1). The surveys, however, show relatively weak support for liberal values such as gender equality, minority rights, freedom of expression and religion, and so on. This combination of strong support for elections and low support for liberal values highlights the dilemmas of democratization in the Middle East: democracy might produce illiberal results.

The Turkish model under study is based on three elements. First, the goal of the state is defined as "civilizing society," thus making it more "modern." Second, social transformation takes place under democratic conditions, where political actors compete in free and fair elections and are allowed to govern as long as they remain committed to the "civilizing" mission of the state. Third, unelected institutions such as the military and constitutional courts are empowered to protect the civilizing mission. In the specific

Table 10.1

Attitudes Toward Democratic and Liberal Values (mean approval)

Type of society	Approval of democratic performance	Approval of democratic ideals	Approval of gender equality	Approval of abortion rights	Approval of homosexuality
Western Christianity	68	86	82	48	53
Islamic	68	87	55	25	12
All others	63	80	67	36	28

Source: Norris and Inglehart, 2002.
Societies were classified according to the historically predominant religion.

case of Turkey, this system has allegedly encouraged democratization by moderating political Islam, but, as I will show, it has done so at the cost of undermining liberalism and the rule of law.

The Kemalist State and the Transformation of Ottoman Society

The Republic of Turkey, established in 1923, is the heir to the Ottoman Empire (1300s– 1923). A Muslim dynasty, the Ottomans ruled over a vast multilingual, multiethnic, and multireligious empire of not only Muslims but also Christians and Jews that covered large sections of Central and Eastern Europe, the Arab Middle East, and North Africa. Although Islam was the religion of the dynasty and the state, the Ottoman sultan afforded considerable internal autonomy to the non-Muslim communities in matters such as marriage, inheritance, and resolving disputes within each community. Under pressure from European expansion and the rising tide of political nationalism, this decentralized system became inoperable in the nineteenth century and accelerated the disintegration of the empire.

By the eve of World War I, the Ottomans had lost control of most of their European and North African provinces to forces of nationalism and European imperialism. Defeat in the war brought the final dismemberment of the empire by Britain and France, along with the formal separation of the Arab provinces, some of which, like Egypt, had been semiautonomous or under European tutelage for decades. In 1923 the Turkish Grand National Assembly, a parliament that had directed the Turkish war of independence, voted to dissolve the Ottoman sultanate and establish the Republic of Turkey, with Mustafa Kemal (later referred to as Atatürk) as its first president, a position that he held until his death in 1938.

An Ottoman general who had led the Turkish troops in their only major victory during World War I (at Gallipoli), and who won Turkey's victory in the war of independence that followed, Atatürk was a nationalist who admired Europe and hoped to create a Turkish

---

Box 10.1

Third-Wave Democracies

In many of today's established democracies, including the United States, liberal values such as gender equality and tolerance of difference became dominant only after political democracy had developed stable institutions. This gradualist path, however, is no longer viable. Many of the new democracies, sometimes referred to as "third-wave democracies," are examples of "democratization backward": universal adult suffrage precedes the development of civil society and state institutions that can establish and maintain rule of law, hold the executive accountable, provide channels for the peaceful expression of societal demands, encourage compromise, and protect the interest and rights of electoral losers. In other words, citizens often obtain the right to vote before a system of "checks and balances" is created, with institutions such as independent courts that can protect electoral losers against the tyranny of the majority.

---

republic similar to a European nation-state in which people identified as citizens based on shared language, culture, and history. Under a new constitution adopted in 1924, legislative power was vested in the Grand National Assembly. While elections were held regularly and universal suffrage for both males and females became the norm in the 1930s—Turkish women obtained the right to vote much earlier than their counterparts in Switzerland—the law permitted only Atatürk's Republican People's Party (RPP) to participate in politics.

The website of the Republican People's Party offers extensive information concerning its history, organization, and political agenda (http://www.chp.org.tr/en).

Atatürk and his inner circle saw their task as the wholesale transformation of Turkish life as lived under Ottoman rule. Politically, this meant the creation of a vast centralized state bureaucracy that allowed the state to impact life in the remotest areas of the country, though this did not always occur in the ways anticipated by the state elite. Economically, it meant centralized state planning, the nationalization of foreign-owned businesses, the creation of state-owned economic enterprises and banks, the expansion of transportation and communication networks, and the creation of a domestic but dependent private sector that relied heavily on the state. Socially, the task before the Republican leadership was the creation of a national identity that distinguished Turkey from its Muslim but non-Turkish neighbors, aligned it with the much-admired European Enlightenment ideals, and advocated loyalty to the state

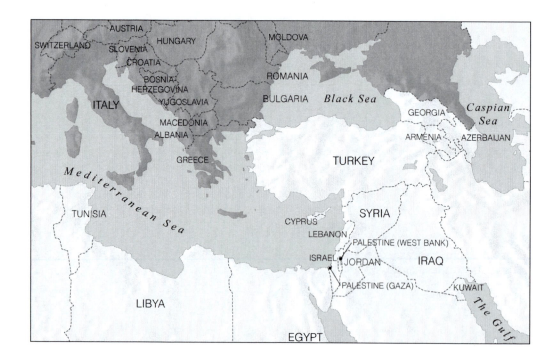

as the supreme value of the Turkish nation. In Atatürk's own words, the aim was "elevating the people to the level of contemporary civilization." Used by Atatürk in a number of speeches to explain the purpose of the reforms, this statement (or variations of it) has appeared in the preamble to all Turkish constitutions (1924, 1961, and the present 1982 constitution). In other words, the task of the Turkish state is to "civilize" the society, not to represent it.

The attempts to create a "modern nation" necessarily raised the question of the proper role of religion in a modern state. For the new leaders of Turkey, the nation, as defined by the leadership of state, was the only legitimate source of identity for the citizens of a modern state. This view denied the existence of alternative sources of identity, such as religion or ethnicity. Hence religion was actively excluded from the public sphere through state-centered social engineering projects. First, the 1924 abolition of the Ottoman sultan's office of the caliph, the head of the global Muslim community, formally severed the ties between the head of the Turkish state and Islam. Second, secularism was introduced as one of the main organizing principles of the state. All Muslim religious schools (*madrassas*), religious courts, and religious orders were legally abolished. The Law on the Unification of Education replaced the religious leaders' historical control over education with a vast system of state schools, which would teach a centrally coordinated secular curriculum. Furthermore, religious law was abandoned in favor of state-created law based on imported European legal codes. After replacing existing religious courts, the state-controlled judiciary became the main setting for the adjudication of both public and private disputes. However, these sweeping measures did not mean the separation of religion and state as it is typically understood in the United States.

The Turkish state's understanding of secularism (*laiklik*) has been called "assertive secularism" (Kuru 2007). Similar to post-revolutionary France, the new Republic of Turkey approached religion with suspicion and as a potential competitor for the loyalty of the citizens. Hence, in Turkey, secularism has not meant the state's withdrawal from the religious arena. In fact, the state deepened the incorporation of the Muslim religious establishment into the state bureaucracy by putting all mosques and their personnel under the control of the Directorate of Religious Affairs. Turkish secularism has encouraged state control of religion, rather than the construction of a "wall" separating the two spheres of public life.

As part of the new national program, the Turkish state introduced a series of social reforms. The most drastic was the alphabet reform of 1928, through which the Latin alphabet replaced the Arabic script that had historically been used to write the Turkish language. As a result, future generations of Turks could no longer read the pre-1928 texts, and thus lost access to their Ottoman past. Other reforms were introduced to "modernize" music, cultural activities and, most importantly, dress. Traditional Ottoman male headgear, such as the *fez*, was banned and replaced with European-style hats. The most dramatic reforms targeted women. The Muslim *hijab*, or headscarf, was strongly discouraged, although not legally banned, and women were encouraged to appear in public in European attire. Although the state continued to view women primarily as mothers and wives, the expansion of the educational system provided new opportunities for women, and they were encouraged to assume more active public roles in the community. Other reforms expanded the political and social rights of women.

The effectiveness and long-term impact of Atatürk's reforms on Turkish society are open to debate. Early scholarship praised Atatürk and assumed that his brand of secularism had fundamentally changed the religious nature of the Turkish society and set Turkey on the path toward "modernization," a concept that, at the time, was equated with Westernization. The more recent emergence of religion as a political issue and Islamism as a political ideology led to the rise of a new scholarship that noted that Atatürk's 1930s reforms remained limited to the larger cities, while the vast majority of residents in rural Turkey and smaller towns remained distinctly traditional and religious. Both groups of scholars—those who considered Atatürk's reforms a success, and those who did not—dismissed political Islam as a product of the "backward" Anatolian region in Turkey's interior and as a threat to "modernity," views that remain strong among some segments of (urban) Turkish society today.

Atatürk's reforms, and those instituted after his death, fundamentally changed Turkish society, but not always in ways anticipated by the state elites. Instead, they have created a modern, educated, nationalist, and secular class that feels threatened by the rise of an equally modern, educated, and nationalist—but also religiously devout and socially more conservative—group. Political Islam, as it is understood today, is another manifestation of modernity, not the remnant of an outdated worldview.

Box 10.2

Protecting Atatürk's Legacy

As founder of the Republic of Turkey, Atatürk holds a very special place in Turkish history books and Turkish society. Indeed, insulting Atatürk is a punishable offense. Controversy ensued in 2008 after the documentary filmmaker Can Dündar released *Mustafa*, based on the diaries and personal letters of the Turkish leader. His goal was to show his personal side, as well as his public persona. Since the film showed Atatürk smoking and drinking heavily during certain parts of his life, the filmmaker was accused of denigrating him. This episode set off a fierce debate over censorship in Turkish society. For a summary of the debate, see the article "Heated Debates Demystify Myths Surrounding Mustafa Kemal Atatürk," published online in *Today's Zaman* (http://www.todayszaman.com/).

The feature film, in Turkish, is available in full on Vimeo at http://vimeo.com/26204380.

Democracy, Turkish Style: Multiparty Politics, the Military, and the Courts

Atatürk's death in 1938 led to divisions among the political elite and the legalization of the other political parties, most notably the Democratic Party (DP). Led by defectors from the RPP, the DP and its leader, Adnan Menderes, appealed to the religious sentiments of Turkish society in mobilizing the voters and defeated the RPP in the parliamentary elections of 1950. During its decade-long rule, the DP lifted some of the restrictions on the public practice of religion, such as the ban on reciting the Muslim call to prayer in Arabic, and accelerated the building of new mosques. The government also established new religious schools under the guise of training religious leaders (imams) for state-controlled mosques. As opposed to the banned traditional religious schools (madrassas), these new imam training schools (*imam hatip okullari*) offered a state-controlled curriculum and included a variety of nonreligious subjects in sciences and other topics. Although these schools have remained controversial, and many among the secular Turks still see them as instruments of Islamization, they proved popular and became the training ground for a new brand of political actors. Some of these political actors became leaders of the Justice and Development Party (JDP), who no longer see a contradiction between modernity and religion.

A military coup in May 1960 ended the DP's rule, yet Turkey's return to multiparty democratic politics was relatively swift, as elected civilian politicians resumed power in 1962. The DP's mantle was picked up by the Justice Party (JP), which remained the largest political party until 1980, when the military staged another takeover. Like its predecessor, the JP was for the most part a secular party that tried to appeal to some of the religious sentiments in Turkish society. At the time, the struggling economy was the main source of divisions in Turkish society, and these struggles led to the emergence of Turkey's first recognizably Islamist party.

Table 10.2

Overview of Main Political Parties in Turkey

Name (English and Turkish)	Founders, leaders	Founded	Ideology	Closings, reincarnations	Present status, notes
Democratic Party (DP; Demokrat Partisi)	Adnan Menderes, Celal Bayar; former RPP leaders.	1945	Center-right	Closed after 1960 coup	JDP and other center-right parties claim it as one of their predecessors
Justice Party (JP; Adalet Partisi)	Süleyman Demirel	1962	Center-right	Closed after 1980 coup	Replaced DP; reorganized as the True Path Party; came to power in the late 1990s
National Order Party (NOP; Milli Nizam Partisi)	Necmettin Erbakan	1970	Islamist (National View, following Erbakan's 1996 manifesto)	Closed by Constitutional Court (CCT) in 1971	Replaced by NSP
National Salvation Party (NSP; Milli Selamet Partisi)	Necmettin Erbakan	1972	Islamist (National View)	Closed after the 1980 coup	Reorganized as WP/VP/FP
Motherland Party (MP; Anavatn Partisi)	Turgut Özal, Mesut Yilmaz	1983	Center-right	Active, not significant	Not significant
True Path Party (Doğru Yol Partisi)	Suleyman Demirel, Tansu Ciller	1983	Center-right	Active, not significant	Founded on behalf of Demirel, who was banned from politics; replaced JP
Democratic Left Party (Demokratik Sol Partisi)	Rahşan Ecevit, Bülent Ecevit	1985	Center-left	Dissolved itself in 2010	Created as a replacement for RPP while the latter was banned; founded by Rahşan Ecevit on behalf of her husband, who was banned from politics
Welfare Party (WP; Refah Partisi)	Necmettin Erbakan	1987	Islamist (National View)	Closed by CCT 1998	Succeeded NSP; reorganized as VP/FP
Virtue Party (VP; Fazilet Partisi)	Recai Kutan	1998	Islamist (National View)	Closed by CCT 2001	Succeeded WP; reorganized as Felicity Party
Felicity Party (FP; Saadet Partisi)	Recai Kutan	2001	Islamist (National View)	Active	Succeeded VP; not significant
Justice and Development Party (JDP; Adalet ve Kalkinma Partisi [AKP])	Abdullah Gül, Turgut Özal, and others	2001	Center-right? Islamist?	Currently in power	Succeeded VP, MP, DP, and various others

Source: Compiled by Hootan Shambayati.

In 1970, Necmettin Erbakan, a former president of Turkey's main industrial and commercial organization, formed Turkey's first recognizably Islamist party, the National Order Party (NOP). Erbakan had outlined his vision for Turkey in a 1969 manifesto called the "National View," and he formed an organization by the same name. He called for industrialization and economic independence, closer ties to the Muslim world based on religious affinity, and warned against further integration with Europe. An engineer by training, Erbakan had close ties to Turkey's religious circles. He recognized that the economic policies of the JP benefitted large enterprises in major urban centers while undercutting businessmen in Turkey's Anatolian hinterland. It is from this Anatolian small-town base that Erbakan drew most of his support. One year later, Turkey's Constitutional Court ruled that the NOP was based on religion and thus violated the principles of secularism. Erbakan then replaced it with the National Salvation Party (NSP). The NSP surprised many observers when it won 12 percent of the vote in 1973 and joined a coalition government led by the center-left RPP under Bülent Ecevit. Although NSP's share of the votes fell to less than 10 percent in the 1977 elections, the party was included in a unity government formed by the JP under Süleyman Demirel.

By the mid-1970s, rising energy prices and poor economic management resulted in a crisis in Turkey's economy and forced the government to borrow ever more heavily. At the same time, political violence between leftists and right-wing nationalists became a daily event, claiming dozens of lives. The inability of a series of weak coalition governments to address these issues further destabilized the country. With no political solution evident, the military took over on September 12, 1980.

The military regime suspended the constitution, dissolved the parliament, and closed all political parties, including the RPP, JP, and NSP. The military junta's new constitution, adopted in 1982, banned Demirel (JP), Ecevit (RPP), Erbakan (NSP), and other pre-coup leaders from politics. The ban on political leaders was lifted in 1987 through a referendum, after which Demirel, Ecevit, and Erbakan resumed their political activities, formed new political parties, and eventually served as prime minister.

The military regime provided the political stability necessary for introducing neoliberal economic reforms aimed at opening Turkish markets to international competition. The architect of these reforms was Turgut Özal. Özal was an engineer by training, and like Erbakan he had close ties to religious circles. He had made his mark as a technocrat working in a number of positions in both the private and public sectors, including at the World Bank and Turkey's State Planning Organization. The military regime charged him with reforming the Turkish economy. In 1983 Özal formed the Motherland Party (MP) and competed in the first post-coup parliamentary elections, easily defeating the military's two favorite parties. As prime minister (1983–1989), and later as president until his sudden death in 1993, Özal oversaw the restructuring of the Turkish economy and the emergence of the "Anatolian Tigers," a group of economic enterprises, such as the food processing conglomerate Ülker (owner of Belgium's Godiva Chocolatiers). Based in Anatolian cities like Kayseri and Konya, these companies provided both the economic basis for the reemergence of political Islam and the economic incentive for its moderation. Many of these businessmen had initially supported Özal's Motherland

Party, but when Erbakan returned to politics they threw their support behind him and his new Welfare Party (WP).

Erbakan shocked Turkey when the Welfare Party won the 1994 municipal elections in Istanbul and Ankara. These two cities had long been viewed as bastions of secularism, and the WP's victories meant that Islamism could no longer be dismissed as a movement contained in "backward" Anatolia. One year later, the WP won 20 percent of the vote in the parliamentary elections, making it the party with the most seats in parliament and allowing it to form a coalition government with the True Path Party (TPP). In retrospect, Erbakan's government did not introduce major changes to the Turkish political system. Nor was Erbakan the first Turkish leader to display his religiosity in public. However, the Welfare Party's rhetoric and symbolic events, such as an *iftar* ceremony for religious leaders, hosted at the prime minister's official residence in January 1997, were enough for the military and its allies to take action.

On February 28, 1997, the military-dominated National Security Council demanded that the government take a serious stand against the threat of Islamism and adopt a number of policies, such as the expansion of mandatory secular education to eight years. The military also issued a series of public statements and reports on the threat of Islamism, and it organized "seminars" for judges and prosecutors, journalists, and civil society organizations at which military officers warned of the dangers of Islamism and encouraged attendees and participants to pressure the government into resigning.

Erbakan's government resigned in June 1997 and was replaced by a minority coalition government, with Mesut Yilmaz of the Motherland Party as the prime minister and Bülent Ecevit from the Democratic Left Party as his deputy. With help from the Republican People's Party, the new government adopted some of the policies demanded by the military. It expanded mandatory education from five to eight years and reclassified religious schools as vocational, thus making it more difficult for graduates of these schools to enter universities.

The Constitutional Court closed the Welfare Party and banned Erbakan and some of the other leaders from political activity. The remaining Welfare leaders then formed the Virtue Party (VP). For all practical purposes a continuation of the WP, and led by one of Erbakan's deputies, the VP caused a mini-crisis in 1999 when one of its deputies, Merve Kavakci, appeared in parliament in a headscarf to take her oath of office. Even though no specific rules existed at the time against a deputy wearing a headscarf on the floor of parliament, the secular parties prevented her from taking the oath. In addition, Prime Minister Ecevit denounced her in parliament and, according to the *Hurriyet Daily News* (May 10, 1999), declared that "parliament was not the place to challenge the state." Kavakci was stripped of her Turkish citizenship because, like thousands of other Turks, she had obtained dual American citizenship without informing Turkish authorities. When it became public that she was in the process of marrying a Turkish citizen, which would have restored her citizenship, the government proposed to change the law to prevent this outcome. The episode contributed to the Constitutional Court's decision to disband the VP in 2001. Thus, in the name of protecting secularism, the government was willing to violate the basic principles of democracy and the rule of law.

Protecting Secularism via Institutional Constraints

Since 1982, Turkey has been functioning under a constitution that severely restricts civil liberties. In addition, up until the mid-2000s, the constitution legitimated the military's repeated interventions in the political process. The post-1982 political system relied on a network of formal institutions such as the Constitutional Court and the Council of State (a system of administrative courts); autonomous boards like the Board of Higher Education; the presidency; and the military-dominated National Security Council to maintain the military's tutelage over the political system. Democracy, of course, requires a system of checks and balances and effective constraints on the powers of elected officials in order to protect the rights of electoral losers and other minorities. However, the kinds of constraints that were imposed by the Turkish model should not be confused with democratic mechanisms of accountability. Democratic checks and balances require the existence of a web of institutions that hold each other accountable. The Turkish judiciary and the military, on the other hand, acted as "guardians of the regime" during this period. Guardianship implies a hierarchical relationship and an imbalance of power between the guardians and those in their charge.

Until the early 2000s, when the European Union pressured Turkey for reforms, these unelected institutions acted with impunity, constraining the parliament and elected officials. During the 1980s and 1990s, the National Security Council acted as Turkey's main political decision-making body. The Constitutional Court, for its part, closed nineteen political parties and frequently annulled parliamentary actions, irrespective of which party was in power.

In 1997, amid fears that the Islamists were trying to establish an Islamic republic, the military, the courts, and the Council of Higher Education launched a campaign to remove Islamism from society, in what became known as "the February 28 process." Thousands of female university students were expelled for wearing the Islamic headscarf, and civil servants and military officers lost their jobs for their alleged Islamist sympathies, sometimes based on little more than accusations that their female relatives wore headscarves. These events alienated both religious Turks and many of their liberal counterparts in secular political groups, paving the way for the rise of the Justice and Development Party.

For information about Turkish relations with the European Union, the website EurActive is a good source (http://www.euractiv.com/enlargement/eu-turkey-relations/article-129678).

For information about Turkish relations with the United States, consult the U.S. State Department's web page "U.S. Relations with Turkey" (http://www.state.gov/r/pa/ei/bgn/3432.htm).

Rise of the JDP and the Dismantling of Constraints

The closure of the VP created an opening for a younger generation of political activists to form the JDP in 2001. Officially, the party was founded by Abdullah Gül and other veterans of the WP and the VP. The real leader, however, was Recep Tayyip Erdoğan, who at the time was legally banned from politics. Erdoğan had first come to public prominence in 1994 as a member of the WP and the elected mayor of metropolitan Istanbul. Many credit the vastly improved municipal services during his mayoral tenure with paving the way for the WP's rise to power in national elections a year later. After the WP's closure in 1998, Erdoğan was tried and imprisoned on charges of "inciting religious hatred" and encouraging the overthrow of the government by reciting a short poem written almost a century earlier. The now defunct State Security Court (a joint civilian-military tribunal) that convicted him also banned him from politics for life.

Erdoğan's candidacy in the November 2002 parliamentary elections was rejected by the election board due to his earlier conviction, but the JDP won the majority of the seats in parliament and formed Turkey's first single-party government in more than a decade. The JDP amended the constitution to allow Erdoğan to run, and then held a special election to elect him to the parliament. He assumed the post of prime minister in early 2003. Since then, the JDP has won two other parliamentary elections, each time increasing its share of the popular vote (47 percent in 2007, and almost 50 percent in 2011).

JDP began its tenure by emphasizing its pro-Western credentials. Whereas Erbakan had begun his term with a tour of Muslim countries, including Libya and Iran, and had expressed ambivalence about Turkey's membership of the European Union (EU), Erdoğan toured the capitals of Europe and moved quickly to adopt a number of reforms long sought by the EU. The democratic reforms also appealed to many liberal, secular Turks who were tolerant of public religiosity, and who had never supported the post-1982 military order and the "February 28 process." Erdoğan also strengthened Turkey's ties with the United States and even indicated that he would allow U.S. troops to invade Iraq through the Turkish border, a proposal that the Turkish parliament rejected shortly before the start of the 2003 Iraq War. By this time, however, the George W. Bush administration was looking at Turkey as a model Muslim democracy, and thus blamed Turkey's military, not the JDP, for the decision not to cooperate with U.S. plans. Military cooperation with the United States, however, continued on other issues. The JDP's overall pro-Western policies had the effect of distancing the military from its erstwhile international supporters at a time when the February 28 process had alienated many liberal Turks. From then on, the military was gradually pushed out of politics and returned to its barracks.

On the domestic front, the JDP initially avoided controversial issues that might provoke the military and its secular allies. The party tried to reassure its supporters that it was committed to addressing their concerns, such as lifting the headscarf ban at the universities, while simultaneously telling its critics that it was committed to secularism and the principles of the Kemalist state. At times the party avoided controversial issues completely, but it did float a reform proposal only to withdraw it in the face of opposition from secular actors who regarded female students wearing headscarves at public universities as

---

Box 10.3

Freedom of Expression in Turkey

In April 1998, the then mayor of Istanbul, Recep Tayyip Erdoğan, was convicted and imprisoned for reciting these lines during a political speech the
previous December:

> minarets are bayonets,
> domes helmets;
> mosques are our barracks,
> and the believers are soldiers.

Taken from a poem by Ziya Gökalp (1876–1924), one of the fathers of secular
nationalism in Turkey, the lines are part of an imaginary dialogue between
Emperor Romanus IV Diogenes (r. 1068–1071 CE) and the Selcuk Sultan
Alparslan. Neither the poem nor Gökalp's writings are banned. Nevertheless,
the court ruled that by reciting these lines, Erdoğan had "incited people to
hatred based on religion."

As prime minister from 2003 to 2014, and now as president of Turkey,
Erdoğan has presided over a judicial system that continues to prosecute
journalists, artists, and others for expressing their views.

---

an attack on secularism. While the party's supporters viewed the legislative retreats as a
prudent and pragmatic strategy, its critics regarded these maneuvers as evidence of JDP's
insincerity. Ultimately, the critics came to doubt that the JDP is committed to democracy,
and instead believe it wants to impose its vision of an Islamic society on Turkey.

For more on the headscarf issue before the ban was lifted, watch "Headscarves:
Mosque and State in Turkey" found on the PBS website (http://www.pbs.org/
newshour/thenews/theglobe/story.php?id=3049&package_id=632); or read
"Turkey: Situation of Women Who Wear Headscarves" (http://www.refworld.
org/docid/4885a91a8.html).

The crisis point was reached in the spring of 2007, when the term of President Ahmet
Necdet Sezer came to an end. (Sezer, a staunch secularist who had voted to close the
WP and VP when he was chief justice of the Constitutional Court, had had an uneasy
relationship with the JDP. Among other things, he refused to host headscarf-wearing
wives of JDP leaders at the presidential palace.) Under the 1982 constitution, the task
of selecting a new president fell to the JDP-dominated parliament. This concerned the
secular segments of Turkish society, who, together with opposition parties, organized large
demonstrations. The opposition did not necessarily object to JDP's candidate, Abdullah

Table 10.3

Parties in the Post–2011 Parliament

Name (English and Turkish)	Founders, leaders	Founded	Ideology	Closings, reincarnations	Present status, notes
Justice and Development Party (JDP; Adalet ve Kalkınma Partisi, AKP)	Recep Tayyip Erdoğan; Abdullah Gül; former WP leaders	2001	Muslim Democrat/ Conservative Democrat	Fined by CCT in 2008	Ruling party since 2002; (49.8 percent of vote; 327 of 550 seats)
Republican People's Party (RPP; Cumhuriyet Halk Partisi)	Mustafa Kemal (Atatürk); Ismet Inonu; Bülent Ecevit; current leader: Kemal Kiliçdaroğlu	1923	Center-left; secular (Kemalist)	Closed after 1980 coup; reorganized 1984 as Democratic Left Party; RPP after 1992	Main opposition party; (25.8 percent of votes; 135 of 550 seats)
Nationalist Movement (Action) Party (Milliyetçi Hareket Partisi)	Alparslan Türkeş; present leader: Devlet Bahçeli	1969	Ultra-nationalist	Closed after 1980 coup; reappeared in 1983	Active (13 percent vote; 53/550 seats); its youth wing, the Grey Wolves, associated with violence in the 1970s
Peace and Democracy Party (Barış ve Demokrasi Partisi)	Selahattin Demirtas	2008	Pro-Kurdish		Replaced a series of pro-Kurdish political parties dissolved by Constitutional Court since 1982; deputies typically run as independents; holds 29 seats in parliament

Source: Compiled by Hootan Shambayati based on Turkey's Bureau of Elections data.

Gül, although they objected to his wife, Hayrünnissa Gül, who wore a headscarf. They questioned the JDP's right to name the next president, even though the party was acting within the legal boundaries of the constitution and was following a tradition established by the Motherland and True Path Parties, both of which had elevated their own leaders (Özal and Demirel, respectively) to the presidency. The opposition was particularly concerned with the future composition of the Constitutional Court and feared that the control of the presidency would allow the JDP to appoint sympathetic justices to the court, thus weakening one of "the guardians" of secularism.

The JDP did not have enough seats in the parliament to elect Gül in the first round of voting, but according to the elaborate procedure set forth in the constitution, it could have easily done so in the third round. The main opposition party, the RPP, boycotted the first round and asked the Constitutional Court to annul the results due to the lack of a quorum.

In a decision criticized by many legal experts, the court granted the petition and annulled the elections. The military joined the opposition, issuing an electronic memorandum warning of the dangers of Islamization. The JDP immediately called for new parliamentary elections in 2007, which it won easily, with 47 percent of the national vote. It promptly elected Gül to the presidency, and then amended the constitution to allow the public to elect future presidents directly.

The opposition, however, was not willing to give up so easily. When the parliament approved a constitutional amendment to lift the ban on headscarves in universities, the Constitutional Court annulled the amendment, even though the constitution clearly forbids the court from reviewing the substance of constitutional amendments. Acting in a separate case, the court also came very close to banning the JDP for its alleged unconstitutional Islamism. In the end, it chose to fine the party rather than close it. These episodes only increased the JDP's resolve to reform institutions such as the courts that constrained its powers.

A series of constitutional amendments in 2010 increased the size of the Constitutional Court from eleven to seventeen judges, expanded the pool of candidates from which justices could be drawn, and restored the role of the parliament in appointing some of the judges. These changes allowed the JDP to appoint justices more open to the party's point of view. Although 58 percent of the Turkish electorate voted for the amendments, and although changes to the Constitutional Court had been long sought by both international and domestic actors, the secularists saw the changes as nothing more than a power grab by the JDP.

The opposition's suspicions found partial support in the JDP's actions. The party has continued some of the more repressive practices of its predecessors in silencing its critiques, including imprisoning journalists, intimidating the media, harsh treatment of peaceful demonstrators, and so on. Particularly troubling have been the ever-widening investigations and trials that have brought hundreds of military officers, academics, journalists, political activists, and others before the courts. Although some see these investigations as positive developments that have brought accountability to previously unaccountable actors, the ways in which they have been carried out, namely through mass arrests, dubious charges, prosecutorial misconduct, and alleged political interference, are reminiscent of earlier tactics used against Islamists and other critics of the regime.

To date, most JDP reforms have concentrated on removing the tutelary powers of unelected institutions such as the military and the courts. The JDP has paid less attention to expanding the protection of civil liberties and removing obstacles to political participation, but it has promised that these issues will be dealt with in a new constitution. Shortly after the 2011 elections, the party convened a committee composed of representatives of all parties in the parliament to draft a new constitution. Writing a new constitution has been on the political agenda since the mid-1980s, and almost all political parties and civil society organizations agree that the existing 1982 constitution is undemocratic and should be replaced, but there has been little agreement among the parties as to the content of the new constitution.

The opposition fears that the JDP is trying to create a semi-presidential system, especially since the election of Erdoğan as the president when President Gül's term ended in 2014. Erdoğan is not the first Turkish leader to favor a presidential system. Presidents Özal and Demirel made similar proposals. Despite the many shortcomings of the presidential system and its greater potential for gridlock when different parties control the presidency and the parliament, the opposition has focused on Erdoğan's presidency rather than the merits of the proposal. Nor has the opposition been able to formulate alternative proposals for a new constitution. The inability of opposition parties to present viable alternatives to the JDP is one of the major shortcomings of Turkish democracy, pointing to one of the side effects of the Turkish model.

Conservative Democrats Versus Secular Opposition Parties

As mayor of metropolitan Istanbul in the mid-1990s, Erdoğan caused a political crisis by proposing to build a mosque in Istanbul's Taksim Square. Twenty years later, in 2013, Taksim was once again the site of large protests in response to plans by JDP to build a replica of an Ottoman barracks and a shopping mall in nearby Gezi Park. These two episodes in many ways indicate the strengths and weaknesses of the Turkish model of democracy.

JDP rejects labels such as "Islamist," "Muslim Democrat," or "moderate Islam," and identifies itself as a conservative democratic party along the lines of Western Europe's Christian Democratic parties. Even JDP's detractors seem to agree that it is more moderate than its predecessors, and more interested in commerce than religion and morality. In the 1990s, the secular opposition attacked Erdoğan and the Welfare Party for attempting to build a mosque in Taksim Square; today, it is the construction of a shopping mall (although the municipality and the prime minister have denied such plans) that has attracted criticism.

The secular opposition has not welcomed JDP's brand of conservatism. An article in the daily *Milliyet* (April 14) less than a week before the 2007 presidential elections, for example, quoted the outgoing President Sezer as warning the graduates of the military academy that "never before has the regime been under so much threat," and declaring that "moderate Islam . . . is a step backward." As long as Islamists and their supporters were characterized as "traditional" or "backward," they could be marginalized through undemocratic constraints. JDP's rejection of radicalism and its embrace of modern life styles, EU membership, free markets, and so forth, however, isolated the extreme secularists, who could no longer count on domestic or international support in repressing the Islamists. Their sense of marginalization is further amplified by the failures of the political parties to present an alternative to the JDP that would appeal to the more liberal elements among JDP's supporters.

In order to remain within the legal boundaries established by the military guardians, political parties had refrained from addressing major issues for almost thirty years. This strategy allowed them to present themselves as mainstream, but also it prevented them from devising bold alternatives or electoral strategies that would have given the electorate actual choices. This electoral failure has continued under the JDP. Instead of formulating policy alternatives, opposition groups question the JDP's commitment to secularism and its right to make policy. The JDP's proposals, whether they concern a new constitution, building a third bridge over the Bosporus, or redeveloping Gezi Park, are not debated on their merits, but instead are questioned as attacks on secularism and unacceptable intrusions of Islamism into the public sphere.

Conclusion

In June 2013, the "Turkish model" began to unravel as protesters took to the streets to denounce the alleged authoritarianism of the JDP and its leader, Recep Tayyip Erdoğan. The immediate trigger for the demonstrations was the government's plan to build a replica of old Ottoman barracks in the small park near Istanbul's Taksim Square. Named after the city's old water distribution system, Taksim is home to the country's main monument to Turkey's war of independence, which includes a statue of Atatürk and other figures from the war. Today, the monument is overshadowed by commercial development and traffic. The square, however, has come to have symbolic meaning for many Turks. Located on the European side of Istanbul but separated from the old city by the Golden Horn and from Anatolia by the Bosporus, Taksim represents modern Turkey and its republican and secular state. The harsh police reaction to the protesters, including the use of tear gas and water cannons, although not unprecedented or uncommon in Turkey, assured that the demonstrations would quickly turn into anti-JDP protests.

Like his secular predecessors, Erdoğan has dismissed those protesting his policies as "hooligans," "terrorists," or "agents of Turkey's enemies," and he has accused foreign powers of inciting the demonstrators; but he is also the first Turkish political leader in modern history to have met with demonstrators and to have promised a compromise. In retrospect, this might have been a political maneuver to justify the government's harsh reaction, but it does suggest a more democratic approach than Turkish demonstrators have experienced historically.

The following organizations offer research and analysis of the human rights situation in Turkey:

- Human Rights Watch (http://www.hrw.org/world-report/2013/country-chapters/turkey)
- Amnesty International (http://www.amnesty.org/en/region/turkey/report-2012)

In addition, the U.S State Department produces yearly reports on human rights and religious freedom in all countries of the world. The reports on Turkey are:

- 2012 Human Rights Reports: Turkey (http://www.state.gov/j/drl/rls/hrrpt/2012/eur/204348.htm)
- 2012 Report on International Religious Freedom (http://www.state.gov/j/drl/rls/irf/2012/eur/208376.htm)

Protesters in front of the Atatürk Cultural Center in Taksim Square, summer 2013.
(Photo by Professor Lerna Yanik, Kadir Has University, Istanbul. Used by permission.)

Turkey clearly meets the minimum electoral requirements of democracy. The JDP came to power through democratic elections, and it has held a number of free and fair national and local elections, in addition to two referendums. JDP's commitment to electoral democracy, however, has not alleviated the party's tendency to see a conspiracy behind every critic, nor has it ameliorated the opposition's fears. Given Turkey's history, these views are not completely unreasonable, but they have poisoned JDP's relations with the political opposition and large segments of the society. New regulations of the sale of alcohol or Erdoğan's declaration that abortion is murder are sufficient evidence for protesters that the JDP's aim is to undermine secularism and establish Islamic law.

The JDP is clearly more moderate than the Islamist parties that preceded it. Its Islamist actions have been limited to lifting restrictions on religious individuals and organizations so they can participate openly in social and political life. The critics see these reforms as an attack on secularism, but democracy requires what Alfred Stepan (2000) has called the "twin tolerations": no religion or religious organization should hold a legally privileged position in determining public policy for freely elected governments, and religious individuals and groups have the right to freely exercise their religion and to organize and advance their values through participation in the democratic process, as long as they do not impinge on the rights of others. The first element points to the importance of competition in developing alternative worldviews, which is at the heart of democracy, while the second concerns the rule of law, without which democracy cannot survive. The Turkish model of democratization has undermined both.

Those who advocate moderating political Islam through institutional constraints assume that secular actors will welcome the moderation of Islamist parties. However, heavy-handed institutional constraints also change the strategies, capacities, and policies of non-Islamist political actors. Instead of developing alternatives to the JDP and encouraging compromise, the other political parties have encouraged the polarization of Turkish society by emphasizing identity-based cleavages. This has left those opposing the JDP without a voice and feeling marginalized and vulnerable to abuse.

Democracy requires both elections and the rule of law. While the first empowers electoral winners, the second protects the rights of electoral losers. Modern democracies establish the rule of law through constitutionalism and a network of state institutions, such as legislatures, executives, independent courts, and autonomous agencies that provide checks and balances. In Turkey, however, these institutions were politicized and have repeatedly violated the basic principles of the rule of law. While the JDP's reforms have removed the tutelage of nonelected guardians over the political system, it is not clear if they have brought the Turkish state closer to the democratic ideal of accountability and the rule of law. In the long term, the reconstructed Constitutional Court and other state agencies might prove their democratic credentials and help establish accountability and the rule of law. In the short term, however, the critics fear that the reforms have actually increased the JDP's potential for abusing its powers.

A Note on Egypt

In early July 2013, millions of Egyptians took to the streets to denounce the incompetence and alleged authoritarianism of Egypt's first democratically elected president, Mohammed Morsi, and to demand his ouster. On July 3, the Egyptian military announced the removal of Morsi from office, the suspension of the newly approved constitution, the transfer of presidential power to the little known head of the Supreme Constitutional Court, and the arrest of the leadership of the Muslim Brotherhood.

Ironically, at the same time that Turks were questioning the efficacy of their democracy, Egyptians seemed to be once again turning to the "Turkish model." After the Arab uprisings of 2011, many Arabs had looked at the Turkey of the past decade as a possible model for democracy in the Middle East. Today, however, it is an older Turkey that is serving as the model for Egyptians. Like their Turkish counterparts in the second half of the twentieth century, Egyptian opponents of the Muslim Brotherhood turned to the military to "save democracy" from a democratically elected president.

Following in the footsteps of the earlier Turkish coup-makers, Egyptian officers promised a quick return to elected civilian leadership. In the spring of 2014, General Abdel Fattah el-Sisi officially gave up his military rank and ran for president of Egypt as a civilian. He won in a landslide. Supporters of the Muslim Brotherhood and President Morsi, of course, saw the military coup as an illegitimate act. For them, Egypt is following the Algerian model, where the electoral victory of the Islamic Salvation Front in 1991 led to military intervention, followed by a decade-long civil war that killed hundreds of thousands of Algerians. Fortunately, to date, Egypt has not become another Algeria. More importantly, however, as suggested in this chapter, the Turkish model imposes its own costs on the long-term prospects for democracy. A democracy under military tutelage is unlikely to produce the kind of democratic institutions capable of maintaining the rule of law, protecting civil liberties, and holding future governments accountable.

References and Further Research

Göle, Nilufer. 1997. "The Quest for the Islamic Self Within the Context of Modernity." In *Rethinking Modernity and National Identity in Turkey*, edited by Sibel Bozdoğan and Resat Kaşaba, 81–94. Seattle: University of Washington Press.

Kuru, Ahmet T. 2007. "Passive and Assertive Secularism: Historical Conditions, Ideological Struggles, and State Policies Toward Religion." *World Politics* 59, no. 4: 568–594.

Müftüler-Baç, Meltem, and E. Fuat Keyman. 2012. "The Era of Dominant-Party Politics." *Journal of Democracy* 23, no. 1: 85–99.

Norris, Pippa, and Ronald Inglehart. 2002. "Islamic Culture and Democracy: Testing the 'Clash of Civilizations' Thesis." *Comparative Sociology* 1, no. 3–4: 235–263.

Shambayati, Hootan. 2004. "A Tale of Two Mayors: Courts and Politics in Iran and Turkey." *International Journal of Middle East Studies* 36, no. 2: 253–275.

Somer, Murat. 2007. "Moderate Islam and Secular Opposition in Turkey: Implications for the World, Muslims and Secular Democracy." *Third World Quarterly* 28, no. 7: 1271–1289.

Stepan, Alfred C. 2000. "Religion, Democracy, and the 'Twin Tolerations.'" *Journal of Democracy* 11, no. 4: 37–57.

Taşpinar, Ömer. 2012. "Turkey: The New Model?" In *The Islamists Are Coming: Who They Really Are*, edited by Robin Wright, 127–135. Washington, DC: United States Institute of Peace.

Tepe, Sultan. 2005. "Turkey's AKP: A Model 'Muslim-Democratic' Party?" *Journal of Democracy* 16, no. 3: 69–82.

Turam, Berna. 2012. "Are Rights and Liberties Safe?" *Journal of Democracy* 23, no. 1: 109–118.

Yavuz, M. Hakan. 2009. *Secularism and Muslim Democracy in Turkey*. Cambridge: Cambridge University Press.

Yesilada, Birol, and Barry Rubin, eds. 2012. *Islamization of Turkey Under the AKP Rule*. London: Routledge.

Government Websites

Constitutional Court of the Republic of Turkey: http://www.anayasa.gov.tr/index.php?lang=1.
The Grand National Assembly of Turkey (Parliament): http://global.tbmm.gov.tr/index.php/EN/yd/.
Presidency of the Republic of Turkey: http://www.tccb.gov.tr/pages/.

Media Websites

Cumhurriyet: http://en.cumhuriyet.com/.
Hurriyet Daily News: http://www.hurriyetdailynews.com/.
The Journal of Turkish Weekly: http://www.turkishweekly.net/.
Today's Zaman: http://www.todayszaman.com/mainAction.action.

Think Tanks

Foundation for Political, Economic and Social Research (SETA): http://setav.org/en.
Turkish Economic and Social Studies Foundation (TESEV): http://www.tesev.org.tr/en/
    homepage.

11

A "Peace by Piece" Look at the Israeli-Palestinian Conflict

MAIA CARTER HALLWARD

The Israeli-Palestinian conflict commands significant international attention and study, even though it is not the largest, deadliest, or longest-lasting conflict in the world. Despite this attention and analysis, however, the Israeli-Palestinian conflict remains intractable. This chapter provides an overview of peace efforts over the past decades, arguing that several factors explain the lack of a resolution to the conflict twenty years after the signing of the Oslo Accords in 1993. Not only do Israelis and Palestinians understand the history and sources of the conflict differently, but, due to their different experiences of the conflict ("terrorism" on the Israeli side and "occupation" on the Palestinian side), Israelis and Palestinians tend to have different conceptions of "peace." In addition to failing to adequately engage with both narratives, official peace efforts have falsely treated the conflict as static and Israeli and Palestinian societies as homogeneous monoliths, overlooking the shifting dynamics of the struggle and the multiple diversities within each population. The international community would do well to learn from Israeli and Palestinian nonviolent efforts for a "just and lasting peace," which have persisted even in times of violent conflict, since the ongoing conflict will continue to affect regional and global politics until a durable resolution is reached.

Background and History

Contrary to popular opinion, the Israeli-Palestinian conflict does not date back to biblical times, but rather has its roots in contemporary movements for nationalism and self-determination; in particular, it is about rival claims to the same land, due in part to conflicting promises made by Western powers. The area between the Jordan River and the Mediterranean Sea, which will be called "Israel/Palestine" here in order to acknowledge competing names for the various territories therein, has been the site of both competition and accommodation between cultures as numerous empires have controlled it over the millennia. Consequently, it is hard to say that any particular community is "indigenous" in the true sense of the word. Arab nationalism emerged as the Ottoman Empire weakened at the beginning of the twentieth century and European empires gained further ground in the Middle East and Africa. Zionism, which sought a nation-state for the Jewish people as a remedy for European discrimination

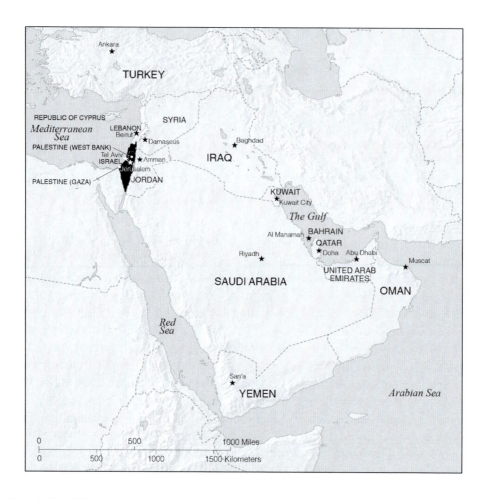

and anti-Semitism, emerged as a political movement in the mid-1800s. Among the different communities of Eastern and Western European Jews, variants of Zionism emerged. They disagreed, for instance, over the extent to which the new state should be a secular-nationalist or a religious-nationalist one. The first major wave of immigration (the first *aliyah*) to Palestine (1882–1904) consisted of 20,000 to 300,000 Eastern European Jews, many fleeing Russian pogroms. Most of these Jews did not have a strong nationalist agenda, and they settled in communities that already had a Jewish presence, including Jerusalem, Safed, Hebron, and Tiberias; at this time Jews numbered only about 5,000 out of the total population of 275,000 to 300,000 (Lesch 2008, 29). The second aliyah (1904–1914), also predominantly from Eastern Europe, brought a different breed of Zionists: younger, more ideologically committed to the idea of creating a Jewish state, and seeking to build a new society. According to the historian Avi Shlaim, although competing strains of Zionism often did not see eye-to-eye, all sought to create new social, economic, and political institutions in Palestine—separate from and exclusive of the Arab population—geared toward building the foundations for a new state.

After their request for support of a Jewish state to the Ottoman Sultan had been turned down, Zionist leaders, including Theodor Herzl and Chaim Weizmann, engaged in extensive diplomacy with European powers. During World War I, Britain and France jockeyed for control over Ottoman lands, agreeing in 1916 to divide the lands between themselves, and they made rival promises to Zionists and Arab nationalists in exchange for their support against the Ottomans during the war. In 1915 Sir Henry McMahon, the British high commissioner of Egypt, in an exchange of letters, offered Sharif Hussein of Mecca an independent Arab state, the exact borders of which were ambiguous. In 1917 the British government issued the Balfour Declaration, giving its approval for "the establishment in Palestine of a national home for the Jewish people" (Lesch 2008, 85). In the end, the British did not honor either promise, but instead took control over what was called "Mandate Palestine" in 1922. The British policy toward Jewish immigration varied over the years of the Mandate, which lasted to 1948, when the State of Israel was established. In fact, one British official contended that Britain had "nothing but fluctuations of policy, hesitations . . . no policy at all," during this period. Despite Britain's lack of consistency in its policies, the Zionists came out ahead—not only of the Palestinians who were competing for statehood, but also ahead of the surrounding Arab states already in existence (Lesch 2008, 94–95).

Over the course of the Mandate period, the British were unable to resolve the rival nationalist claims, despite numerous commissions—such as the 1937 Peel Commission that recommended partition, and the 1946 Anglo-American Committee that recommended a single binational state—and tensions (with outbreaks of violence) continued to mount between the Palestinians and Jews. In 1947 the British submitted the problem to the United Nations, which recommended partition, with Jews receiving a state on 56.47 percent of the territory, Palestinian Arabs receiving a state on 42.88 percent of the territory, and an international zone that included Jerusalem and Bethlehem receiving 0.65 percent.

Of the 905,000 people living in the area of the proposed Jewish state, over half were Palestinian Arabs; less than 10,000 Jews were located in the proposed Arab state. With the passage of UN General Assembly Resolution 181 on November 29, 1947, a civil war broke out between Jews and Arabs in Palestine. Britain withdrew from the Mandate on May 14, 1948, without any formal transfer of powers to a new government, and on the same day, David Ben-Gurion announced Israel's independence, which turned the ongoing civil war into an international war. The chronology of what followed the announcement varies considerably according to different sources. Israeli history books call the war their War of Independence, won bravely against a numerically superior enemy bent on Israel's destruction. Palestinian history books call the same war al-Nakba, "the Catastrophe." The Jewish forces were better organized than their Arab counterparts, who lacked equipment and trained personnel, and whose leaders were pursuing rival aims. During the course of the war, some 700,000 to 800,000 Palestinians became refugees (Morris 1999, 252). The war ended in 1949 not with a formal peace treaty, but with armistice agreements, signed on the Greek island of Rhodes, between Israel and the Arab nations fighting against it. The resulting new boundaries, called the "Green Line," gave Israel control of 78 percent of the territory, rather than the 56 percent allocated by UN

Resolution 181. The Green Line demarcated the de facto borders of the Israeli state; however, to this day, these borders remain contested.

> Maps on the disposition of the land during the 1948–1949 civil war are produced, published, and made available online by the Palestinian Academic Society for the Study of International Affairs (http://www.passia.org/palestine_facts/ MAPS/1947-un-partition-plan-reso.html).

After 1949, Palestinians remaining in what had been the British Mandate were divided under many different forms of rule. Some Palestinians remained in what had become Israel, living under martial law until they received citizenship in 1966. Egypt controlled the Gaza Strip, and Jordan controlled what is called the "West Bank," referring to the west side of the Jordan River. Palestinian refugees were scattered throughout the Middle East—largely in Jordan, Lebanon, and Syria—stateless and without rights, many living in United Nations refugee camps that have transformed over the years from collections of tents to crowded concrete cities lacking proper infrastructure and facilities. This situation changed as a result of the 1967 Arab-Israeli War (called the Six-Day War in Israel, and al-Naksa, "the Setback," by Palestinians), when Israel gained control of the Sinai Peninsula from Egypt, the Golan Heights from Syria, and all of the remaining Mandate territory. In response to this war, the United Nations Security Council issued Resolution 242 in 1967, which, amid much debate, granted the right of all states in the area "to live in peace within secure and recognized boundaries" and called for "withdrawal of Israeli armed forces from territories occupied in the recent conflict," as well as a "just settlement of the refugee problem" (Lesch 2008, 216). Since Israel felt unsafe and threatened in its boundaries (which were not officially recognized), Israeli troops did not withdraw from the territories it occupied.

For many religious Israelis, the post-1967 territorial configuration, including the newly occupied areas not surrendered as demanded in Resolution 242, provided the opportunity to "redeem" the land they called "Judea and Samaria" by building Jewish communities in the land of their forefathers, whereas for many secular Israelis it provided the opportunity to exchange "land for peace" in future negotiations. Indeed, the 1979 Egyptian-Israeli peace treaty, through which Israel returned the Sinai Peninsula to Egypt, and the 1993 Oslo Accords (discussed below) were grounded in the assumption that peace can be achieved by territorial concessions of land taken in the 1967 war.

The land Israel annexed as a result of its 1967 victory included East Jerusalem (and land from twenty-three surrounding villages); it also placed the rest of the West Bank and Gaza Strip under military rule. Neither move was legitimate under international law. When Arab armies challenged the new territorial status quo in the 1973 Arab-Israeli War (called the Yom Kippur War in Israel and the October War in Arab countries), Israel won the war but realized it might not be sufficient to rely on military solutions in the conflict. UN Security Council Resolution 338, adopted in 1973, proposed a cease-fire and called on all parties to implement Resolution 242 immediately.

With the defeat of the Arab states in 1967, the focus had shifted from an interstate conflict to one between the Israelis and Palestinians. Under the leadership of Yasser Arafat, the Palestinian Liberation Organization (PLO) became recognized by the Arab League in 1974 as the sole legitimate representative of the Palestinian people, and in 1975 the PLO was granted observer status at the United Nations. Until November 1988, when at its historic meeting in Algiers it voted to recognize Israel, renounce terrorism, and accept a two-state solution on the basis of UN Resolutions 242 and 338, the PLO was committed to armed struggle for the full "liberation" of Palestine from Israeli control, and it committed numerous attacks against Israeli civilian targets during this period. Israel refused to recognize or talk to the PLO, which it considered a terrorist organization, and it treated Jordan as the representative of the Palestinian people. Meanwhile, Israel began to build Jewish settlements in the West Bank, for both religious and strategic reasons. The government supported the settlement enterprise financially and made all "state-owned" land in the West Bank (50 percent of the surface area) available for settlement (Morris 1999). By 1972, a total of 10,608 Jewish Israelis lived in lands occupied in 1967; by 1983, the number had grown to 106,595, with the vast majority (76,095) in East Jerusalem, the Arab sector of the city. By 1985, there were over 100,000 settlers in East Jerusalem alone, and over 44,000 elsewhere in the West Bank. Many settlers were motivated by economic incentives, including free land or low mortgages, rather than by an ideology that sought to establish the Jewish identity of the land. After the election of the right-wing Likud Party in 1977, the pace of settlement activity quickened, with over 100 settlements in the West Bank alone by the mid-1990s (Morris 1999).

Changing Conflict Dynamics and Efforts at Peace

The First Intifada

In December 1987, massive demonstrations followed the deaths of four Palestinian workers who were killed when an Israeli army truck collided with their car at an army roadblock in the Gaza Strip, setting off Palestinian anger at the Israeli military occupation and also frustration with the PLO leadership, in exile in Tunisia. The resulting *intifada*——literally "shaking off" the occupation—used predominantly nonviolent tactics, including strikes, sit-ins, demonstrations, noncooperation with authorities, tax resistance, and even creation of Victory Gardens, set up to grow fruits and vegetables to make Palestinian households more self-sufficient. According to Mary King, a professor of peace and conflict studies, this was due in part to the leadership of a group of Palestinian intellectuals who had spent years laying the groundwork by conducting workshops and circulating booklets about strategic nonviolent resistance. The shift to nonviolence marked a significant transition in Palestinian resistance. Not only had the PLO largely engaged in armed struggle prior to the intifada, but also it intentionally targeted Israeli civilians and operated outside Israel/Palestine, including in Jordan, Lebanon, and Tunisia. It was also hierarchical in nature and dominated by the Fatah faction of Yasser Arafat. The PLO also represented a shift from a more static *sumud* (steadfastness) of earlier generations to more active participation and mass mobilization in grassroots committees, which were built on the voluntary associations (popular committees for women, trade unions, students, and farmers) created in the 1970s.

The intifada brought a new kind of international attention to the Palestinian cause, as pictures of unarmed Palestinian boys facing Israeli tanks were circulated by the media. Although Palestinians used overwhelmingly nonviolent tactics, some did participate in armed resistance, but the Israeli military was instructed to follow a "break their bones" policy, not differentiating between armed and unarmed protest. In a four-year period, according to an Israeli military spokesperson, 706 Palestinian civilians were killed, in contrast with 12 Israeli soldiers. By comparison, 650 Israelis, three-fourths of whom were civilians, were killed by PLO factions in the fifteen-year period between 1969 and 1985. And while most Israelis did not change their view of the conflict during the intifada, some Israelis partnered with Palestinian activists to pursue a path of reconciliation.

The intifada has been deemed both a success and a failure. It refocused international attention on the Israeli-Palestinian conflict, raised the issue of the occupation in domestic Israeli politics, and portrayed Israel as the aggressor with vastly superior force at its disposal. While it failed to bring about a Palestinian state, the pressure resulting from it, both on the PLO and Israeli leaders, brought them to the table at the 1991 Madrid Peace Conference and the 1993 Oslo Accords, even though leaders of the PLO, who were out of touch with the situation on the ground in the West Bank and the Gaza Strip, never fully understood the intifada's nonviolent strategy. Indeed, the intifada was a major factor in Arafat's decision to declare Palestinian independence in November 1988 in Algiers, part of the strategic shift in Palestinian goals from a single binational state in all of historic Palestine to the recognition of the State of Israel and an acceptance of the two-state solution.

The intifada mobilized a minority of the Israeli left wing: new groups like Women in Black, which has held a vigil against the occupation every Friday since January 1988, and B'Tselem, which documents human rights violations in the occupied territories, emerged. However, although elements of the Israeli peace movement, such as Shalom Achshav (Peace Now), grew during the years of the intifada, the Israeli peace movement as a whole remained small, and was criticized for failing to genuinely understand the Palestinian perspective. Nevertheless, it did have some impact on public attitudes and policy considerations, such as territorial compromise.

The Oslo Process

The 1993 Oslo Accords were the result of backchannel negotiations mediated by Norway. They preempted the official (deadlocked) negotiations that were simultaneously being conducted by the U.S. State Department. Although the accords were widely heralded, they were also widely misrepresented as a "peace agreement"; instead, the Oslo Accords consisted of an exchange of letters of mutual recognition and a Declaration of Principles (DoP) that established a "transitional period not exceeding five years, leading to a permanent settlement based on Security Council Resolutions 242 and 338." Thus, the accords represented an agreement to begin a process of negotiation in pursuit of "a just, lasting and comprehensive peace settlement and historic reconciliation through the agreed political process." The accords took a piecemeal rather than a comprehensive approach, and extremists on both sides rejected them. In a dramatic example, Yitzhak Rabin, seen as too conciliatory in the negotiations, was assassinated in November 1995, following a political rally in Tel Aviv, by a Jewish settler who believed in Israel's God-given right to all of the land between the Jordan River and the Mediterranean Sea.

> The Declaration of Principles on Interim Self-Government Arrangement—one of the documents resulting from the Oslo process—is available at the Israeli Ministry of Foreign Affairs website (http://www.mfa.gov.il/mfa/peace%20process/ guide%20to%20the%20peace%20process/declaration%20of%20principles).

In many ways, the Oslo Accords represented both a new Israeli strategy for containing the Palestinian national movement and a PLO effort to regain its control over it. The Palestinian National Authority (PNA), the newly established governing body of the West Bank and Gaza Strip, was to exercise autonomy over the territory, and, in fact, it developed numerous police and security apparatuses to exert its power and to establish security, including Israel's. Meanwhile, Israel insisted it had to protect its settlers, leading to the construction of hundreds of miles of Israeli-only bypass roads on land confiscated from Palestinians, dividing the Palestinian population geographically and socially. For many of those who had been active in the intifada, this was not an experiment in self-rule, but rather another form of occupation. Furthermore, the Oslo Accords shifted issues covered by international law, such as the status of Jerusalem, Palestinian refugees, and Israeli settlements, to items up for negotiation in the framework of future permanent status talks between Israel and the Palestinians. The frame of reference was thereby shifted away from what Palestinians saw as a "historic compromise" of agreeing to the two-state solution (as opposed to a single binational state) and toward the need to compromise over the 22 percent of territory that they had settled for. Palestinians felt they were getting the "holes" of what they called a "Swiss cheese map," referring to the 1995 interim agreement (Oslo II) that divided the West Bank into areas A, B, and C, with differing degrees of Palestinian autonomy.

> The Palestinian Academic Society for the Study of International Affairs (PASSIA) has produced and published a map online on the division of the West Bank under the Oslo II interim agreement (http://www.passia.org/palestine_facts/ MAPS/newpdf/Oslo-II.pdf).
>
> The areas resulting from the Oslo II interim agreement are shown on this map. Area A, under direct Palestinian control, included six major cities and 2 percent of West Bank territory. Area B, under Palestinian civil control and Israeli security control, included 420 villages and 26 percent of the West Bank. Area C, under Israeli control, included the remaining 72 percent of the West Bank.

During the decade of the Oslo process, the Israeli settler population doubled, with 230,000 new settlers added in an effort to consolidate as much territory in the West Bank as possible. If the vast expansion of settlements and increased restrictions on movement symbolized the failures of Oslo to deliver to the Palestinians peace and self-determination, suicide bombings by groups such as Islamic Jihad and Hamas symbolized the failure of the accords to deliver peace and security to the Israelis. In February and March 1996, for example, suicide attacks killed fifty-nine Israelis and wounded hundreds more (Lesch 2008, 338).

For all intents and purposes, the Oslo process ended with the Camp David Summit between Israeli prime minister Ehud Barak and Palestinian president Yasser Arafat in July 2000. Barak sought to end the interim period and the Oslo redeployment process by presenting a final offer to the Palestinians (and the Israeli public) prior to Israeli elections. Barak's offer regarding Jerusalem went farther than those of previous Israeli leaders, who refused to discuss the status of the city, calling it the "indivisible Jewish capital." Instead, Barak offered Palestinians clusters of authority in an expanded "Greater Jerusalem." Yet, at the same time, Israel was to annex and make permanent large settlement blocks and retain control of water resources, bypass roads, airspace, and borders; and Palestine was to be divided into three major canton blocks. The final straw for Palestinians, however, was the failure to resolve the Palestinian refugee issue. The talks ended in disaster, and many Israelis and Palestinians began to talk about the end of the peace process. The mainstream Israeli peace movement collapsed, concluding that there was "no partner for peace" (Malley and Agha 2001), and the Palestinian NGO network called for a discontinuation of joint activities with Israelis.

Neither "Peace" nor "Process": Problems with the Oslo Framework

One of the major problems with the Oslo Accords was their tentative nature. They set up an interim process with no guarantee that a settlement of core issues—including Jerusalem, borders, Palestinian refugees, water, security, and settlements—would be reached. Moreover, the accords did not take into account the inherent asymmetry of the two parties: Israel as a sovereign state with a developed economy, the fourth largest military in the world, and a supportive, influential Jewish diaspora, had a significant advantage over the stateless PLO leadership in Tunisia, which lacked a military and was, like the Palestinian communities in Israel and the occupied territories, relatively impoverished. In the Oslo exchange of letters, Arafat recognized the State of Israel's right "to exist in peace and security," affirming his commitment to UN Security Council Resolutions 242 and 338 and to the peace process, and renounced terrorism. In contrast, the brief letter from Yitzhak Rabin stated, "In light of the PLO commitments included in your letter, the Government of Israel has decided to recognize the PLO as the representative of the Palestinian people and commence negotiations with the PLO within the Middle East peace process." Rabin did not mention UN resolutions, Palestinian statehood, or a commitment to final status negotiations. He simply agreed to recognize the previously banned PLO, long considered a terrorist organization by Israel.

The exchange of letters between Arafat and Rabin under the Oslo Accords can be found at the website of the Jewish Virtual Library (http://www.jewishvirtual-library.org/jsource/Peace/recogn.html).

A second major problem with the Oslo process was its secrecy. With limited transparency, neither side was prepared for what the agreement meant for them in practice, nor was the cause of peace "sold" to either Palestinians or Israelis. Because the PLO leaders had been living in exile, they were out of touch with the situation on the ground in the Palestinian territories; when they returned, many officials built new villas and drove fancy cars, while the economic situation of average Palestinians declined and their freedom of movement was restricted due to the new system of Israeli bypass roads and checkpoints. A double tax structure had been put in place, in effect requiring Palestinians to pay taxes to both the PNA and Israel, since all major utility companies remained ultimately under Israeli control. The PNA received only those powers Israel wished to devolve, including the provision of social services and the policing of rival Palestinian factions like Hamas. (Israel still collects taxes on behalf of the PNA, and selectively releases or withholds those funds as a way of exerting control.)

Perhaps the most fundamental problem was that Israelis and Palestinians, because of their different experience of the conflict, had different understandings of "peace." Peace and conflict resolution scholars and practitioners distinguish between "negative peace" (the absence of war or armed violence) and "positive peace" (the presence of freedom, equity, and human rights). Israelis tend to emphasize the need for "peace with security" (i.e., "negative peace"), due to their experience of the conflict through suicide bombings, Qassam rocket bombardments, and war with its neighbors. Palestinians emphasize the need for "peace with justice" (i.e., "positive peace"), since they tend to experience the conflict not only in terms of direct violence, but also in terms of socioeconomic hardships and lack of political freedom and self-determination. This lack of a shared conception of "peace" is a primary reason that the mainstream peace movement collapsed with the outbreak of the second intifada in 2000. The civil society groups that did continue their work, despite the outbreak of violent conflict, tended to have strongly democratic and equal decision-making processes, a clear understanding that "peace" required an end not only to direct forms of violence, but also an end to the Israeli occupation of Palestinian territories, and an organizational structure that embraced diversity of opinion.

The al-Aqsa Intifada

The second (al-Aqsa) intifada began in September 2000, after Ariel Sharon, then Israeli minister of defense, made a visit with an estimated 1,000 armed Israeli police and security agents to the Al-Aqsa Mosque in Jerusalem. Al-Aqsa is part of the sacred Muslim space called Haram al-Sharif that includes the Dome of the Rock. The Haram al-Sharif is built on top of what is believed to be the remains of the Jewish temple the Romans destroyed in 70 CE, which makes this piece of land the most contested piece of territory in all of Israel/Palestine. The visit by Sharon, known for his support of increased Israeli settlement in the West Bank, enraged Palestinians, who viewed it as a deliberate provocation. The tension between the two sides had been increasing steadily before the visit to the mosque, as it became clear that the Oslo Accords would not lead to the promised peace negotiations, especially when the July 2000 Camp David Summit produced no results. In contrast with the first intifada, the second intifada became known for its militant actions and for intra-Palestinian rivalries. According to the Israeli human rights group B'Tselem, between the end of September 2000 and December 26, 2008, more than 4,900 Palestinians and 580 Israelis were killed.

Despite the return to armed conflict, Palestinian and Israeli negotiators met in the Red Sea town of Taba in January 2001 to move forward from where they had left off at Camp David in July of 2000. The election of Ariel Sharon as Israeli prime minister and George W. Bush as U.S. president, combined with al-Qaeda's terrorist attacks in New York City and Washington, DC, in September 2001, resulted in a freeze of the political process until all "terror" was halted. In March 2002, Saudi Crown Prince Abdullah issued a peace plan that would have included the recognition of Israel by Arab states in exchange for a withdrawal to the 1967 borders. The proposal was overshadowed by a suicide bombing killing thirty people celebrating Passover in the Israeli town of Netanya, which provided the impetus for Israeli invasion of the major Palestinian cities in the West Bank, including Ramallah, Bethlehem, and Nablus.

In June 2002, Israel began constructing a 440-mile-long physical barrier—which it calls a "security wall"—separating Israel and the West Bank, although most of the route winds back and forth through the West Bank and not along the Green Line. The barrier, which consists of a series of fences, electronic monitoring equipment, patrol roads in rural areas, and a 20- to 25-foot-high concrete wall in urban areas, has been the site of much nonviolent protest by Palestinian communities, often with the support of Israeli and international activists. Construction of the barrier has resulted in the destruction of millions of olive trees, the staple of the Palestinian economy, and many villages were separated from their farmlands. Consistent nonviolent protests in villages such as Budrus and Bil'in, often supported by Israeli and international solidarity activists, managed to alter the route of the barrier in places. Although both villages still lost land, they lost less of it.

In 2003 the United States, the European Union, Russia, and the United Nations, known as "the Quartet," issued a "Performance-Based Road Map," which offered a phased approach toward a Palestinian state with "provisional borders" and recycled many of the ideas and plans presented previously. The plan was met with a series of reservations outlined by Israeli Prime Minister Ariel Sharon, especially against the Phase I requirement to freeze settlement expansion. On the Palestinian side, conflict within the PLO hierarchy and among Palestinian political factions undermined Phase I requirements of Palestinian institutional reform. Like previous plans, the 2003 road map was neither implemented nor enforced, thereby allowing the status quo, including the ongoing construction of settlements, to continue.

The second intifada ended in 2005, although violent clashes between the Israeli Defense Forces and Palestinian groups did not. Palestinian suicide bombings claimed hundreds of Israeli lives, while Israeli military operations—including reclaiming control over most of the West Bank and targeted assassinations of Palestinian leaders and family members—claimed several thousand Palestinian lives. Conflict began to ease when Ariel Sharon announced, in 2004, the unilateral withdrawal of Israeli troops and settlers from the Gaza Strip, which was implemented by September 2005.

Civil Society Efforts for Peace Since the al-Aqsa Intifada

Despite the media's focus on violence, most Israelis and Palestinians simply want to live their lives, and many have continued to work for a secure, just, and lasting peace with their neighbors. However, structural changes to the conflict resulting from actions taken by Israelis and Palestinians since the second intifada have made such efforts increasingly difficult, and many have turned to work for unity and understanding within their own society as a precursor to working across national lines. Increasingly, high-level individuals in mainstream politics and the media are noting that time may be running out for a two-state solution, and some civil society groups suggest it is time to focus on a single, binational, democratic state for all living between the Jordan River and the Mediterranean. Sizeable constituencies of Israelis and Palestinians are against this option, as Israelis fear the loss of a Jewish majority and Palestinians fear it would enshrine their second- or third-class status in perpetuity. However, officials in the United States, Europe, and elsewhere point to the ongoing expansion of Israeli settlements, particularly in East Jerusalem, as a major obstacle to a viable Palestinian state. A number of track-two initiatives have occurred over the years, such as the 2003 Geneva Initiative, which brought together former Israeli and Palestinian government officials and demonstrated that negotiating partners on each side could be found. Also, a variety of commissions looking at options for addressing final-status issues have been organized by the Israel Palestine Center for Research and Information (IPCRI).

> See the website of the Israel Palestine Center for Research and Information, the only Israeli-Palestinian bilateral think tank in the world, for information on final-status solutions and policies the organization is working on (http://ipcri.org/httpdocs/IPCRI/Home.html).

While most in the West tend to think of "peace" efforts in terms of dialogue, the Palestinians and Israelis who continued to work for peace after the Oslo process ended have not defined their work in those terms. In fact, some groups resist describing their work in terms of "peace" efforts, given that "peace" is seen as "political" in Israel, and that the Oslo process is so discredited in both societies. Rabbis for Human Rights (RHR), for example, focuses on Jewish teachings urging Israelis to "remember when you were a stranger in Egypt," or that all humans are made in the image of God. Working alongside Palestinian farmers, they help them gain access to land occupied by Israeli settlers so they can tend their crops and harvest olives; in doing so, they thereby reduce the likelihood of attacks by settlers (although settlers sometimes even attack RHR rabbis) and provide a positive image of Jewish Israelis to Palestinians. Even those groups that follow more of the traditional "dialogue" model, such as the Parents Circle Families Forum–Bereaved Families, engage in action to change the status quo by going out in pairs (one Israeli and one Palestinian) and sharing the stories of their loved ones who died as a result of the conflict. Due to the segregation of schools within Israel, the ban on teaching the Arab/Palestinian historical narrative in Israeli schools, and the separation of Israelis from Palestinians in the West Bank and Gaza Strip, sharing the two narratives—and demonstrating that Israelis and Palestinians who have experienced loss can still embrace the other—are courageous political acts.

During the second intifada, Israeli groups such as Ta'ayush organized large solidarity actions in which Israeli Jews and Palestinian citizens of Israel went to the West Bank to support Palestinians in villages there. Ta'ayush activists worked with their Palestinian partners to demonstrate against the building of Israel's separation barrier, to plant olive trees, and to assist those, such as the villagers in Yanoun, seeking to remain on their land despite pressure from violent settlers. Ta'ayush members spent days helping pick up poison pellets that settlers scattered across the grazing grounds of Palestinian shepherds in the South Hebron Hills. The Israeli women's group Checkpoint Watch monitored the checkpoints and roadblocks throughout the West Bank and sought to raise awareness within Israeli society (and abroad) regarding the restriction of movement enforced at the checkpoints. For example, Checkpoint Watch members informed Israelis that the majority of checkpoints actually separated Palestinians from Palestinians, and were not on the border between Israel and the Palestinian Territories, as was commonly assumed. Checkpoint Watch activists also did research into the permit system, learning that Palestinians could be put on the black list simply for having a relative who was arrested or hurt by Israeli soldiers. Also, Palestinian organizations including the Holy Land Trust conducted nonviolence training sessions for villages in the path of the separation barrier.

To learn more about Israeli and Palestinian civil society efforts to end the Israeli-Palestinian conflict, see the websites of the following peace groups:

- Alternative Information Center   http://www.alternativenews.org/english/
- Bil'in Village   http://www.bilin-village.org/english/
- Breaking the Silence   http://www.breakingthesilence.org.il/
- Coalition of Women for Peace   http://www.coalitionofwomen.org
- Israel Palestine Center for Research http://www.ipcri.org
  and Information
- Just Vision   http://www.justvision.org
- Parents Circle Families Forum—   http://www.theparentscircle.com
  Bereaved Families
- Rabbis for Human Rights   http://rhr.org.il/eng/
- Other Voice   http://www.othervoice.org/welcome-eng. htm

Increasing Obstacles

Civil society peace efforts that bring together Israeli and Palestinian citizens have grown increasingly difficult since Oslo and the second intifada, due to the increasing physical, legal, and psychological barriers to contact between Israelis and Palestinians. During the second intifada, Israel made it illegal for Israelis to enter Area A, the cities nominally under Palestinian control, and it is extremely difficult for most Palestinians to obtain the necessary permits to travel into Israel. However, interaction and solidarity efforts continue in villages like Bil'in and Nabi Salih, where Palestinians are joined by Israelis and international activists in their weekly protests against the occupation and the confiscation of their lands, and in East Jerusalem neighborhoods like Silwan and Sheikh Jarrah, where Israeli settlers and Israeli government officials are displacing Palestinian families.

Increasing political fragmentation within both societies has also compounded the challenge of working for peace. Prime Minister Netanyahu's right-wing coalition government, in power since 2009, can only hold together, according to many analysts, on the condition that no substantive peace negotiations are underway. Laws targeting left-wing activists and Arab citizens are increasingly common. The rift between a Hamas-controlled Gaza and the Palestinian Authority (PA)–controlled West Bank, along with the continued international political isolation of Hamas, means that without reconciliation between the PA and Hamas, negotiations with Israel will exclude a sizeable portion of the Palestinian people, and therefore be deemed less legitimate.

The trauma inflicted on the young generation through the violence of the second intifada and the ongoing siege of the Gaza Strip, the encircling of entire communities in the West Bank, such as Qalqilya, by the separation barrier, the political divides between Fatah and Hamas, and the growing rift between the religious right and the more secular left in Israel make reaching peace more difficult than ever. This does not mean, however, that peace is impossible; rather, it means that concerted effort needs to be applied to address the root causes of the conflict and to find ways to motivate political leaders to make moves toward peace, particularly when their domestic political structures do not provide incentive for them to do so. Outbreaks of intensified violence in Gaza in 2008–2009, November 2012, and the summer of 2014 indicate that military solutions are still deemed viable by Israeli and Palestinian leaders. Israelis and Palestinians affected by the violence in Gaza and southern Israel have come together and called on their governments to change their policies. Groups like Other Voice seek to use shared pain as a foundation for working to stop ongoing violence.

The general contours of a lasting peace agreement have been outlined in the Clinton Parameters of 2000, the 2003 Geneva Accord, and the Arab Peace Initiatives of 2002 and 2007. However, previous initiatives have not been implemented, and with time running out for a two-state solution, Defense Minister Ehud Barak noted at a conference in 2010 that Israel (the de facto sovereign over all of historic Palestine) is left with the option of maintaining a democracy but losing its identity as a Jewish state, or becoming an apartheid state in which a Jewish minority rules over the majority Palestinian population (*The Economist* 2010). Earlier generations of Palestinians and Israelis had much more contact with each other, but the growing separation of ordinary Israelis and Palestinians since the second intifada makes it all too easy for Israelis and Palestinians to believe the worst about "the enemy."

Ways Forward?

Disagreements over what constitutes "peace efforts" continue. In November 2012, Palestinian president Mahmoud Abbas, frustrated with the lack of progress in negotiations, gained "non-member observer state" status for Palestine, with a vote of 138 to 9, and 41 abstentions. Although this nonviolent bid for self-determination contrasted greatly with the violent tit-for-tat exchange between Hamas and Israel occurring around the same time, the Netanyahu government denounced it as a move against peace and announced the construction of 3,000 new settlement units in the West Bank. While peace and conflict resolution scholarship suggests that, indeed, negotiation between the parties is the best way to achieve a lasting agreement, Palestinians sought status at the United Nations to raise international attention on the lack of progress on the Road Map established in 2003 under the Quartet. Rather than rejecting negotiations, Palestinians and Israelis supporting Abbas saw the UN move as a way of jump-starting the negotiating process and creating more equality between the two parties. Not all Palestinians supported the move, however, saying that it ignored the issue of Palestinian refugees, and did nothing to change the situation on the ground.

   In contrast, some of these Palestinian critics are part of the 2005 call by over 170 Palestinian civil society organizations for a global Boycott, Divestment, and Sanctions (BDS) movement aimed at putting pressure on Israel to end its occupation of the Palestinian territories. Some Israelis, as well as a number of Jews living in the diaspora, believe that Israel's survival as a democratic Jewish state depends on ending the occupation. Other Israeli peace activists, however, see the BDS movement as counterproductive, since sanctions tend to harm civilians and rarely change the policies of governments.

   The Israeli civil society group Boycott from Within explains why it supports a boycott of Israel in a video available on YouTube entitled "Boycott from Within" (http://www.youtube.com/watch?v=kdYfrAUFL90).

Conclusion

By 2013, "peace" had become a dirty word in parts of both Israeli and Palestinian societies. The *language* of peace has been largely discredited by the inability of politicians to perform the *actions* of peace. At the same time, however, Israelis and Palestinians do know how to live together. Before the Oslo Accords carved up the territory between the Jordan River and Mediterranean Sea, Israelis and Palestinians could travel freely, and many in the older generation tell stories of their Jewish or Palestinian neighbors during the British Mandate. Since the second intifada, policies of fragmentation and separation have intensified, and new generations of Israelis and Palestinians know the other mainly through the mostly negative stereotypes produced in the media. This makes it more urgent for civilians and political leaders on all sides to step up their efforts to build trust and practice reconciliation.

Most Israelis and Palestinians want to live their lives without violence; most want to simply be left alone and be free to pursue their dreams. In order to reach this goal, however, policymakers need to be aware of the different orientations Palestinians and Israelis have toward "peace." For Israelis, peace means an end to any outward expression of violence, as well as "security" at home and in the broader region, whereas for Palestinians, peace requires a transformation of the current system, which restricts their movement, hinders social and economic development, and withholds the national right to self-determination.

Most analysts agree that ending the Palestinian-Israeli conflict is critical to the stability of the Middle East. In the wake of the political change engendered by the so-called Arab Spring in 2011, Arab regimes are called to be more accountable to their populations, including demands to support Palestinian self-determination and freedom. Regional unrest is troubling to Israelis concerned for their security and for the endurance of peace treaties with Egypt and Jordan, although these countries have maintained the peace agreements with Israel despite periods of intensified conflict in the past. The violence in Syria has again raised the problems of unresolved historical tensions between Syria and Israel, as well as the dilemmas of the stateless Palestinian refugees, who are unable to flee Syria given their lack of identity papers and their inability to attain a visa.

It is unclear whether the decision of the United Nations General Assembly to recognize Palestine statehood will have any real implications. If it remains words on paper without international action to realize such statehood, the declaration will join the list of agreements or plans that have been relegated to the dustbin of history. However, popular opinion is shifting, and if Israel is to avoid becoming an international pariah state, as many Israelis and diaspora Jews increasingly fear, a more intensive effort to reach a negotiated peace with the Palestinians is crucial. As policymakers work for peace, however, they should interrogate the underlying principles at play, especially those concerning the proposed parameters of a Palestinian "state," not only in terms of the borders, but also in terms of the powers reserved to the state.

If Israeli and Palestinian negotiations are to achieve success, they should draw from the lessons of those civil society groups that were able to keep working during the second intifada, who deliberately engaged different, oppositional viewpoints. They should include parties such as Hamas and the settler leadership in discussions rather than isolate them, but not let them veto the process; they should seek equality, finding ways to offset Israel's superiority in power and resources in the negotiation process; and they should work to address the root causes of the conflict, including the psychological traumas experienced by Israelis and Palestinians over the last decades.

By transforming past losses into efforts to prevent future pain rather than endless cycles of revenge, both Israeli and Palestinian leaders can promote a long-term view that goes beyond short-term, domestic political interests. And in the broader context, the international community should realize that in its desire to remain "neutral," it is actually endorsing the status quo of a very imbalanced conflict—between the State of Israel and a much challenged Palestinian Authority.

References and Further Research

Baskin, Gershon, and Zakaria al-Qaq. 2004. "YES PM: Years of Experience in Strategies for Peacemaking: Palestinian-Israeli Relations." *International Journal of Politics, Culture and Society* 17, no. 3: 543–562.

The Economist. 2010. "Ehud Barak Breaks the Apartheid Barrier." Democracy in America blog, February 15. http://www.economist.com/blogs/democracyinamerica/2010/02/israel_demography_democracy_or_apartheid.

Hallward, Maia Carter. 2011. *Struggling for a Just Peace: Israeli and Palestinian Activism in the Second Intifada*. Gainesville: University Press of Florida.

Hermann, Tamar. 2002. "The Sour Taste of Success: The Israeli Peace Movement, 1967–1998." In *Mobilizing for Peace: Conflict Resolution in Northern Ireland, Israel/Palestine, and South Africa*, edited by Benjamin Gidron, Stanley Katz, and Yeheskel Hasenfeld, 94–129. New York: Oxford University Press.

King, Mary. 2007. *A Quiet Revolution: The First Palestinian Intifada and Nonviolent Resistance*. New York: Nation Books.

Lesch, David W. 2008. *The Arab-Israeli Conflict: A History*. New York: Oxford University Press.

Malley, Robert, and Hussein Agha. 2001. "Camp David: The Tragedy of Errors." *The New York Review of Books*, July 12. http://www.nybooks.com/articles/archives/2001/aug/09/camp-david-the-tragedy-of-errors/?pagination=false.

Meital, Yoram. 2006. *Peace in Tatters: Israel, Palestine, and the Middle East*. Boulder, CO: Lynne Rienner.

Morris, Benny. 1999. *Righteous Victims: A History of the Zionist-Arab Conflict, 1881–1999*. New York: Alfred A. Knopf.

Shlaim, Avi. 2009. *Israel and Palestine: Reappraisals, Revisions, Refutations*. London: Verso.

Short Films

Budrus. 2010. Directed by Julia Bacha. Washington, DC: Just Vision. http://www.justvision.org/budrus.

Encounter Point. 2006. Directed by Ronit Avni. Washington, DC: Just Vision. http://www.justvision.org/encounterpoint.

Five Broken Cameras. 2011. Directed by Emad Burnat and Guy Davidi. New York: Kino Lorber Films. http://www.imdb.com/title/tt2125423/.

New Hope for Peace: What America Must Do to End the Israel-Palestine Conflict. 2009. Directed and edited by Glen Pearcy. Washington, DC: Foundation for Middle East Peace. http://www.youtube.com/watch_popup?v=CoXuRJVpB8A&vq=medium.

Searching for Peace. 2006. Directed by Mischa Scorer. Written by Landrum Bolling. Washington, DC: Foundation for Middle East Peace. http://www.fmep.org/searching_for_peace_in_the_middle_east.html.

12

The Green Movement and the Struggle for Human Rights in Iran

MAHMOOD MONSHIPOURI

The 2009 Iranian presidential elections resulted in a second term for Mahmoud Ahmadinejad, as well as a series of public protests against alleged election fraud. These protests came to be called the Green Movement. The protesters were predominantly young, but members of Iran's reformist factions, who have long sought more democratic rights, also participated. Facilitated by digital interactions via instant messaging and postings on Facebook, Twitter, and YouTube, the protests were reported worldwide, while the Iranian regime struggled to shape public perceptions of the events. Although the regime's security apparatus ultimately suppressed the Green Movement, it undoubtedly felt threatened by the efficiency and organizational skills that allowed opposition groups to inspire popular protests on a scale unseen since Iran's 1979 revolution that overthrew a monarchy. Thirty years later, the protesters demanded individual freedoms and rights, and thereby gave evidence of the normative diffusion of human rights language into everyday Iranian politics. According to the human rights expert Anthony Chase (2012), the regime countered the language of human rights on the streets by invoking Iran's national security, sovereignty, and cultural exceptionalism.

Since its inception, the Islamic Republic of Iran has guaranteed its political longevity by defending itself against real and imagined external enemies, thereby garnering nationalist support. In 2009, however, the Islamic Republic faced a new challenge: a "green wave," reminiscent of the post-communist "color revolutions" that transpired in Georgia (the Rose Revolution of 2003), Ukraine (the Orange Revolution of 2004), and Kyrgyzstan (the Tulip Revolution of 2005). These revolutions demonstrated that political opposition groups, together with civil society, can successfully use nonviolent strategies to overthrow governments. The Green Movement presented a similar homegrown and popular challenge to the Iranian regime. The protesters' use of social networking services diminished the effectiveness of the regime's "external enemy argument" that had been a convenient foil in previous conflicts. The 2009 protests pitted Iran's national security apparatus against a coalition of forces demanding and promoting human rights in Iran. That particular internal political dynamic, however, is representative of a larger trend throughout the Middle East.

The specific conditions under which the "green wave" of opposition in Iran emerged will be examined in this case study, which also looks at the contradictions and uncertainties

facing the Islamic Republic in the coming years. Profound socioeconomic and demographic shifts have taken place since the 1979 Iranian Revolution. A new generation of Iranian protesters drastically altered Iranian political culture, and the political uprising in Iran in 2009 echoed throughout the region in subsequent years. The chapter ends with a brief comparative discussion of the 2011 Arab Spring.

Brief History of the Islamic Republic

The 1979 Islamic Revolution that overthrew Shah Mohammad Reza Pahlavi's monarchy was made possible by the actions of a broad array of secular as well as religious groups by discontent with the monarchy's economic policies, which had created growing class disparities; and by the growing influence of security and intelligence forces in society. Acts of civil resistance began in 1977, and strikes and street demonstrations became increasingly common in 1978. The Shah's regime was friendly to, and had the backing of, the United States, and the revolution was fueled by anti-Western and anti-American slogans. Iranians mobilized to stop the Westernization of Iranian society.

The third day of the Green Movement protest rally in Tehran near Azadi Tower. (*Wikimedia Commons. Photo by Hamed Saber.*)

The main opponents against Western influences in Iran were members of the Shiite religious establishment, which ended up being led by the charismatic Ayatollah Ruhollah Khomeini. The cleric had long been under surveillance by the Shah's security forces, and when the revolution broke out, he was living in exile in Paris. When the Shah left Iran in 1979 in response to nationwide demonstrations, Khomeini returned. He became Iran's "supreme leader," advised by an appointed Council of Guardians as well as an elected parliament. Iran's monarchy was replaced by an Islamic government (*velayat-e faqih*, or "rule of the jurist"), and the primacy of Islamic law was enshrined in Iran's constitution.

Early promises of the Islamic Republic's government to protect and promote civil liberties and basic freedoms gradually faded, as the leading clerics started to carve out their space in Iranian politics. Power struggles between conservative and reformist factions intensified within the new regime, resulting in sharp policing of dissent. When Iraqi forces invaded Iran in September 1980, a grossly miscalculated act by the Iraqi president, Saddam Hussein, they inadvertently bolstered the clerical establishment's position vis-à-vis the more pragmatic and liberal elements within the regime. In fact, this bloody and senseless war, which lasted for eight years (1980–1988), consolidated the theocratic republic by allowing it a nationalist self-defense platform that silenced all opposition.

During the first ten years of the Islamic Republic, the civil and human rights situation of the Iranians deteriorated. Internal opposition to the Islamic regime was restricted. The only opposition group that was tolerated was the Freedom Movement of Iran, founded in 1961. Large numbers of Iran's intelligentsia and educated elites left the country.

The fifth day of the Green Movement protest rally in Tehran at Haft-e Tir Square. The woman's sign reads, "They killed my brother because he asked, 'where's my vote?'" *(Wikimedia Commons. Photo by Hamed Saber.)*

Paramilitary groups such as the Revolutionary Guards and *basijis* (literally, "those who are mobilized") created a climate of fear as they hunted down books, tapes, and videos that promoted Western ideas and culture. Islamization programs, such as the enforced veiling of women who had previously chosen not to wear the veil, were initiated as a way to repel Western ideas through the proper moral education of Iranian citizens. The theocratic regime defined civility and citizenship largely in religious terms, which created new categories of inclusion and exclusion of citizens in the society. Secular, left-leaning ideologies were declared Western in origin and banned, turning a large segment of the Iranian population—many of whom had participated in the overthrow of the Shah—into enemies of the state.

Ayatollah Khomeini died in June 1989. He was replaced as supreme leader by the incumbent president, Ali Khamenei, while Ali Akbar Hashemi Rafsanjani, then speaker of the parliament and a proponent of free-market economics, was elected president. At the time, this was taken to mean that the velayat-e faqih would no longer dominate the political sphere. Such an important internal political change would signal a transition to a reconstruction phase of the Islamic Republic. Parliamentary elections in April and May

1992 curbed the influence of radical conservative politicians. With their electoral defeat, the country's need to implement Islamic ideals became a much lower priority. Instead, President Rafsanjani focused on dismantling economic protectionism, removing virtually all barriers to foreign investment in Iran, including regulations that limited foreign ownership of industries and firms to 49 percent of shares and capital investments. This was a signal to the West that Iran wanted to be back in business.

In 1994, public discontent over deteriorating economic conditions and increasing political repression led to riots in several Iranian cities. Violent confrontations between demonstrators and security forces were reported in Tehran, Tabriz, Zahedan, Qazvin, and Najafabad. Officially sponsored vigilantism became widespread in 1995. Domestic human rights organizations—including the Parliamentary Human Rights Committee, the Organization for Defending Victims of Violence, and the Human Rights Commission—were no longer allowed to operate effectively. The mounting popular discontent led to the election of a new president, Mohammad Khatami, on May 23, 1997.

Khatami, although a cleric with close ties to the Iranian religious establishment, was well known for his pragmatism. He had served as the minister of culture and Islamic guidance from 1982 to 1992, but was forced to resign when conservatives criticized his relatively permissive stance on issues such as allowing access to television satellite dishes. Khatami's lopsided victory—he received almost 70 percent of the vote—was a firm rebuke to hardline clerics who had dominated Iranian politics since the 1979 revolution. Khatami brought greater freedom and tolerance not just to the political scene, but to Iranian society as well. Perhaps the most striking facet of the 1997 election was Khatami's overwhelming support from both young people and women. In gaining young people's votes, Khatami succeeded in winning the trust of a generation that had not participated in the revolution. Khatami's presidency, however, was overshadowed by the intense internal power struggles between Iran's reformists and hardline conservatives. Power struggles were most obvious in cultural politics, that is, in the struggle over whose vision of an Islamic society would prevail. Prominent Iranian intellectuals and journalists began to challenge the underlying concepts of Islamic governance. In response, in April 2000, many newspapers were closed down, and many journalists and editors were imprisoned or called before what became known as "the Press Court."

During Khatami's presidency, the judiciary—which is accountable to Supreme Leader Ali Khamenei rather than the elected president—was at the center of human rights violations. Many abuses were carried out by the nation's "parallel institutions" (*nahad-e movazi*), plainclothes intelligence agents and paramilitary groups who would intimidate or attack members of the opposition, including students, writers, and reformist politicians. The parallel institutions also included secret prisons and interrogation centers run by intelligence services. The operation of these parallel institutions alongside government institutions demonstrated the executive branch's lack of control over any of them. This was perhaps most notable in the serial murder case of prominent secular dissidents after President Khatami's election in 1997. On November 22, 1998, Dariush Forouhar and his wife Parvaneh, who ran a small opposition party, were stabbed to death. In the following weeks, three outspoken secular writers—Majid Sharif, Mohammad Jafar Pouyandeh, and

Mohammad Mokhtari—disappeared, and their bodies were later found dumped on the outskirts of Tehran. The closed trials of those accused of the murders, which occurred during December 2000 and January 2001, led to guilty verdicts. On January 27, 2001, a judge sentenced several "rogue agents" from the intelligence ministry to death or life imprisonment. The Iranian security apparatus remained intact, however, and it continued to wield extraordinary powers in politics.

Ahmadinejad's Rise to Power

Analysts argue that Mahmoud Ahmadinejad, who was the mayor of Tehran, won the presidency in 2005 by promising to bring Iran's oil revenue to the tables of the people. During his electoral campaign, he adeptly spoke to the financial worries of the majority of the Iranian population. As a way of arguing that Iran needed more social and economic justice, Ahmadinejad used religious slogans, such as "Islam without justice is not Islam." Ahmadinejad's populist message of economic equality proved more attractive at the polls than the promises of neoliberal economic development espoused by other candidates. The notion of liberal democracy and its related free-market reforms failed to resonate with the masses of people in Iran, 30 percent of whom lived below the poverty line. At the time, 80 percent of the economy was controlled by the state. All presidential candidates, with the exception of Ahmadinejad, talked about the need for privatization, without mentioning the corrupting influences—or "crony capitalism"—engendered by the sale of state-owned firms to people loyal to the regime. Ahmadinejad, instead, promised in plain language to bring oil revenues to people's tables, and to privatize state-owned firms by handing out "justice shares" directly to Iranian families.

Once Ahmadinejad was in office, he faced the challenge of operationalizing his election promises. He had to find a way to redistribute the wealth in shares of stock to each Iranian family, while at the same time pushing for state subsidies and welfare packages such as health insurance and low-interest loans. His protectionist economic policies shielded Iranian companies from global competition, but also they cut off Iran from the global market. Quite understandably, the same populist campaign platform that brought him to power spelled trouble for him in the 2009 presidential election, in large part because his policies had failed to bring about economic justice.

A biographical profile of Mahmoud Ahmadinejad can be found on the Middle East section of the BBC News website (http://www.bbc.co.uk/news/world-middle-east-10866448).

Challenges From Without: Wars and Sanctions

Since its inception, the Islamic Republic of Iran has suppressed domestic reform-oriented movements in the name of confronting external threats to its survival. Foremost among these threats were the Iraq-Iran War (1980–1988) and continued sanctions aimed at undermining the Islamic Republic. In the post-Khomeini era (1989–present), Iran has encountered continued sanctions, boycotts, and political isolation by the United States and some of its Western allies. These policies have enabled the Islamic Republic to exploit a narrative of an ongoing foreign conspiracy that requires constant vigilance and legitimizes the restriction of individual freedoms.

Iran's history contains sufficient evidence of foreign interference, which can be, and has been, marshaled by contemporary politicians for political gain. For instance, in 1953 the narrative of Soviet interference in Iranian affairs through the Soviet Union's manipulation of the Iranian communist Tudeh Party seriously weakened Prime Minister Mohammad Mossadeq, especially in the eyes of the clerical establishment and its supporters. At the same time, the perceived Soviet influence led to the involvement of U.S. intelligence services, which were instrumental in organizing and executing a coup against Mossadeq. The United States then proceeded to support the reinstated Shah with a combination of economic and military aid, which led to the identification of the United States with an increasingly brutal, authoritarian regime. This narrative explains the popular support among Iranians when Khomeini endorsed the taking of hostages at the American embassy in Iran in 1979. The hostage crisis lasted for 444 days, isolated Iran in the world community, and severely damaged the country's international standing. The students who held the American hostages demanded that the United States extradite the Shah, who was in the United States seeking medical treatment, so he could face trial in Iran. A botched 1980 rescue attempt of the hostages (Operation Eagle Claw) damaged the standing of President Jimmy Carter, who lost his bid for reelection against Ronald Reagan. It came as no surprise, then, that the United States chose to support Saddam Hussein during the subsequent Iran-Iraq War.

On November 4, 2004, National Public Radio (NPR) broadcast a commemorative radio program titled "25th Anniversary of the Iran Hostage Crisis," which examined the reasons behind the student takeover of the U.S. Embassy in Teheran. The program is available on the NPR website (http://www.npr.org/templates/story/story.php?storyId=4144174).

In the 1990s, the Clinton administration adopted a "dual containment" policy toward Iran and Iraq. The Iranian half of dual containment was based on a "five part challenge" that Iran posed to the United States and the international community: (1) support for "terrorism and assassination across the globe," (2) opposition to the Arab-Israeli peace process, (3) efforts to subvert pro-West governments, (4) military build-up aimed at dominating the Persian Gulf region, and (5) quest to acquire nuclear weapons. Although the dual containment policy drove a wedge between the United States and its main allies, Europe and Japan, the United States pursued unilateral sanctions against Iran. In August 1996, President Clinton signed the Iran-Libya Sanction Act (ILSA) to punish Iran and Libya for alleged state-sponsored terrorism. ILSA required the U.S. president to impose sanctions against any foreign or domestic company that invested $40 million or more a year in oil and gas projects in either Iran or Libya. The law was questioned by U.S. allies—Canada, the European Union (EU), Australia, and Japan—on the grounds that it violated international law.

The attacks of September 11, 2001, on New York and Washington, DC, prompted a brief convergence of interests between the United States and the Iranian government: both wanted to drive the Taliban out of power in Afghanistan, and both opposed the spread of terrorism and the drug trade in the region. But President George W. Bush's "Axis of Evil" speech in January 2002, which labeled Iran, along with Iraq and North Korea, as rogue states, convinced Iran's hardliners that the Islamic Republic would become the next target in Bush's "war on terror." The threat of U.S. or Israeli military action put Iran's Islamic radicals back in business, and layers of mistrust between Iran and the United States deepened. The U.S. invasion of Iraq in 2003, along with Washington's threat of possible military attacks against Iran, pushed hardliners and populists to the forefront of Iran's 2005 presidential election.

In 2005, American troops were on both sides of Iran's border, in Iraq and Afghanistan, and U.S. aircraft carriers were in the Persian Gulf, a vital sea-lane for oil shipments. At the same time, Western powers and Israel demanded that Iran dismantle its uranium enrichment operations and its presumed plan to develop nuclear weapons. In 2006, the United Nations (UN) Security Council issued Resolution 1696, giving Iran one month to end uranium enrichment, as well as related research and development. President Ahmedinejad remained fiercely unmoved, insisting that Iran's nuclear program was civilian in nature. The UN Security Council then began to impose sanctions of increasing severity—via Resolutions 1737 (2006), 1747 (2007), 1803 (2008), and 1929 (2010)—blocking the import and export of sensitive nuclear material and equipment, freezing assets of and imposing travel restrictions on persons involved in Iran's nuclear program, and blocking weapons sales. Additionally, President Obama signed into law the Comprehensive Iran Sanctions, Accountability, and Divestment Act of 2010 in order to pressure foreign governments and companies to divest from Iran's oil industry, in particular Iran's oil refineries, thereby restricting Iran's own gasoline supply. This last measure has been controversial both in Iran and the United States, because this kind of sanction harms Iranian civilians as well as U.S. business interests. Subsequent rounds of nuclear diplomacy have remained inconclusive.

On June 5, 2013, Al-Jazeera's *Inside Story* presented a discussion on "Iran: The Real Cost of Sanctions" (http://www.aljazeera.com/programmes/insidestory/2013/06/201365928843270.html). One of the significant effects of sanctions is the devaluation of the Iranian currency against the U.S. dollar, making it very difficult for Iran to pay for imports.

Challenges From Within: The Green Movement

The 2009 elections, Iran's tenth presidential election, placed the incumbent, Mahmoud Ahmadinejad, against his political rival, Mir Hossein Mousavi, who had served as

Iran's prime minister from 1981 to 1989 under Supreme Leader Khomeini. The office of prime minister had been abolished in a constitutional referendum after Khomeini's death. Mousavi reemerged into the political limelight in 2009 as a reformist presidential candidate. He chose green, the color of Islam, as his campaign color. The election took place on June 12, and a high voter turnout led to an extension of voting time. Shortly after midnight, the official Islamic Republic News Agency announced that Ahmadinejad had won the election with more than 60 percent of the votes. The ensuing days and weeks were filled with massive protests throughout Iran. Mousavi and his "Green" supporters claimed large-scale voting fraud, releasing a statement to the effect that the people's movement "would not surrender to this charade." An appeal was submitted to the Council of Guardians, the appointed twelve-member council that possesses enormous influence in the Islamic Republic of Iran, to recount the votes. The council recounted the votes, amid protests from the opposition that millions of ballots were missing, and subsequently announced that Ahmadinejad had won the election.

This result further galvanized the opposition, which by now included Islamic reformists (among them former political authorities of the Islamic Republic of Iran), human rights activists and lawyers, university professors, a wide array of nongovernmental organizations (NGOs), and large numbers of young people with secular ideas. In spite of the Islamic Republic's intense efforts to portray the Green Movement as an *enqalob-e makhmalee* (velvet revolution) financed and directed from the West, evidence suggests that the Iranian public was well aware of the Green Movement's homegrown origin. The movement was not formulated along strict ideological lines; that is, it was neither a class struggle against a populist government nor a secularist uprising against religious rule. Instead, it represented a post-Islamist democracy movement to reclaim human rights and dignity. The protesters indeed asked, "Where is my vote?" However, they also asked to live a dignified life free from fear, moral and political surveillance, corruption, and arbitrary rule. Essentially indigenous and nonviolent, this movement aimed to restore the civil liberties promised, but not delivered, by the 1979 Islamic Revolution. Many Iranians, according to journalist Hooman Majd (2010), were no longer resigned to the increasingly undemocratic aspects of the Islamic Republic's political system.

Some analysts believe that the Islamic Republic is preparing the way for its own demise by educating its people. Iran has become a middle-class society imbued with rising expectations and demands for political freedoms. A quick glance at the demographics behind the Green Movement explains why educated young women were at the forefront of this reformist movement. In the 1970s, toward the end of the Pahlavi monarchy, nearly 5 percent of college-age youth went to college. By 2009, the figure had reached 31 percent. Since the 1990s, females had come to outnumber males in secondary schools (1996), primary schools (1999), and higher education (2001) (see Hashemi and Postel 2010).

The Green Movement was fully aware of the means of suppression at the disposal of the Iranian government, so its leaders and followers opted for a method of nonviolent civil disobedience. They were eventually suppressed by a combination of coercive means. The leaders were placed under house arrest, protesters were attacked and killed in the streets or imprisoned and tried on charges of treason, and media freedoms were severely restricted for international as well as Iranian journalists. The regime portrayed the protesters as a minority of pro-Western urban elites, out of touch with the majority of Iran's population in the provinces. The regime also staged pro-Ahmadinejad rallies that, unlike the protest rallies, were allowed to be televised.

Uniqueness of the Green Movement

What distinguished the 2009 Green Movement from previous protests was that this time a significant portion of the populace rejected the state's narrative of foreign conspiracy and replaced it with its own, unique language of citizen's rights. As a prelude to the Green Movement, the human rights discourse in Iran had gained considerable traction. The relatively open social and political climate of the Khatami years (1997–2005) had strengthened Iran's civil society and expanded the freedom of expression. For instance, Khatami had allowed secular feminists to participate in discussions of women's issues and concerns.

Iran's first female judge, Shirin Ebadi, had faced several difficulties in her efforts to promote legal reforms immediately after the 1979 Iranian Revolution. Following the victory of the Islamic Republic, she and other female judges were dismissed from their posts on the grounds that Islam forbids women to serve as judges. In 1992, she obtained a lawyer's license and set up her own practice. During the Khatami years, she operated in a far less restrictive environment than women in the earlier years of the revolution. In 2003, Ebadi was awarded the Nobel Peace Prize, the first Iranian and the first Muslim woman to be so honored. She now lives in exile. Iranian women's support for internationally recognized human rights standards is crucial to the advancement of their rights in Iran.

> Biographical information about Shirin Ebadi, as well as footage from her Nobel Prize ceremony, can be found on the official website of the Nobel Prize (http://www.nobelprize.org/nobel_prizes/peace/laureates/2003/ebadi-facts.html).

Likewise, the July 8–14, 1999, student protests, a reaction against the closure of a reformist daily newspaper called *Salaam*, had made it clear that students would voice their dissent over the suppression of free speech. In the absence of legitimate political opposition parties, the press became not only a bastion of the struggle against the conservatives, but also a driving force behind the country's political development. In many respects, the press—especially those media outlets supporting reform—took the place of political parties in Iran, a development that threatened the right-wing clergy and their supporters. It is worth noting that students' demands in 1999 were more broadly political in nature. They expressed a growing resentment of the public—and not just among students alone—against the restriction of Iranians' fundamental civil liberties and universal rights.

Since 1999 the spread of information and communication technologies (ICTs) has further bolstered the human rights discourse, particularly among youth and women. The Islamic Republic had established a monopoly over the means of mass communication—comprising all six national television channels, dozens of radio networks, and all but a few newspapers and magazines. In 2009, however, students with access to the Internet were able to communicate with their peers across the country and outside it, transmitting images of their demonstrations and the violence of regime forces, challenging the messages of state-censored media. The regime tried to counter this by blocking websites and proxy servers that were used to circumvent the restrictions. To this day, regime hardliners are struggling to maintain control over the flow of information that reaches urban centers. Internet saturation in Iran's provinces is not yet very high.

What was also remarkable about the Green Movement was that opposition figures, such as Mousavi, responded to sentiments on the street rather than directing them. Perhaps the most important facet of this movement was, in the words of one observer, the fact that Iran suffered political cracks in 2009 precisely because the Iranian establishment had split so openly, with former members of the Iranian government raising a critical voice alongside more secular dissidents. Significantly, the 2009 Green Movement in Iran will be remembered around the world because of images of the protests documenting the willingness of Iranians to take their opposition to the streets. Although the 2009 demonstrations in Iran were not as widespread as those of 1979 that ushered in the Islamic Republic, the experience of activism created new political opportunities in Iran.

Under the watchful eyes of the international community, it became obvious that the Islamic Republican train had veered off track. The government has to address how to secure internal legitimacy and credibility if it wants to remain a dominant, regional power. Although one should not underestimate the resilience of the Islamic Republic and its proxies outside the country, it is far more difficult for Iran's ruling elites to pursue formidable foreign policies in the region when their credibility is questioned internally. Iran's supreme leader, Ayatollah Ali Khamenei, declared the election of Ahmadinejad in 2009 a "divine assessment." Whereas Ayatollah Khomeini was on the side of the Iranian people against the Shah, Ayatollah Khamenei opted for the opposite course.

While some Western commentators see a democratic transition in Iran as a realistic possibility, others see that as wishful thinking. The Islamic Republic remains in firm control of its military and intelligence apparatus. During the presidency of Mahmoud Ahmadinejad (2005–2013), Iran's Islamic Revolutionary Guard Corps (IRGC), gained unprecedented control over the country's economy and levers of power. The IRGC will likely continue to consolidate its power and gradually diminish independent clerical influence, without openly displacing the clerics from their constitutional offices. Other experts point to the centralized clerical hierarchy—not religion—as a major barrier to political and economic reform that could lead to democracy. This structural barrier, they argue, along with widespread coercion, the regime's counterinsurgency tactics, and Iran's ability to use its oil revenue to co-opt its citizens, will prolong the current regime.

In 2011, the Council on Foreign Relations (CFR) published a short slide show titled "Crisis Guide: Iran" on its website (http://www.cfr.org/interactives/CG_Iran/index.html?cid=oth-redirect-crisis_guide_iran). It gives an overview of Iranian revolutionary history, and it discusses the policy options of both Iran and the United States.

The Green Movement and the Arab Uprisings

Views differ as to whether Iran's Green Movement inspired or had a palpable impact on the subsequent Arab revolts that began in Tunis in December 2010. While the Islamic Republic and its state media maintained that the 2011 Arab uprisings in the Middle East and North Africa were similar to Iran's 1979 Islamic Revolution—which overthrew a secular ruler who enjoyed Western support and replaced him with an Islamic political system—Mir Hossein Mousavi took the opposite view. In a statement on Facebook on January 29, 2011, he wrote, "The starting point of what we are now witnessing on the streets of Tunis, Sanaa, Cairo, Alexandria, and Suez can be undoubtedly traced back to June 2009, when people took to the streets of Tehran in millions shouting 'Where is my vote?' and peacefully demanded the restoration of their denied rights" (Radio Zamaneh 2011).

Some analysts have tried to explain why the revolution succeeded in Tunisia but failed in Iran. To begin with, the Tunisian army refused to shoot at demonstrators. More importantly, however, Tunisian political power and control over the economy was increasingly concentrated in the hands of an isolated, ruling family. The Tunisian president, Ben Ali, and his family held a tight grip on the country's political and economic power, which disenfranchised everyone else. In Iran, by contrast, the current regime has an extensive institutional base and retains popular support among some segments of Iranian society, especially the poor, who count on the government for welfare payments and other financial support. Finally, the Tunisian uprisings began in the provinces, and then moved to the capital, demonstrating support for the revolution across the rural-urban divide, something that cannot be said about the Green Movement. Of course, Tunisia's population is also much smaller and more homogenous than Iran's, which makes it easier to mobilize.

There are many who question the notion that the Arab uprisings can be termed successful in any meaningful sense. They point to the instability and economic losses that followed the toppling of Arab dictators from Saddam Hussein to Muammar Qaddafi and the embattled Bashar al-Assad, even threatening the survival of some of those states.

Speaking Truth to Power

As an effective and legitimate campaign of internal civil disobedience, the Green Movement undermined the legitimacy of the Iranian government, which appears incapable of meeting its demographic challenges and coming to grips with one of the youngest and most educated populations in the region. Its repressive tactics and methods have yet to silence the people's cry for human rights and dignity. An emphatically homegrown and indigenous movement, the Green Movement demonstrated contrasting visions among members of the Iranian leadership, along with their sharply different interpretations of reform and Islamic law. Perhaps the single most important aspect of these oppositional movements has been the revelation of further divisions within the ruling establishment regarding how to lead the country in a digitally revolutionized world.

Even with the Green Movement's leaders under house arrest and banned from external contact, the 2013 election of the reformist candidate Hassan Rouhani as president of Iran was proof that the suppression of the 2009 protests did not put an end to the dynamics that had given rise to the Green Movement. While regime hardliners have blocked Rouhani's reform efforts at every turn, the pressures continue to build. The increasingly severe international sanctions imposed on Iran for violating the Nuclear Non-Proliferation Treaty have had a crippling effect on the industrial, energy, and financial sectors. The worsening economic situation, high unemployment rates, and the oppressive political climate not only intensify tensions within the Iranian regime itself, but also further undermine the regime's legitimacy. As in the rest of the Middle East and North Africa, the Iranian regime is challenged by its demographic youth bulge and educated young people who view regime corruption as stripping them of their future. Despite the fact that street protests in Iran have largely vanished in the face of the government's machinations, the political divisions among the ruling elites continue unabated and a new generation of activists is working behind the scenes to sustain the movement's momentum. The Green Movement has expanded far beyond university campuses to encompass diverse groups, including human rights activists, women, disgruntled clerics, and the unemployed. In sum, the struggle for democracy, the rule of law, and modern human rights has become integrated into the consciousness of Iranians, and the Islamic Republic increasingly finds itself in a race against time.

References and Further Research

Chase, Anthony Tirado. 2012. *Human Rights, Revolution, and Reform in the Muslim World.* Boulder, CO: Lynne Rienner.

Dabashi, Hamid. 2010. *Iran, the Green Movement, and the USA: The Fox and the Paradox.* London: Zed Books.

Hashemi, Nader, and Danny Postel, eds. 2010. *The People Reloaded: The Green Movement and the Struggle for Iran's Future.* New York: Melville House.

Ibish, Hussein. 2012. "Was the Arab Spring Worth It?" *Foreign Policy* 194 (July/August 2012). http://www.foreignpolicy.com/articles/2012/06/18/was_the_arab_spring_worth_it.

Kamrava, Mehran. 2001. "The Civil Society Discourse in Iran." *British Journal of Middle Eastern Studies* 28, no. 2: 165–185.

Majd, Hooman. 2010. *The Ayatollahs' Democracy: An Iranian Challenge.* New York: W.W. Norton.

Miller, Debra A., ed. 2012. *The Iranian Green Movement.* San Francisco, CA: Greenhaven Press.

Radio Zamaneh. 2011. "Mousavi Says Upheaval in the Arab World Extension of Iranian Election Protests." Radio Zamaneh, January 29. http://archive.radiozamaneh.com/english/ content/mousavi-says-upheaval-arab-world-extension-iranian-election-protests.

Web Resource

Radio Zamaneh is an Amsterdam-based Persian radio station, funded in large part by the Dutch Ministry of Foreign Affairs and the European Union. Its English-language summary website can be found at http://archive.radiozamaneh.com/english/.

13

State-Society Relations and Protest in the Kurdistan Region of Iraq

NICOLE F. WATTS

In late November 2012, half a dozen disabled men went on a hunger strike in the city of Sulaimaniya, one of the largest cities in the Kurdistan region of Iraq. They spent their days sitting in a tent, occasionally hosting guests who joined them in drinking water and banana-flavored milk drinks. Outside, on the streets and in front of government buildings, dozens of people marched in support of the men and the rights of the disabled, calling for more government assistance in meeting their needs.

Coming, as it did, in the context of a bloody civil war in Syria and constitutional struggles for control of post-uprising Egypt, this quiet if poignant campaign for the rights of the Kurdish disabled might have escaped most people's notice. But the campaign was significant for more than those involved: it represented part of a sustained wave of protests in the Kurdish north of Iraq, the most significant example of which involved two months of daily demonstrations that swept across Sulaimaniya Province in early 2011. The 2011 protests were some of the largest ever in the history of the Kurdistan region, but in sharp contrast to demonstrations of earlier decades, the protesters targeted their own Kurdish authorities, not the Iraqi regime in Baghdad.

This chapter examines the new politics of protest as it unfolded in the Kurdistan region of Iraq in the years 2010–2013. Why would ordinary people challenge a government that, on the surface, seemed to embody their greatest hopes and dreams? For much of the twentieth century, the focal point of Kurdish politics in Iraq was the drive for autonomy and Kurdish rights, and Kurdish authorities have traditionally enjoyed considerable public support, or at least quiescence, based on perceptions of their role in leading the Kurdish nationalist struggle. The impetus to maintain a unified Kurdish front against the Iraqi state has further discouraged internal criticism of the Kurdish regime. Unlike other protest zones across the Middle East and North Africa, the Kurdistan region is not an independent state but a region in a federal (Iraqi) state structure; its status is contested and relatively vulnerable, and its leaders recently and quite fairly elected. The fact that charismatic Kurdish leaders whose parties have dominated politics for four decades could be subject to sustained public and popular criticism is thus important both for what it can tell us about the nature of political legitimacy in the Kurdistan region of Iraq and for the insights it offers into some of the broader dynamics transforming state-society relations in the Middle East and North Africa.

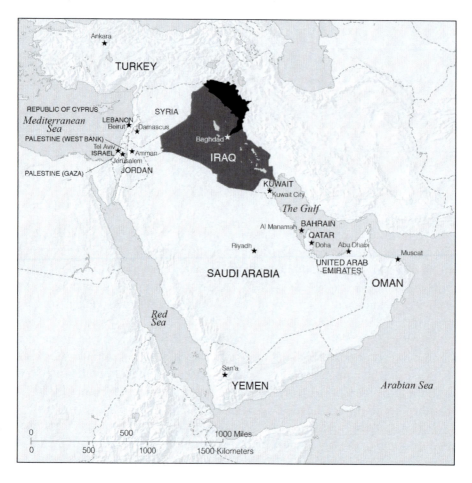

Although mobilization patterns, regime types, and demands vary considerably among the Kurdistan region, Egypt, Tunisia, Libya, and elsewhere, lessons can be drawn from these localized protests that are applicable to studies of resistance and mobilization across the region and beyond. First, the 2011 "Sulaimaniya Spring" protests highlight the emergence of a new governing paradigm that grants the right to rule based on performance in office and accountability, rather than on older forms of patron-client relations and credentials earned in national liberation struggles. The way this "good governance" paradigm is resonating in broad sectors of society shows that even in fragile "quasi-states" such as the Kurdistan region of Iraq, ordinary people will prioritize good government. The innovative political relevance of this new governing paradigm points to a second lesson: critical to the emergence of protest politics in Kurdistan and beyond is a new mobilization capacity that has translated widespread grievances into a powerful presence on the street. A third lesson is a more sober one: the new wave of protests draws our attention to the ways decentralized and inclusive models of protest may generate mass support, but also it illustrates the limitations of street demonstrations as a way to negotiate complicated systemic reforms.

The first part of the chapter examines Kurdish efforts to establish self-governance up to and after the overthrow of the Iraqi Baath regime in 2003, when de facto Kurdish autonomy became codified into law through the 2005 Iraqi Constitution, thus formally establishing the Kurdistan Regional Government (KRG) as the primary governing authority in three northern provinces. The second part describes the protests that began in 2005 and 2006, culminating in mass protests of early 2011. The third part examines some of the reasons that ordinary people were dissatisfied with KRG governance and how they began to reconceptualize the role and responsibilities of authorities in the region. The next section analyzes why activists were able to begin to mobilize on a large scale, drawing our attention to the new mobilization capacity in the region and the organizational characteristics of the protests themselves. The chapter concludes with a discussion of some of the broader lessons and implications of the case.

Visit the website of the Kurdistan Regional Government (http://www.krg.org/) for news about the Kurdistan region and government (click on "English" on the top right for the English-language version).

Governance and Legitimation

Establishing the authority to govern is, as the scholar Joel S. Migdal (2013) puts it, "no easy business." Although rulers may put themselves in power through force of arms, they cannot keep it for long without resorting to numerous other means of convincing ordinary people that they should support or at least comply with state authority. Such questions about why ordinary people obey states—about how political legitimacy is created and maintained—have fascinated scholars for centuries. How do states (or would-be states) establish and maintain the right to rule, and when and why do ordinary people challenge them? The Arab uprisings that began in December 2010 in Tunisia show that such questions are not simply a matter of academic debate but are driving real-life politics across the region, with the traditional legitimacy regimes had enjoyed—in some cases for decades—very much up in the air.

Establishing authority involves fending off challenges from external powers that lay claim to the same human and physical terrain, and from competing "internal" players who vie for the leadership of the (national) community. Neither process takes place in a vacuum but rather in the context of an international network of states and markets that raise and lower the stakes, empower some actors more than others, and can dramatically change the playing field. In all these respects the Kurdistan region of Iraq is a case in point. For more than four decades, state-society relations in the region have been profoundly shaped by three main factors: the fight against the Iraqi state, an internal schism between two rival Kurdish nationalist parties—the Kurdistan Democratic Party (KDP), formed in 1946, and its rival Patriotic Union of Kurdistan (PUK), formed in 1975—and extensive regional and international involvement in Kurdish affairs and fortunes.

For Kurds who sought to rule the Kurdish-populated north of Iraq, the primary competitor for the right and capacity to govern has been the central Iraqi state. Throughout the twentieth century, Kurdish leaders and *peshmerga* (fighters) fought on-again, off-again wars with the Iraqi armed forces in an effort to protect Kurdish national rights within Iraq and establish some measure of autonomy. From 1987 to 1988, in the last years of the Iran-Iraq War, the ruling Iraqi Baath Party launched several campaigns to ensure the territorial security of the north and eliminate Kurdish resistance once and for all. Around 50,000 to 100,000 people, mostly civilian boys and men, were murdered en masse; tens of thousands of people were forcibly relocated; hundreds of villages were destroyed; and thousands of Kurdish villagers and townspeople were killed in chemical weapons attacks by Iraqi warplanes (Hiltermann 2007, 2008; McDowall 1996). For many Kurds, self-governance has seemed the only way to protect Kurdish communities and Kurdish ways of life from falling prey to the politics of Arab nationalism, authoritarianism, repression, and centralization.

The year 1991 marked a first turning point in Kurdish political fortunes. A failed uprising in the northern and southern parts of Iraq in the wake of the First Gulf War (1990–1991) was followed by the mass exodus of tens of thousands of Kurds to the borders and an acute humanitarian and political crisis, resulting in the creation of a no-fly zone north of the 36th parallel that removed the region from central Iraqi control. As British, American, and Turkish warplanes patrolled the area, Kurdish parties held parliamentary and presidential elections, and in 1992 they established the Kurdistan Regional Government (KRG). After more than half a century of fighting for rights and autonomy, Kurds found themselves suddenly, and somewhat paradoxically, in charge. This did not end conflict and suffering, however: the two major Kurdish national parties fought a civil war over financial and physical resources between 1994 and 1998, and the region's inhabitants suffered intensely from the "double embargos" of international sanctions against Iraqi president Saddam Hussein and the central Iraqi state's embargo against the Kurdish north. But by the end of the 1990s, a blueprint for Kurdish self-governance had been created, and Kurds had some experience in self-rule.

A second turn in fortune came in 2003 with the American-led invasion of Iraq, when Iraqi Kurds aided the American and British forces in their ousting of Saddam Hussein's Baath regime in Baghdad. This, and initial Sunni Arab unwillingness to participate in the new system of government that replaced Baath rule, put Kurdish parties in a strong position to negotiate the post-Saddam political arrangement. De facto Kurdish autonomy, in existence since 1991, was legally ratified by the new 2005 Iraqi Constitution, which gave three Kurdish-majority provinces—Erbil (sometimes spelled Arbil), Sulaimaniya, and Duhok (sometimes spelled Dohuk)—collective status as a recognized region within the new federal Iraq state. It also recognized the Kurdistan Regional Government and its related institutions as the legislative and executive authority of the region, and guaranteed it 13 percent of the central Iraqi budget. The Kurdistan Regional Government thus received significant governing powers over budgetary policies, policing and security, health, education, and infrastructure development, while maintaining important economic, legal, and educational links with the central Iraqi state.

Having, to a large degree, established their capacity to govern vis-à-vis Baghdad, Kurds then turned to arranging their affairs at home. After a short period of split governance, with territorial divisions and two capital cities, in early 2006 the PUK and KDP unified the two administrations, making Erbil (known locally as Hawler) the official and united capital of the Kurdistan region. In sharp contrast to other parts of Iraq, Kurdish rule kept the region largely free of political violence, and international companies—particularly from Turkey—flooded in, creating an investment boom. Elections for the 111-person Kurdistan National Assembly in 2005 and 2009 sent representatives from the two major parties to the parliament, as well as several major opposition groups, minority representatives from the region's Christian and Turkmen communities, and (in 2009) thirty-six women. The efforts of more than six decades of struggle seemed to have come to fruition.

Dissent in the Dreamland

Local protests that began in 2005 and 2006 suggested, however, that quasi-independence had not ended conflict between society and state in Kurdistan. This fact was brought vividly to international attention on March 16, 2006, in the town of Halabja, when student protesters tried to prevent Kurdish authorities from holding a commemoration event at the Halabja Monument of Martyrs built to honor the thousands of men, women, and children killed in the 1988 chemical gassing of the city by the Iraqi military (see Box 13.1). Activists argued that Kurdish officials had failed to deliver on promises to the city—especially service- and infrastructure-related pledges to help the town's inhabitants—and had thus lost their right to hold a ceremony there. In the course of the demonstration, the monument was burned and destroyed. The Halabja protest was followed by other demonstrations, among the most important of which were a series of marches against a new anti-demonstration law in December 2010 and January 2011, and, in May 2011, marches in protest of the murder of a young journalist, with activists accusing party officials of complicity.

By far the largest and longest campaign was that in early 2011. Inspired by Tunisian protesters' successful ousting of President Zine Ben Ali on January 14, and the mass demonstrations then occurring in Egypt, the Gorran Party (Movement for Change), the main opposition party in the Kurdistan National Assembly, in late January issued a seven-point program for reform that called on the KRG government to resign, accusing it of corruption and partisanship. On February 17, in the midst of the tense political standoff and acrimonious debate, a little-known group called the Network to Protect Rights and Demands of the People held a legal gathering in Sulaimaniya's Sara Square. Although it was announced as a demonstration of solidarity with the people of Egypt and Tunisia, some speakers raised criticisms of the KRG. The demonstration itself ended without incident, but a group of protesters peeled off from the square and marched to the Kurdistan Democratic Party headquarters on Salim Street. Demonstrators threw stones and broke some windows, and, after some hesitation, security forces ended up shooting at protesters, killing a fourteen-year-old boy and injuring another youth who died a few days later.

Protesters at the Halabja Memorial, March 16, 2006. *(Photo by Hunar Hamad Rashid. Used by permission.)*

After several days of street clashes between roaming groups of angry youth and KRG security forces, as well as attacks by government supporters on the opposition media, civic opposition leaders stepped in and, working with students and other activists, facilitated a transition from generalized street protests to an organized movement. Protesters built a stage and erected a podium in the square, which activists renamed Maidani Azadi, or Freedom Square, after Tahrir Square in Egypt. Activists formed a loose association—the Ad Hoc Committee of Maidani Azadi—to serve as a mouthpiece and coordinator of the protests; they arranged a daily afternoon protest schedule; and they issued a specific set of demands that revolved around calls for government transparency and accountability and an end to the party-state. On February 19, protests also began and then continued in Rania, Darbandikhan, Halabja, and other towns and cities around the province.

These protests continued for two months, and some demonstrations attracted crowds in the tens of thousands. Although they were mostly peaceful, clashes between security officials and protesters took their toll, and ten people were killed, including two police officers and several youths under the age of eighteen (Amnesty International 2009). KRG authorities responded to the protests with a mixture of repression, alarm, and offers of concessions, but on April 18, security forces arrived en masse in Sulaimaniya to break up the gathering in the square by force. The next day the Security Committee for Sulaimaniya Province banned all unlicensed demonstrations, and the protests ended.

Box 13.1

The 1988 Chemical Gassing of Halabja

Halabja—an Iraqi Kurdish town in Sulaimaniya Province near the border with Iran—
was bombed by Iraqi warplanes on March 16, 1988, in one of the worst single chemical
gassings of civilians of the twentieth century. The event occurred in the waning days of
the Iran-Iraq War just after Halabja was taken by Kurdish fighters working alongside
Iranian Revolutionary Guards. It is generally reported that about 5,000 men, women, and
children died in the attack, mostly from nerve gas. After the overthrow of Iraqi president
Saddam Hussein, Kurdish authorities built a monument just outside the gates of Halabja
to honor the victims.

Omar Khawar cradling his infant son. Original photograph taken by Ramazan Ozturk after
1988 gas attack in Halabja. Framed and on display at Halabja Memorial. *(Photo by Nicole
F. Watts)*

Although no demonstrations of comparable size occurred in 2012 or early 2013,
activists took to the streets again for a number of causes: in February 2012 on the anniversary of the Sulaimaniya Spring protests; in June 2012 to protest the KRG budget
and its lack of transparency; in December 2012 to support hunger strikers calling for
rights of the handicapped; and in March 2013 in support of women's rights. Protests,
while not exactly an everyday occurrence, had become a regular part of political
culture.

A report about the June 2012 protest against the Kurdish budget is available from
Kurd Net (http://www.ekurd.net/mismas/articles/misc2012/6/state6325.htm), an
online news source about Kurdish issues.

Grievances and Framing: Toward a New Governing Paradigm?

The emergence of a politics of street protest in Iraqi Kurdistan mirrors similar phenomena around the Middle East and North Africa, and indeed the 2011 protests in Iraqi Kurdistan share many of the same features as Arab uprisings elsewhere. These include individuals or martyrs who serve as initial catalysts and ongoing symbols for mobilization; decentralized and horizontal leadership of the protests; youth communication via Facebook and cell phones; popular but largely nonviolent street protest; popular reclamation of public and official spaces; the involvement of parties, associations, and nongovernmental organizations (NGOs) that serve as "mobilizing structures" for action; and an ambiguous regime response that vacillates between repression and promises for reforms.

Nonetheless, the Kurdistan region of Iraq has a substantially different status than other places in the Middle East, something that should discourage us from assuming a protest movement there would be a natural by-product of the Arab uprisings. Unlike Tunisia, Egypt, and other countries facing recent unrest, the Kurdistan region is not a fully independent state but a region in a federal government structure, and its autonomous status is fragile and contested. Unlike most other regimes, the Kurdistan Regional Government (KRG) was relatively fairly and freely elected. Although the duopoly of the KDP and PUK uses repression and force against dissidents, the depth and degree of systematized violence against its citizens in no way matches the police states of countries such as Tunisia and Egypt prior to the uprisings there. Moreover, although protests did occur in February in Baghdad, Iraq as a whole did not experience sustained, anti-regime demonstrations in early 2011. Given these many differences, the protests in Sulaimaniya cannot be taken as a given or as something that would "naturally" or inevitably occur.

As with the study of social movements more generally, to explain them demands that we examine the grievances that motivate activists. We need to ask how they represent or "frame" their grievances so that they resonate with large portions of the population, and also how they are able to mobilize the public (see, e.g., Tarrow 2011). At the heart of these protests is a series of grievances concerning the KRG administration, which, on paper, is governed by a popularly elected president, a prime minister, and the Kurdistan National Assembly, which includes many different parties. In reality, the KRG often functions more like a party-state: a regime in which state institutions have very little autonomy and in which party membership and status—and relations to the ruling families—largely determine employment and promotions in government, civil service, universities, and other public and many private institutions. As the two largest and most important parties, the Kurdistan Democratic Party (KDP) and the Patriotic Union of Kurdistan (PUK) became the key players in the new political apparatus, banking on their role in the nationalist struggle, extensive powers of patronage, and close international allies to perpetuate their authority. The merger of their two administrations in 2006 has been characterized as a duopoly in which the two parties shared the spoils of lucrative construction, business, and petrol-related contracts.

Although political freedoms and civil rights (e.g., religious freedoms) have been considerably greater than in the rest of Iraq—and indeed greater than in many countries—the KRG has come under both domestic and international criticism for nepotism and corruption. Specific complaints include the persecution of dissident journalists; torture at the hands of the Asayish (the security forces); a weak judiciary and very little political or business accountability; a lack of budget or governmental transparency; a lack of business accountability; overly centralized rule with little real power at the local level; a lack of institutional autonomy; and the influence of two major parties in virtually all business, educational, and political decision-making institutions (see, e.g., Amnesty International 2009). A glaring example of controversies concerning alleged abuses of power, for instance, surfaced in April 2012 with the arrest and then death in Sulaimaniya prison of Mayor Zana Hama Salih, who was accused of corruption.

More details on these grievances can be found in Amnesty International's 2009 report, "Hope and Fear: Human Rights in the Kurdistan Region of Iraq," which has been made available on several websites, including the following:

- Amnesty International   http://www.amnesty.org/en/library/info/ MDE14/006/2009
- Refworld.com, an online   http://www.refworld.org/docid/49e6e8922.html resource of the UNHCR, the UN Refugee Agency
- Kurdipedia.org, an online   http://www.kurdipedia.org/?q=62435&lng=8 "wiki-style" repository of Kurd-related material

Legitimation Through Reform and Rights

Many of these grievances are long-standing. What is new is the way they have served to justify a call for a new governing paradigm that prioritizes good governance, institutional autonomy, and accountability. Activists argue that Kurdish authorities can no longer expect people to grant them the right to govern on the basis of their historic struggle against Baghdad. Nor can such authorities wave aside internal criticism with reference to the need for national security. Instead, critics argue, political authority in the Kurdistan region should rest with transparent and democratically elected institutions, and with parties held accountable for their performance.

This reform and rights model is not so much about moving beyond nationalism as it is an effort to reconstitute conceptions of Kurdish national interest so that "the good of Kurdistan" is as much about good governance at home as it is about the need to protect Kurds from external aggression through independence or autonomy. Zana Rauf Hama, a former member of the Kurdistan National Assembly from the opposition Gorran Party, put it this way in an interview in June 2012: "They [the ruling parties] are creating imaginary enemies to try and bury internal dissent. . . . If you go to a tall building that looks nice from outside, but you go inside and there is no electricity, do you think the people from outside and in will have the same idea about the building? I think it's the same for Kurdistan."

In their effort to frame their dissent as patriotic, protesters have flown the Kurdish flag, organized huge protests around Kurdish Newroz (New Year) celebrations, and made frequent references to the Kurdish nationalist struggle. They have also used religious imagery and activities to portray criticism of the KRG as a religious duty, or at least justifiable through Islamic teachings. Most obviously, this was done through huge public Friday prayer protest services conducted in Sara Square by opposition mullahs. Combining both religious and nationalist frames, demonstrators have also made frequent use of the symbolic politics of martyrdom, which was generally defined to include all who died in the course of the protests, whether they be activists or police. Banners with photographs of the dead were hung in Sara Square and elsewhere. These victims were constructed as a new sort of national martyr, martyred not at the hands of the Iraqi Baath Party but at the hands of KRG's security forces. Cumulatively, these demands were framed in ways that suggested it was both a patriotic and religious duty to support the protests.

New Mobilization Capacity

Such ideas about the basis on which authorities may claim the right to govern have been given new force not just by the Arab uprisings, which broadly legitimated a "reform and rights" discourse, but by structural changes that have given ordinary people new resources with which to promote such ideas and pressure authorities. In Iraqi Kurdistan, as elsewhere, the onset of regular and large-scale protests was made possible through the development of a new "mobilization capacity." In the Kurdish case, this derived from the creation and strong electoral performance of a well-funded opposition party led by a former leader of the Kurdish nationalist struggle; from the development of an opposition and independent media that has challenged taboos and raised many criticisms of the ruling parties; and from the development of autonomous nongovernmental organizations and clusters of opposition groups that have worked closely together to challenge the KRG.

Gorran

Dissatisfaction with the ruling parties and the changing balance of power was clearly evidenced in the formation of, and then popular support for, the Gorran Party, or "Movement for Change." Established in 2009 through an internal schism within the PUK leadership, the Gorran Party rapidly became the KRG's first serious opposition movement. Gorran's platform calls for the depoliticization of government institutions, making them independent of political parties; for the elimination of corruption; for the establishment of a democratic constitution; and for a more equitable distribution of wealth. In the 2009 elections for the Kurdistan National Assembly, Gorran won twenty-five seats. It is particularly strong in Sulaimaniya governorate, and in the 2009 election won about

303,000 votes there, compared to the 260,000 for the Kurdistani List shared by the KDP and PUK, according to figures supplied by the Gorran Election Office. In the March 2010 Iraqi parliamentary elections, Gorran won six of its eight parliamentary seats from Sulaimaniya Province. Gorran figures suggest that 61 percent of the party's support is from Sulaimaniya governorate.

> Search the website of the Gorran Party (http://www.gorran.net/En/) for more information on its activities.

Along with taking seats and forming a new opposition bloc in the parliament, Gorran provided the opposition movement significant new material, as well as human and ideological resources. Gorran founder Nawshirwan Mustafa was a key figure in the nationalist struggle against Saddam Hussein, and thus bestows "nationalist credentials" on the movement, as well as considerable charismatic authority. Although Gorran is internally divided by an "old" and "new" guard, its significant presence in the Kurdistan National Assembly, the electoral threat it posed the PUK, and its willingness to join forces with other smaller opposition parties all translated into increased visibility and leverage for opposition groups and activists.

Opposition Media

The growth of an opposition and independent media has also altered the balance of power between state and society in the Kurdistan region. The newspaper *Hawlati*, which began publication in 2000; *Lvin*, a trimonthly magazine started in 2002; the newspaper *Awane*, which began in 2006; the Speda TV satellite channel created by the Kurdistan Islamic Union party in 2008; and the satellite news channel KNN, launched by Gorran's Wesha company, have challenged the ruling parties for control over historic memory and have broken numerous taboos—especially concerning KDP and PUK leaders such as Massoud Barzani and Jalal Talabani. Collectively, they have played an important role in creating a new "information politics" that readily publicizes grievances and protesters' demands. By 2010, the organization Reporters Without Borders would describe a "veritable media boom" in the region, with around 850 recently registered new media outlets.

> Reporters Without Borders' complete 2010 report on the media in Kurdistan, *Between Freedom and Abuses: The Media Paradox in Iraqi Kurdistan*, can be found on the organization's website (http://en.rsf.org/IMG/pdf/rsf_rapport_kurdistan_irakien_nov_2010_gb.pdf).

The spread of new media also, as elsewhere, provided valuable new tools for activists seeking to garner support and challenge the government. Iraq as a whole has one of the lowest rates of Internet penetration in the Middle East and North Africa, with an estimated 7 percent penetration, compared to 35 percent in Egypt and around 40 percent in Tunisia (Freedom House 2012). But in the Kurdistan region an estimated 2 million people—around half the population—now regularly access the Internet, according to the KRG's Ministry of Transportation and Communication. Among students and young people, the number of Internet users is extremely high and students now use social media extensively, especially Facebook. According to a March 2011 *New York Times* article, activists also have ready access to reliable cell phones. Cell phone penetration in Iraq overall is around 75 percent, and cell phone companies have been operating in the Kurdistan region since 1999. As with analyses of uprisings elsewhere in the region, it is important not to exaggerate the importance of social media and cell phones, but they did facilitate communication, offer platforms for the airing of grievances, and help bring together clusters of activists around common goals (as discussed further below).

New Associational Networks

Increased mobilization capacity in the Kurdistan region is also a result of the expansion and development of civic and associational networks there. In general, the Kurdistan region of Iraq has a very low level of associational autonomy, and the vast majority of "nongovernmental" organizations in the region are affiliated with one of the major parties and receive stipends from the Kurdistan Regional Government. However, particularly after 2006, a small but important group of more independent associations, particularly from Sulaimaniya, began to work together and became more active in lobbying and pressuring the KRG. These groups were largely independent of the parties, although many later came to be sympathetic to Gorran.

Nongovernmental organizations (NGOs) and the new opposition media played a crucial role in the months following the Halabja protest of 2006 by defending those who were detained, publicizing protesters' demands, and putting direct pressure on authorities to deliver on their promises to the town. The NGOs involved in these campaigns created a coordination center that later became the Federation of Civil Society NGOs, an umbrella group of about fourteen active NGOs (Watts 2012). Several new NGOs were also established to focus more closely on political activism. Thus, out of Halabja came a new level of associational cooperation and coordination and an expanded political space with more aggressive and more independent nongovernmental actors. In December 2010 and January 2011, many of these civic groups came together to stage a series of protests against a new anti-demonstration law proposed by the Kurdistan National Assembly; these were networks that were reinvigorated in the Sulaimaniya protests that began a month or two later.

The Power of Human Decisions: Movement Characteristics

The new phase of contention in the Kurdistan region of Iraq cannot be explained only by reference to grievances, frames of action, or broader structural changes. It also is due to decisions and actions of activists themselves, testifying to the importance of challengers' strategies and the way such choices can promote large, broad-based, long-term protests. It is these decisions that help explain how activists, particularly in Sulaimaniya province, were able to convert the symbolic meaning and moment of opportunity that came with the Arab uprisings into the most serious internal challenge to KRG authority the region had yet seen.

The protests across Sulaimaniya evince several characteristics that facilitated their size and durability. They were horizontally and loosely organized, which allowed many different groups to participate. It is best to conceive of the Sulaimaniya Spring protests, for example, as consisting of networked clusters of overlapping groups and individuals rather than deeply rooted or institutionalized associations with clearly demarcated identities. Clearly, the movement was influenced and supported by several main opposition parties—the Kurdistan Islamic Union and Gorran, as well as the Communist Party—but these did not control or run it. Rather than a top-down hierarchy or centralized management system, which might have alienated some groups, the protests were structured through many different actors from different social sectors, and many of the organizations involved in the protests were formed at that time and did not survive past mid-April. The Ad Hoc Committee of Maidani Azadi, formed by a group of activists in the first days of the Sulaimaniya Spring protests, had a fluid and open membership that saw itself as responding to popular demand rather than directing the demonstrations. As its spokeswoman, Nasik Kadir, a Canadian trained sociologist and health worker, said in an interview at the time, "We don't represent the people—we are here to make sure the people are a little more organized, that's all. It is the street that moves us; it is not us that moves the street. We are not like a party telling people what we need them to do" (2011).

A second characteristic of the protests was their inclusiveness, particularly the incorporation of both civic and religious opposition as well as students. Those involved in the 2011 demonstrations included the new civil opposition (groups of activists who had worked together previously to call for an end to corruption, protection for journalists, and improvements in hospitals, among other changes); the longer-lived Federation of Civil Society NGOs; and professional organizations representing doctors, lawyers, and journalists. Students, especially from Sulaimaniya University, were critical for mobilization, working via Facebook and through cell phones and word of mouth. Numerous groups in support of the protests formed on Facebook: Shaqam, which by early 2013 had around 65,000 "friends"; 17 Shobat; Sulaimani Youth; and "We are all Rizhwan Ali" (named after Egypt's "We are all Khaled Said") were some of the most important Internet-based communities. These were formed by different individuals and groups (mostly students) and did not belong to the political parties. Although many of the protesters were young men, the demonstrations around the region exhibited some demographic diversity as well. Especially after the first week, when the protests became more peaceful and better organized, young women (especially university students) began to participate in the demonstrations, as did older men and women, sometimes bringing along young children.

In a striking departure from past demonstrations, religious opposition figures and organizations also supported the protests. This was one of the first times the non-Islamist civil-society-based opposition cooperated with the religious opposition, although co-operation between Islamic and other opposition parties had been more routine. Along with Islamic political parties, the Kurdistan Islamic Union (which has loose links to the Muslim Brotherhood) and a number of mullahs joined the protests and became prominent spokesmen. This diversity and breadth of societal representation—especially religious leaders and women—helped refute accusations that the protesters were simply a bunch of "troublemakers" (as some party press referred to them).

A third characteristic of the protests was activists' use of nonviolent repertoires of contention that allowed for mass participation and sustained protest. Afternoon demonstrations featured an open microphone, speeches, marches, music, tents, and the re-occupation of a nationalized space: Sara Square, which had great symbolic import to the Kurdish national struggle. After a few early skirmishes between protesters and security forces, some demonstrators and civic leaders formed a group of about 200 people known as the White Group—loosely modeled on the Muslim Brotherhood in Egypt's work in Tahrir Square—to patrol Sara Square and maintain the peace. Other groups cleaned the square each evening. Religious opposition leaders also led Friday prayer protests that involved thousands of people in the protests.

KRG Responses: The Power and Limitations of Protest Politics

Mass, sustained protests can achieve many different things: they can call attention to issues; change the agenda domestically, regionally, and internationally; provoke regime responses that in turn attract new supporters; create new communities and protest cultures; forge new relationships that may develop later into important associations or networks; embarrass or shame officials into conceding to activist demands; and, if large and widespread enough, create mass "ungovernability," bring economic production to a standstill, and force leaders to resign and regimes to promise change.

In Sulaimaniya, the demonstrations of 2010–2013 changed the agenda domestically and raised international awareness about problems of KRG rule. They forced a series of debates over governance in the area and extracted a series of promises from party leaders and government officials. They created new networks and connections between activists, giving them valuable experience in mobilization and protest. KRG officials also learned from the protests, and began, for instance, training security forces in crowd control to try and prevent bloodshed during protest events.

However, if limited in geographic scope or to one sector of the population, street demonstrations may attract attention and some promises of reform, but activists may have little else in terms of immediate policy change to show for their efforts and the risks they take. They can fizzle out as activists exhaust themselves, and they can lead to factionalization. Moreover, decentralized, mass protests in and of themselves are rarely effective mechanisms for negotiating complicated institutional reform. This was amply demonstrated in countries such as Egypt and Tunisia in the aftermath of their Arab uprisings, and became very clear in Kurdistan as well.

Protesters' efforts to use mass protest to promote reform within the KRG were complicated by several factors. First, they did not seek a revolutionary overthrow of the regime
but a series of democratizing reforms. Although these might seem more modest goals
than ousting a dictator, they can be equally difficult to achieve because the "solution" to
institutional corruption, inefficiency, and lack of autonomy is complicated, involves many
different actors, and requires long-term commitments to change that are often stymied
by individual self-interest. Second, the fact that they were largely limited in geographic
scope to Sulaimaniya Province limited activists' leverage and credibility. That there were
no sustained demonstrations outside of Sulaimaniya was not due to lack of effort; in fact,
there were some short-lived protests, and many attempts at organizing beyond the region.
However, none produced sustained daily demonstrations such as those that occurred in
Sulaimaniya and other cities.

A number of factors help explain the lack of mass protest in Erbil Province. Efforts to
mobilize there were more fragmented, and there was some competition for movement
control between religious elites and civic activists. There is a higher level of repression
and political control in Erbil than in Sulaimaniya, which is well known as a cultural,
NGO, and "movement" capital. Many activists in Erbil reported preemptive crackdowns
on activists before protests even began there, for instance. More generally, the rights and
reform framing of the Arab uprisings was less influential in Erbil due to the different
nature of state-society relations there and the nature of KDP governance. KDP-society
relations are more closely linked to tribal structures, for example, which are more important to the political and social fabric in Erbil. Finally, both KRG officials and ordinary
people worried that internal dissent might jeopardize Kurdish stability, prosperity, and
the gains of the past decade.

The mixed impacts of the protests are reflected in government and party responses
to them. These indicated a clear tension within the KRG between the desire to maintain
order and protect the "House of Kurdistan," on the one hand, and traditional KRG and
party sensitivity to domestic and international opinion, on the other. In response to the
Sulaimaniya protests, the Kurdistan National Assembly held a number of emergency
meetings, and in early March Prime Minister Barham Salih survived a proposal for a
vote of no confidence over his handling of them. KDP leader and KRG president Massoud Barzani initially referred to the protesters as "enemies trying to create sedition and
chaos" (see, e.g., the *Los Angeles Times* of February 18, 2011), but by early March and
April he offered more conciliatory statements in which he promised substantial reform.
In mid-March 2011, Prime Minister Salih issued a four-page response to the protesters'
demands and issued an apology for shortcomings of the KRG and the deaths of activists.
Also in mid-March, PUK leader and President Jalal Talabani of Iraq gave a conciliatory
statement in support of the protesters, saying that "We, the Patriotic Union of Kurdistan,
express support for peaceful meetings, demonstrations and sit-in occasions; and strongly
oppose any violence acts or the use of arms against the demonstrators" (Kurd Net, March
17, 2011).

An article on Iraqi President Talabani's remarks about the Sulaimaniya protests can be found at the Kurd Net website (http://www.ekurd.net/mismas/articles/misc2011/3/state4857.htm).

Meanwhile, security forces used tear gas and other anti-riot techniques on protesters on the street, hundreds of activists were detained, opposition TV stations were attacked and set on fire, journalists and civil society leaders were harassed, and party-affiliated militias roamed the streets. Counter-demonstrations in support of the KDP were also held. Pro-KRG media sources, such as the KDP-affiliated Kurdistan TV, showed hundreds of KDP supporters on the streets of Erbil with yellow armbands, driving around the city with pictures of Masoud Barzani and the KDP's flag, and dancing to the music in the background. In March, masked men with firearms and clubs attacked protesters, set tents alight in Sara Square, and drove away protesters while security forces stood by; in April, security forces arrived en masse to break up the gathering in Sara Square by force; and on April 18, they destroyed the podium and ended the protests. On April 19, the government's Security Committee for Sulaimaniya Province banned all unlicensed demonstrations. Legislation passed by the Kurdistan Regional Government in December 2011 gives authorities wide discretion to decide whether to approve a license for a protest. There was also a legal crackdown after the protests: hundreds of people were detained, and many put on trial.

Conclusion

Conceptually and theoretically, the study of dissent under the Kurdistan Regional Government (KRG) demonstrates how ordinary people may begin to renegotiate the terms of a hierarchical and sometimes authoritarian state-society relationship in a state that is not fully independent. Through mass mobilization and the effective use of symbols and frames that resonated with many members of the population, activists have begun to change the balance of power between rulers and ruled.

The Sulaimaniya Spring and the wave of protests across the Kurdistan region can be understood as part of a growing but geographically differentiated effort by ordinary people to redefine what is understood by the "national interest" and to lay claim to the symbolic politics of national memory and conversation, rather than leaving such domains to political elites. Activists in the Halabja protest of 2006 wanted Halabjans themselves to be able to define and manage the city's memory and resources. Activists in 2011 wanted to decide what kinds of policies and governance would be in the best interests of Kurds. Disabled activists in 2012 identified themselves as citizens with rights and needs that the government was not adequately addressing. All of this indicates a new emphasis on accountable and democratic government, rather than an almost exclusive focus on the nationalist mission. At the same time both the emergent protest culture in Sulaimaniya Province and the relative rarity of protests in other parts of the Kurdistan region point to the fact that state-society relations are not uniform across territories; that levels of "stateness" and legitimacy can vary significantly; and that even in a nationalizing community such as Kurdistan-in-Iraq, we should not assume a uniform response to processes of state-building and governance.

———————

Much of the information in this chapter was gathered during multiple research trips to the Kurdistan region of Iraq between 2009 and 2013. The author wishes to thank Peshawa Ahmad and Shadman Hiwa for their invaluable research assistance and translations from Sorani Kurdish to English, as well as everyone who gave generously of their time to speak with me.

References and Further Research

Amnesty International. 2009. "Hope and Fear: Human Rights in the Kurdistan Region of Iraq." http://www.amnesty.org/en/library/info/MDE14/006/2009.

Bengio, Ofra. 2012. *The Kurds of Iraq: Building a State Within a State*. Boulder, CO: Lynne Rienner.

Fischer-Tahir, Andrea. 2012. "Searching for Sense: The Concept of Genocide as Part of Knowledge Production in Iraqi Kurdistan." In *Writing the History of Iraq: Historiographical and Political Challenges*, edited by Jordi Tejel, Peter Sluglett, Riccardo Bocco, and Hamit Bozarslan, 227–246. Hackensack, NJ: World Scientific Publishing.

Hiltermann, Joost R. 2007. *A Poisonous Affair: America, Iraq, and the Gassing of Halabja*. Cambridge: Cambridge University Press.

———. 2008. "The 1988 Anfal Campaign in Iraqi Kurdistan." In *Online Encyclopedia of Mass Violence*, edited by Claire Andrieu. http://www.massviolence.org/IMG/article_PDF/The-1988-Anfal-Campaign-in-Iraqi-Kurdistan.pdf.

McDowall, David. 1996. *A Modern History of the Kurds*. London: I.B. Tauris.

Migdal, Joel S. 2013. "Foreword." In *The Everyday Life of the State: A State-in-Society Approach*, edited by Adam White. Seattle: University of Washington Press.

Natali, Denise. 2010. *The Kurdish Quasi-state: Development and Dependency in Post–Gulf War Iraq*. Syracuse, NY: Syracuse University Press.

Reporters Without Borders. 2010. *Between Freedom and Abuses: The Media Paradox in Iraqi Kurdistan*. http://en.rsf.org/IMG/pdf/rsf_rapport_kurdistan_irakien_nov_2010_gb.pdf.

Stansfield, Gareth. 2013. "The Unravelling of the Post–First World War State System? The Kurdistan Region of Iraq and the Transformation of the Middle East." *International Affairs* 89, no. 2: 259–282.

Tarrow, Sidney. 2011. *Power in Movement: Social Movements and Contentious Politics*. 3rd ed. New York: Cambridge University Press.

Watts, Nicole F. 2012. "The Role of Symbolic Capital in Protest: State-Society Relations and the Destruction of the Halabja Martyrs Monument in the Kurdistan Region of Iraq." *Comparative Studies of South Asia, Africa and the Middle East* 32, no. 1: 70–85.

Interviews Cited

Zana Rauf Hama, June16, 2012, Sulaimaniya, Kurdistan region, Iraq.
Nasik Kadir, March 29, 2011, Sulaimaniya, Kurdistan region, Iraq.

Related Websites

News Outlets

Rudaw English: http://rudaw.net/english/kurdistan. Website of online Kurdish newspaper.
Kurdistan Islamic Union: http://www.kurdiu.org/en/. Click on "News" for news in various
   categories (National, KIU, Iraq, General, Technology).

Political Parties

Gorran (Movement for Change) Party: http://www.gorran.net/En/Default.aspx.
Kurdistan Democratic Party (of Iraq): http://www.kdp.se/.
Patriotic Union of Kurdistan: http://www.pukpb.org/en/.
Patriotic Union of Kurdistan media: http://www.pukmedia.com/EN/EN_Sereta.aspx.

Think Tanks and Agencies

Freedom House. 2012. Freedom of the Press, 2012: Iraq. http://www.freedomhouse.org/
   report/freedom-press/2012/iraq.
International Crisis Group (ICG): http://www.crisisgroup.org/en/regions/middle-east-north-
   africa/iraq-iran-gulf/iraq.aspx. The ICG has many useful reports on Kurdish politics in
   Iraq and on the Arab uprisings.

14

Energy and Geopolitics in the Gulf
Mixing Water and Oil

ASLI ILGIT

In the early 1930s, King Abdulaziz Al Saud (Ibn Saud) invited American geologists to Saudi Arabia to survey the kingdom's natural resources, with the immediate concern being water. The search, however, led to the discovery of oil in the eastern part of the country. This was the beginning not only of a long-term relationship between the United States and Saudi Arabia, but also of intertwined politics of oil and water in the kingdom. Today, Saudi Arabia, along with the other Gulf countries—Bahrain, Qatar, Kuwait, the United Arab Emirates (UAE), Yemen, Oman, Iraq, and Iran—are among the top ten oil and natural gas producers in the world, holding 50 percent and 40 percent of proven reserves of crude oil and natural gas, respectively (see Tables 14.1 and 14.2). Yet, with the exception of Iraq and Iran, all remaining Gulf countries are also among the ten most water-stressed countries, with the least available water per capita, according to the most recent estimates of Maplecroft, a British risk consulting firm.

This abundance of oil but lack of sufficient natural freshwater compelled the Gulf countries to implement water and energy policies and to invest in technologies that help them convert their oil into water. The Gulf countries have long been applying their oil wealth—17 percent of their own oil production—to generate water. The oil-for-water usage increased the Gulf's energy consumption, which is one of the highest worldwide. According to Alterman and Dziuban (2010), the Gulf countries' desalination of seawater accounts for more than half of global desalination, around 57 percent, with Saudi Arabia and the UAE together representing about 30 percent of that amount.

The Gulf states' energy policy in the first decade of the twenty-first century has undergone important rethinking, as leaders there began to understand the demographic, economic, environmental, and political challenges arising from their energy security. Some of the old policies—mainly for maintaining domestic political stability, ameliorating poverty, and managing consumption habits of Gulf societies—continue to shape energy dynamics in the region. Despite the increasing population and energy demand at home, governments in the Gulf continue to subsidize the costs related to water and energy use, thus further encouraging energy consumption of their citizens.

Yet at the same time, new concerns—such as rapidly depleted Gulf aquifers, the worldwide overuse of water, a global economic crisis beginning in 2007–2008 with a highly volatile oil market, soaring global food prices, and climate change—are prompting local and regional initiatives to manage the remaining energy resources. One of the examples

227

Table 14.1

Key Statistics: Oil and Natural Gas in the Gulf States, 2011

Country	Proven oil reserves (billion barrels)	Total oil production (1,000 barrels/ day)	Total oil consumption (1,000 barrels/ day)	Crude oil exports (1,000 barrels/day)	Proven natural gas reserves (billion m³)	Natural gas production (billion m³)	Natural gas consumption (billion m³)	Natural gas exports (billion m³)
Bahrain	0.13	48	52	153	92.03	12.25	12.25	0
Iran	137.00	4,226	1,700	2,295	33,070	146.10	144.60	8.42
Iraq	115.00	2,629	720	2,600	3,171	1.30	1.30	0
Kuwait	104.00	2,692	410	1,365	1,798	11.73	12.62	0
Oman	5.50	891	123	253	849	35.90	17.50	11.49
Qatar	25.40	1,641	160	704	25,201	116.70	21.80	94.90
Saudi Arabia	263.00	11,154	2,620	6,844	8,028	99.23	99.23	0
UAE	98.00	3,088	630	2,036	6,088	51.28	60.54	7.65
Yemen	3.00	165	130	191	479	6.24	0.80	5.48

Sources: Compiled from OPEC *Annual Statistical Bulletin* 2013 (http://www.opec.org/opec_web/static_files_project/media/downloads/publications/ASB2013.pdf), CIA *World Factbook* (https://www.cia.gov/library/publications/the-world-factbook/index.html), and U.S. Energy Information Administration (http://www.eia.gov/countries/data.cfm#undefined).

Table 14.2

World Producers of Crude Oil and Natural Gas

Producers of crude oil	Million tons	Percent of world total	Proved reserves, percent of world total
Saudi Arabia	517	12.9	16.1
Russian Federation	510	12.7	5.3
United States	346	8.6	1.9
Iran	215	5.4	9.1
China	203	5.1	0.9
Canada	169	4.2	10.6
UAE	149	3.7	5.9
Venezuela	148	3.7	17.9
Mexico	144	3.6	0.7
Nigeria	139	3.5	2.3
Rest of the world	1,471	36.6	29.3
World	4,011	100.0	100.0

Producers of natural gas	Billion cubic meters (m^3)	Percent of world total	Proved reserves, percent of world total
Russian Federation	677	20.0	21.4
United States	651	19.2	4.1
Canada	160	4.7	1.0
Qatar	151	4.5	12.0
Iran	149	4.4	15.9
Norway	106	3.1	1.0
China	103	3.0	1.5
Saudi Arabia	92	2.7	3.9
Indonesia	92	2.7	1.4
Netherlands	81	2.4	0.5
Rest of the world	1,126	33.3	37.3
World	3,388	100.0	100.0

Sources: Compiled from Key World Energy Statistics, International Energy Agency, 2012 (http://www.iea.org/publications/freepublications/publication/kwes.pdf); BP *Statistical Review of World Energy*, June 2012 (http://www.bp.com/statisticalreview).

of this policy initiative is Saudi Arabia's decision in 2010 to establish a fully funded and tax-exempt renewable energy center, the King Abdullah City for Atomic and Renewable Energy (KACARE), to draft policies for renewable and nuclear energy deployment plans and to coordinate the action of the different national renewable energy centers, research institutes, and private sector enterprises. In sum, in the face of twenty-first-century challenges, Gulf governments have to consolidate their increasingly contested power at home, while also working to secure their place in a changing global energy market. This chapter examines the causes and dynamics of the struggle over oil and water, and analyzes the implications of petroleum and hydropolitics of the Gulf states for regional and global energy politics. First addressed are issues surrounding oil and natural gas, after which issues of water use and challenges to water security in the Gulf region are examined. Finally, an estimate of future prospects regarding energy, water, and geopolitics in the Gulf region is presented.

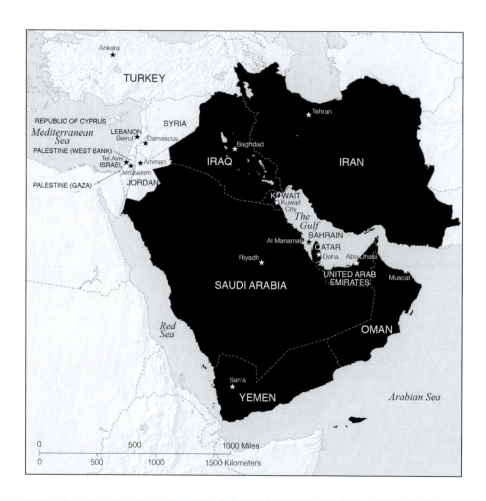

The King Abdullah City for Atomic and Renewable Energy (KACARE) website (http://www.kacare.gov.sa/en) offers information on the research and investment strategies of this major initiative of the Saudi government's renewable energy policy.

Oil in the Gulf Region

In the Gulf region, oil was first discovered in Iran and Iraq in the early twentieth century. The discovery of oil brought about wide-ranging economic, social, and political changes in these countries, whose economies had previously relied mainly on the trade of dates, fish, and pearls.

History and Background

Oil fields and refineries in the rest of the Gulf region began to emerge in the 1930s as the rulers of Bahrain, Saudi Arabia, Kuwait, and Qatar signed concession agreements with major oil companies such as Standard Oil of California and Gulf Oil (both currently Chevron), and the Anglo-Persian Oil Company (currently BP).The burst of oil exploration activities in the region continued throughout the 1930s, with the first crude oil shipment from Saudi Arabia to refineries abroad in 1939. World War II stopped major oil exploration activities and delayed oil development in the region. In these early decades of Gulf oil politics, foreign oil companies took over the ownership and management of the Gulf oil industry under the generous concession agreements they had initially negotiated with the Gulf states. By the 1950s, with the increase in oil production and knowledge of oil reserves in the region, the Gulf rulers began to demand an equal share of profits in addition to the royalty fees that the oil companies had agreed to pay.

This change in Gulf oil deals was the result of a transformation in the relationship between oil-producing states and international oil companies, which had begun in the 1930s and gained steam in the context of anticolonial nationalist movements. Mexico's nationalization of its oil industry in the late 1930s and Venezuela's demand for a "fifty-fifty deal" in the early 1940s, in which the taxes and royalties due to Venezuela would be equal to the oil company's net profit, fundamentally altered the relationships and balance within the international oil market. After World War II, Iran nationalized the Anglo-Persian Oil Company in 1951, an action that would eventually prompt a Western-supported coup of the Iranian government. Gulf countries obtained their independence in the 1960s and 1970s, and they subsequently nationalized their oil and natural gas industries. With Britain's withdrawal from its former "protectorates," Kuwait, Bahrain, Qatar, and the UAE became independent and negotiated with the international oil companies and major oil-consuming states to take control over their own natural oil resources. The energy nationalization process was complete by the end of the 1980s and early 1990s with Saudi Arabia's acquisition of Aramco—the Arabian American Oil Company, a consortium of mainly American oil companies—which became Saudi Aramco. This era also witnessed the discovery of a natural gas field, the so-called North Field, in Qatar in 1971, which is considered the largest single natural gas reserve in the world.

By the 1960s, the Gulf countries had also come to realize the power they had over oil markets if they coordinated their policies, especially pricing. Meeting in Baghdad in 1960, Saudi Arabia, Kuwait, Iraq, and Iran, along with Venezuela, established an oil cartel, the Organization of the Petroleum Exporting Countries (OPEC), to work together in their negotiations with international oil companies. They were able to test their newly acquired collaborative powers by organizing a boycott of oil sales to any country that supported Israel against the Arab states in the 1973 Arab-Israeli War. Through OPEC, the Gulf countries organized an oil embargo against Israel, the United States, and several European countries, resulting in a quadrupling of the price of oil within weeks. Saudi Arabia was instrumental during this time, both within OPEC as it negotiated with its main rival, Iran, to keep a united front, and with outside partners in the oil-consuming world, such as the United States. The embargo lasted from October 1973 until March 1974, resulting in a reduction of oil sales by 4 million barrels, which affected the international market significantly. By replacing the marketing power of big international oil companies with a consortium of sovereign countries, OPEC changed

---

Box 14.1

National Oil Companies of the Gulf States

Abu Dhabi National Oil Company (ADNOC)

Bahrain National Oil Company (BANOCO)

Kuwait Petroleum Corporation (KPC)

National Iranian Oil Company (NIOC)

Petroleum Development Oman (PDO)

Qatar Petroleum (QP)

Saudi Aramco

---

the geopolitical context of the oil market and proved it was a force to be reckoned with on the international energy market.

The Organization of the Petroleum Exporting Countries (OPEC) was founded in Baghdad in 1960 by Iran, Iraq, Kuwait, Saudi Arabia, and Venezuela. Qatar, Indonesia, Libya, the United Arab Emirates, Algeria, and Nigeria joined later. The "About Us" page on its website (http://www.opec.org/opec_web/en/17.htm) offers general information on the organization, including material on its history and member countries.

The Gulf states today harbor 50 percent and 40 percent of proven worldwide reserves of crude oil and natural gas, respectively, and they currently produce 30 percent of the world's oil and 15 percent of the world's natural gas. Their state-owned oil and gas industries are the major players in the global oil market and the single largest economic sector in all Gulf countries, accounting for about 80 percent of their government revenue, according to the estimates of the Economist Intelligence Unit (*The GCC in 2020: Broadening the Economy* 2010). According to the National Bank of Abu Dhabi (NBAD), oil production by the Gulf Cooperation Council countries (see Box 14.2) reached a record level in 2012, with crude oil output averaging about 17 million barrels per day.

Domestic Consumption of Oil

Saudi Arabia's oil reserves have long been considered a "cushion" for the global oil market. It is the only OPEC country with a production capacity that can make up global supply shortfalls whenever they happen. In the long run, other Gulf countries such as Iraq and Iran are likely to increase their oil and natural gas production in competition with Saudi Arabia, in order to meet global demand. Yet, importantly, the Gulf countries

---

Box 14.2

The Gulf Cooperation Council

The Gulf Cooperation Council (GCC) (http://www.gcc-sg.org/eng/index.html) is a coalition formed in 1981 by six Arab monarchies on the Gulf: Bahrain, Kuwait, Oman, Qatar, Saudi Arabia, and the United Arab Emirates. The tumultuous events of the late 1970s in the region—the Iranian Revolution, the Soviet invasion of Afghanistan, the Iran-Iraq War—triggered a response by these Arab monarchies to promote political and economic coordination, security, and unity in the region.

---

have also become one of the best customers of their own oil. Between 1980 and 2011, for example, Saudi Arabia's domestic oil consumption increased more than fourfold. In 2011, Saudi Arabia consumed about one-fourth of its own production, or nearly 3 million barrels per day. It has consequently become the seventh largest oil-consuming state, according to the U.S. Energy Information Administration (EIA). Other Gulf countries' thirst for their own oil has also been growing by more than 50 percent since the beginning of the twenty-first century.

This increase in domestic oil consumption is a result of three developments in the region. First, the rapid population growth in the Gulf countries, driven by a young population with high birth rates and an influx of expatriate workers from other countries, generates more demand for energy. The population of the six Gulf Cooperation Council countries grew from 33 million in 2004 to about 47 million in 2011, according to a recent report by Booz & Company (AlMunajjed and Sabbagh 2011), a global management consulting firm. Citizens under the age of twenty-five account for one-half to one-third of their population, while expats make up one-third of the total GCC population. In Saudi Arabia, for example, nearly 51 percent of the population is under twenty-five, while in the United Arab Emirates and Qatar, foreign nationals constitute nearly 80 percent and 75 percent of population, respectively. These demographic trends generate political and social challenges for the governments, especially in the larger context of Arab unrest, yet their implications for energy consumption patterns also loom large.

Second, despite the efforts to diversify their economies, Gulf countries still rely heavily on income from oil and natural gas. Energy income is used to subsidize other economic sectors and to fund initiatives to create new jobs within existing underperforming sectors. In other words, the oil economy is the main engine of growth for other areas of economic development, and it will continue to be until newer economic activities become self-sustaining. Moreover, as the demand for energy continues to increase, these state-led economies need more of their income from energy exports to produce more energy for their own use. Saudi Arabia is a good illustration: 10 percent of the country's energy output is already being used by Saudi Aramco, the national oil company of Saudi Arabia, to produce energy, according to the U.S. Energy Information Administration.

Third, the Gulf governments have had to focus on strengthening their internal political power and legitimacy. Although all the Gulf monarchies weathered the uprisings that, beginning in 2010, shook the Arab world and deposed several long-time leaders in other countries, the challenges of meeting the expectations of their subjects still exist. For instance, alleviating poverty, especially among their Bedouin populations, through social welfare programs, is important, as is relieving social and economic pressures on their citizens via subsidies. The monarchies subsidize energy, agriculture, and industrial sectors as well as domestic consumption of energy at home. Rulers of the Gulf countries have also used their oil wealth to provide their citizens with annual cash stipends and free college education and health care. In 2011, for example, the Kuwaiti emir distributed US$4 billion and free food items to citizens over the span of fourteen months, while Saudi Arabia announced a financial aid package that includes jobs, interest-free home loans, pay raises, and student scholarships for its citizens, at a price tag of about US$36 billion, as reported by Jennifer Koons (2011), a *Congressional Quarterly* researcher.

Geopolitics of Gulf Oil

Energy security has become a major priority for both oil-consuming and oil-producing states, leading to a constant search for and bolstering of new, reliable, and sustainable technologies, sources, and partners. In today's oil market, new discoveries in other parts of the world, such as a surge in North American shale oil production and rising African oil exports, seem to take much of the pressure off the Gulf oil producers. For the United States, these new sources of energy allow it to import less crude oil from the Middle East. However, China's energy needs have been rising, and Middle Eastern energy sales to China are surging. Moreover, with the current United Nations, United States, and European Union sanctions on Iranian oil and natural gas exports, the Gulf oil producers remain strategically important. Therefore, the Gulf countries are still producing at or very near capacity, with Saudi Arabia producing around 11 million barrels per day and the UAE and Kuwait both pumping around 3 million barrels per day in 2011 (see Table 14.1).

In the face of these domestic and global challenges, Gulf countries work toward diversifying their energy economies. Kuwait, for example, has entered bids for hydrocarbon exploration licenses in Afghanistan, and Saudi Arabia opened old reservoirs and plans to build more refineries in order to sell refined products in addition to crude oil. Even though these investments in new energy initiatives are, to a large degree, intended to help sustain Gulf countries' domestic economic and political power, international players in the energy market watch these efforts with caution and concern. Saudi investments in refineries, for example, not only raise questions about its crude oil supply capacity, but they also intensify competition with the major refinery powers in Asia, such as India, China, and Japan.

Despite the increasing role of other oil suppliers, the countries of the Gulf region, and Saudi Arabia in particular, remain significant players in the global oil market. With approximately 263 billion barrels, Saudi Arabia holds the world's largest proven oil reserves. Equally important is the fact that the cost of oil extraction in Saudi Arabia is one of the lowest in the world, less than two dollars per barrel, because of the location of its crude oil near the surface of the desert and the size of its oil fields. This makes Saudi oil the most affordable on the market, compared to the global average cost of about eleven dollars per barrel in 2011.

The Implication for Water Consumption

Energy production—extraction, transport, and processing of oil, gas, and coal; irrigation for biofuel crops—is not only expensive financially, it is also costly in terms of water. The International Energy Agency (IEA) projects an 85 percent rise in water consumption worldwide over the period to 2035, which indicates, among other things, more water-intensive energy generation. The competition for water resources is already intense due to worldwide population and economic growth. The Gulf, a water-stressed region to start with, has followed the increasing competition over water with great concern.

Water in the Gulf Region

The Gulf countries are characterized by high temperature and humidity levels, as well as limited or irregular rainfall. Despite the fact that a number of international rivers bring freshwater to the region, including the Tigris and Euphrates Rivers and their tributaries, nearly all Gulf countries suffer from water scarcity, and their water consumption exceeds total renewable water resources.

Water Uses and Resources in the Gulf

Despite these climactic and geological challenges, and with already scarce freshwater resources, the Gulf countries have undertaken various water-intensive economic development projects. For example, Saudi Arabia, despite its arid climate and unreliable surface water, was for decades the world's sixth largest wheat producer, and is still home to the world's largest single integrated dairy farm, Al Safi Dairy, which milks approximately 450 cows every eight minutes. At this farm, 2,300 gallons of water or more are needed to produce one gallon of milk. A similarly staggering statistic is that, on a per capita basis, Saudi citizens consume 91 percent more water than the international average, according to the country's Saline Water Conversion Corporation. Urban centers and industrial parks all around the kingdom rely on approximately thirty desalination plants and a network of 3,100 miles of pipelines to get their water. Other Gulf countries are no different. The global consulting firm Booz & Company reported that on a per capita basis, citizens in the United Arab Emirates consume 83 percent more water than the global average, which is about six times more water than the British average. Qatar and Oman are also above the global average for water consumption.

Box 14.3

Water Resources: Terminology

Aquifer   An underground layer of rock or soil that stores water.

Desalination   The process of converting seawater to freshwater.

Freshwater   Water that theoretically can be used for drinking, hygiene, agriculture,
                   and industry; but not all of this water is accessible. Only 2.5 percent
                   of the earth's water is freshwater, of which less than 1 percent is in
                   liquid form on the surface—such as rivers, streams, and lakes.

Renewable water   Water that is replenished yearly in the process of water turnover on
                   the earth.

Water scarcity   A complex concept that includes different dimensions, such as scarcity
                   in availability, in access to water services, and lack of adequate water
                   infrastructure. In general, experts refer to "absolute" water scarcity when
                   people have less than 500 cubic meters of water per year per capita.

Water stress   Similarly, water stress refers to conditions under which people have
                   between 500 and 1,000 cubic meters of water per year per capita. Or,
                   by another definition, countries could be defined as water-stressed if
                   they extract more than 20 percent of their renewable water resources.

For more information on Saudi Arabia's Al Safi Dairy, the world's biggest integrated dairy farm, see the video on YouTube (http://www.youtube.com/watch?v=KL3aUuDjMTw) produced by DeLaval, the company that manufactures the farm's milking equipment.

DeLaval's website (http://www.delaval.com/) offers insight into the company's philosophy, practices, and customers.

Water is allocated predominantly to three sectors: agriculture, industry, and home use (see Table 14.3). The amount of water used for agriculture is more than that for industry and home use combined. For instance, 54 percent of Kuwait's water and 88 percent of Saudi Arabia's water go to agriculture. The Gulf countries invested in domestic agriculture with the goal of becoming self-sufficient. Because of this policy goal, the Gulf governments, until very recently, heavily subsidized their agricultural sector, increasing water demand and pressure on water resources. In the meantime, population growth, a rising standard of living, and increasing urbanization also have increased pressure on water use.

Table 14.3

Water Sources and Use in the Gulf States, 2009

Country	Total renewable water resources (m³/capita/ year)	Freshwater withdrawn as a percent of total renewable water resources	Percent of municipal water withdrawal	Percent of agricultural water withdrawal	Percent of industrial water withdrawal
Bahrain	99.0	219.8	49	45	6
Iran	1,880.0	68.0	7	92	1
Iraq	2,461.0	87.0	6	79	15
Kuwait	7.6	2,465.0	44	54	2
Oman	526.0	87.0	10	89	1
Qatar	36.0	455.0	39	59	2
Saudi Arabia	90.0	943.0	9	88	3
UAE	22.0	2,032.0	15	83	2
Yemen	90.0	169.0	8	90	2

Source: Compiled by Asli Ilgit from Frenken (2009).

With almost no surface water resources, water used in these countries comes mainly from fresh groundwater sources or from desalinated seawater. The UAE, for example, gets 72 percent of its water from groundwater, 21 percent from desalination, and 7 percent from recycled water, according to the Environment Agency of Abu Dhabi. Similarly, in Saudi Arabia, already the world's largest producer of desalinated water, desalination accounts for about 70 percent of drinking water consumption. The kingdom has invested nearly US$25 billion over the last eighty years developing the technology for desalination and building desalination plants. Given its extensive experience with desalination technology, and its escalating need for more water in the foreseeable future, the kingdom plans to build the world's largest desalination plant, with a capacity of 600,000 cubic meters of water per day, by 2018.

Challenges to Water Security

In the late 1980s, Boutros Boutros-Ghali, the former foreign minister of Egypt and later the UN Secretary General, famously stated that the next war in the Middle East would be over water, bringing global attention to the militarily securitized water resources in the region. Even though his main concern was the potential for interstate water conflicts, water security issues have increasingly become a global issue. Today, the Gulf region faces major challenges due to its fast demographic growth, potentially unsustainable economic development to meet the demands of its population, and the mismanagement of water resources. Additionally, global trends such as climate change and soaring food prices exacerbate the challenges.

One of the major hydropolitical concerns in domestic politics in the Gulf is ensuring citizens' access to freshwater. This is becoming a challenge for two reasons. First, major cities throughout the Gulf region are located far from their water sources, and it is becoming increasingly costly to bring water to populations living in these cities. For example, Riyadh, the capital city of Saudi Arabia, is located almost at the center of the kingdom, far from its desalination plants along the coasts. The water used in Riyadh arrives through long pipelines that are costly to build and maintain. Similarly, in Sanaa, Yemen's capital city, the major sources of drinking water are private tankers that dock at the country's ports. The water is then trucked to and sold in urban areas. As urban population growth remains high, both through birth rates and migration—already over 75 percent of the Gulf's citizens live in cities—the demand for urban water supplies will remain high. The increased urban consumption will only raise pressure on the very limited water supplies, which are already drained by the agriculture sector. In some areas in Saudi Arabia, underground aquifers have been totally depleted. These underground water reserves formed over centuries, and they cannot replenish at the same rate that they are depleted.

Concerns about limited quantities of available water are compounded by concerns about water quality. Major groundwater aquifers on the coastline have been contaminated due to saltwater intrusion from over-pumping from desalinization plants. Contamination has also resulted from a rise in sea levels, while pesticides and fertilizers from agricultural production and pollution from oil industries endanger both the limited surface water resources and groundwater. Water quality and quantity problems coupled with the region's extreme climate make the Gulf countries particularly susceptible to the effects of climate change, which include increased soil temperatures, droughts, increased sea levels, and water salinity.

All this intensifies the competition for water and creates an environment ripe for political instability and conflict. Conflicts over water at the subnational and local levels have already occurred throughout the Gulf. For example, in Yemen, where annual per capita water availability is only 125 cubic meters, compared to the global average of 2,500 cubic meters, local communities, tribes, farmers, and politicians have been in constant conflict over water allocation to agriculture. As Gerhard Lichtenthaeler (2010)—an expert working for the German Technical Cooperation Agency in Yemen—reports, the irrigated area in Yemen increased tenfold, from 37,000 to 407,000 hectares (91,000 to 1 million acres), between 1970 and 2004, and 40 percent of that water came from pumping deep groundwater aquifers. In Sanaa, this heavy reliance on wells stirs tension, especially between local villagers, whose drinking-water source is usually a spring or a cistern, and farmers, who insist on drilling more wells for their water-intensive cash crops such as qat (a mild narcotic leaf, chewed by most Yemenis on a regular basis), citrus, and bananas. Local communities also try to subvert authorities: in 2009, almost 100 new wells were drilled without permits. The lack of government legitimacy and local people's resistance to regulations and laws further intensify tensions among different stakeholders.

Addressing Water Challenges

The Gulf states have become increasingly aware that water mismanagement and unsustainable levels of water consumption are serious issues that need to be addressed. In fact, Dr. Abdullatif bin Rashid Al-Zayani, the Secretary General of the GCC, acknowledged in

2012 that "the challenge of water is the most important and dangerous challenge facing the Gulf" (Malek 2012). Government officials in the Gulf have realized that they must move from awareness to action quickly to confront these concerns.

Despite their heavy investments and subsidies in the domestic agriculture sector, the Gulf states have limited domestic agricultural capacity and are heavily dependent on food imports. This makes Gulf countries susceptible to global food shortages and price fluctuations, confirmed most recently by the 2007–2008 global food crisis, which not only led to soaring food prices, but also made the Gulf states realize that, despite their wealth, they were unable to buy all the food staples they needed, because the producer countries limited food exports to feed their own citizens first.

In order to reduce the burden on domestic energy resources and as a response to the global food crisis, the Gulf states have developed various strategies. One policy is to invest in agricultural ventures abroad. Establishing intensive farming overseas and importing produce back to domestic markets is part of a larger strategy that considers "food security" a top national priority. These foreign land acquisitions are executed by government agencies and private enterprises. The Gulf governments encourage domestic corporations to invest in Canada, Argentina, and Brazil, in addition to economically poor countries around the world. The Saudi Arabian government, for example, purchased farmlands in the developing world, in places like Sudan, Ethiopia, Senegal, Pakistan, and Egypt, with the stated purpose of directly supplying corn, soybean, fodder, rice, palm oil, pineapple, and other produce for the kingdom. According to *Bloomberg BusinessWeek* in 2012, Saudi Arabia had spent US$11 billion in agricultural and livestock investments abroad. Moreover, Kuwait has invested in Asian countries such as Cambodia, Laos, and the Philippines to secure its rice and corn supplies.

However, these "land grabs," as they are sometimes referred to, involve risks and raise questions and concerns about their consequences. Because of the heavy involvement of private corporations whose main concern is profit, it is unclear whether these projects actually provide food security for Gulf nations. More importantly, these agricultural ventures have an unprecedented impact on the local people in the countries the Gulf nations invest in, since their domestic food supply is reduced as foreigners invest in their lands. These land deals are already considered a new form of "economic colonialism" or "agro-imperialism," because the oil-rich Gulf countries and their corporations conduct their investments without regulation and oversight. A particular segment of local governing elites might profit from the arrangement, but their populations are likely to suffer.

The efforts to outsource agricultural production target the supply side of the water problem, with the goals of preserving the domestic water supply and encouraging more sustainable water management. Still, most Gulf citizens remain ignorant about the condition of their water resources, because most of their energy consumption is free or subsidized. Since the cost of water use is so low, there is no incentive for or burden on consumers to save or consume sustainably. This situation has begun to change, however. With the realization that they have to address challenges resulting from water demand, and not just from water supply, the Gulf governments have started to implement economically and environmentally beneficial policies to curb demand for water. For example,

```
┌────────────────────────────────────────────────────────────────┐
│                           Box 14.4                               │
│                                                                  │
│        Examples of National Water Policy Bodies and Agencies     │
│                                                                  │
│   Bahrain                 Ministry of Works, Power and Water     │
│   Oman                    Public Authority for Electricity and Water (PAEW) │
│   Qatar                   Permanent Water Resources Committee (PWRC) │
│   Saudi Arabia            Ministry of Water and Electricity      │
│   United Arab Emirates    Ministry of Environment and Water      │
└────────────────────────────────────────────────────────────────┘
```

the United Arab Emirates (UAE) has cut subsidies, increased fees for water usage, and introduced new water tariffs. To regulate water consumption more effectively, the governments in the Gulf have improved their legal systems regarding water and the environment by introducing new water conservation or groundwater utilization laws. Yemen and the UAE, for instance, have established laws requiring drilling contractors working in their countries to have a drilling license.

Equally important is the widespread realization at the interstate level that comprehensive water management is necessary for sustainable development. To coordinate their water policies, all GCC countries have established centralized authorities such as the UAE's Ministry of Environment and Water. These new, centralized national institutions have streamlined the decision-making process and worked as information clearinghouses to collect and distribute data on all water-related sectors, such as agriculture, fisheries, urban planning, and environment.

In addition to individual state-level policy changes, regional cooperation initiatives have increased since the early 2000s. The Gulf states, in collaboration with private sector and international and nongovernmental organizations, organize annual summits and conferences to bring together key players and decision makers to discuss and debate the regional challenges on water-related issues, such as wastewater management, power and desalination, and cross-border water sharing. Similarly, the Gulf governments, along with other Arab states in the region, set up the Arab Water Academy in the UAE in 2008 to promote innovation regarding policies to deal with water scarcity in the Middle East as a whole. By focusing on education and development, this academy aims to shift the attention from supply-side management to a more integrated water management approach that includes both supply and demand.

The website of the Arab Water Academy (http://www.awacademy.ae) offers information on its programs, as well as resources pertinent to its work in promoting innovation relating to water scarcity issues.

The Arab Water Council (http://www.arabwatercouncil.org/index.php) is another example of interstate cooperation regarding water issues in the Middle East.

Conclusion

Energy security has become a major priority for both energy producers and consumers in the world. As the above discussion illustrates, a combination of local, regional, and global factors has influenced, and continues to influence, the petroleum and water politics in the Gulf region. As the global energy market has become more integrated, increasing numbers of new players, both state and private, have intensified the competition over scarce resources. Energy consumption has increased due to demographic and economic trends in major producing and consumer countries. In the meantime, the search for and discoveries of oil outside the Gulf, as well as the push for alternative energy sources in oil-consuming countries, have become important factors for the future prospects of the Gulf energy industries.

More recently, regional and domestic challenges such as the rise of political Islam, sectarian tensions, popular unrest, population growth, and migration have also led the Gulf states to reconsider their relations with the other actors in the global energy market. Since the beginning of the 2000s, Gulf countries have become more active and multidimensional in their energy policy and have begun to collaborate on various oil- and water-related problems. They also have increased their engagement with major energy consumers in Asia, especially China. In the 2008 global recession, for example, when the demand for and consumption of oil dropped significantly in major Western consumer countries, Saudi Arabia's exports to China doubled from previous years. The kingdom now accounts for one-quarter of all Chinese oil imports.

Political, economic, and strategic conditions within and beyond the region have also brought new opportunities for the Gulf states. The earlier attempts to diversify their economies and make them less energy dependent have had mixed results. But the most current renewed and strengthened attempts to invest oil money in projects within industry, education, and the service sector seem to be generating real economic diversification.

In the changing geopolitics of oil, new alliances and collaborations have appeared on the horizon. Similarly, in hydropolitics, given the increasing need for water in energy production in addition to domestic and agricultural consumption, water will increasingly become a security issue. Despite future projections that emphasize the increasing oil production in the United States and an emphasis on U.S. energy independence, the countries of the Gulf region will remain important players and decision makers in the well-integrated global energy market.

References and Further Research

AlMunajjed, Mona, and Karim Sabbagh. 2011. *Youth in GCC Countries: Meeting the Challenge*. Ideation Center Insight. Abu Dhabi, UAE: Booz & Company, September 26. http://www.booz.com/media/file/BoozCo-GCC-Youth-Challenge.pdf.

Alterman, Jon B., and Michael Dziuban. 2010. *Clear Gold: Water as a Strategic Resource in the Middle East*. CSIS Middle East Program Report. Washington, DC: Center for Strategic and International Studies. http://csis.org/program/clear-gold-water-strategic-resource-middle-east.

Frenken, Karen, ed. 2009. *Irrigation in the Middle East Region in Figures*. FAO Water Report 34. Rome: Food and Agricultural Organization of the United Nations. ftp://ftp.fao.org/docrep/fao/012/i0936e/i0936e00.pdf.

The GCC in 2020: Broadening the Economy. 2010. A report from the Economist Intelligence Unit, Sponsored by Qatar Financial Centre Authority. London: Economist Intelligence Unit, October 31.

Jones, Toby Craig. 2010. *Desert Kingdom: How Oil and Water Forged Modern Saudi Arabia*. Cambridge, MA: Harvard University Press.

Koons, Jennifer. 2011. "Future of the Gulf States: Can the Monarchies Survive in a Changing Region?" *CQ Global Researcher* 5, no. 21: 525–548. http://library.cqpress.com/globalresearcher/document.php?id=cqrglobal2011110100&PHPSESSID=k4sshg0fd77p5988nhicneflo7.

Lichtenthaeler, Gerhard. 2010. "Water Conflict and Cooperation in Yemen." *Middle East Report* 254 (Spring): 30–36. http://www.merip.org/mer/mer254/water-conflict-cooperation-yemen.

Malek, Caline. 2012. "Water Plan Needed to Tackle Scarcity, Says GCC Chief." *The National*, April 23. http://www.thenational.ae/news/uae-news/water-plan-needed-to-tackle-scarcity-says-gcc-chief.

Rice, Andrew. 2009. "Is There Such a Thing as Agro-Imperialism?" *New York Times Magazine*, November 16. http://www.nytimes.com/2009/11/22/magazine/22land-t.html?pagewanted=all&_r=0.

Shepherd, Benjamin. 2012. *GCC States' Land Investments Abroad: The Case of Cambodia*. Summary Report 5. Washington, DC: Center for International and Regional Studies, Georgetown University School of Foreign Service in Qatar. http://www12.georgetown.edu/sfs/qatar/cirs/CambodiaSummaryReport.pdf.

Websites

Food and Agriculture Organization of the United Nations (FAO): http://www.fao.org.

FAO-AQUASTAT: http://www.fao.org/nr/water/aquastat/main/index.stm.

Gulf Cooperation Council (GCC): http://www.gcc-sg.org/eng/.

International Energy Agency (IEA): www.iea.org.

Organization of the Petroleum Exporting Countries (OPEC): www.opec.org.

UN-Water: http://www.unwater.org/index.html.

UN World Water Development Report 4: http://www.unesco.org/new/en/natural-sciences/environment/water/wwap/wwdr/wwdr4–2012/#c219661.

U.S. Energy Information Administration (EIA): www.eia.gov.

15

Central Asian Cotton in Global Perspective
Uzbekistan's Monoculture and Its Impact on Rural Society

RUSSELL ZANCA

People who live in cotton-growing villages in Uzbekistan, adjoining enormous cotton farm fields, continue to plant and harvest "white gold" in ways similar to ongoing practices of the last 100 years. Until very recently—the past fifteen years or so—Uzbek villages, extending from the humid Ferghana Valley in the east to the arid lands of Khorezm in the west, existed almost as self-contained and self-maintained units of production and economy. In keeping with a model developed by the Soviet Union from the 1920s onward, rural places were developed as they increased their range of basic consumer goods, used technological innovations, and offered new educational, entertainment, and other leisure facilities and activities that reflected urban aspects and tastes.

The Soviet Union elevated the status of workers and peasants to the highest level in an attempt to achieve an egalitarian socialist society. It hoped to limit the trend of migration to cities, which is typical in the capitalist version of industrialization, whereby workers search for better, more diversified lives and higher incomes. Using a combination of legal residency requirements (known as the *propiska*, or "permission license"), forced labor in all facets of cotton growing, and leveling mechanisms, the Soviet regime, for the most part, enabled rural Uzbeks to survive and even flourish within the cotton *qishloq* (Uzbek village). Indeed, what the local peasant population would associate with genuine progress—more varied foodstuffs and a higher-protein diet, agricultural mechanization, more rapid communication networks, payments or salaries in money, and more widespread availability of electricity, among other factors—began to characterize village Uzbek life from the mid-1950s on. The 1960s through the late 1980s were widely considered to be the "golden age" of socioeconomic life in Soviet Uzbekistan. It was a time of abundance, although many rural people admit that they had little freedom of choice, and they often were commanded to work in the cotton fields and on collective farm laboring projects, whenever local authorities deemed it necessary or crucial to the success of the state's agricultural prerogatives, as I explored in my 2010 book, *Life in a Muslim Uzbek Village: Cotton Farming After Communism*. After the collapse of the Soviet Union in 1991 and the subsequent complete restructuring of the interconnected Soviet system, many Uzbeks with whom I lived and conducted interviews from the mid-1990s through 2010 explained that their lifestyles of relative material comfort and security had been lost.

Cotton grows abundantly in Uzbekistan. So much grows, in fact, that Uzbekistan is the world's third-biggest exporter of cotton, behind the United States and Africa. Cotton is a global agricultural commodity supported by an insatiable demand across the globe, and it is a vital component of Uzbekistan's overall economy, comprising 25 percent of the country's export revenue. In monetary terms, cotton provides Uzbekistan with more than $2 billion per year (Djanibekov et al. 2010). Given that approximately 50 percent of the country's entire population earns its keep either directly in cotton production or through secondary, related economic sectors, such as cotton processing, machine repair services, and so forth, it would be logical to think that rural folk make a decent living from cotton. The government, however, monopolizes control over every aspect of the cotton-growing sector, and it pays or remunerates ordinary people in ways only it sees fit. As a result, for the last twenty years, more and more Uzbek citizens have been trying to move away from cotton farming and the cotton industry.

Although the state's leadership realizes this, it has not considered liberalizing the sector or increasing wages and compensation. Instead, it relies on the increasing numbers of the country's population that are both vulnerable and pliable, including middle-aged women, university students, and even grammar school children. It has no compunction about pulling young people and children away from their educational institutions, especially during the peak harvesting period, from early September until often well into November. Such practices are well-documented in anti–child-labor initiatives, such as the Cotton Campaign. These measures clearly indicate that the government does not have enough labor available to harvest the cotton, or is not willing to pay what ordinary people would consider fair or acceptable compensation. Thus, the overall effect on rural society is mass migration: millions of Uzbeks either leave their villages for the country's cities or migrate abroad to neighboring states, such as Kazakhstan, or slightly farther, to Russia, where the majority of Uzbekistan's labor migrants now reside. Uzbeks will even migrate to Western Europe and the United States if they can obtain visas.

> The Cotton Campaign website (http://www.cottoncampaign.org/) presents information about the Uzbek cotton industry and forced labor conditions and child labor in the cotton fields across Uzbekistan.

For the past decade or so, social scientists, including anthropologists (such as myself), have begun trying to make sense of what these large-scale movements (involving no less than 2.5 million people) away from the cotton-growing villages and farms will mean for rural life and Uzbek culture. In a 2009 work, *Labor Migration in Central Asia: Implications of the Global Economic Crisis*, Erica Marat explores these implications. The only thing we are sure of, however, is that the previous Soviet model of collective farming, replete with mainly large, patrilineally structured family households rooted to their natal villages, is fast becoming something of the past.

Mobility in Uzbek sociocultural life marks a significant break with the past. The ethnographic literature has characterized rural communities as rarely venturing far from their natal villages. But the fact that cotton is a global commodity, coupled with the state's control over cotton production, has brought many rural Uzbeks out into the world. By the mid-1990s, it had become apparent to many rural Uzbeks that the worst elements of the collective farming system were to remain, while the best elements of state support and development were rapidly disappearing. With few paying jobs available on the farms, the choices became starker and starker for villagers, and the one way out of economic stagnation and creeping impoverishment was literally to get out of Uzbekistan, even if only temporarily, so that people could make money outside the country in order to return, or repatriate their earnings, and maintain a way of life they had grown accustomed to before the break-up of the Soviet Union.

Historical Background

Uzbekistan, situated in the Central Asian heartland, has enjoyed a long and complex history that includes numerous lifestyles, languages, waves of immigration, and artistic and intellectual developments. But prior to its incarnation as a modern nation-state, Uzbekistan, literally the "Land of the Uzbeks," had never been politically unified, except for relatively brief periods during medieval and contemporary eras.

A main thoroughfare in Tashkent, the capital of Uzbekistan. The signboard reads: "Uzbekistan is a free and equal country in the world." *(Photo by Russell Zanca)*

The linguistic character of Uzbek, the language most of the country's 27 million people have spoken since birth, reveals much about its history. It is Turkic in origin, which links it closely to several other modern languages, such as Kyrgyz, Turkish, Uyghur, and Turkmen. Today's Uzbek has also been strongly influenced by Persian and Arabic (and much more recently by Russian). The linguistic ties to Persian and Arabic, according to Scott Levi (2007) and Peter B. Golden (2011), reflect the historical periods when Uzbekistan was in more direct contact with the Islamic world that shaped and influenced what we consider to be contemporary Uzbek.

Indeed, the overwhelming majority of Uzbeks are Muslims. Less than fifty years after the death of the Prophet Muhammad in 632 CE, Islam came to the "Land Beyond the River," or Mawar-an-nahr, which is Arabic for the land north of the Amu Darya (*darya* or *dario* is the Uzbek word for "river"), a natural border separating Afghanistan from Turkmenistan and Uzbekistan. Once Arab armies crossed the Amu and invaded Central Asia, a gradual process of Islamization among the indigenous inhabitants began. The peoples of these areas would not become Muslims in great numbers for many centuries; however, this would occur during the medieval era, and according to Carter Vaughn Findley (2005), until the post-Mongol era (after the 1400s), many people of today's Uzbekistan retained earlier religious beliefs and practices, including Judaism, Christianity, Buddhism, and Turko-Mongolian forms of animism and shamanism.

By the tenth century, however—and despite the Mongol invasion and devastation some 300 years later (in the 1220s)—urban centers of contemporary Uzbekistan functioned as renowned sites of Islamic learning and culture, as well as commerce and industry. Among these cities, Bukhara (in south-central Uzbekistan), Marw (in southwestern Turkmenistan), and, later, Samarkand (in eastern Uzbekistan) stand out. Both Persian and Arabic enabled

Samarkand Street with Bibi-Khanym Mosque. *(Photo by Russell Zanca)*

much of the intellectual development in these cities, according to Beatrice Forbes Manz (1991), although Persian rapidly superseded Arabic as the main language through which literary Islamic civilization spread throughout Central Asia. The ascendance of Persian continued for many centuries. Whereas the various regions of Central Asia were never ruled by Middle Eastern polities for very long, the direct human contacts and exchanges between the peoples of Central Asia and the Middle East were substantial, shaping ideas, customs, practices, and material culture. We continue to see this today. For example, Middle Eastern influences in Central Asia, including Uzbekistan, can be found in a range of cultural practices beyond religious beliefs, such as its cookery, architectural styles, artistic and decorative motifs, language, music, dress, agricultural organization, gender relations, and even home furnishings.

Conditions for Uzbekistan's Agriculture

As Islam spread from the Arabian Peninsula and became more readily accepted in towns and urban areas located in river valleys or oases, the agricultural innovations employed in the Middle East, including technologies adapted to such valleys and oases, also spread. The development of elaborate networks of canals became crucial to agricultural production, given the aridity of much of the land in Central Asia. Indeed, like much of the Middle East, Central Asia is very dry. In Uzbekistan only about 10 percent of the land is suitable for farming, and of that 10 percent only a relatively minor portion is conducive to dry-land farming, the practice of raising crops with no need for constant irrigation. While the Middle East historically engineered two types of irrigation agriculture (open-air-channel canal systems, or underground piping systems—*kariz* or *qanat*, respectively, in Arabic) Central Asia has relied predominantly on the former system in modern times.

Major mountain ranges, such as the Tien Shan and Pamir, considered a part of the greater Himalayan chain, provide enormous reserves of water in the form of melted ice and snow from late spring until early fall. The huge rivers, including the Syr and Noryn (in the north) and the Amu (in the south), also historically provided the peoples living in the territory of modern Uzbekistan with plentiful water for centuries. For people living more than 100 miles from the rivers themselves, elaborate systems of large and small canals were dug and maintained from the Central Asian soils. Locally in Uzbekistan, these feeder canals—which bring water from rivers, streams, and larger grand canals— are known as *ariq*.

Present-day Uzbekistan was known from antiquity as agriculturally productive, as described in histories of Alexander the Great's campaigns through southern Uzbekistan and northern Afghanistan (330s–320s BCE). Grains—such as barley and rice—and fruits—such as apricots, pomegranates, and melons—were cultivated with relative ease throughout the area. For example, Uzbekistan's long association with delicious musk melons resulted in their being exported, according to Peter Green (1991), stretching back nearly 2,000 years, from the very inception of the silk routes (known as the "Silk Road") that connected China in the east to the Byzantine Empire in the west.

Cotton also has been raised on Uzbekistan's lands for at least 2 millennia. Both Chinese chroniclers and archeological finds have supported this conclusion. However, evidence does not suggest that cotton was widely raised, or that extensive cultivation played a prominent role in commodity exchanges. Rather, it seems cotton was used for local needs and probably sold or traded locally, perhaps involving exchanges with pastoral nomadic peoples, or even with regional buyers from China. Up until the modern era, cotton did not assume the major role that textiles, such as silk, wool, and even flax, once did.

While cotton grows well in Central Asia's mainly warm and dry climates, as well as in warm and more humid oasis areas, such as the Ferghana Valley, it requires a heavy reliance on resources such as water and nutrients, and this can result in a severe depletion of those resources. Furthermore, cotton cultivation requires a high level of labor intensity. In particular, the crop needs continual care during its cycle, including watering, weeding, pest control, loosening of soils, and defoliating of the plants once the cotton wool begins to emerge from the bolls. Continuous maintenance of the crop is necessary from spring plantings in late March or early April all the way through the main harvesting period from late August to early November (depending upon locations throughout the country).

Making Uzbekistan a Cotton Monoculture

The story of Uzbekistan's ongoing reliance on cotton as the country's number one export crop begins shortly after the Russian Empire's colonizing push into southern Central Asia in the 1850s. At that time, most of what would become Soviet Central Asia was known as Turkestan. Perhaps the major reason that the Russian Empire tried to dominate peoples in Central Asia was related to Russia's desire to become both a world power and to stave off the imperial ambitions of Great Britain, which at the time controlled nearly all of South Asia, including present-day India, Pakistan, and Bangladesh, as well as sections of northeastern Afghanistan. Today these countries are regional neighbors to the Central Asian states.

Thus, during the second half of the nineteenth century, Central Asia formed the fulcrum of what came to be identified as the "Great Game," which referred to the Anglo-Russian rivalry for imperial supremacy in much of western and southern Asia. Peter Hopkirk, who wrote a book with this title in 1992, showed that contemporary identities of Central Asian peoples, including the Uzbeks, underwent a significant degree of change because of their submission to Russian colonial power, which lasted about sixty years, from the second half of the nineteenth century up to the Bolshevik Revolution of 1917. Whereas Russia's leaders of the mid-nineteenth century knew that Central Asian peoples had long practiced and refined all sorts of agricultural activities, they considered Central Asia a backwater in terms of technology and scientific advancement. Russian leaders insisted that Turkestan's governing, economic, and sociocultural organizations and structures had stagnated for some 300 years. They also reckoned that, in addition to subjugating the people of the region, they would force their agricultural techniques and practices to become considerably more productive.

The relatively short period of conquest in southern Central Asia, from the late 1850s through the mid-1880s, coincided with Russia's own industrial revolution. Among other industries, Russia became a substantial textile producer, and one of its core textile industries was cotton, centered especially in the large factories that operated in Ivanovo in western Russia. While southern Russia and Ukraine provided some harvested cotton for the rapidly growing industry, Russia imported much of its raw cotton from the highly productive southern United States. The international trade network between the United States and Russia, however, practically ceased during the American Civil War (1861–1865), and some historians attribute the increased and rapid attention to southern Central Asia—much of today's Turkmenistan, Uzbekistan, and Tajikistan—to the internal conflict in the United States (see Becker 2009; Massell 1974; and Soucek 2000). From the 1860s on, Russian industrialists came to believe that Central Asia provided a way out of their dependence on foreign cotton production.

By the turn of the twentieth century, cotton cultivation and production had increased astronomically in comparison to what Central Asians had been producing less than fifty years earlier. The Russians invested heavily in all of the technical aspects of cotton cultivation, from gathering dedicated agronomists to finding the best adapted seeds and fertilizers and developing the most efficient means of access to massive supplies of water. On the whole, all types of agriculture became increasingly important in Central Asia, especially in Uzbekistan, because from the 1860s on, tens of thousands of freed serfs (basically indentured peasants) from Russia moved to Central Asia as part of a settlement policy that expanded colonization beyond military personnel and administrative bureaucrats (Brower 2003).

In the early twentieth century, then, the primary agricultural lands of Central Asia enjoyed diverse crop profiles—including wheat, flax, oil seeds, clover, fruits, vegetables, and so on—but cotton was fast becoming the primary cash crop. With the defeat of the Russian Empire and the onset of the Bolshevik Revolution in 1917, this shift intensified. Although authorized and essentially run by Russian and Slavic actors, the Bolshevik Revolution resulted in the establishment of the Union of Soviet Socialist Republics

(USSR), which generally corresponded to the parameters of the erstwhile Russian Empire. One of the most basic political premises of the new communist state was that it should become a vast partnership of culturally distinct but equal ethnic nations. As part of this transition, Uzbekistan was established as one of the fifteen constituent Soviet socialist republics in 1924.

While many Uzbek elites led the new Soviet republic, it is also true that Uzbekistan's economic and political choices were subject to full approval by the overarching Soviet—largely Russocentric and Russophonic—system. Hence, from the mid-1920s on, it became clearer to rural Uzbek people that the most important crop in the new republic had to be cotton. From that point forward, the entire range of scientific, technical, and resource investments in Uzbekistan centered on the increased productivity of cotton fields, and Uzbekistan soon became a cotton-growing country par excellence.

From the early 1950s until the late 1980s, the increase in cotton productivity would see Uzbekistan become one of the world's top producers, reaching harvests of nearly 4 million metric tons by the mid-1980s, according to Soviet statistics (as reported in Zanca 2010). Uzbekistan's record harvests were eclipsed only by cotton harvests in much larger cotton-producing countries, such as the United States and China. Of course, cotton quality is a key to strong export earnings, and Uzbekistan did not always produce cotton of the finest quality, such as what one would associate with a smaller but powerful cotton country such as Egypt. Still, cotton dominated the twentieth-century Uzbek way of life and became inextricably associated with everything Uzbek, a fact seen in artistic motifs in the advanced Tashkent metro stations, gold leaf tea sets and housewares designs, architectural motifs of modern apartment buildings, and even Tashkent's football team, called Pakhtakor, or "Cotton Worker."

Explaining Popular Attitudes Toward Cotton

The Soviet system operated neither democratically nor pluralistically, and people who raised and picked cotton never had a say in how their economic lives should be organized, or in the decisions that were made about the use and maintenance of their lands. From the 1920s onward, the USSR forced farming people, or peasants, to live and work on collective farms, which meant, among other things, that almost all agriculturally productive land was owned and controlled by the state. Common people could not decide for themselves what to do with the land or which crops they could raise. They could make decisions only with regard to the tiny plots of land that adjoined their own homes; that is, they could grow food and raise small numbers of animals within their own *hovlis*, Central Asian household compounds with a backyard. Seeds, fertilizers, and other agricultural inputs were controlled and distributed mainly by state-licensed agents who managed village shops or stores. The only freedom allowed peasants of the collective farms—which used to be called *sovkhozes* and *kolkhozes* (two variations on agricultural lands and their products that belonged entirely, or mostly, to the state)—was in the production of fruits, vegetables, nuts, and animal products (such as eggs, dairy, and meat) on their hovlis. They could bring small amounts of their "surplus" produce to weekly or biweekly

Uzbek teapot with cotton plant and cotton boll motif. *(Photo by Russell Zanca)*

farmers' markets (*dehqon bozor* in Uzbek) to sell or exchange at prices or values they themselves negotiated, but they paid taxes for rental space in the markets as well as taxes on their earnings. Of course, there have always been peasants who have raised cotton and smuggled it for private sale, but this was illegal in Uzbekistan, and with rare exceptions it remains illegal today.

Despite these restrictions, Uzbeks do not necessarily share an American or Western perspective about economic opportunities, the role of the state in regulating daily life, and how work or labor itself should be compensated. While Uzbeks certainly have questioned their living conditions and have often expressed resentment at the state's demands for their labor, they also accommodated to the communist system, and since the fall of that system to post-Soviet developments, in ways that are uniquely their own. While they have borne the brunt of a punishing and commanding system of labor in the form of cotton work and cotton farming, they still embrace the transformation of their country into an enormous cotton-farming hub.

Indeed, the transition came at a considerable cost to Uzbek farmers. The Soviet system forced millions of people to work very hard, often to the point of physical exhaustion and sometimes early death, in the construction of massive public works projects. In the Uzbek countryside, for example, this meant the manual digging of new canals hundreds of kilometers in length and several meters in depth. It also entailed relentless construction of new pumping and hydraulic works to channel water to an ever-expanding network of fields.

In an effort to understand the response of Uzbeks to these extensive demands, I conducted ethnographic fieldwork in the 1990s among very elderly peasants, focusing on their

An Uzbek child hauls a bale of cotton from the field. *(Photo by Russell Zanca)*

earliest recollections of the Soviet public work projects that coincided with the organizing of people into collective and state farms. A colleague, the historian Marianne Kamp, and I organized a team of young Uzbek researchers to help us identify elderly farming people who could recollect and would be willing to share their memories of this period.

Whenever we expressed a kind of sympathy for the hardships of the time, our interviewees often agreed, but also they often expressed that their suffering was for a greater good. This "greater good" only marginally—and theoretically—meant the establishment of socialism; in practical terms it meant bringing permanent supplies of water to the areas in which they lived. When we asked if the price they paid was too high, or if progress might have occurred in a freer, less harsh way, the question seemed not to make sense to some. They said that despite the harsh conditions and deprivations, including hunger, the end result was development in the countryside in the form of more productive lands, the gradual mechanization of agriculture, the establishment of schools and literacy, and the creation of institutions of culture—material and intellectual. In a sense, for better or for worse, the Soviet drive to make Uzbekistan a cotton-focused country also led to its development.

The Day-to-Day Life of Contemporary Cotton Workers

People of the formerly large-scale state cotton farms naturally privileged tools and technology that they considered "advanced" and modern. They had been raised to understand that Soviet life in connection to labor and productivity was tightly linked to the development of technology. Indeed, peasants often seemed to treat *tekhnologiia* as the solution to nearly every problem—particularly questions relating to high harvest yields or the quality of cotton wool—especially in light of what they considered their relative backwardness. When productivity was low or the cotton not highly valued, people would mention how they could have turned things around if only they had the right technology. This even extended to other realms of agricultural work, such as the lack of a good wine industry. As an anthropologist, I was always deciding whether or not to argue against what I considered a kind of fetishizing of this "god" known as technology. Sometimes, perhaps, more basic qualities or properties are needed—such as good soils; high-quality seed; long stretches of hot, dry weather; and a minimizing of harsh chemical fertilizers. And while I sometimes challenged those consultants I interviewed, I also realized that it was important simply to understand their perspectives, and also to realize that the Soviet system itself created, in a large part, this notion that technological control and improvement over agriculture marked the difference between advanced and underdeveloped countries.

I was often struck by how extensive many aspects of cotton field labor could be. If one is going to study the impact of cotton on rural life and how people are involved in cotton work, then spending as much time as possible in the fields themselves is critical. I tried to do this as often as possible in my research during the 1990s, on several research trips to examine aspects of rural life and political economy in the Ferghana Valley. On a typical cotton farm, anywhere from several hundred to a thousand or more people may be directly involved in various aspects of sowing and harvesting processes from late March through November. Many families and their members make up work brigades to which the farm's administration has assigned them. With a leader or brigadier, these teams are given tasks that involve preparing fields, watering, weeding, clearing, planting, aerating soil, and, later, picking and packing the cotton wool. According to many of my interviewees during those years, the economic situation had deteriorated on the farms from its height of relative wealth and prosperity in the mid-1980s. As a partial result, tractors and harvesters had become too expensive to keep running, partly due to the costs for general maintenance and repair, new parts, and gasoline. As a result, more and more people were working on all aspects of the harvest by hand.

Picking cotton and then carrying a full, compressed load in one cloth waist apron requires skill, endurance, strength, and flexibility. Women account for the vast majority of cotton pickers. The hardest-working pickers can sometimes bring in hauls of nearly 200 kilograms (440 pounds). That is a lot of cotton. Having tried to pick cotton myself on numerous occasions, I know how much skill and perseverance it takes. First of all, the weather can be taxing, especially when late summer temperatures reach above the ninety-degree mark, with relatively high humidity. Second, picking the wool itself requires speed and caution, because the cotton boll's petals, which start out soft and pretty, become hard and sharp before finally withering. There is a good chance pickers will scratch, or even cut, their hands in the process. By mid-September one frequently sees cotton workers with bandaged fingers as a result of harvesting the cotton and working with sharp tools. Third, as the soft and fluffy cotton wool accumulates in one's waist sack, it gets heavier and heavier. Because one also has to bend and stoop to get to the lower bolls that grow on stalks that reach a height of four or five feet, lower back pain and discomfort are common.

Box 15.1

Ethnographic Methods

Ethnographic fieldwork—such as the work I conducted in investigating cotton farming in Uzbekistan—entails spending extended periods of time in a particular community and getting to know daily routines and practices. Ideally, ethnographers speak the language of the communities they study, while others work through interpreters. One of the famous early anthropologists, Bronislaw Malinowski (1884–1942), called the practice of fieldwork the "inexhaustible attention to the minutia of everyday life." Fieldwork requires taking detailed notes of even the most mundane circumstances that can be observed on a daily basis, in addition to recording interviews. Importantly, fieldworkers need to render the other person's point of view as clearly as possible, without any imposition of their own opinions and possible biases.

People who work in these fields dress appropriately for the season. When the weather is hottest, women wear light flowing dresses—akin to nightgowns—and they tie their hair back in kerchiefs. Despite the hot sun, Uzbeks rarely wear the kind of wide-brimmed headwear we associate with peasant farmers in, say, China or Southeast Asia, though women sometimes loosen their large kerchiefs (*rumol*), wear some extra material on their heads, or even craft a makeshift brim from a piece of newspaper. Men's ubiquitous headwear is the small, brimless skullcap known as a *duppi*. Equal parts a mark of one's ethnic identity and of Muslim piety, the duppi does not offer much protection from the sun for the face, ears, and eyes. Men in the fields, however, will make either a more protective turban framed around the skullcap, or they will pull a shirt over their heads and place the skullcap back on top. The only state of undress in the fields is a boy or man's purview: only when working in the fields or within one's own courtyard will a man strip down to an undershirt or go bare-chested. Modesty and decorum would prevent a man from doing this in nearly any other public, rural setting.

Generally, people dress in worn and ragged work clothes, even if these include old sports jackets or threadbare dresses. As the weather turns colder or is chilly, women will don shawls, sweaters, and velvet-covered and cotton-stuffed vests, whereas a man may wear an old sweater and a heavy robe known as a *chopon*, or an old European-style jacket or overcoat. Footwear ranges from sandals to firm, low-cut rubber galoshes, known as *kalosh*, and when the weather is colder or the fields are wet and muddy, both men and women will wear soft leather boots, or *maksi*, that they place inside the *kalosh*. In the colder months this combination of maksi and kalosh makes it convenient for entering indoor spaces without dragging in dirt, since people can simply slip out of the kalosh.

Many people and children walk anywhere from a couple of hundred yards to a half-mile to reach their fields, and then spend from eight to twelve hours there, so they need to be supplied. Women will pack for themselves and their families. They always bring thermoses of tea, bread, and leftover food from the previous day's dinner or breakfast.

Men and boys resting after cotton work during the fall in the Ferghana Valley. *(Photo by Russell Zanca)*

With no plastic wrap or silver foil, people mainly wrap their food, sometimes filling a small enamel basin, in a thin, clean cloth. During the day, adults or children may return home for a number of reasons, including caring for animals, resting, taking care of general housework, or doing chores around their own small garden plots.

Because each large farm may work on three or four field sectors, small shelters and canteens exist in each one. Generally, the cotton workers will get some sort of a communal hot lunch, and if they bring their own quilts or pillows, they can lie down in the simple barrack-like shelter and rest. Men always seem to have playing cards, a backgammon or chess set, and a comfortable spot to while away the hottest part of the day. Some people, more often the men than the women, may spend one to two hours eating, smoking, playing, and snoozing. Most women, however, will not take more than a half hour or so to eat and rest before turning back to their tasks.

The work cycle in the fields begins to slow by the end of October, once the best grades of available cotton have been picked. After the daily pickings are collected and hauled off, they are then cleaned or ginned, and eventually brought to local processing centers to be bailed and made ready for shipments to large cities, including Tashkent, Moscow, Dhaka, Beijing, Seoul, and even cities of Western Europe and the United States.

Uzbek Cotton and the Global Market

Even though Uzbekistan continues to make over 10 percent of its export earnings from the sale of cotton, the industry has been in decline since the turn of the new millennium. Some of the decline has resulted from the state's own decisions about removing land from cotton cultivation since its peak production in the late 1980s. Other factors, such as poor infrastructure, increasingly less mechanization, the salinization of soils, and decreasing irrigation capacity, have damaged the industry. Moreover, Uzbek people have come to understand how poorly they are paid for their work, and how the state control of the industry precludes them from gaining a fair market value for their cotton (perhaps less than one-third of what they should expect). They have therefore increasingly looked for work and income outside of the cotton sector. Nevertheless, Uzbekistan exports somewhere in the area of 600,000 metric tons of cotton a year (its peak in about 1990 was over 800,000 metric tons), according to a paper written by Stephen MacDonald (2012). While some of this cotton fiber is directly imported by the United States and goes into mattresses, much of the better-quality fiber is sent to other countries and used to make denim, towels, and cotton knits. In other words, while the clothing worn across the globe may have labels reading "Made in China" or "Made in Bangladesh," it is quite likely that your T-shirts, polos, and jeans contain Uzbek cotton.

With a virtually insatiable world demand for cotton products, it is unlikely that Uzbekistan will consider this primary cash crop a thing of the past. The real question is whether it can modernize the industry and maintain its profitability. It is likely that Uzbekistan will decline as a leading global cotton exporter because it continues dictating terms to peasant farmers, including relying on manual labor for roughly 90 percent of the work, and because it disregards international allegations of inhumane working conditions, not the least of which is child labor during harvest time. Thus, if Uzbekistan fails to modernize and legitimize its industry, buyers may be harder to secure. Therefore, while cotton puts Uzbekistan firmly on the map of contemporary economic globalization, it has also had the untoward consequence of practically forcing millions of Uzbeks to seek alternative livelihoods. While many of these alternatives include simply leaving the farming areas and moving to large cities, such as Samarkand, Andijan, and Tashkent, as internal migrants, urban Uzbekistan offers few truly worthwhile job options for rural people, who often have limited educational backgrounds. In the next and final section, I briefly discuss the phenomenon of mass labor migration that has brought Uzbeks into the globalized economy in ways not seen during the entire Soviet era.

Cornell University's Program in Food Policy for Developing Countries presents a case study, "Pros and Cons of Cotton Production in Uzbekistan" (http://cip. cornell.edu/dns.gfs/1279121771), which looks at Uzbekistan's cotton industry from the point of view of four stakeholders: the government, the farmers, the textile industry, and the rural population.

Conclusion: Uzbek Labor Migration as a Major Link in Globalization

Uzbekistan is "missing" about 3 million people from its population at any given time, depending on whose estimates one trusts. This means that somewhere between 10

After the harvest, the cotton is processed through a cotton gin. *(Photo by Russell Zanca)*

and 15 percent of the entire Uzbek population now resides outside of Uzbekistan. For comparison's sake, imagine if 30 to 45 million Americans lived abroad due to a lack of sufficient wages and economic freedom. Although Uzbeks are not starving at home, they wish to maintain a particular way of life. Much of their wealth earned abroad is returned home, not only to put children through college or buy an extra bag of groceries, but also for hosting life-cycle ceremonies, such as weddings, circumcision parties, and remembrance days for departed loved ones, that will earn them the respect of other community members. Moreover, they also pay the onerous costs of additions to large and ever-increasing extended family homes. As societies undergo change in a globalizing world, ever-expanding requirements for rural family life are likely to change, too. Thus, it is likely these financial demands will persist.

In addition to leaving the country, Uzbeks have also responded to oppressive government policies with public protests. One such demonstration led to what Human Rights Watch calls "the Andijan Massacre" in the city of Andijan in the Ferghana Valley on May 13, 2005. On that day, thousands of unarmed Uzbeks gathered in protest outside of Andijan Prison, where armed gunmen had earlier made an attempt to free political prisoners. Security forces shot into the crowd indiscriminately. The government claims it was responding to a prison break, but the protesters claim they were voicing grievances peacefully. The government put the death toll at 187, but unofficial counts are much higher. In the aftermath, the government imprisoned and harassed human rights lawyers, activists, journalists, and members of civil society groups.

Human Rights Watch published its findings on the Andijan Massacre, "Uzbekistan: No Justice 7 Years After the Andijan Massacre" (http://www.hrw.org/news/2012/05/11/uzbekistan-no-justice-7-years-after-andijan-massacre) on May 12, 2012.

Throughout the early twenty-first century, young Uzbek men, mainly, have been moving to cities in Kazakhstan and Russia for temporary work in agriculture, construction, marketplace sales, and low-level jobs that often force them to endure exploitative conditions. In the judgment of most, however, the hardships outweigh the alternative of staying put on cotton farms or migrating to work as common laborers in other Uzbek cities. Today, Uzbeks, as well as neighboring Tajiks and Kyrgyz, help make Russia the second-largest labor migrant recipient country in the world after the United States.

For further analysis of labor migration from Uzbekistan and other Central Asian countries, explore the 2009 report titled "Labor Migration in Central Asia: Implications of the Global Economic Crisis" (http://www.silkroadstudies.org/new/docs/silkroadpapers/0905migration.pdf), a joint publication of the Central Asia–Caucasus Institute and the Silk Road Studies Program.

Uzbeks also have settled in the Scandinavian countries, Germany, Ireland, England, and, increasingly, the United States. Large urban centers such as New York, Columbus, Atlanta, Los Angeles, Phoenix, Chicago, and St. Louis attract tens of thousands of Uzbeks. While not all of these people intend to settle abroad for good, it is becoming increasingly obvious to many young Uzbeks that the world's centers of global capital and development offer them far more opportunities for a better quality of life than they can find at home.

Where this trend will go, or how many more Central Asians will choose, or try, to leave their respective countries, is unknown. Insofar as Central Asian countries struggle to provide decent wages, or even jobs, for their citizens, it seems likely this out-migration will continue. These economic concerns, coupled with a denial of basic human rights, as well as severe punishments for members of human rights organizations or those perceived or alleged to be members of extremist organizations, make it likely that the upsurge in people leaving or trying to leave their countries will continue.

In conclusion, there is a certain irony relating to globalization that embodies Uzbekistan as a center of global cotton production. The rules of the game, as it were, in the Uzbek cotton industry have more or less made life unbearable for millions directly and indirectly tethered to the industry. The government's monopoly and virtual stranglehold over cotton and the peasant population has caused a genuine rebellion in the country. This rebellion, however, does not involve pitchforks or Molotov cocktails, but rather a kind of global resettlement for a better way of life—the old immigrant's song, with its own

---

Box 15.2

Uzbeks in Russia

In June 2013 the president of Uzbekistan, Islom (or Islam) Karimov (the only president Uzbekistan has had since it became an independent country in 1991) called those Uzbeks who have chosen to migrate, especially to Russia, "lazybones" and an "embarrassment to the people of Uzbekistan." This likely did not please most Uzbeks, since there is probably not a single citizen without a relative living and working abroad, and sending money back home to support relatives in Uzbekistan.

Interestingly, while the Uzbeks in Russia and abroad continue working in what most people in the United States and other Western countries would consider low-skilled and dead-end jobs, one extraordinary development is the increasing popularity and reputation of Uzbeks as chefs and restaurateurs. Uzbekistan enjoys a wonderful cuisine, one which is little known outside of Uzbekistan but now appears to be ascendant in Russia. Who knows how long before it becomes a new trend in international dining in other parts of the world?

The Ferghana News Information Agency published a report on the president's comments, "Islam Karimov: Far from Reality" (http://enews.fergananews.com/articles/2837), on its website on June 24, 2013.

---

particular, twenty-first-century Central Asian twist. Rather than allowing one form of global capitalist order to dictate terms of working and living that their own despotic state mediates and perverts in its own way, Uzbeks have taken themselves out of the cotton equation by embracing alternative pathways. Seeking these new options, they hope, will help them merge and meld with global capital in ways they perceive as personally more advantageous. Ordinary people cannot now challenge the state's power directly, so they simply leave Uzbekistan, at least temporarily, for job opportunities that pay them genuine living wages. What the social and physical structure of the old cotton collective villages may look like in another decade or so cannot be predicted accurately, but it is unlikely that they will remain the domain of state engineering, which has been the case for the past eighty-five or so years.

References and Further Research

Adams, Laura L. 2010. *The Spectacular State: Culture and National Identity in Uzbekistan.* Durham, NC: Duke University Press.

Allworth, Edward A. 1990. *The Modern Uzbeks: From the Fourteenth Century to the Present; A Cultural History.* Stanford, CA: Hoover Institution Press.

Becker, Seymour. 2009. *Russia's Protectorates in Central Asia: Bukhara and Khiva, 1865–1924.* London: Routledge.

Brower, Daniel. 2003. *Turkestan and the Fate of the Russian Empire.* London: Routledge-Curzon.

Davies, R.W. 1980. *The Soviet Collective Farm, 1929–1930*. Cambridge, MA: Harvard University Press.

Djanibekov, Nodir, Inna Rudenko, John P.A. Lamers, and Ihtiyor Bobojonov. 2010. "Pros and Cons of Cotton Production in Uzbekistan." Case Study No. 7–9 of the Program "Food Policy for Developing Countries: The Role of Government in the Global Food System." Ithaca, NY: Cornell University. http://cip.cornell.edu/DPubS?service=UI&version=1.0& verb=Display&handle=dns.gfs/1279121771.

Findley, Carter Vaughn. 2005. *The Turks in World History*. New York: Oxford University Press.

Golden, Peter B. 2011. *Central Asia in World History*. New York: Oxford University Press.

Green, Peter. 1991. *Alexander of Macedon, 356–323 B.C.: A Historical Biography*. Berkeley: University of California Press.

Hopkirk, Peter. 1992. *The Great Game: The Struggle for Empire in Central Asia*. New York: Kodansha International.

Kamp, Marianne. 2006. *The New Woman in Uzbekistan: Islam, Modernity, and Unveiling Under Communism*. Seattle: University of Washington Press.

Khalid, Adeeb. 2007. *Islam After Communism: Religion and Politics in Central Asia*. Berkeley: University of California Press.

Levi, Scott. 2007. "Turks and Tajiks in Central Asian History." In *Everyday Life in Central Asia*, edited by Jeff Sahadeo and Russell Zanca. Bloomington: Indiana University Press.

Liu, Morgan. 2012. *Under Solomon's Throne: Uzbek Visions of Renewal in Osh*. Pittsburgh: University of Pittsburgh Press.

MacDonald, Stephen. 2012. *Economic Policy and Cotton in Uzbekistan*. Washington, DC: U.S. Department of Agriculture. http://www.ers.usda.gov/media/935015/cws12h01.pdf.

Manz, Beatrice Forbes. 1991. *The Rise and Rule of Tamerlane*. Cambridge: Cambridge University Press.

Marat, Erica. 2009. *Labor Migration in Central Asia: Implications of the Global Economic Crisis*. Washington, DC: Central Asia-Caucasus Institute.

Massell, Gregory J. 1974. *The Surrogate Proletariat: Moslem Women and Revolutionary Strategies in Soviet Central Asia, 1919–1929*. Princeton, NJ: Princeton University Press.

Northrop, Douglas. 2003. *Veiled Empire: Gender and Power in Stalinist Central Asia*. Ithaca, NY: Cornell University Press.

Rasanayagam, Johan. 2010. *Islam in Post-Soviet Uzbekistan: The Morality of Experience*. Cambridge: Cambridge University Press.

Soucek, Swat. 2000. *A History of Inner Asia*. Cambridge: Cambridge University Press.

Stronski, Paul. 2010. *Tashkent: Forging a Soviet City, 1930–1966*. Pittsburgh: University of Pittsburgh Press.

Zanca, Russell. 2010. *Life in a Muslim Uzbek Village: Cotton Farming After Communism*. Belmont, CA: Cengage Learning.

———. 2011. "Cotton Farming in Uzbekistan: Interview with American Scholar Russell Zanca." Human Rights Society of Uzbekistan. http://en.hrsu.org/archives/1870.

Further Links

CESS Blog (www.centraleurasia.org) is both a news and scholarly research site and a resource pertaining to Central Eurasian Studies.

Eurasianet (http://www.eurasianet.org/) provides all manner of news-related items pertaining to Central Asian societies.

Ferghana News Information Agency (http://enews.fergananews.com/index.php?cid=2) covers newsworthy events pertaining to Central Asia.

The Institute for War & Peace Reporting (http://iwpr.net/) provides good analysis of Central Asian events and political and social processes.

The Jamestown Foundation's "Eurasia Daily Monitor" (http://www.jamestown.org/edm) provides in-depth journalistic coverage of events in Central Asia.

Registan (http://registan.net/) is an independent site focusing on Central Asian news and analysis.

16

Images of Place
The Legacy of the Ottoman House in Modern Turkey

CAREL BERTRAM

There is a distinctive type of house that once was found wherever the Ottomans lived. From the seventeenth century until the first days of the twentieth century—when regions such as Bulgaria, Greece, Bosnia, and Turkey claimed a private title to their own part of the once great Ottoman Empire—timber-framed houses with protruding upper stories characterized a wide landscape, giving it a distinctive Ottoman stamp. Just by looking at these houses, you knew you were in Ottoman territory. Most noticeably, their upper floors would jut out over the lower ones to take advantage of the free space of the street. These cantilevers were lined with uniform windows to maximize ventilation and views, and they were protected by expansive, overhanging eaves. Such facades and profiles once defined the streetscapes of many Ottoman towns, from modern-day Bosnia to Syria.

Although these old Ottoman houses have a common style, this chapter is not about their architectural vocabulary. Instead of looking at its roof, or its window, or its profile, I explore what went on inside the Ottoman house. More specifically, I will examine what type of life is associated with this house *in memory*, looking at its social and cultural meanings in the part of the Ottoman Empire that became modern Turkey. I have found by analyzing how the Ottoman house has been represented in Turkey over time, such as how it appears in paintings or novels, one sees how it began to take on a larger-than-life power. This power emerged at a crucial time of transition between the beginning of the early twentieth century and the late 1930s, as a young Turkish Republic struggled to release itself from its Ottoman past and to reconceptualize itself as a nation of Turks.

Methodology

When investigating any kind of built structure, architectural historians study building processes, materials, and styles, but also they ask questions about how a building was understood by the builder and the patron, as well as by the user, and what its uses were. Architectural historians might also ask how a building fit in with a social system of thought; for example, they might ask what style of building was thought to be beautiful, or even holy. Art historians, on the other hand, are more concerned with artistic *representations*—in this case, how a building appears in paintings or magazine illustrations. Art historians also ask about the meanings an image conveys to the viewer. For this meaning, art historians

A street in Tokat in northern Turkey, 1993. *(Photo by Carel Bertram)*

look at a defined body of work, asking how houses were represented in a certain era. Also, they can go more deeply into the way that images evoke, or once evoked, *feelings*. For this information, art historians must consult texts. If the text is a novel in which the building is important in the life of the people using it, it may provide information about how people thought about these buildings as well as about how they were used.

By interpreting both visual and textual images, I expand from architectural and art history into the realm of social and cultural geography. A social geographer asks how people live in spaces, including houses, neighborhoods, and nations; what places mean; and how that meaning comes to exist. In other words, how do the ways that people configure their spaces represent who, in fact, people feel they are? Through the use and meaning of space, people answer questions about deeply held identities.

Thus, visual or textual images of places, through their symbolism, are central to giving meaning and identity to groups, small or large. Examples of the image-laden, symbolic universe of the Ottomans include their architecture, art, and public ritual. For example, the skyline of Istanbul is dominated by imperial mosques built by successive sultans and

Illustration of the carrying of a model of Suleiman's mosque during a festival, 1582. *(Photo by Walter B. Denny. Used by permission.)*

their families, including Mehmed II (the Conqueror), Suleiman I (the Magnificent), and Ahmed II (the Warrior Prince). These imposingly beautiful, domed structures with their graceful minarets constantly proclaimed a nexus of imperial power, piety, and continuity. One proof of the significance of this image is the fact that a model of Suleiman's mosque was carried in a fifty-two-day public festival organized in 1582 by a later sultan, and an image of it was later reproduced in an illustrated text about this festival.

My investigation of how the Ottoman house became a meaningful visual image began when I was a Fulbright Scholar in Turkey in 1993, investigating the architecture of what was then known—because the Ottoman Empire was long over—as "the Turkish house." People were forever asking what a foreigner like me was doing in Turkey, and my simple answer was that I had come to do research on "the Turkish house." What I found, to my surprise, was that I only had to utter those three words to induce a sort of glow, as they repeated the words with a reverent love: "the Turkish house . . ." After the glow, and a pause for reverie, would come stories about a specific house that they knew, or ones they had missed knowing. Where they lived now, they had heard, was once filled

Postcard of Istanbul's Suleimaniya Mosque. 1910 *(Photo by Carel Bertram)*

with such houses. They had heard that one always sleeps so well in these old wooden houses. Or perhaps they remembered their grandfather's or uncle's house; or stories about those houses that had been torn down; or about houses that were in villages they had not visited, or that they *had* visited, and how they wished to live in one, if only they could. And so I began to ask about how this old wooden house had come to evoke such strong emotions and memories of the past; how an *image* of this house could become lodged in the Turkish imagination all the way to the present day. And I asked what exactly these emotions and memories expressed.

Information and images of the Turkish house can be found in the "Architecture: Houses" section of the Turkish Cultural Foundation website (http://www.turkishculture.org/architecture/houses-27.htm).

Imagining a New Nation in the Image of Home

The Ottoman Empire understood itself as a pluralistic mosaic inclusive of minority ethnic and religious groups. However, when the empire was partitioned by the victorious powers of World War I in 1918, new nation-states ended this pluralism. Turkey, like the other nations that emerged from this division, had new demographics and a new nationalist ideology that actively excluded minorities. With the vast Ottoman territorial losses of the

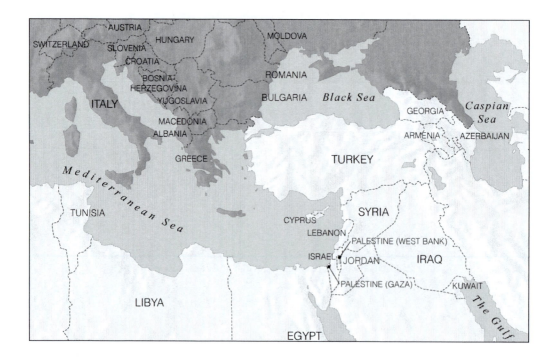

Balkan Wars of 1912 and 1913, Muslim refugees fled from massacres or marginalization in formerly Ottoman territories that had come to define themselves as Christian nations, such as Bulgaria, Serbia, and Greece. On the other hand, the new nation of Turkey underwent comparable cataclysms in a similar purging of non-Muslims from within its national boundaries. Prior to 1923, when Turkey was established, Christian Armenian, Greek, and Syriac Orthodox made up at least one-third of the population in Anatolia, the land that would primarily compose the new country. The Ottoman capital of Istanbul had nurtured thriving communities of Christians and Jews. But after the establishment of today's Turkey, with a new capital in Ankara, Turkey's population became almost completely Muslim. It is at this moment of significant, and at times traumatic, demographic change that the old Ottoman house began to emerge in the new Turkish imagination as a marker of identity. In other words, during a period of rupture and pain, when the losses of the Ottoman Empire became finalized, the old Ottoman house began to emerge as a concept rather than as a place to hang one's fez.

The first images of the house appear in paintings by Hoca Ali Riza (1858–1939), who illustrated what he considered to be a disappearing past. In fact, the old houses were indeed disappearing quickly, some due to fire, some to decay, and some as they were subdivided for use by new immigrants. As a teacher at the military academy, where the study of art was required, Hoca Ali Riza influenced a generation of political players, setting the stage for "imagining" the old house. In 1911, some members of this intelligentsia who had studied with Hoca Ali Riza, and had even learned to paint these houses, formed what they called "The Turkish Hearth Society," a group that would become an ideological arm of a new Turkey. Its president, Hamdullah Suphi, took up

Painting of a street in Üsküdar, a neighborhood in Istanbul, by Hoca Ali Riza (1858–1939). *(From the archive of Antik A.S., Istanbul. Used by permission.)*

the idea of the house in a series of talks and articles, which he entitled "The Turkish House." This may have been the first time that the term "Turkish house" was used. Thus, among the national elites, the house that Hoca had drawn pictorially as a marker of the past was given both a name and textual depth as an official site of national memory. "How did you feel when you left [your old houses]?" Suphi would ask when showing people images of old Ottoman houses. "Were you sad when you grew up and moved away?" (Suphi 1912, 1217).

Hamdullah Suphi did not want to move out of his own fine apartment into a wooden house that was drafty, expensive to maintain, and probably had mice in the rafters; and he certainly did not want to revive the Ottoman past. Rather, his aim was to persuade his audience of "new Turks" that they had a common Turkish past. He made it seem obvious that they—or at least their parents or grandparents—had once lived in the Turkish house that he was imagining for them.

He did this at the right time. Beginning with the establishment of the new Republic of Turkey in 1923, and under the country's new leader, Mustafa Kemal Atatürk, who was committed to ideas of progress and reform, the old symbolic universe of the Ottoman world was attacked. Within ten years, Atatürk had closed the Ottoman palace and ended the Ottoman Sultanate that had been the highest (Sunni) Muslim religious authority. Furthermore, religious schools were made illegal and replaced with Western secular education. In fact, all public religious practices were curtailed. Sufi dervish lodges were shut down and even visits to the graves of the sultans or religious figures were prohibited. Religious forms of dress, such as the dervish hat, and Ottoman forms of dress, such as the fez, were also made illegal. Polygamy was abolished and women were encouraged to take off their scarves, to wear Western clothing in public, and to take jobs. Even the Ottoman language was dismantled. It was now illegal to use Arabic and Persian words, and the Arabic script, which was so closely associated with Islam, was, in a single day, replaced by the Western alphabet. Western music was the only type allowed on the airwaves, and all forms of art could portray only secular subjects. In fact, the Ottoman past and its symbolic universe were made into one of the new state's most strictly supervised domains.

Primed by Hamdullah Suphi and the Turkish Hearth Association, the imagined Turkish house was introduced into this reformed symbolic space. Once it was established that the old house belonged, at least officially, to every "Turk," forward-looking Turkish nation-builders had to convince this "Turk" that the house represented modern ideals. The irony in this strategy, successful as it may have been, was remarkable, for the idea was to construct an image as a representation of a common past, and then to make that past represent the ideals of the modern state. Thus, instead of emphasizing the original ideas behind the house's architectural forms, which allowed for privacy inside yet also allowed free use of the streets, the house was now touted as "civilized," meaning intrinsically modern (and Western), with a design that met contemporary requirements of hygiene, light, and clean air. In this way, the new Turks in the new republic could imagine that they were not imitating Western modernity, but that modernity was their birthright—one that emerged from their own past.

Thus, when the new nation attempted to formulate its own national architectural style, it would seem only natural that this new style included overhanging eaves and uniform rows of windows, for this represented modern and Western republican ideals, as well as ideals that were specifically Turkish. Under the leadership of the architect and teacher Sedad Hakki Eldem and his students, this national style was used for public buildings that represented secular institutions. In other words, the architectural vocabulary of the Turkish house was used on buildings that were meant to create attachments to a new form of modern public life among all residents in the newly formed nation. What was forgotten in this translation of style from private to public use was the idea of home, of the inside, and perhaps even of the soul of its residents.

However, the novels written at the time and that take place in these old houses suggest that the house might not have accepted its role as an image of the modern; rather, it insistently tied itself to traditions and religious values of the past. Perhaps this is not a surprise. The new Turkish citizen was not only to be ethnically Turkish, but also a Turkish Muslim. At the same time, however, his or her religious values were being forced off the streets and out of the public realm, and the symbolic universe of the past was being stripped of its Islamic identity. In this environment, where better could this part of the Turkish identity be expressed? Textual images of the Turkish house in national literature thus suggest that part of national memory went indoors to fight back against the insistent public secularism.

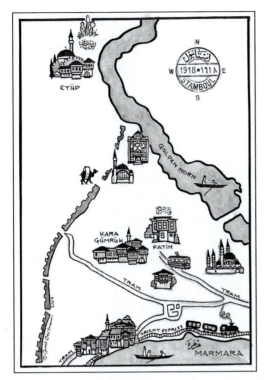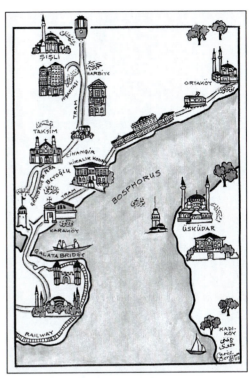

Map of Istanbul, 1918, illustrating the tramline from Fatih, west of the Golden Horn, to Harbiye, to the east. *(Drawing by Carel Bertram)*

The Turkish House in Safa's Novel *Fatih-Harbiye*

The novel *Fatih-Harbiye*, published in 1931 by the well-known author and nationalist Peyami Safa (1899–1961), presents fertile textual ground for exploring the complex cultural meanings of the Turkish house. Fatih and Harbiye are two areas of Istanbul on opposite sides of an inlet of the Bosporus called the Golden Horn. The neighborhood of Fatih is in the heart of Istanbul's historic peninsula. In the 1920s and 1930s, it was a symbol of the religious and cultural heritage of "the East," as it is today. On the opposite side, across the Golden Horn, at the other end of a tramline, is Harbiye, the northernmost section of the neighborhood of Beyoğlu. Because Beyoğlu was the home of Ottoman Latin, Orthodox, and Armenian Christians, and some Jews (as well as foreign merchants and ambassadors), it has always been a symbol of the *non*-Muslim world, and of "the West."

The heroine of *Fatih-Harbiye*, seventeen-year-old Neriman, lives in an old wooden house in Fatih with her widowed father, Faiz Bey. Their house is clearly described with all its visual attributes: it has an upper floor that protrudes over the street, it is lit by gas lamps, "and when the front door closed, the old house shook and its window panes rattled." Like all the old Ottoman-Turkish houses of Istanbul, it was starting to fall apart; but it was described with warmth, as a place where one could be happy.

Old Istanbul Street, ca. 1870–1910. *(Photo by G. Berggren [1835–1920]. Reproduced courtesy of the Library of Congress, Prints and Photographs Division, lc-dig-ppmsca-03851)*

Neriman is a student at the music conservatory, where she plays the *oud* (a lute-like string instrument). Neriman's sweetheart, Shinasi, is also from Fatih; he studies the *kemanje* (a type of fiddle) at the same conservatory. Her father, Faiz Bey, spends his evenings reading the great Ottoman philosophers, as well as mystical, spiritual poetry. These details—Neriman's and Shinasi's playing of classical Oriental instruments and the subjects Faiz Bey is interested in—associate the characters, without saying so explicitly, with the religious thought of the Ottoman world and the East. In fact, Islam and religion are never mentioned in this novel. Doing so would go against secular Kemalism, as Mustafa Kemal Atatürk's ideas were called. Under Kemalism, secularism and Westernization were the only ideologies allowed a public voice, forcing authors of novels to resort to codes.

As the plot progresses, the dramatic tension between the worlds of the past and the present deepens. It is clear that if Neriman and Shinasi—who are tied to the classical past by their houses and their music—would just marry, modern life would go on, but with

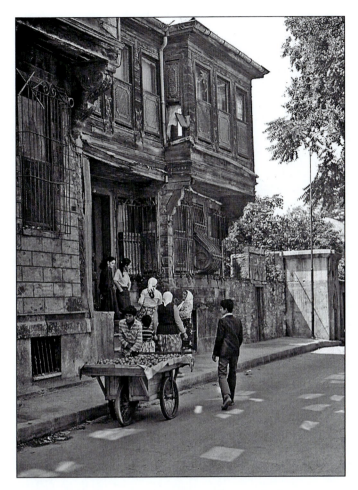

Istanbul Street, 1983. *(Photo by Fred M. Donner. Used by permission.)*

the old values intact. But Neriman is attracted by the lights of Beyoğlu, and she takes the tram there, the Fatih-Harbiye tram.

After spending time in the cafes of "Westernized" Harbiye, Neriman gives up playing the oud. Not only does she give up the oud, she starts to play the violin, partly because she is star-struck by a young male violinist from the conservatory who is enamored by everything Western. Neriman even dreams of going with him to a formal ball. This was a period when people would talk about "hat and ball longings," the desire to wear a hat instead of a scarf, and to go to dances. And the more often she visits Beyoğlu, the darker the houses of Fatih appear to her, the more sleepy and silent they become.

Neriman's father does not try to stop her visits; instead, he wants only to nurture and protect her. He has encouraged her education and her independence, and in fact he loves her so much that he tries to sell family valuables so she can have a dress for the ball. But he does understand, and he does say that his daughter is having "a spiritual crisis," again code words, along with oud, for Eastern, Muslim values.

Young women at an oud lesson at the Turkish Conservatory of Music, Istanbul, 1919. *(The Istanbul Ansiklopedisi, Vol. 2, edited by H. Ayhan, p. 557. Istanbul: Kültür Bakanlığı ve Tarih Vakfı'nın Ortak Yayınları, 1993.)*

Postcard of the Fatih-Harbiye tram in Beyoğlu, on what is now Independence Street (Istiklâl Caddesi), Istanbul, ca. 1918. *(From the collection of Carel Bertram.)*

Her spiritual crisis is made clear as she tries to rationalize her attraction to the West. In defining the two cultures that are tugging at her soul, she has an epiphany:

> Neriman thought and suddenly understood why Easterners loved cats so much and Westerners loved dogs. In Christian houses there were lots of dogs, in Muslim houses lots of cats, because Easterners resembled cats and Westerners resembled dogs! Cats eat, drink, lie down, sleep, give birth. Their life is spent on a cushion and passes in a dream; even if their eyes are open, it's as if they are dreaming, they are languid, lazy and day-dreaming creatures who can't stand work. Dogs are vigorous, swift, and bold. They do useful work—a lot of useful work. Even when they are sleeping they are wakeful. If they hear even the slightest sound, they jump up and bark.

When Neriman's father comes home, she bursts at him with her new intelligence:

> "Look!" she said. "Gülter [the housekeeper] is sleeping and so is Sarman [the cat] . . . and they're not the only ones who are sleeping! All of Fatih is asleep!" (Safa 1931, 46)

Her wise and kind father understands her inner dilemma and gently offers another interpretation to the great East-West divide. Whereas his daughter thinks of the East as lazy and the West as active, Faiz Bey suggests that the cat may be inactive because it is thinking about ideas that might benefit man; the dog merely acts, offering no spiritual depth. He thus suggests that the difference between the East and West is that the East emphasizes the spiritual, whereas the West emphasizes the material:

> There are some men who sit and think from morning to evening. They have a *hazine-i efkâr*, a treasury of ideas, I mean they are rich on the side of thought. Then there are some men who work on their feet from morning till night, for example peasants, . . . but the work that they do consists of laying four bricks on top of each other. At first people may appear lazy, but really, *velâkin!*, they are hard-working. Other people appear hard-working, but really, *velâkin!*, the work they do is weak. Because one's work involves mental endeavors using the spirit, the other's work is physical and uses the body. *The spirit is always great, the body destitute. The difference between what they do is because of this* [emphasis added]. (Safa 1931, 47)

Faiz Bey, in the passage above, places what appears to be the hard work of material progress in an inferior position to the work of the intellect. In their sitting room, lit by gas lamps, he explains to his daughter that the houses that appear dark, sleepy, and silent conceal something that is deep and meaningful—the depth of an Ottoman legacy of spiritual thought. This he places in opposition to the West and Harbiye, with its shops, bright lights, and a materialism that must not be accepted uncritically, without asking how they fit into one's larger set of values.

The roles of the family father, the old house, and the values of "the East" come together late in the story when Neriman confronts a "friendly ghost of the past" who inhabits an old wooden house in her neighborhood. Neriman and Shinasi used to pass this house every day as they walked home from the music conservatory:

Old house in Fatih, Istanbul, 1990. *(Photo by Walter Denny. Used by permission.)*

> Every part was run down, the windows had lost their rectangularity. The eaves had lost some of their planks, the zinc cladding had fallen in. . . . This Konak [mansion] was in such ruins that even a three year old child could push it down. But there were still curtains on the windows; so was anyone inside? And if there was, who? (Safa 1931, 66–67)

Over the years, Neriman and Shinasi would imagine an old man inside watching them as they walked home from school. Each time they walked by, they would add to their story about him, until he felt entirely real:

> He had a long white beard, the cap that he put on his bald head was plain and simple, he sat by the right-hand window and fiddled with his prayer-beads, his lips always mumbling a prayer. He would think, but he wasn't thinking about people or work; he had large ideas about the world, about humanity, about God and death. When he heard a footstep on the street, his trembling head would look out the window behind the grills, and when he would see Neriman and Shinasi walking by, he would shut his eyes and pray that they were happy. (Safa 1931, 68)

This "friendly ghost of the past" could even sense Neriman's "inner struggle," when she was giving in to her "hat and ball longings," and perhaps her thoughts about that other violin-playing suitor, and rejecting her old neighborhood, as well as the ideas and values attached to it. As she was experiencing her internal turmoil,

> Neriman was caught up with a strange feeling, as if she had heard a footstep in the house; then she thought the door opened and she thought she saw the image of the old man on the threshold. He still had his prayer-beads in his hands, [but] this time his face was as white as his beard and his night cap; and he asked with eyes that tried to conceal a deep, sad, astonishment: What has happened, children? What happened to you? (Safa 1931, 68)

It seems that this "ghost" wanted Shinasi and Neriman to be together, to live a traditional life with the promise of spiritual peace. Her own vision is so disturbing to Neriman that she faints in Shinasi's arms.

Clearly, the old house was taken seriously as a symbol of Turkish identity. But the house also represented the larger nation as a place where new Western ideas, such as women's education, dances, and even violins, could be thought about, based on Ottoman religious and philosophical ideas. Neriman's father was like other fathers and grandfathers written about in other contemporary novels; like Neriman's friendly ghost, they wanted the children and grandchildren of the new nation to move successfully into their new world, and to be happy. But also they wanted them to have an inner, examined happiness, with room for Muslim values. Inside the house, Islam and the nation were not diametrically opposed to one another; instead, it was a place where the two could coexist.

The Turkish House and the Turkish Diaspora

As discussed, the new nation defined itself as a nation of ethnically Turkish Muslims. One of the reasons for this was a belief—or fear—that the non-Muslim Ottoman populations were aligned with other nationalist programs (such as Orthodox Christian Russia or Orthodox Christian Greece), and were thus a threat to the new Turkey. This fear was so strong that even those minorities who had generally been loyal Ottomans, and who also saw the new Turkey as their home, were often perceived as dangerous. Once a representation of the ideal of Ottoman pluralism, these Ottoman Jews and Ottoman Greek, Armenian, and Assyrian Christians became the new outsiders; this was true not just conceptually, but literally, as most were forced to leave. Thus, although many minorities once lived in the old Turkish houses, they do not appear in the nationalist novels of this period, and the houses in these novels do not represent them. In fact, the very memory of these groups seems to have been erased.

Nonetheless, the descendants of Ottoman Jews and Ottoman Greek, Armenian, and Assyrian Christians, although they now almost all live outside of Turkey, have not forgotten that their pasts can be found in Ottoman houses. Hence, in the twentieth and twenty-first centuries, these descendants have begun actively to reclaim their memory of them, if not the actual homes. Descendants of Ottoman Jews in Israel recall or visit the houses of their ancestors in Istanbul neighborhoods such as Kuzguncuk; contemporary Anatolian Greeks return to visit family houses in Anatolian towns such as Safranbolu; and U.S. citizens of Anatolian

Family photo of the Armenian Arakelian family, taken in Yozgat, Ottoman Turkey, before World War I. *(Used by permission of Mary Ann Arakelian Kazanjian.)*

Armenian descent find ancestral houses in cities such as Yozgat or villages such as Lidje. The old wooden houses appear as sites of memory in their films and memoirs, and the images address the rupture with their past, as well as the pain that goes with it.

Descendants of Armenians, who were able to leave Anatolia after Ottoman authorities targeted their ancestors (and other non-Muslim minorities) in systematic massacres and death marches (centering on 1915), are an important example. Traveling to Turkey today from the Americas, Europe, and the Middle East, they frequently find the houses of their ancestors. They also frequently meet Turkish citizens with Armenian roots, descendants of Armenian children saved from the death marches or given over to the care of kind neighbors. Conservative estimates put the number of Turkish citizens with Armenian roots today in the very high thousands. Thus, it is not surprising that these traverlers often wonder if they are meeting descendants of the lost siblings of their own grandparents. In fact, along with finding family houses, some actually do find family members, even their own first cousins.

When they arrive in their ancestral towns, Armenians with roots in Anatolia almost always feel "at home," for the stories they carry are not only of trauma and atrocities, but also of a life once shared with Muslim neighbors who today still share much of their culture, including music and food, or who live in ways that fit their cultural memories. Thus, in the memoirs, journals, films, and writings that recount these journeys, the house becomes a marker in the imagination that evokes not just loss, pain, and injustice, but also shared origins.

However, although many Turkish citizens are beginning to cope with the idea of shared pain in the transition from the Ottoman Empire to the Turkish Republic, the image of the

An Ottoman mansion (*konak*) in Yozgat reflecting Arakelian family memory; today a Turkish House Museum. *(Photo by Carel Bertram)*

Turkish house has not yet begun to reflect its multicultural or multiethnic history or what caused its rupture. Rather, it seems that the meanings attributed to the image of the Turkish house are changing in other ways. Whereas the early republic repudiated the Ottoman period, the ruling Justice and Development Party is reconnecting to it as it celebrates Turkey's ties to an Ottoman past, both to its political might of empire and to its Sunni Muslim heritage. As of this writing in 2013, Prime Minister Recep Erdoğan aims to build an enormous Ottoman-style mosque in Greater Istanbul, on a hilltop overlooking the Bosporus, or perhaps in one of the vibrant centers of the modern city. Resembling the Suleimaniya Mosque, the important feature of the skyline during the sixteenth century mentioned above, this new mosque would publicly tie government ideology to Sunni values of piety, once associated with the Ottoman world.

In addition, restrictions on Islam in the public sphere have been lifted, if not reversed, and thus the house's old message of Muslim piety no longer needs to be kept hidden or referred to in secret coding, as in Safa's *Fatih-Harbiye*. Since 1996, for example, the Ramadan festival, an important municipal celebration in Istanbul, has been using miniature Turkish houses as concession stands, thereby reconnecting the memory of home with a public expression of Islam. Indeed, Kemalist and secularist symbols may retreat into the private realm in the future, in a curious inversion of history.

Celebration of Ramadan, in the Sultan Ahmet neighborhood, Istanbul. *(Photo by Carel Bertram)*

What remains clear, however, is that the tools of art and architectural history combined with those of social and cultural geography allow us to question how images of the past bring that past into the present, laden with new meanings. Walter Benjamin (1968, 255) reminds us that that "every image of the past that is not recognized by the present as one of its own concerns threatens to disappear irretrievably." The Old Turkish house has not disappeared; it remains active in the imagination of all the children of the Ottoman Empire, and it still has restorative work to do.

References and Further Research

Atasoy, Nurhan. 1997. *1582 Surname-i Hümayün: An Imperial Celebration.* Istanbul: Koç Bank Publications.

Benjamin, Walter. 1968. "Theses on the Philosophy of History." In *Illuminations: Essays and Reflections.* Translated and edited by Hannah Arendt, 253–263. New York: Schocken.

Bertram, Carel. 2008. *Imagining the Turkish House: Collective Visions of Home.* Austin: University of Texas Press.

———. 2010. "Journeys to Historic Armenia: 'There Is Something There!'" *Armenian Reporter*, December 14. http://www.reporter.am/go/article/2010–12–14-journeys-to-historic-armenia—there-is-something-there—.

Cagaptay, Soner. 2004. "Race, Assimilation and Kemalism: Turkish Nationalism and the Minorities in the 1930s." *Middle Eastern Studies* 40, no. 3: 86–101.

Kezer, Zeynep. 2000. "Familiar Things in Strange Places: Ankara's Ethnography Museum and the Legacy of Islam in Republican Turkey." *Perspectives in Vernacular Architecture: People, Power, Places* 8: 101–106.

Landen, Robert G., ed. 1971. *The Emergence of the Modern Middle East: Selected Readings.* New York: Van Nostrand Reinhold.

Nereid, Camilla Trud. 2012. "Domesticating Modernity: The Turkish Magazine *Yedigün*, 1933–9." *Journal of Contemporary History* 47, no. 3: 483–504.

Safa, Peyami. 1931. *Fatih-Harbiye.* Istanbul: Ötüken Yayınevi. Reprinted in 1976.

Suphi, Hamdullah. 1912. "Eski Türk Evleri." *Türk Yurdu* 5: 1216–1221.

17

Counterinsurgency and Culture
The 2003 U.S. Invasion of Iraq

ROCHELLE DAVIS

With the U.S. wars of the twenty-first century, the concepts of "counterinsurgency" and "culture" were reintroduced into U.S. foreign policy calculations and military strategies. These concepts were an element of past wars the United States had fought, such as the Pacific War against Japan during World War II and the Vietnam War. In both of these cases, the enemy was understood to be culturally distinct and fighting in an unconventional way. Thus, for the war effort to be successful, the U.S. military had to train for new methods of fighting and for understanding the cultural differences it would encounter.

Counterinsurgency wars differ from conventional wars in that they involve different kinds of enemies: a conventional war pits two trained, organized, well-equipped militaries against each other, whereas a counterinsurgency war pits an organized military against an unregulated configuration of fighters who rely on civilians and often live among them. These fighters use a variety of guerrilla tactics with more or less sophistication. Soldiers on one side face "rebels" or "insurgents" on the other, who might wear uniforms but might also dress in civilian clothing. The battleground for insurgency can be anywhere, can shift at any time, and can be in or near civilian areas. Since they are facing superior forces in terms of equipment and training, insurgency forces rely on the element of surprise. The U.S. war against Iraq in 2003 started as a conventional war between U.S. forces and the Iraqi forces under Saddam Hussein, but with the defeat of the Iraqi army the U.S. military began to describe it as a counterinsurgency effort, which required a change in strategy.

This chapter discusses the U.S. invasion and occupation of Iraq from 2003 onward, looking specifically at the shift from conventional warfare to a counterinsurgency (COIN) doctrine that emphasized the importance of understanding Iraqi culture in fighting the enemy and running the government for the occupied population. As a cultural anthropologist, I chose this research topic in order to understand the direct and indirect influence of U.S. foreign policy decisions, agreed upon in Washington, DC, on the everyday lives of U.S. troops and Iraqis, and to elaborate on one element of how these wars were fought and how the people involved came to perceive and understand each other. Important to these discussions are the experiences of Iraqis. It was, after all, their country that the United States invaded and occupied, and they rightfully should be heard and allowed to evaluate the failures and successes of the U.S.-led war in their country.

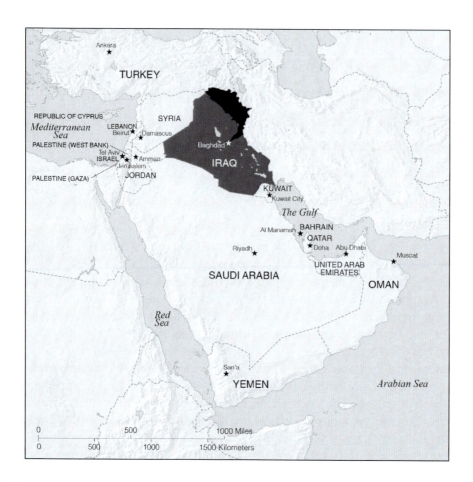

After a brief history of the U.S. invasion and occupation of Iraq (2003–2010), this chapter focuses on how the U.S. military's approach to dealing with Iraqis shifted over time. It will present accounts of troops on the ground concerning how various policies and practices affected Iraqis as well as the troops' abilities to accomplish their missions. It shows how many believe that the U.S. military's attempt to use cultural understanding in its interactions with Iraqis should have eased the harshness of the U.S. occupation of Iraq on Iraqis. It suggests that despite the widespread adoption of the COIN doctrine—the aim of which was to use cultural knowledge as a way to defeat the insurgency and win "the hearts and minds" of Iraqis—the counterinsurgency strategy did not address the underlying imbalance of power and force that made "winning hearts and minds" a nearly impossible task to accomplish in the context of war.

Brief Chronology

The goal of the U.S. invasion of Iraq in March 2003, as stated by President George W. Bush, was "to disarm Iraq of weapons of mass destruction, to end Saddam Hussein's support for terrorism, and to free the Iraqi people" (radio address, March 22, 2003). However,

Box 17.1

Methods: Interviews and Analysis

The investigation in this chapter combines two research methods. First, my research assistants and I conducted more than ninety open-ended interviews with U.S. troops who served in Iraq (and some who had also served in Afghanistan), and with Iraqis who had contact with U.S. service personnel between 2007 and 2012. We used a variety of means to find troops and veterans, primarily through personal contacts, but also through outreach to veterans groups. Those who agreed to be interviewed were sent a list of questions about their experiences serving in Iraq, were assured of absolute anonymity, and were asked to donate one to two hours of their time to speak with us. Second, I undertook a critical textual analysis of the cultural training materials produced by and for the U.S. military, as well as the materials describing COIN strategies that were developed, with the purpose of understanding the role that culture has played in U.S. military strategies in the wars of the twenty-first century. Thousands of pages of manuals and materials have been produced by or for the different branches of the U.S. military since 2001.

investigators found no weapons of mass destruction, and no links were proven to have existed between Saddam Hussein and al-Qaeda or other Muslim terrorist organizations tied to the September 11, 2001, attacks on the United States. By May 1, the Iraqi regime had fallen, and on that day, after a televised landing in a fighter jet on an aircraft carrier in the Gulf, President Bush declared "Mission Accomplished."

With the end of major combat operations, the war in Iraq shifted from the initial "invasion" phase to a period of occupation, officially termed a "rebuilding." Since major combat operations had ended, it was expected that the military would take on a security role in Iraq, and that the U.S. State Department and other civilian governmental bodies would take over the tasks of rebuilding. However, the Department of Defense (DoD), under the leadership of Donald Rumsfeld, maintained control in Iraq through the establishment of the Coalition Provisional Authority (CPA), which functioned as the transitional government of Iraq. With this move, the DoD and the U.S. president sidelined the civilian components of government—specifically the State Department and U.S. Agency for International Development (USAID), which have the most experience in rebuilding political systems, aiding in the development of democratic institutions, and directing the reconstruction of post-conflict infrastructures. Military officials acknowledge that this rebuilding task was not part of the initial conception of their role in the war, and that they had therefore not prepared for it. In large part this lack in planning for rebuilding was the direct result of the organization of the military chain of command: the U.S. military has no direct say over larger decisions about going to war; the president of the United States, as the commander in chief, and the second in command, the secretary of defense, are both civilians. Thus, in this case, the U.S. military followed the orders given to it by President Bush to invade Iraq, and then abided by the decisions of Secretary of Defense

---

Box 17.2

The Baath Party

The Baath Party was the only legal political party in Iraq from the late 1970s until 2003, and the entire country was run through it. A secular and nationalist party, it enforced obedience to the regime. For instance, Baath Party members had to attend pro-regime rallies. To serve in most positions of authority, such as the principal of a school, or even a school teacher, one had to join the Baath Party. Hence, the membership in the party as of 2002 was close to 4 million individuals, compared to the total population of around 25 million. Many members of the party joined for pragmatic rather than ideological reasons, because they wanted to get, or retain, their jobs. The vast majority (2.3 of the 4 million) were at the lowest level of "sympathizers," and thus likely had little involvement with the party (Sassoon 2003).

When Saddam Hussein was overthrown, Baath membership lists were used to determine who had supported the regime, and a program of "de-Baathification" began (similar to a program of "de-Nazification" in Germany after World War II). It did not distinguish between people who had actually believed in the Baath Party and those who pretended to be loyal in order to make a living.

Rumsfeld, who put the military in charge of rebuilding with no preparation and a very limited number of troops on the ground.

The way that the occupation of Iraq was planned and executed was disastrous for both individual Iraqis and Iraq as a country, as well as for American foreign policy and U.S. domestic politics. In late May 2003, the newly appointed head of the CPA, J. Paul Bremer, disbanded the Iraqi army. As a result, the once ubiquitous Iraqi security forces were put out of work, and the U.S. military was handed the job of security with little knowledge of the country and a limited presence on bases well-removed from the population. Bremer also ordered the "de-Baathification" of the civil service, thus removing tens of thousands of Baath Party members (formerly the ruling party in Iraq) from jobs running essential services. Thus, all mid- and high-level governmental employees who had stayed in Iraq and were keeping the governmental, service, and economic infrastructure running were dismissed from their jobs. As a result, one month after the U.S. president declared "Mission Accomplished," there was no longer a functioning state or security apparatus in the country.

For more insight into the policies of the CPA in Iraq, see "Disbanding the Iraqi Army," a clip from Charles Ferguson's film *No End in Sight* (2007), available on YouTube (http://www.youtube.com/watch?v=9VFnHEOb2eI).

The invasion of Iraq, followed by the disbanding of the Iraqi military and the de-Baathification of the civil service, and the limited number of troops on the ground, resulted in high levels of insecurity and chaos. Other issues, such as Saddam Hussein's release of criminals from prisons, aggravated the breakdown in security. Iraqis began to engage in a growing and violent resistance to the U.S. occupation. This resistance was labeled an "insurgency" by the U.S. forces. The insurgents attacked the U.S. military via improvised explosive devices (IEDs), car bombs, sniping, and, less often, face-to-face battles. They were not immediately seen as tied to any one particular ideology, faction, or sect, although with time the insurgents became affiliated with various groups and leaders, both Iraqi and foreign.

The insurgency, its growing size and power, the security vacuum, and the ensuing chaos continued through 2003 and 2004. The military tried to assert its control by doing what it was trained to do: using overwhelming force to achieve military control and squash the insurgency. This strategy failed, at least in part, because of the nature of insurgencies. In the process of using overwhelming force, the U.S. military alienated huge swaths of the civilian Iraqi population; and, despite its heavy-handed tactics, U.S. troops were unable to prevent lootings, provide security, and guarantee a stable infrastructure, including the provision of electricity. After 2005, different political and religious Iraqi factions began to fight each other, as well as the Americans, over access to postwar power.

The Turn to Culture

It was in this precarious environment that the U.S. military leadership seized on the idea of a counterinsurgency doctrine emphasizing the winning of hearts and minds as a way to stabilize and govern Iraq. Instead of escalating military firepower, the U.S. military would now follow a strategy that emphasized human interactions, with the goal of approaching nonmilitary tasks in a "culturally appropriate" way and using cultural knowledge as an intelligence asset to better understand the Iraqis and those attacking U.S. forces in the country. This new strategy was articulated in the 2007 Army Field Manual 3-24, *Counterinsurgency* (FM 3-24), created under the leadership of General David Petraeus. In the military, field manuals are detailed, how-to documents, and in the case of counterinsurgency, the manual was also very much about educating troops about what insurgency is and how to fight against it. Using the manual and other strategic planning documents, the military created a counterinsurgency doctrine, which was used to reconfigure the approach the military took regarding the occupation of Iraq (and also Afghanistan).

The Army Field Manual 3-24, *Counterinsurgency*, is accessible in a range of places online, including on the website of the Federation of American Scientists' Intelligence Resource Program (http://www.fas.org/irp/doddir/army/fm3-24.pdf).

The most crucial shift in the military's approach was to no longer think of Iraq as a country that it occupied and ran, but rather to think of Iraqis as partners in rebuilding Iraq. For example, FM 3-24 states the following:

Long-term success in COIN depends on the people taking charge of their own affairs and consenting to the government's rule. Achieving this condition requires the government to eliminate as many causes of the insurgency as feasible. This can include eliminating those extremists whose beliefs prevent them from ever reconciling with the government. Over time, counterinsurgents aim to enable a country or regime to provide the security and rule of law that allow establishment of social services and growth of economic activity. COIN thus involves the application of national power in the political, military, economic, social information, and infrastructure fields and disciplines. Political and military leaders and planners should never underestimate its scale and complexity; moreover, they should recognize that the Armed Forces cannot succeed in COIN alone. (FM 3-24, 1-1)

One crucial element of the COIN doctrine is that the insurgents are part of the local population and not a uniformed enemy, as is common in other wars. According to the manual,

in almost every case, counterinsurgents face a populace containing an active minority supporting the government and an equally small militant faction opposing it. Success requires the government to be accepted as legitimate by most of that uncommitted middle, which also includes passive supporters of both sides. (FM 3-24, 1-20)

Thus, the COIN strategy developed ways of dealing with all Iraqis, including, but not limited to, ways to use cultural knowledge to better train the Iraqi army and police, to deal more respectfully with the leaders of a local village, and to interrogate more effectively those detained in prisons. The goal of acquiring and using cultural knowledge in the COIN doctrine was always to advance the performance of the mission and its effectiveness. Thus, underlying the COIN doctrine was a twin philosophy: (1) to not offend supporters of the government and "that uncommitted middle" and thereby turn them against the U.S. mission, and (2) to capture and disable insurgents who were attacking U.S. troops.

While the COIN strategy touted the importance of "insight into cultures," it presented an understanding of "culture" that never clearly showed how to make "culture" applicable to actions on the ground. In part, the issue was the amorphous nature of "culture" and how best to turn it into a strategic asset. Defining culture is not easy. In American English, "culture" is used colloquially to mean "a way of doing things." The term "corporate culture," for example, refers to the way that corporations and the people who work for them do business and create relationships. "Culture" is also used as a term to generalize about the characteristics of a people or a way of being. But such generalizations may not be accurate. When thinking about French culture, Americans might think of an obsession with food, a certain stuffiness, and the wearing of berets. However, not many French persons exhibit these features or define themselves in this way. Thus the generalization may say more about how Americans understand and see the French than what French culture actually is. When using the word "culture" in the context of the Middle East, it has become acceptable to talk about "Muslim culture" (or, incorrectly, "Islamic culture"), despite the fact that some 1 billion Muslims, or about one-sixth of the global population, come from many different countries and backgrounds. Additionally, rarely will one see in American English media a reference to "white culture" to explain politics, economics, or social events, but observers often write or talk about "black culture" or "Hispanics," for example, as explanatory paradigms.

Academic definitions of culture, however, convey a sense of both the universal and changing nature of a people. As part of the domain of anthropology for more than a century, "culture" is defined as beliefs and practices that are shared, change over time, and transmitted from one generation to the next and between people (i.e., cultures mix with and shape each other). The U.S. military's FM 3-24 defines culture in the same ways, largely because the section of the manual concerning culture was written by anthropologists. This marked an important shift in how the military thought about "culture," going from a static notion of culture to one more in line with how malleable cultures actually are, and acknowledging how actions have meanings that are shaped and learned (Davis 2010).

The COIN manual encapsulates detailed information about what culture and society are, how to think about identity, and so forth, in the chapter on "Intelligence in Counterinsurgency." Its placement in "Intelligence" suggests that the U.S. military should use "culture" to understand other people and why they do things, which will help soldiers collect crucial information in order to help their war efforts. Yet the manual does not provide direct instructions about how to better interact with the people they encounter in executing their mission. In that sense, the COIN embrace of culture was one-sided:

> Intelligence in COIN is about people. U.S. forces must understand the people of the host nation, the insurgents, and the host-nation (HN) government. Commanders and planners require insight into cultures, perceptions, values, beliefs, interests and decision-making processes of individuals and groups. These requirements are the basis for collection and analytical efforts. (FM 3-24, 3-1)

In the years following the appearance of the COIN doctrine, this new approach to culture (and language) was adapted into the military's larger philosophy and made part of training courses developed throughout the U.S. military branches. This change was most prominent in the creation of forums and programs about culture and language for troops to be deployed. Building on the prominence and vision of the well-respected Defense Language Institute (DLI), between 2005 and 2007 each branch of the U.S. military either established new bodies or enhanced the capacity of existing ones to produce cultural training materials and to provide cultural training.

Other cultural training programs and materials were specific to certain areas, such as Iraq, Afghanistan, Somalia, and Korea, among other locales. Following the emergence of the COIN doctrine, the military created culture-specific courses and training packages to teach troops; but it was not clear what the troops were to do with, or how to operationalize, that knowledge. That was left to the individual or unit to figure out. An interview with an Iraqi who worked daily with the U.S. military between 2004 and 2009 illustrates the vagueness that resulted from expectations raised during cultural training:

Box 17.3

Courses on Culture at the AFCLC

Below are examples of courses offered by the Air Force Culture and Language Center (AFCLC). The descriptions are taken word-for-word from the AFCLC's website.

Introduction to Culture
"Introduction to Culture" *(ITC)* is a lower level college course for enlisted Airmen that presents students with basic concepts and skills that will build their cross-cultural competence. . . . The course explores the many aspects of human life that are influenced by culture, such as family relationships, religion and belief systems, sports, health practices, history and myth, and others. It is offered twice a year by the Air Force Culture and Language Center and the Community College of the Air Force.

Introduction to Cross-Cultural Communication
"Introduction to Cross-Cultural Communication" is the second course offered by the Air Force Culture and Language Center aimed towards the development of cross-cultural competence among Airmen. This on-line, self-paced course is designed to help Airmen better understand the process of communicating across cultural boundaries and will include learning units devoted to: nonverbal communication, paralanguage, cross-cultural communication conflict styles, active listening, and interaction skills, among others.

For more information, see http://www.au.af.mil/culture/.

In reality, I saw a lot of things and situations which the American soldiers dealt with in different ways, in different places, meaning there was a difference from one city to another and in their consideration and respect for religious occasions and customs and inherited traditions, depending on the city that they came to. . . . In some areas that were a bit calm, you would see them deal better and more closely with the Iraqis, helping them in building and providing services. But in the hot zones [where there was fighting], they would be more violent and harsh, and they would not differentiate between civilians and terrorists, considering everyone guilty and punishing them all, ignoring all the customs and traditions of Iraqis and forgetting that the terrorists and militias were just a very small, criminal minority. (Anonymous interview, April 2012)

Thus, while the focus on COIN resulted in increased cultural training programs and cultural knowledge among the troops, the situation on the ground dictated whether troops put the doctrine to use. Another Iraqi who studied in the United States and worked as a translator for the Americans thought that the Americans "had information about Iraqi traditions and about the month of Ramadan, but they did not have enough. Their information was less than what they should have known given the training they received from their government" (Anonymous interview, April 2012).

COIN and Civilians in Iraq

General Petraeus's critique of U.S. strategy during the first years of the Iraq war, and one that my own research with Iraqis affirms, is that from the outset the U.S. military prioritized its own security far above the security and well-being of Iraqi civilians (Ricks 2009). This was particularly true from 2003 until 2006. While many Iraqis celebrated that the U.S. forces had liberated them from the dictatorial regime of Saddam Hussein and the Baath Party, they also found that the condition of their lives following the 2003 invasion contradicted the liberator rhetoric of the U.S. government. With the passage of time, Iraqis found it increasingly difficult to reconcile their freedom from despotic rule with the unprecedented danger and fear they faced on a daily basis. In our interviews, they mentioned the unexpected threats to their personal safety by U.S. troops during house searches, or random attacks by U.S. troops on Iraqis and their families while they were driving down the street or standing on the roofs of their houses. Iraqis questioned why the most powerful military in the world, which was occupying and running their country, could not keep their neighborhoods and children safe, ensure a regular supply of electricity and water, or establish routine garbage pick-up. They saw U.S. troops living in well-protected bases and patrolling the streets heavily armed, armored, and geared up, often with guns drawn. They described being yelled at, fired upon, and interrogated by masked interpreters after being thrown on the ground with an American boot on their head or neck. In this general atmosphere, which went on for years, Iraqis did not feel liberated, they felt occupied. An Iraqi living in a Baghdad neighborhood commented on the situation:

> Their manner of dealing with us was "dry" and cautious, a sort of contempt from the soldiers and a lack of respect for Iraqis. Some of the things that the Iraqis had to endure generally included cutting off the roads and not allowing anyone to pass beside them, stopping for long hours without reason and ignoring all human rights and respect for the elderly, children, and cases of illness, who would then have to walk long distances, very slowly, making people late to their work and creating traffic jams that would last for a long time. . . . I was one of those people who feared to even look at them, in particular because in our region there were many arrests for no reason when there was an attack or arms or missiles fired. (Anonymous interview, April 2012)

The video "House Raids in Iraq," available on YouTube (http://www.youtube.com/watch?v=-q4pyG6fGB8) and created from footage and interviews from U.S. soldiers in Iraq by David Iles, provides a glimpse into what it was like to experience a house raid in Iraq; it was posted on YouTube on September 11, 2007.

See also "The Other War: Iraq War Vets Bear Witness" (http://www.thenation.com/article/other-war-iraq-vets-bear-witness-0), published in *The Nation* on July 30, 2007, which presents stories of U.S. military personnel serving in Iraq, selected from interviews by Chris Hedges and Laila Al-Arian.

So while the COIN doctrine and the resulting cultural training programs were designed to win over Iraqis, many of the Iraqis we talked with described heavy-handed actions (particularly by enlisted men and women). They did not feel the military made an effort to win their hearts and minds.

From the perspective of U.S. troops, force protection was, of course, a priority. The U.S. troops did not want to lose service members to gunfire, snipers, car bombs, or suicide bombings. But in failing to protect Iraqi civilians from those same dangers, they lost the goodwill that the overthrow of Saddam had generated. As a consequence, when it came time to implement counterinsurgency strategies on the ground, which required local partners and interlocutors, the U.S. troops had difficulty finding Iraqi partners that trusted them or that they felt they could trust. In short, U.S. troops paid a heavy price for not having more foresight about the consequences of their military actions in terms of postwar "reconstruction."

In our phrasing of the interview questions for U.S. troops, we particularly emphasized what role culture had played in the carrying out of their work, since COIN proponents believe cultural knowledge in interaction with civilians will prevent alienating the population. For example, the following story, related by an Air Force sergeant about his experiences in Iraq in 2007, suggests that the prioritization of his specific mission and the overall goal of getting the "bad guys" endangered Iraqis who were not the target:

> We did a raid one night in Iraq off of the Tigris River with some Rangers conducting area-wide clearances of homes. The first house we raided, there were no men in the home, just half a dozen women with children, and one older gentleman in there. It was a huge fiasco on this one—so why were we there? We needed info. So instead of being a dick about it, we could have brought them in and said, sorry we have to do this raid, we're looking for these people, and if we were smart, we'd bring a woman in with them, let the wife get dressed, calm them down and talk to them. When they're getting shot at, bombs are going off, people go into fight or flight. Instead, the interpreter beat the old guy to get information and got nothing—another problem—the respect for the older guy is gone. So here is the interpreter, who doesn't have to abide by LOAC [Law of Armed Conflict] and is a third country national representing [the] U.S. . . . . So we go to another house. Here I watched a family get completely mortified. We woke up the family—husband, son, and wife. The husband is educated but we didn't find this out until later. We are throwing people around, yelling at them. We didn't have any intel [intelligence information] on this particular house, just that we were doing an area-wide clearance of homes. The father and son spoke English—therefore they were rolled up and taken to base for interrogation. And we then left a single female alone in house in the middle of the night after a raid. (Anonymous interview, February 2, 2012)

The sergeant was highly critical of the way this raid had happened, and he suggested that the process could have been more culturally sensitive. In his answers to our questions, the sergeant indicated that letting women cover themselves, or gathering them with other women, or not being disrespectful of elders were important cultural considerations. And while that is likely true—respect for women and elders are important in Iraqi culture— from the point of view of the Iraqis, their experience of the same event was *not* about their culture. Regardless of a people's ethnic or religious background, it is unlikely that they would respond positively to having their house searched in the middle of the night by armed men yelling in a language they do not understand; to seeing their wife, mother, sister, or daughter in their nightgowns patted down by strange men; and to having family members cuffed and hooded.

Why might U.S. troops have conducted raids and kill or capture actions in ways they knew alienated the population through their violence and disregard for basic human dignity? Initially, it might have been about the power of the occupying military to intimidate and cause fear, and thus achieve acquiescence. However, by 2004, this tactic of raw power was no longer working and Iraqis had become openly hostile to the soldiers. In addition, from this point forward, the U.S. military felt it was faced with a constantly shifting "enemy." The war began with a fight against the Iraqi army of Saddam Hussein. After the war was declared over, U.S. troops were told the enemy was no longer the Iraqi army but was now the Baathist resistance and Iraqi nationalists. And then it was also al-Qaeda in Iraq, and the Mahdi army (an Iraqi Shia militia loyal to Muqtada al-Sadr, created in 2003, and in the first few years very antagonistic to the Americans), and Iranian and Arab sympathizers, among others. With such a long list of insurgents and enemies, every Iraqi was suspect. Thus, U.S. troops went from freeing oppressed Iraqis to scrutinizing and suspecting every one of them as potential "bad guys"—and treating them as such. Many Iraqis wondered how they suddenly had become the enemy after they had welcomed the Americans as liberators. According to an Iraqi man in his fifties who owned a real estate business,

> there was a general difference in their behavior in the beginning, when the Americans first arrived. Their manner was better, less hostile and less violent. . . . Later, their manner changed to become dry, more violent, particularly after the increase in terrorist operations after 2005. . . . The difference came when they stopped differentiating between terrorists and Iraqi civilians, when everyone became the same to them. (Anonymous interview, May 2012)

A Marine colonel told the following story that occurred during his deployment in 2006 in Iraq, and that illustrates the lack of trust in Iraqis and the Iraqi response to it:

> We went to Camp Fallujah . . . and General Diyya, an Iraqi general, briefed the U.S. general in charge on battlespace. He said, "I want to take battlespace. I want to take responsibility for this area over here." He gave a real good brief, especially for an Iraqi, and the U.S. general approved. He got the battlespace and the Marine unit that was there was going to leave and the Iraqis were going to control their own battlespace. We walk out of Camp Fallujah, the briefing area, and Diyya is ecstatic, he's got his own battlespace, he is making progress, we are slowly turning over. . . . Well, we go to the PX [the store on base] and Diyya says I'm going to buy you something, a Coke or something, so we go there and the guards are from Uganda, contracted guards, and they don't let Diyya in the PX. So an Iraqi general, and he can't go into a PX. Diyya is livid, and what do I say, he is a general officer, he is an ally, if he was a Brit or anything else they would have let him in. But an Iraqi . . . there isn't that trust . . . well they're our allies. They wouldn't let him in, and he is in front of his officers

and so Diyya does—and I took it, and I took it like a man—he screamed and yelled at me, "This is my country, this is Iraq," and on and on, and rightfully so, and I was going to take him to chow [the dining facility], but he wouldn't go. He pulled me aside, and you know how they hold your hand, he grabs my hand and pulls me aside, and he looks at me and he has watery eyes and he says, "You know what the real thing is here, I'm hurt." I understood that, hell, I was hurt. (Anonymous interview, June 5, 2007)

This Marine colonel's story shows how the U.S. government and military wanted to be seen as helping Iraqis rebuild their country. The Iraqi general does the right "military thing" (in both his brief to the U.S. command and in wanting to take responsibility for an area), yet he cannot be allowed into the store because he is Iraqi. He is judged not by his actions but by his nationality, and the suspicions automatically engendered because of that identity.

The research that forms the basis of this chapter revealed the changing experiences of troops and their responses to the cultural training programs. Many of the people interviewed *post*-2007 wanted more cultural training because, in retrospect, they thought they could have done their jobs better if they had known more or had more resources available to them. Describing her experiences in Iraq in late 2007, a Marine staff sergeant described how she had been trained before going to Iraq:

It was more than just knowing how to use your weapon and rebuild infrastructure. It's because we were taking a different cultural approach. If we hadn't taken that approach, we wouldn't have seen the progress that we did. For example, it's really important to be respectful of an elder. If I'm talking to her like she's a child, and she goes back and tells her son this, then he will get angry. . . . But engaging with them and their culture lowered their defenses. [We learned] the value of caring about someone else's culture and giving them the space to be who they are. (Anonymous interview, February 6, 2012)

Indeed, unlike the majority of those who served pre-2007, those who served during the COIN period found the cultural training relevant (in military jargon, there was a better alliance between mission and training for the mission). In addition, the troops interviewed repeated that they were constantly being told that culture was important, that this was one of the messages that trickled down from the implementation of the COIN doctrine. Thus, whatever their feelings were about the effectiveness of COIN, they had learned the framework and the "way to think" about culture as part of their mission.

The more positive responses to cultural training could be due to the better content of the material and the more effective means of teaching it, as well as the importance placed on cultural training and knowledge. More training is now computer-based or delivered through real-life simulations, targeting kinetic and visual learning skills rather than oral and aural learning alone. For example, Computer-Based Trainings (CBTs) are modules that troops watch and click through, transferring information sometimes through lectures, and other times through "pretend-you-are-in-X" interactive scenes. Additional real-life simulations occurred in mock-Iraqi and Afghani villages located in Fort Polk, Louisiana, the Playas in New Mexico, and Camp Pendleton in southern California, among other locations.

Our interviews with troops revealed how these new types of training modules were received by some U.S. service members. One Marine staff sergeant who was in Iraq in late 2007 described the mock Iraqi village training as useful:

> I thought it was helpful; realistic is a relative term, when you are using paintballs rather than bullets. . . . But the training helped build my confidence and my understanding, so through having these interactions with Iraqis, it gave me a chance to talk through some of the things that I was unsure about. . . . I went to Iraq knowing what I was going to be doing there, so being able to engage in the faux scenarios in town and understand how they felt about being searched and our mission and how to say stuff, enough Arabic to get by, and please and thank you kind of stuff, that goes a long way. . . . We had the chance to mess it up all over again, by not talking to them correctly and respectfully. I couldn't have learned that from a book. (Anonymous interview, February 6, 2012)

Conclusion

Given the types of training that the troops we interviewed recall as important, the more effective and successful skills they acquired for dealing with the populations are less related to culture and more about patience, perspective, communication, and respect; they are skills more centered on dealing with others as equals on the global stage. The troops' responses suggest that cultural knowledge was not really the solution for dealing with Iraqis; instead, the skills they saw as successful were anchored in understanding Iraqis' perspectives and their desire to be treated with respect. These skills, while they can be taught as part of a counterinsurgency strategy, are also likely to develop as part of living as equal citizens in a globalized world.

Looking back historically, the question remains as to what pushed the invasion from a conventional war to an insurgency. And it is worth asking whether the rise of the insurgency could have been prevented by a better-trained and more culturally sensitive military at the outset. But if we think about what it means to invade another country, it is not clear whether cultural sensitivity is truly an option with an occupying military force, no matter how much training is involved. Can the U.S. military, or any military force, figure out how to train soldiers to be culturally sensitive, or even simply patient or respectful of others, when that force is tasked with missions that involve violence and are done within the framework of a military occupation of another country?

In fact, the turn toward cultural knowledge as a tool in the military has never been wholeheartedly adopted, whether by the leadership or by the troops. Complaints about it from interviews we conducted suggested that it was ineffective, that it was a "touchy-feely" fix and not something that troops joined the military to learn. Many thought that more force was needed to show the Iraqis what could happen to them if they did not comply with U.S. demands. These responses point up the fundamental contradictions in the shift toward adding culture as an important component in the military arsenal. Is it possible to bomb and build simultaneously?

References and Further Research

Chandesekaran, Rajiv. 2006. *Imperial Life in the Emerald City: Inside Iraq's Green Zone*. New York: Alfred Knopf.

Davis, Rochelle. 2010. "Culture as a Weapon System." *Middle East Report* 255 (July): 8–13. http://www.merip.org/mer/mer255/culture-weapon.

Elder, Ralph. 2007. "Arab Culture and History: Understanding Is the First Key to Success." *Armor* 116 (January–February): 42–44.

González, Roberto. 2010. *Militarizing Culture: Essays on the Warfare State*. Walnut Creek, CA: Left Coast Press.

Kelley, John, Beatrice Jauregui, Sean T. Mitchell, and Jeremy Walton, eds. 2010. *Anthropology and Global Counterinsurgency*. Chicago: University of Chicago Press.

McFate, Montgomery. 2005. "Does Culture Matter? The Military Utility of Cultural Knowledge." *Joint Forces Quarterly* 38: 42–48.

Pfiffner, James. 2010. "US Blunders in Iraq: De-Baathification and Disbanding the Army." *Intelligence and National Security* 25, no. 1 (February): 76–85.

Ricks, Thomas. 2009. *The Gamble: General David Petraeus and the American Military Adventure in Iraq, 2006–2008*. New York: Penguin.

Sassoon, Joseph. 2003. *Saddam Hussein's Ba'th Party: Inside an Authoritarian Regime*. Cambridge: Cambridge University Press.

Sewall, Sarah, John A. Nagl, David H. Petraeus, and James F. Amos. 2007. *The U.S. Army/ Marine Corps Counterinsurgency Field Manual*. Chicago: University of Chicago Press. Also available at www.fas.org/irp/doddir/army/fm3-24.pdf.

18

Lebanese War Diaries in the Digital Age
Blogging About the Home Front During Times of Violence

NADINE SINNO

Yes, I speak English
Yes, I carry explosives
They're called words
And if you don't get up
Off your assumptions,
They're going to blow you away
—Mohja Kahf, *E-mails from Scheherazad* (2003)

The recent proliferation of online writing, blogging, and diary keeping in response to current affairs has not passed over the Middle East. Arabs—and Arab women in particular—have kept war diaries that have attracted worldwide audiences. These innovative narratives include Suad Amiry's *Sharon and My Mother-in-Law: Ramallah Diaries* (2004); *Baghdad Burning: Girl Blog from Iraq* (2005), by an Iraqi woman who goes by the pseudonym Riverbend; and Laila el-Haddad's *Gaza Mom: Palestine, Politics, Parenting, and Everything in Between* (2010). The Palestinian writers Amiry and el-Haddad provide personalized accounts of the struggles of everyday Palestinians in Ramallah and Gaza, respectively. They highlight the plight of farmers, mothers, children, and other civilians whose lives are frequently disrupted by the violence of the Israeli occupation. Similarly, Riverbend's online diary deals with the American invasion of Iraq from the perspective of a young Iraqi woman who, exasperated by the mainstream, or corporate, media's coverage of the war, decided to tell her side of the story.

Rasha Salti's "Lebanon Siege" (http://rashasalti.blogspot.com/) and Zena el-Khalil's "Beirut Update" (http://beirutupdate.blogspot.com/) are two blogs that offer eyewitness accounts of the 2006 Israel-Hezbollah war. Published electronically and in print, these online diaries crossed multiple genres, including weblogs (or blogs), memoirs, creative nonfiction, and news. They are also claiming their spot in the expanding canons of Arabic and world literatures, academic curricula, and alternative media. For instance, excerpts from el-Khalil's blog have been published by *The Guardian* and in the edited volume *Lebanon, Lebanon* (Wilson 2006). Her blog was also publicized by news media, including CNN and BBC. Similarly, Salti's blog was excerpted in various outlets, including *The Electronic Intifada* and the *London Review of Books*, and in print in *The War on Lebanon: A Reader* (Hovsepian 2008).

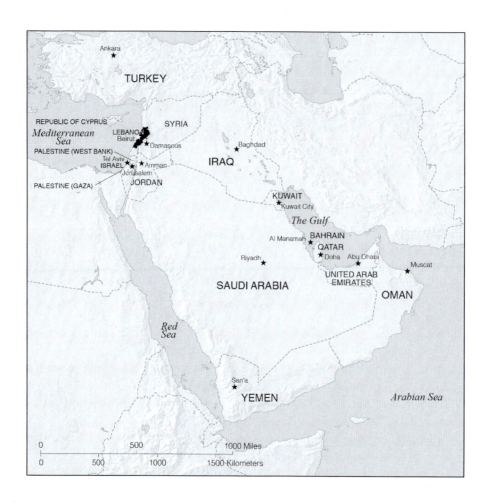

In this chapter, using el-Khalil's "Beirut Update" and Salti's "Lebanon Siege" as case studies, I highlight the role of online diaries in providing personal and humanized accounts of war. These diaries contribute to debunking pervasive stereotypes about Arabs, especially Arab women. As this chapter shows, these transnational writers bear no resemblance to the "silenced" and "oppressed" woman, whose image remains engraved in the Western imagination. In addition, I show that blogs complement and critique the mainstream media, whose war reporting typically focuses on military operations, casualty figures, and questions of battlefield victory or loss. This does not necessarily mean that mainstream reporting cannot be critical of the war itself, or critical of one or both sides in the conflict, but reporting from these traditional outlets generally offers a form of writing that deemphasizes the suffering and pain caused by militarization.

I am looking at blogs in particular because they offer an alternative mode of producing and consuming the news. As the communication scholar W. Lance Bennett argues, "People who have long been on the receiving end of one-way mass communication are now increasingly

---

Box 18.1

Media: Context and Definitions

The consumption of media has undergone radical shifts since the advent of Internet-mediated communications technologies. Nowhere have these new tools for communication, commonly referred to as social media, been more pronounced than in the dissemination of news on local, regional, and international scales.

These instruments—such as weblogs (or, more simply, blogs), the microblogging system Twitter, and YouTube channels—are used for a wide range of activities, including entertainment and interpersonal social interaction. But as they have evolved and become more effective and widespread, they have come to occupy an alternative stance in political spheres, especially regarding what is commonly referred to as "mainstream media."

This chapter uses the term "mainstream media," therefore, to denote a particular type of mass communication, one that is typically controlled by for-profit corporations and that offers relatively monolithic coverage of current events geared toward satisfying a large portion of the media-consuming public. Given this definition, the term "corporate media" is used synonymously in the chapter. On the other hand, social media outlets—as their control is decentralized and can more easily be originated by individuals with no capital investment—can offer more varied options for disseminating news, communicating different points of view, and creating alternative narratives.

It is in the context of an alternative media landscape that this case study unfolds.

---

likely to become producers and transmitters. With the advent of interactive communication and information systems . . . the distinction between producers and consumers will become increasingly difficult to draw" (2003, 34). Blogs have served as platforms from which writers and readers can express dissenting opinions—ones that counter the perspectives offered by official governments as well as complacent corporate news channels. By offering firsthand experiences of war and encouraging participation through readers' comments, war bloggers have the opportunity to create democratic platforms that not only resist the corporate media's monopoly of the news but also encourage cross-cultural dialogue and understanding. War blogs offer a space for average civilians to tell their own story, instead of relying solely on information provided by journalists who may not be present at the scene of violence or who may not be invested in highlighting the detrimental effects of war and in seeking solutions to global conflicts. Furthermore, war bloggers can often report about conflicts in "real time," as war is unfolding, rather than in retrospect. The immediacy with which war bloggers are able to report often offers them an advantage over professional journalists who may not have access to hard-hit areas in the midst of a conflict.

This chapter seeks to answer several questions: How do the diaries demonstrate the impact of war on the everyday lives of civilians? Are civilians always victims, or can they demonstrate agency during a war? How do writing, technology, and activism intersect in these texts? A critical analysis of these diaries will provide complex answers to such questions, thus adding nuance to mainstream perceptions about war in the Middle East and highlighting female Arab agency. My case study revolves around the Israel-Hezbollah War, or the "July War" (*harb tammouz*), as the Lebanese call it. It started on July 12, 2006, when the Lebanese resistance group Hezbollah (or Hizbullah, meaning "Party of God") abducted two Israeli soldiers on the Lebanon-Israel border.

Overview of the "July War"

During my summer break from teaching in 2006, I returned home to Beirut for my annual family visit and some much-needed sun bathing and relaxation on one of Lebanon's famed beaches. A Beiruti native, I was used to the news of skirmishes between Lebanese resistance fighters and the Israeli army. Therefore, I did not consider the abduction of two Israeli soldiers at the border a cause for immediate alarm. Such kidnappings had happened before: they were preludes to prisoner exchanges, where Israeli soldiers were released in return for Lebanese resistance fighters in Israeli jails. But shortly after the July 12 event, Israel bombed the Beirut Airport. I was not the only one taken by surprise. Thousands of residents, Lebanese expatriates, and foreign tourists found themselves trapped under fire as a result of the blockade instituted by Israel. International evacuation efforts were soon mobilized to transport foreign nationals out of Lebanon. Clearly, the tourist season of which the Lebanese and their visitors had been dreaming was aborted before it even started, and it was time to gear up for a full-fledged war. Summer in Beirut was going to be a different kind of blast this time around.

Israel proceeded with airstrikes that targeted civilian infrastructure, in addition to the airport in Beirut. This was followed by a ground invasion of southern Lebanon, as well as an air and naval blockade. The war lasted for thirty-three days. It resulted in extensive loss of human life and environmental damage. Approximately 1,200 Lebanese died, and 1 million people, especially from southern Lebanon and the Dahiye, a southern suburb of Beirut—both areas with predominantly Shiite populations—were displaced. A catastrophic oil spill spread over the Lebanese and Syrian coasts, and major infrastructure and thousands of civilian homes were destroyed. Some villages in the south of Lebanon remained uninhabitable in the aftermath of the war because of the hundreds of thousands of unexploded cluster bombs, which were dropped by the Israeli military prior to the United Nations–brokered cease-fire agreement that went into effect on August 14, 2006.

When news of the abduction first broke, many Lebanese assumed that this was just another skirmish that would result in some unrest on the border to be followed by talks and a resolution. When friends of Rasha Salti, the author of the blog "Lebanon Siege," wrote her asking if everything was okay, she assured them that the violence would not escalate, since the Israelis were busy fighting Hamas in Gaza at the time and "will not want to open a second front" (personal interview, 2012). Even Sayyed Hassan Nasrallah, the leader of Hezbollah, did not anticipate such a disproportionate response from Israel. He admitted that Hezbollah had carried out the kidnapping operation in order to free Lebanese and Palestinian prisoners whom Israel had held back, unexpectedly, during a previous prisoner exchange. At that time, Nasrallah had promised not to rest until those last prisoners were freed as well. Hezbollah military operations in South Lebanon often went unnoticed in the Lebanese headlines, let alone the international news. But this time, Prime Minister Ehud Olmert of Israel declared the soldiers' abduction an act of war. Two weeks prior, another Israeli soldier had been kidnapped in a cross-border raid from Gaza in a separate incident, in a similar attempt to force a prisoner exchange. From Israel's perspective, the Lebanon incident opened a second front that needed decisive action. From Lebanon's perspective, the abduction provided a pretext for a war against Hezbollah that had been preplanned.

This brief but bloody war represents an episode in the much longer narrative of the Arab-Israeli conflict, rather than an isolated incident. While providing a detailed overview of the Arab-Israeli conflict is beyond the scope of this chapter, it is important to understand the context. Although the war officially began on July 12, 2006, it would not have occurred at all, nor continued as it did, were it not situated within a specific framework of conflict beginning with the establishment of Israel and the dispossession of hundreds of thousands of Palestinians in 1948; the 1967 Arab-Israeli War, which resulted in the Israeli defeat of neighboring Arab states and increased the Palestinian refugee population; the 1982 Israeli invasion of Lebanon, which included a siege of Beirut; the Israeli occupation of South Lebanon from 1978 to 2000, which gave legitimacy to and enhanced the reputation of Hezbollah as a resistance movement; and ongoing Palestinian-Israeli hostilities, particularly the series of escalating battles between Hamas and the Israeli Defense Forces (IDF) in Gaza in June 2006.

In other words, the Lebanon war of 2006 unfolded in the larger context of the Arab-Israeli conflict: Israelis defending the safety and security of their state versus Palestinians and other resistance groups fighting for the liberation and national independence of Palestine. Depending on whose side of the conflict you are on, you will call the State of Israel or the Palestinians and resistance groups such as Hezbollah "terrorists." The U.S. State Department lists Hezbollah on its list of terrorist organizations, and U.S. media routinely report on "the terrorist group Hezbollah." That designation is not generally used in Arab mainstream news, however, where Hezbollah has the status of a liberation organization, one that is brave enough to face the militarily superior IDF.

That Hezbollah has obtained such a widely popular status is the result of several factors. First, Lebanon's army has historically been weak—it disintegrated into militia groups during the 1975–1990 Lebanese Civil War—so Hezbollah's armed contingents were able to fill a power vacuum. Second, Israeli forces occupied South Lebanon from 1978 to 2000, as part of its strategy to protect Israeli soil against Palestinian incursions, and the Israeli presence in southern Lebanon gradually engendered support for Hezbollah, which came to be the primary Lebanese militia in that area. Third, Lebanese Shiites, who have historically been marginalized, started to obtain political power within Lebanon's government after the country's civil war, at a time when traditional parties had lost much credibility. Even Lebanese who did not support Hezbollah's ideological platform conceded that Hezbollah was less tainted by corruption.

Lebanon possesses a multicommunal identity, a matter of pride for most Lebanese. There are eighteen officially recognized religious groups (sects) in Lebanon, namely Sunni and Shia Islam, Syriac Catholic, Alawite, Armenian Catholic, Armenian Orthodox, Assyrian Church of the East, Chaldean Catholic, Copts, Druze, Greek Catholic, Greek Orthodox, Ismaili, Jewish, Maronite, Protestant, Roman Catholic, and Syriac Orthodox. These various religious denominations are represented in Lebanon's parliament via a complex quota system. Traditionally, the largest shares of seats went to Sunni Muslims and Maronite Christians, and overall, Christian representatives had more seats than Muslim representatives. Shiite politicians, up until the 1970s, did not have much of a voice. The Shiite community asserted itself during the Lebanese Civil War via political parties and armed militias. Two main rival Shiite groups, Amal and Hezbollah, emerged during that time, and they continued to exert increasing levels of political influence—in Hezbollah's case supported by a continued armed militia presence—after the civil war ended. As a new post–civil war constitution recalibrated the quotas for seats in parliament, Shiite parties kept pushing for more influence. Hezbollah's actions in July 2006 need to be understood in the context of its search for increased political legitimacy and popular support in Lebanon.

To Blog or Not to Blog: Embracing Writing and Technology

Rasha Salti is a visual art curator, programmer, and freelance writer. She was raised in Lebanon during the Lebanese Civil War and lived in New York for about eight years prior to moving back to Lebanon on July 11, 2006, a day before the war erupted. She jokes about running into an old friend the next morning on her way to an Internet café to check in with friends and relatives. Upon responding "yes" to the friend's question about whether or not she had returned to Lebanon for good, the friend replied, jokingly, "Wow, welcome to Lebanon. The war has just started" (personal interview, 2012). Born in 1975 in London, Zena el-Khalil has lived in Nigeria, London, New York, and Beirut. She is a visual and installation artist, painter, and environmental activist. El-Khalil and Salti share a transnational background that is often reflected in their work. Both their diaries demonstrate secular, nonsectarian, and nonpartisan politics.

Zena el-Khalil and Rasha Salti were not active in the blogosphere prior to the outbreak of war. They did not see themselves as "civilian journalists." When the war first erupted, el-Khalil and Salti wrote e-mail messages to family and friends abroad in order to assure them of their safety. Eventually, however, their audience expanded as their initial recipients started forwarding their messages to other people who were interested in obtaining an "insider" and "alternative" perspective to the narrative provided by the mainstream Western media.

In one of her early entries, el-Khalil establishes that, as someone who was fully devoted to her fine art projects, writing about the war was not on her agenda. Her summer plans included creating art installations, selling paintings, and coordinating international workshops and art exhibitions. She tells us in one of her early entries that her "whole life has changed and I did not ask for it. . . . People bought artwork from me, I am supposed to cash my checks. I am supposed to deliver art to people" ("Beirut Update," http://beirutupdate.blogspot.com/2006_07_01archive.html). El-Khalil's candid discussion of her aborted summer plans and her disappointment that she has to spend her time writing about war is revealing. From the outset, she establishes that she is not a seasoned journalist and that her story is personal, informal, and subjective. In doing so, she humanizes civilians such as herself, whose lives were suddenly disrupted by the events.

Similar to el-Khalil, Salti discusses the spontaneous birth of her blog. She emphasizes that her primary audience was limited to a group of friends and family and that her blog was transformed into an alternative source of news after her friends starting sharing her emails with others. She says she "started writing these diary notes to friends outside Lebanon to remain sane and give them my news. . . . They were more intended to fight dementia at home, in my home and in my mind, to bridge the isolation in this siege, than to fight the media black-out, racism, prejudice and break the seal of silence" ("Lebanon Siege," http://rashasalti.blogspot.com/2006/07/lebanon-siege-day-5.html).

By asserting that her intended primary audience was restricted to friends and family, Salti guards against the criticism and demands of her progressively larger audience. She explains the dilemmas she faced once her e-mails reached beyond her close circle of friends and were now being judged by anonymous cybercitizens:

> I am more than ever conscious of a sense of responsibility in drafting them. They have a public life, an echo that I was not aware of, that I experience now as some sort of a burden. . . . Should I remain candid, critical, spiteful, cowardly, or should I transform into an activist and write in a wholly different idiom? There is of course a happy medium between both positions, but I don't have the mental wherewithal to find it now. ("Lebanon Siege," http://rashasalti.blogspot.com/2006/07/lebanon-siege-day-5.html)

Salti's "Day 5" post can be read in its entirety on the "Lebanon Siege" blog (http://rashasalti.blogspot.com/2006/07/lebanon-siege-day-5.html).

Despite their initial reluctance to write for a virtual audience they knew very little about, both el-Khalil and Salti ultimately embraced the responsibility of providing alternative news to anyone who was willing to hear it, including readers who did not necessarily share their political views. Therefore, while the online diaries were an unintended result of the war, born out of a feeling of helplessness in a moment of crisis, they ultimately altered the landscape of the reportage on the war as they started to gain visibility. Referring to the Lebanese blogs as "living archives," the literature professor Carol N. Fadda-Conrey argues that "by drawing the reader into the 'now' of the war, thus implicating him/her in the experience of trauma, the cyberblog-as-testimony changes the topography of the war experience, both at home and abroad, thus broadening the impact of this experience and the way it affects its subjects, whether directly or indirectly" (2010, 164). The blogs did indeed serve multiple purposes, including providing alternative news to global readers; empowering the authors themselves by providing a forum for expressing their emotions and disseminating crucial information; and mobilizing readers to participate in the protest against war (and relief efforts), both inside and outside the country. The republishing of their blogs on various websites and ultimately in anthologies contributed to creating a wider readership and preserved the unofficial, firsthand accounts of the war.

Humanizing "Collateral Damage"

One of the main advantages of these blogs compared to mainstream news war reportage, some would argue, is their concern for and expression of humanity. Written by eyewitnesses, these texts provide access into the intimate lives of civilians caught up in a war zone, such that these civilians no longer appear (or disappear) as "collateral damage" or statistics. The Lebanese victims and survivors have names, faces, and stories that the diarists recount vividly, inviting their worldwide readers to experience empathy and outrage at the violence inflicted on civilians. Sometimes, the diarists share their own experiences and testimonies of violence; other times, they focus on those of others.

The autobiographical texts revolve around the lives and emotions of the diarists themselves as they struggle to find meaningful ways to combat fear and agony amid ongoing shelling. Contrary to the calm and collected professional news reporters that typify mainstream media, these unofficial reporters present themselves as average human beings who experience a range of complex emotions, such as compassion, love, fear, and hope. Sharing these personal aspects of themselves—which became important to the diarists as a public outlet when they felt trapped in their homes—moved online readers to genuinely care about the fate of the writers and the fate of some other civilians.

In one post, el-Khalil describes a heavy night of shelling:

> Last night after I went to sleep, we heard three bombs dropped on Dahiye, our bed shook, but I looked into my husband's eyes and felt safe. I hugged him so tight and thought to myself, "if this is my time to die, I wouldn't want to have it any other way." ("Beirut Update," http://beirutupdate.blogspot.com/2006/07/thank-you.html)

In sharing an intimate moment in her life, el-Khalil allows us a glimpse into the mindset of a young woman caught up in a war zone. War threatens to end her life, while at the same time war engenders a heightened sense of appreciation for things often taken for granted in times of peace, such as the deep human relationships that sustain us. In another entry, however, el-Khalil is not as positive in her outlook. She talks about breaking down after watching all the foreign nationals being evacuated, saying that "it really hit me hard. I was crying all day. . . . and I'm not ashamed to share this with you . . . I cried and cried. . . . Because I felt an incredible wave of fear and sadness take over my mind. . . . Combine fear and lack of sleep and you get one big breakdown" ("Beirut Update," http://beirutupdate.blogspot.com/2006/07/today-i-cried-lot.html). El-Khalil is worried that, with the evacuation of foreign nationals, Israel might step up its military operations, because without potential foreign victims the world's focus would turn away from Lebanon. Here, and in other places in the diary, we become privy to el-Khalil's moments of weakness and despair, not just her resilience. Through such confessions, her readers become emotionally attached to the diarist herself and not merely to the "alternative news" she offers. The readers' responses to the diary demonstrate that they eagerly wanted to know what would happen to Zena, her family, and her friends as the war unfolded. When she did not write, they needed reassurance that she was still alive.

Similar to el-Khalil, Salti's tone in "Lebanon Siege" is subjective and personal. Throughout the diary, readers accompany Salti on her emotional roller coaster. She is sarcastic, acerbic, angry, desperate, resilient, and everything in between. Salti's vulnerability is most palpable when she speaks of her ambivalence about writing. While broadcasting the news gives her a sense of purpose and order, it does not always alleviate the grief caused by the deaths, explosions, and evacuations around her. Revealingly, at one point she confesses that "writing is becoming increasingly difficult. Writing . . . has begun to lose its meaning and its cathartic power. I am consumed with grief. There is another me trapped inside me that cries all the time" ("Lebanon Siege," http://rashasalti.blogspot.com/2006/07/lebanon-siege-day-8_28.html). Salti's struggles with grief remind us that, despite her eloquent reporting, she is *in* the situation, and that we must not lose sight of the living, grieving woman behind the words.

On a more public level, the diarists focus on humanizing others who endured more devastating fates because they resided in hard-hit areas, or because their lower socio-economic status put them in harm's way. Through recounting stories of the dead, the injured, and the displaced, they stress that no matter what the Israeli military or Israel's allies might proclaim about the legitimacy of "the global war on terror," "targeted killings," and "surgical airstrikes," it is innocent civilians that most often end up injured or dead. In addition to reporting about the shelling and the rise in the death toll of civilians in southern Lebanon, Salti describes makeshift refugee centers sprouting up all over the country so that her readers can witness the devastation of the most vulnerable: the elderly, the sick, and children. Through her detailed description, the aftermath of a massive attack comes alive, and faces are attached to the news coming out of Lebanon: the nine-year-old child begging volunteers to allow him to find work so he can save his family from the humiliating life of the shelter; or the disabled and ill refugees who were left behind or who arrived at the relief centers without their medications, wheelchairs, or crutches. By highlighting the effects on innocent civilians, the diarists deconstruct the mainstream media's discourse on "collateral damage" and invite the readers to recognize the vulnerability and "grievability" of Arab lives. They thereby challenge the reader to an emotional response as well. Which one is a more normal reaction to the devastation of war: detached objectivity or unsettled emotions?

Complicating the Discourse of Victimhood: Celebrating Solidarity and Civil Society

The diaries demonstrate that while pain and loss were at the core of the civilian experience during the July War, survivors often devised creative ways of negotiating the new reality of war. Without glorifying war, they show that while violence inevitably leads to moments of fear and paralysis, it also engenders a sense of empowerment that enables those impacted to move forward against all odds. At the heart of this empowerment is the coming together of the community during times of crisis.

Rasha Salti's diary captures the sense of solidarity that is born out of tragedy. Her diary pays tribute to the various volunteers who came together to help those most affected by the Israeli invasion, namely the refugees from the southern villages of Lebanon. Salti discusses the schools-turned-shelters that emerged in the wake of the Israeli invasion, demonstrating the work done on the ground. We accompany her to the Nazareth Nuns School, a public school that was turned into a refugee camp, in Beirut. She speaks of the "band of volunteers," a group of men and women under thirty, who took care of everything from setting up sleeping quarters and preparing meals to cleaning bathrooms and screening DVDs for children in the school's courtyard. In a debt-ridden country like Lebanon, where government expenditures on social services are very low, such volunteer efforts became crucial in helping affected civilians re-create some level of normalcy, despite their dispossession. That these young volunteers offered the crisis management normally expected of governmental institutions is a remarkable feat, given the paucity of the resources at their disposal.

Salti contrasts the willing and spontaneous efforts of community volunteers with the sense of apathy of Lebanese leaders. She writes of these leaders that "they parade on TV and in the streets, with their neat hair and pressed suits, moving from their air-conditioned meeting rooms to restaurant for 'power lunches' and so-called coordination meetings, while hundreds and hundreds of volunteers are actually carrying the burden of this problem" ("Lebanon Siege," http://rashasalti.blogspot.com/2006/07/lebanon-siege-day-11_115411578172301070.html). Salti's biting criticism of the Lebanese government and her documentation of the relief efforts of civilians, who represent a foil to these leaders, is a major feature of her blog. It speaks to her commitment to engaging in a double-critique of both the Lebanese/Arab leadership and the Israeli military. She does not simply point fingers at Israel, the "outside enemy," but also directs her criticism at the Arab leaders, the "insiders," who failed to do their part in providing timely relief and in supporting their people in the face of Israeli aggression.

Salti's "Day 11" post can be read in its entirety on her blog (http://rashasalti. blogspot.com/2006/07/lebanon-siege-day-11_115411578172301070.html).

Similar to Salti, el-Khalil celebrates the volunteers whose meager resources did not stop them from assisting war refugees. She speaks of her young sister's involvement with NGOs, including Zico House and Helem, that established bank accounts for collecting donations for food, medicine, water, and mattresses in an effort to provide refugees with basic necessities. While her criticism of the government is less scathing than Salti's, she still reiterates that "the ministries of health and social affairs have proven to be ineffective," and that "it is up to the civil society now to help out" ("Beirut Update," http://beirutupdate.blogspot.com/2006/07/beirut-update-3.html). Both Salti's and el-Khalil's diaries reflect a strong sense of disillusionment with the Lebanese government. However, they both also manifest a renewed hope in a growing Lebanese civil society, particularly among the country's youth, who end up shouldering some of the responsibilities that the state fails to execute. Whereas extended families still represent the main support group for individuals, massive crises such as the July War demand a societal response that crosses ethnic and religious divides.

Both Zico House and Helem were civil society institutions that existed before the 2006 war and that shifted their efforts toward providing relief during the crisis. Built in 1935 and located in the Sanayeh district in Beirut, Zico House used to be the family home of Moustapha Yamouth (alias Zico). In the 1990s, following the Lebanese Civil War, Zico transformed the building into "an alternative space that housed contemporary art," and in 1999 it was officially established as a civil society organization for culture and development. The organization hosts art exhibitions, dance and theater performances, and concerts, and it provides a space for ecological, social, and cultural organizations.

Helem advocates for the civil, political, economic, social, and cultural rights for lesbian, gay, bisexual, and transgender (LGBT) people in Lebanon. Even though the specialized causes of Zico House and Helem may differ, their progressive agendas overlap in their attention to issues of social justice and human rights. The 2006 war allowed for cross-community alliances among these organizations and individuals from all walks of life.

The websites of Zico House (http://www.zicohouse.org/) and Helem (http://helem.net) offer additional information about the goals and activities of the organizations.

The rallying of Lebanese citizens to help each other during Israel's invasion of Lebanon in 2006 echoed their communal efforts and solidarity in the wake of the April 1996 Israeli attack on the southern village of Qana that killed over 100 civilians. In the aftermath of that event, many volunteer groups of different religious and ideological affiliations worked together to provide material support and financial aid to the people of Qana. Similarly, in the summer of 2006, the Lebanese people banded together across communities, and rather than oppose Hezbollah—as Israel had hoped—supported their military efforts publicly. As el-Khalil notes, "Israel is trying to bring Lebanon to its knees. . . . Israel is trying to turn Lebanese against each other. Israel is trying to turn us into animals scrounging for food, water, and shelter. . . . Well you can tell them that I'm not leaving. And there are many of us who are not leaving" ("Lebanon Update," http://beirutupdate.blogspot.com/2006_07_01_archive.html). By highlighting the coming together of the Lebanese, I do not mean to downplay the prominence of sectarian divides in Lebanon, which, in part, explain the country's bloody civil war between 1975 and 1990. Yet wartime devastation caused by an "outside enemy" appeared to engender a sense of unity among those Lebanese who still had access to resources, particularly while the crisis was still unfolding, and before the dust and smoke of war had settled.

Zena el-Khalil's "Beirut Update 2" post can be read in its entirety on the "Beirut Update" blog (http://www.beirutupdate.blogspot.com/2006/07/beirut-update-2.html).

That the summer of 2006 saw the emergence of a more unified civil society among Lebanon's youth is evidenced by the organization of a civilian resistance march to the south of Lebanon. The march was organized by a group of young people who decided to confront Israeli violence by organizing a "civil convoy" that would head to the heavily shelled south of Lebanon and demand an end to civilian killings. Both Salti and el-Khalil worked on rallying people of various political affiliations to join the demonstration. In her entry "Call for Action," el-Khalil published the announcement regarding the purpose and logistics of the convoy. The announcement, which provided information by various organizations that came together in solidarity, created and endorsed the necessity of civilian resistance in the absence of national and international governmental action:

> We urge you to join us in defying Israel's aggression against our country and in defending the rights of inhabitants throughout Lebanon, and particularly the South, to live on their land. When the United Nations, created to preserve peace and security in the world, is paralyzed, when governments become complicit in war crimes, then people must show their strength and rise up. When justice and human rights are scorned, those who care must unite in their defense. ("Beirut Update," http://beirutupdate.blogspot.com/2006/08/call-for-action.html)

The announcement not only calls for unified civilian action, but also it serves as a critique of the United Nations and the international human rights discourse as just words. This act of civilian resistance also defied and critiqued the United States' response to the war. Because the administration of President George W. Bush did not call for an immediate cease-fire, and explained that ending the war too soon would return the region to an unacceptable status quo—with Hezbollah armed, and thus threatening Israel—the Lebanese saw the U.S. government as complicit in war crimes, specifically in the death and anguish of Lebanese civilians. In a news conference, reported in the *Washington Post* on July 21, 2006, Secretary of State Condoleezza Rice expressed concern about "innocent people who are suffering from violence, Lebanese, Israeli, and Palestinian," and emphasized that she had urged Israel to keep "humanitarian corridors open." Yet she strongly supported Israel's "right to defend itself" and even referred to the conflict optimistically as "the birth pangs of the new Middle East" (CQ Transcripts Wire 2006). The Lebanese took Rice's statement to mean that additional Lebanese civilian deaths were an acceptable price to pay for Israeli security.

Zena el-Khalil's "Call for Action" post can be read in its entirety on the "Beirut Update" blog (http://beirutupdate.blogspot.com/2006/08/call-for-action.html).

Even though the march itself was diverted by Lebanese officials who stopped the convoy from proceeding to the city of Sidon for "security reasons," that act of civilian participation undeniably left its mark on the lives of those who took to the streets in defiance of Israeli aggression. Rasha Salti recalls the transformative effect that the experience of participating in that march had on her personally. Her eyes lighting up, she said that it was "the most radical action [she] could undertake," and she pointed out that two days after the convoy headed south, the cease-fire was put into effect (personal interview 2012). For Salti, her involvement in civilian action was necessary in helping her feel useful after she had exhausted all other means through writing and volunteer work. Reflecting on her decision to participate in the march, she says, "there were so many [other] blogs, I couldn't go more places, the political situation was overwhelming, my fear was so overwhelming. So I became involved with civilian action" (personal interview 2012).

Whether the march did expedite the cease-fire agreement cannot be known. The march, nevertheless, shows that mobilization to political action can and does occur among those without a clear political agenda or a prior history of political activism. It also helps complicate the discourse of victimhood. The women's diaries reiterate that while war victimizes civilians through violence, it also can lead to the creation of pockets of resistance. Stripped of government support and disillusioned by the United Nations' and the international community's failure to act, the youth groups described by el-Khalil and Salti decided to act by drawing attention to the predicament of innocent civilians. As such, the mobilization of young Lebanese from across religious lines sets a hopeful signal for a country that was torn apart by civil war one generation earlier.

Calling for Transnational Action

Rasha Salti and Zena el-Khalil ensured that their call for action took a transnational journey as they reached out to worldwide audiences via their blogs. They asked for more than simply passive reading, and invited their audience to respond to the events. More specifically, like many bloggers inside and outside Lebanon, they prodded their readers to spread the word, write letters to political representatives, demand a cease-fire or an end to human rights violations, join the civilian resistance march to the south, or, at the least, take a public antiwar stance. The diarists were thus interventionist in not only providing their interpretations of global events, but also in attempting to influence the trajectories of war, relief efforts, and protest movements by reaching beyond their national borders. In doing so, they also empowered the readers residing outside Lebanon by giving concrete suggestions in response to the familiar question, "What can we do to help?" Readers of the two blogs could now respond in ways that went beyond sending mere comments of support to the bloggers and the Lebanese people.

In her second blog post, el-Khalil provides a summary of Israeli military actions that had transpired since the first day of the attacks, including bombing of the south with chemical weapons, shelling of civilian neighborhoods in the suburbs of Beirut, destroying the roads that lead to the mountains (thereby cutting off escape routes for civilians), and targeting infrastructure, such as electricity and gas factories. Following her update, she addresses her worldwide readers directly, asking them to spread her message. She asks them to "please help in any way you can. Please pass on the message, this email—reprint if you wish. Please tell people what is going on. Please put pressure on your respective governments to step in and do something." She even asks readers to reach out to Israeli citizens: "Tell the Israeli citizens what their government is doing to us. Tell them that violence begets violence" ("Beirut Update," http://beirutupdate.blogspot.com/2006/07/beirut-update-2.html). In this entry, el-Khalil emphasizes the readers' responsibility in circulating the news. Appealing to their sense of shared humanity and justice, she attempts to recruit the international community in a collective information and antiwar campaign.

> Zena el-Khalil's "Beirut Update 2" post can be read in its entirety on the "Beirut Update" blog (http://beirutupdate.blogspot.com/2006/07/beirut-update-2.html).

> Reports addressing Israel's alleged use of chemical weapons in Lebanon can be found online at:
>
> Human Rights Watch: http://www.hrw.org/news/2006/08/17/lebanon-israeli-cluster-munitions-threaten-civilians; http://www.hrw.org/news/2006/08/30/convention-conventional-weapons-ccw-first-look-israel-s-use-cluster-munitions-lebano.
>
> *The New York Times*: http://www.nytimes.com/2006/10/22/world/africa/22iht-mideast.3251081.html?_r=0.
>
> *Haaretz Online*: http://www.haaretz.com/news/israel-admits-using-phosphorus-bombs-during-war-in-lebanon-1.203078.

Conclusion

The moment a war is declared, or sometimes before its official declaration, the daily lives of civilians in a war zone are forever altered. From the time civilians start stocking up on food, fuel, and water until well after the day they remove the duct tape plastered on their windows, they are enlisted into the battle and engage in their own warfare and militarization, no matter how apolitical, antiwar, or pacifist they might be. War can be simultaneously spectacular and quotidian, and civilians must learn to navigate it in all its facets. Depicting the physical and psychological transformation of daily life in a war zone to the average Western reader, who may have never experienced war first-hand, is a heavy burden. It is a particularly challenging task for persons, such as Zena el-Khalil and Rasha Salti, who take up writing, literally, "under the gun."

The dramatic events characterizing the July War inevitably shaped the purpose, form, and tone of this blog literature: the urgent tone of el-Khalil and Salti in their blogs was clearly a result of the unexpected escalation of violence between Hezbollah and Israel. One of the main goals of all the Lebanese diarists during the 2006 war was to circulate information immediately so they could elicit equally fast responses from their readers, which might help mitigate the damage. As this chapter has shown, el-Khalil and Salti did not intend to tell a story that would demonstrate their journalistic skills. They needed their readers to fight for their lives and for the lives of other civilians in the war zone. And their calls for action became more powerful as they revealed their own humanity and the humanity of civilians in their country. They became vehicles for telling other people's stories. Their diaries would document the collective pain, grief, hope, and feelings of resistance experienced by the Lebanese people, in addition to their own personal predicaments. For these writers, blogging became a nonviolent explosive used to draw attention to the crisis. Their writings also aimed to honor the dead and the survivors of the war.

Indeed, the diaries of el-Khalil and Salti are reminiscent of earlier literary war narratives by Arab women who wrote before the advent of the Internet, such as the works of the so-called "Beirut decentrists," a term coined by the literary scholar Miriam Cooke in her book *War's Other Voices* (1988). It refers to a group of authors who wrote about the Lebanese Civil War in ways that highlighted the "dailiness" of war and deconstructed traditional male war narratives that focused primarily on victory and defeat in battle. These Beirut-based authors include Emily Nasrallah, Ghada Samman, Hanan al-Shaykh, and Etel Adnan. Like the Beirut decentrists, the bloggers under study confirm the blurring of public and private spaces in times of crisis. They demonstrate the inevitable militarization of ordinary civilians and the devastating impact of war on their lives. They expose the futility of thinking about war in terms of victory and defeat, when the truth is that everybody in society loses. Like the traditional writing and publishing of their predecessors, the selected online war diaries attest to the fact that Arab women are not passive victims of violence. By producing their own narratives of war and its discontents, they continue to resist the stories of disempowerment that are told about them in the mainstream broadcast media and Western pop culture.

The Arab women bloggers featured in this essay are fierce, witty, and irreverent. They have no reservations about critiquing authority or engaging in a reinterpretation of news events and antiwar activism. Quite simply, these narratives urge us to move beyond the "oppressed Arab woman" discourse and brace ourselves for more female-authored missives from the Middle East. By embracing new technologies, Arab women in the Middle East are increasingly able to participate in the public sphere, nationally and internationally, thus achieving more visibility. In her discussion of literary and cultural blogs, literature professor Hoda Elsadda points to the power of this online forum for women:

> In cyberspace, the private/public dichotomy is blurred, making room for creative transgression of old taboos. Blogs, as personal diaries that are made public instantly rather than being stashed away in a drawer, have cracked the protective shell of a somewhat inhibitive obsession with privacy and have enabled many women to take their first steps to the outside world. (Elsadda 2010, 330)

Taking advantage of the Internet revolution, bloggers such as Salti and el-Khalil, and many others in countries like Iraq and Palestine, have turned their painful experiences of war into personal yet public testimonials. Excavating and analyzing Arab women's war blogs, a burgeoning literature that can only grow with the proliferation of the tools of social media, is necessary for achieving a fuller understanding of war as a day-to-day experience of ordinary civilians, particularly women. Bringing this literature to the forefront is also crucial for acknowledging the cultural artifacts created by budding women writers who—by taking fingers to keyboards in war-torn countries—are remaking their lives as well as the literary and social landscapes of the modern Middle East.

References and Further Research

Amiry, Suad. 2004. *Sharon and My Mother-in-Law: Ramallah Diaries*. New York: Pantheon.

Bennett, W. Lance. 2003. "New Media Power: The Internet and Global Activism." In *Contesting Media Power: Alternative Media in a Networked World*, edited by Nick Couldry and James Curran, 17–37. Lanham, MD: Rowman & Littlefield.

Cooke, Miriam. 1988. *War's Other Voices: Women Writers on the Lebanese Civil War*. Cambridge: Cambridge University Press.

CQ Transcripts Wire. 2006. "Secretary Rice Holds a News Conference." *Washington Post Online*, July 21. http://www.washingtonpost.com/wp-dyn/content/article/2006/07/21/AR2006072100889.html.

Elsadda, Hoda. 2010. "Arab Women Bloggers: The Emergence of Literary Counterpublics." *Middle East Journal of Culture and Communication* 3, no. 2: 312–332.

Fadda-Conrey, Carol N. 2010. "Writing Memories of the Present: Alternative Narratives About the 2006 Israeli War on Lebanon." *College Literature* 37, no. 1: 159–173.

el-Haddad, Laila. 2010. *Gaza Mom: Palestine, Politics, Parenting, and Everything in Between*. Charlottesville, VA: Just World Books.

Harb, Zahera. 2009. "The July 2006 War and the Lebanese Blogosphere: Towards an Alternative Media Tool in Covering Wars." *Journal of Media Practice* 10, no. 2–3: 255–258.

Hovsepian, Nubar, ed. 2008. *The War on Lebanon: A Reader*. Northampton, MA: Olive Branch Press.

Kahf, Mohja. 2003. *E-mails from Scheherazad*. Gainesville: University Press of Florida.

Riverbend. 2005. *Baghdad Burning: Girl Blog from Iraq*. New York: Feminist Press.

Shadid, Anthony. 2012. *House of Stone: A Memoir of Home, Family, and a Lost Middle East*. Boston: Houghton Mifflin Harcourt.

Sultan, Kathy. 2008. *Tragedy in South Lebanon: The Israeli-Hezbollah War of 2006*. Minneapolis: Scarletta Press.

Ward, Will. 2007. "Uneasy Bedfellows: Bloggers and Mainstream Media Report the Conflict in Lebanon." *Arab Media & Society* 1 (Spring). http://www.arabmediasociety.com/?article=17.

Wilson, Anna, ed. 2006. *Lebanon, Lebanon*. London: Saqi.

Blog Sites

Zena el-Khalil's "Beirut Update": http://beirutupdate.blogspot.com/

Laila el-Haddad's "Gaza Mom": http://www.gazamom.com/

Rasha Salti's "Lebanon Siege": http://rashasalti.blogspot.com/

19

Language and Identity in Tunisia
"Without Tunisian Arabic, We Are Not Tunisians"

KEITH WALTERS

The smallest of the North African countries, Tunisia juts into the Mediterranean where Algeria and Libya meet; it is less than 100 miles south of Sicily and forty miles west of the island of Pantelleria, administratively part of Sicily. Over 98 percent of the Tunisian population identifies as Arab Muslims of the Maliki rite (one of the four Sunni legal traditions), making it the most ethnically and religiously homogeneous country of the Arab world. Yet Tunisia is characterized by great linguistic diversity, as are the Arab world and the Middle East generally. This diversity reflects the history of the region, including forces such as colonization and, more recently, globalization. This chapter examines Tunisia's changing linguistic characteristics, demonstrating how such forces continue to shape language use there. It also presents two case studies, one focusing on language choice at an international conference on politics and the other analyzing language use on the Internet.

Background and History

Nearly all Tunisians today speak Tunisian Arabic as their native language. Arabic came to Tunisia and the rest of North Africa as a result of the spread of Islam, beginning in the seventh century. Arabic began displacing Tamazight, the indigenous language, a process that never reached completion. Tamazight, the increasingly preferred name for Berber, is part of the Afro-Asiatic family of languages, which includes Arabic, Hebrew, and several other Middle Eastern languages. It is spoken today in communities in all the North African countries—Mauritania, Morocco, Algeria, Tunisia, Libya, and Egypt—as well as Burkino Faso, Mali, and Niger. It is also spoken by many emigrants from these countries to Europe, the United States, and Canada. The Tamazight term for a person belonging to this ethnic group is *Amazigh*, the plural of which is *Imazighen*.

The only remaining communities of Tamazight speakers in Tunisia speak a variety of the language called Shelha, and they are found in fairly remote mountainous towns in the southern part of the country and on the island of Djerba. Men from these communities also speak Tunisian Arabic, which they learned at school or in dealings with the dominant community; girls and women who have gone to school likewise speak Tunisian Arabic. (Like anyone who goes to school in Tunisia, speakers of Tamazight also learn Modern

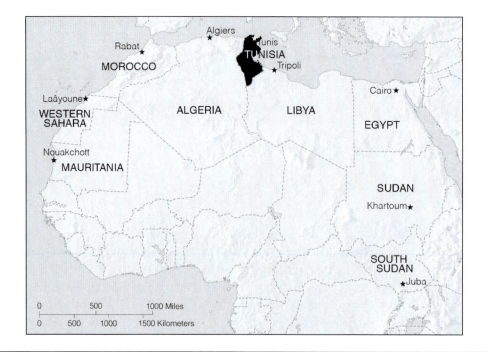

Box 19.1

Methods

This chapter combines the methods of two fields: sociolinguistics, the branch of linguistics that examines language use in society, and the overlapping discipline of linguistic anthropology, which considers how language reflects, and in many ways constructs, societies and cultures. Both are concerned with the consequences of a clear and simple fact: communicative resources—whether languages or language varieties—are never equally distributed across any community. In a multilingual society, not everyone will speak the same language(s). Even in societies where a single language predominates, as in the United States, some dialects are valued more than others. For example, many people think of broadcast English as being Standard English, whereas regional dialects such as Appalachian English, those of other rural areas, and ethnic varieties of American English are generally stigmatized.

In investigating language in society, sociolinguists and linguistic anthropologists use many similar tools and methodologies. Models from linguistic theory have helped them understand the systematic nature of code-switching and the ways that bi- or multilinguals use their languages strategically in communities around the world. Insights from various social theories—theories of the nature of identity, nationalism, technology and new media, and social inequality—give the researchers frameworks for interpreting the data they collect. A commonly used technique for data collection is participant observation, which involves long-term involvement in communities, where the analyst systematically observes the nature of social organization and interviews people formally and informally. Sociolinguists or linguistic anthropologists analyze any instance of language—including the languages chosen by speakers at a conference or the language used on a web page, in a radio interview, or written in comments posted on a website.

Box 19.2

Tamazight and Tunisian Arabic

Although Tamazight once formed what linguists call a "dialect chain," where speakers from one community could always understand those from the next community but not necessarily those who lived several hundred or thousand miles away, the situation today is quite different. Because of the spread of Arabic, which drove speakers of Berber into mountainous regions (as in Morocco and Tunisia) or into geographically peripheral regions (as on the island of Djerba or the Kabyle in Algeria), Berber is best thought of as a collection of dialects mutually intelligible to varying degrees. *Tamazight* is the cover term for this family of dialects, though it is also the name of one of the varieties of the language spoken in Morocco, a situation that often leads to confusion.

North African varieties of Arabic have all been influenced by Tamazight, especially in terms of vocabulary. Here is a list of words in Tunisian Arabic borrowed from the variety of Tamazight widely spoken there in the past:

najjez	jump (verb)
najjem	be able to
shlarum	moustache
babbush	snail
fukroon	turtle

Standard Arabic, French, and English, as described below.) Thus, the only monolingual speakers of Tamazight in Tunisia are children who have not been to school, whether because they are too young or live too far from an elementary school, or women who never attended school.

Standard Arabic and National Dialects

Every country of the Arab world has its own national dialect of spoken Arabic, and within each country there are regional variations (e.g., the coastal versus the inland areas); religious variations (Muslim—sometimes Sunni and Shia—and, in some cases, Jewish and/or Christian varieties); variations related to social class or education; and variations based on gender. These dialects vary widely—so much so that someone from the Arabian Gulf must spend about six weeks in Morocco to be able to understand and use Moroccan Arabic. Thus, the differences across dialects are much greater than the differences across native varieties of English, in which fewer differences exist.

When Tunisians begin school, they are not educated in their national dialect. Like students across the Arab world, they learn Modern Standard Arabic (MSA), a variety that differs markedly from any of the national dialects. These differences are so great that someone who speaks only Tunisian Arabic (or any national variety) would have considerable difficulty understanding news broadcasts, which are in MSA. While Arabs generally assume that MSA is the same across the entire region, it is possible to tell a

Tunisian from an Egyptian or a Saudi when she or he speaks MSA (much as speakers of English can distinguish among speakers from Ireland, Canada, and New Zealand). Thus, while MSA is the variety of Arabic that educated speakers across the Arab world share, speakers from each country have their own distinguishable accent when speaking it.

As noted in the earlier chapter on languages in the Middle East, MSA descended from Classical Arabic, the language of the Quran, early Arabic literature, and the texts of the Islamic tradition. As part of the development of Islamic thought, Classical Arabic was standardized around the eighth century, centuries before any European language was standardized. (English was standardized during the period between the Renaissance and the eighteenth century.) Standardization is the process whereby the elite users of a language work to minimize variation in order to maximize the range of communication. Thus, when using a standardized language, everyone "agrees" to follow the same set of rules, thereby facilitating communication across time and space.

From a purely linguistic point of view, the national dialects would be considered distinct languages, and MSA would be considered a different language still, although there is some degree of mutual intelligibility among the dialects and between the dialects and MSA. Importantly, however, Arabs perceive the national dialects, MSA, and Classical Arabic to be a single language: Arabic. In fact, many argue that the major thing which unites the Arab world is Arabic and that what defines an Arab is speaking Arabic.

Traditionally, the national dialects were spoken varieties that developed independently of Classical Arabic, whereas Classical Arabic and, later, MSA were used for writing or reading written texts aloud. As societies have changed, and as a larger percentage of the population across the region has become educated, so have the functional uses of the dialects and MSA. Today, in addition to being used for writing, MSA is used, as noted above, for news broadcasts and in discussions in the media, especially when speakers from different national dialects are participating, as well as in other formal contexts.

While the national dialects continue to be used for everyday spoken interactions, they are also written (though nobody is ever taught how do to so). Words from the dialects have long shown up on restaurant menus or receipts, especially handwritten ones, and the dialects are also used for writing scripts for soap operas and plays, novels, and cartoons where characters sound like everyday people. For the past few decades, however, words and expressions from the dialects have also shown up in print advertising. Their use represents what rhetoricians term *emotional appeals*, referring to the fact that it is much easier to sell people a product by using the language they use every day than by using a language that is associated with school or formal situations. Interestingly, dialects are also written in interactive electronic contexts, an issue discussed later in the chapter. The logic of this practice should be easy to see, since the written language of most electronic interactions is similar to spoken language in many ways.

Although Arab intellectuals have long been concerned with keeping MSA pure by protecting it from the influence of foreign languages, there has been no such concern with the spoken national dialects, a factor contributing to their continuing differentiation. Tunisian Arabic, for example, has many, many words borrowed from Tamazight, Italian, and French, but far fewer from English. In contrast, because of its history, Egyptian

Arabic has far more borrowings from English, since the British colonized Egypt for a long period, but fewer from these other languages.

Linguists use the term *diglossia* to refer to the situation in which two varieties of a single language are in contact but used for different functions. In fact, Arabic is the best example of diglossia. In the case of Arabic, the national dialects are associated with everyday life and lived experience, whereas MSA is associated with formal contexts because in such situations one is, in some sense, speaking like a book. Therefore, many Arabs do not generally like to speak MSA, although they have studied it throughout their educational careers. As society changes, the relationship between the language varieties used in a diglossic situation, although stable in many ways, is also subject to change, and such changes are occurring across the Arab world today.

Bilingualism and Multilingualism in Tunisia

In addition to speaking Tunisian Arabic and studying MSA, Tunisian children begin learning French, the language of the colonial power that ruled the country from 1881 until 1956, in elementary school. (The French established the first "modern schools" in Tunisia and set up the educational system that later became the basis for the current system of schooling there.) Whereas the educated among earlier generations of Tunisians received some or all of their education in French, sometimes not studying MSA at all, younger Tunisians receive nearly all their education in MSA, although they currently study both French and English beginning in primary school.

Over the decades since independence, Tunisians have hotly debated the proper role of each language in their society and the impact of educational language policy on national identity. At an earlier time, French was seen as ensuring access to education in and information about modern science and technology, a role increasingly usurped by English. Arabic, on the other hand, represents links to the thought and culture of the Arab world, including Islam. During the mid-1970s, two decades after independence, public banners, often political in nature, and bureaucratic forms in public buildings such as post offices were bilingual, in Arabic and French. In later decades, Arabic was used more and more in those contexts, at the expense of French, in an effort to strengthen ties between Tunisia and the rest of the Arab world. With economic liberalization and the continuing move toward a market-driven economy, French, English, and, as noted, written versions of spoken dialects are increasingly common in domains such as advertising, whether print or electronic.

Thanks to the widespread presence of satellite television and the growing number of national and pan-Arab channels, Tunisian children today hear speakers of MSA from across the Arab world, and as a result they begin developing an understanding of the broad range of accents that speakers from various countries use when speaking this variety of Arabic. In fact, elementary school teachers often report that pupils use Egyptian forms in their written schoolwork because Egyptian Arabic has traditionally been the most commonly used variety of Arabic for broadcasting. In making these errors, children are assuming that because they heard these forms on television and knew they were not Tunisian, they

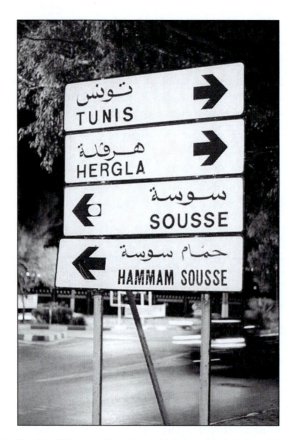

A bilingual road sign in Tunisia. The Arabic script, which is written right to left, is on top in each case, while the Latin script, which is written left to right, is on the bottom. The Latin-script spellings of the place names reflect French spelling rules, providing evidence of Tunisia's colonial past. *(Wikimedia Commons.)*

must be MSA, evidence of their growing understanding of diglossia. Tunisian children also hear broadcasts in French, English, and Italian. In fact, many Tunisians, especially those in the north, speak Italian to some degree, and they claim to have learned it by watching Italian television, aided, of course, by the fact that they have studied French, a related language, and speak it, whether in limited fashion or fluently.

The experiences that Tunisian children have growing up with multiple languages differ greatly from the experiences of their parents and particularly their grandparents. Whereas well over 95 percent of school-aged children in Tunisia today attend school, many university-aged Tunisians have at least two grandparents—their grandmothers—who are illiterate and speak only Tunisian Arabic. These women likely understand at least some Egyptian Arabic because of the many Egyptian soap operas and other television programs they have watched over the years. In many cases, their grandfathers have some limited knowledge of Classical Arabic, likely gained through Quranic schooling at a mosque, or

French, thanks to contact with colonial institutions. These university students' parents might be well educated and multilingual, or they might speak only Tunisian Arabic and some French they picked up. Among their aunts and uncles, there might be some with university degrees as well as some who had not completed elementary school.

Thus, each generation has had very different experiences with and attachments to the languages of the country and those that can be heard in the Arab world. Such stark differences across generations in terms of access to education, and hence languages or language varieties, characterize many countries of the developing world. These social changes of the past seventy years are sometimes difficult for Westerners to imagine.

Importantly, Tunisians see the languages they speak as resources, and they are generally good language learners. Equally significant, Tunisians do not see fluency in languages other than Arabic as a threat to their "Arabness," a fact distinguishing them from Arabs in many, but not all, other Arab countries, and a situation that reminds us of the complex relationship between attitudes toward and beliefs about the links between language and identity.

Thus, Tunisia is a bilingual, and increasingly a multilingual, society, and it is proud to be so. Tunisians generally see French as their second language—not a foreign language—and English continues to gain ground. During Tunisia's Jasmine Revolution of 2010–2011, which heralded the beginning of the Arab Spring, Tunisians on the street frequently spoke English when interviewed by international television correspondents reporting from the country—something that could not have happened a decade or two before.

One can understand Tunisians and their attitudes toward language, language learning, and language use in the context of their history. For most Tunisians, the country has been a "crossroads of civilizations" around the Mediterranean across the centuries for Berbers, Phoenicians, Romans, Vandals, Arabs, Italians, Maltese, and the French. Likewise, the country is small, and one of its most important sources of income and hard currency is foreign tourism, mainly from Europe. Especially in resorts along the coasts, it is common to find merchants and guides who speak several languages to some degree, in addition to Arabic, French, and English. From their perspective, multilingualism is part of Tunisia's heritage, something that helps Tunisia and Tunisians in an increasingly globalized economy. At the same time, it is important to acknowledge a growing minority of Tunisian Islamists, the Salafists, who emphasize Tunisia's Muslim and Arabic heritage; their goal is a drastically different Tunisia, one with fewer foreign influences and one where citizens focus on a more conservative interpretation of Islam and greater use of Arabic, particularly MSA, which is closer to the Arabic of the Quran than any of the dialects.

Two Case Studies

In Tunisia, as in all societies that are bi- or multilingual, languages and language varieties come to have distinct, if sometimes diffuse, social meanings. The same is true to a lesser degree, of course, in societies where a single language predominates. One can safely predict that American rappers will never use Standard English when they perform—except perhaps mockingly so—because of the conflict between the social meanings of Standard

Graffiti from the Jasmine Revolution on a street in Tunis, the capital of Tunisia, in French *(left)*, English *(center)*, and Arabic *(right)*. While all three languages are used in Tunisia, the use of Arabic is aimed at audiences in the Arab world, whereas the use of French and English can be seen as a clear effort to communicate with audiences outside the Arab world—and to claim membership in that larger world. *(Wikimedia Commons.)*

English and the oppositional stance hip-hop artists take in their lyrics. In fact, the same relationship is found in hip-hop around the world: whatever language or languages rappers use, they are socially stigmatized by the majority culture in some way. Here, I examine two cases where language choice by Tunisians carries specific social meanings, which will demonstrate the dynamics of language use in multilingual contexts and in Tunisia in particular. The first case study looks at the choice of language for speeches about politics at an international conference, while the second examines instances of language use on the web pages of a radio station.

Case Study 1: Language Choice at an International Conference on Politics

On March 28–29, 2013, the Center on Democracy, Development, and the Rule of Law at Stanford University sponsored a conference on building viable democracies in Tunisia, Egypt, and Libya—the three countries where dictators were overthrown during the Arab Spring. The conference was held in Tunis at the Centre d'Etudes Maghrébines à Tunis (CEMAT), the overseas research center of the American Institute for Maghrib Studies. Among the speakers were three important Tunisian political figures: Sheikh Rached

Ghannouchi, the president of Ennahda, the ruling moderate Islamist party; Beji Caïd Essebsi, the president of Nida Tounes, the secularist opposition party; and Saïd Ferjani, the spokesperson for Ennahda. This was the first event where the leaders of the party in power and the major opposition party were both present and spoke. Everyone in attendance understood the occasion to be one of great significance.

Ghannouchi is among the world's leading Muslim intellectuals, and his writings are concerned with Islam and modern life, especially the links between Islam and democracy. From early in his career, Ghannouchi has asked questions about why the Arab Muslim world, which during certain historical periods was the most advanced civilization in the world, ended up being seen as underdeveloped and backward, left behind in the contemporary world. Not surprisingly, Ghannouchi, the leader of an Islamist party in an Arab country, delivered his speech in MSA, which shows an influence from Classical Arabic.

As noted, MSA is the most appropriate variety of Arabic for very formal contexts, and it is one that Ghannouchi, as an Islamic sheikh, or scholar, would be expected to have mastered. Using this variety of Arabic demonstrated not just that Ghannouchi is highly educated, but also that he was educated predominantly in Arabic and could speak authoritatively from an Islamic perspective. (It is worth recalling that Muslims believe the Quran to be actual words of God dictated to Muhammad, the Prophet, in what came to be known as Classical Arabic; thus, Islam and Arabic are inevitably linked for believers and for others as well.)

In fact, Ghannouchi, who was born in 1941 in a rural town in southern Tunisia, received his education in Tunis, and later in Egypt and Syria, countries where the language of higher education was Arabic. As he spoke, Ghannouchi was also using the country's official language. The 1959 constitution of independent Tunisia named Arabic—and MSA was clearly intended—as the country's official language. In the aftermath of the events of the Arab Spring, the Tunisian Constitution is being revised, but Arabic will no doubt be the official language if one is listed. (Some countries—the United States, for example—have no official language, though, of course, English is the country's de facto national language.) Ghannouchi spoke MSA with a Tunisian accent and was, therefore, demonstrating to his listeners his Tunisianness. In public debates about many aspects of Tunisian life, Arabic and things Islamic are often associated with the notion of "authenticity," and the Arabic word used for this idea can also be translated as "rootedness." For Tunisians, this word connotes tradition and strong bonds to Islam and their country's Islamic past.

Essebsi, who leads the opposition party, which contends that religion should play no direct role in the country's politics, made his remarks in French. Doing so demonstrated that he, too, was highly educated, but in a very different tradition. Born in 1926 into an elite family, Essebsi, like many of the future political leaders of independent Tunisia, attended a bilingual high school in Tunis that trained its students, all male, to be equally comfortable in Arabic and French, teaching them to be at home with both intellectual traditions. Again, like most of those of his generation who received advanced degrees, Essebsi studied in France, and he later returned to Tunisia to become an attorney. From the beginning, he strongly supported the Neo-Destour Party of Habib Bourguiba, Tunisia's first president, who served in that post from 1956 until he was overthrown in a blood-less coup in 1987 by Zine al-Abidine Ben Ali, who was later overthrown in the Jasmine Revolution.

While Essebsi is perfectly comfortable speaking French, he speaks it with a marked Tunisian—that is, Arabic—accent, a practice found among many highly educated men of his generation. By speaking perfect, sometimes even bookish, French with a Tunisian accent in this way, these men are sending a message to the French: "We have mastered your language and your ways; you may have colonized our land, but you have not colo-nized our souls." At the same time, in public debates about many aspects of Tunisian life, French and things Western are often associated with "openness" and a willingness, even a desire, to be fully part of the contemporary world—in the way that that notion is understood in Europe and the West more broadly.

By speaking French, Essebsi aligned himself not merely with the West but also with secularism as those familiar with French culture understand it. Importantly, French no-tions of secularism differ markedly from American ones. In the United States, the notion of the separation of church and state still allows for expressions of religious beliefs in the public arena. U.S. coins state "In God We Trust"; newly elected politicians are sworn in by placing their hand on a book of scripture, most often the Christian Bible; and one finds nativity scenes (and increasingly menorahs, a Jewish religious symbol celebrating Hanukkah) in public places during December. In contrast, French understandings of secularism (*laïcité*) assume a much stricter separation of the church and state. Despite the fact that, both culturally and historically, Catholicism has played a significant role in France, laïcité prohibits any notion of a state religion, and it further presumes that religious beliefs are private matters and should, therefore, not be expressed or evident in the public sphere, particularly by persons in public office.

In a newspaper interview prior to the conference, Essebsi had stated that his dream for Tunisia after the revolution was "a republic whose religion is Islam, not an Islamic republic." (In fact, the phrase "a republic whose religion is Islam" comes from Tunisia's earlier constitution, which dates to the Bourguiba era, and is understood by Tunisians to mean a republic where Islamic understandings of values form the bedrock of the society.) Tunisians hearing Essebsi's remarks would assume he identifies as a Muslim, but as a different sort of Muslim than Ghannouchi.

Across the Middle East generally, a person is born into membership in a religious group—the major ones being Muslim, Jewish, or Christian—which is an essential part of her or his identity. Such identifications based on religion are different, however, in the Middle East than in most communities of the United States or Europe. Thus, the debate among Tunisians and Muslims in many countries of the Arab world is largely about what it means to be Muslim and what role religion should play in public life, in the govern-ment, and in the constitution. Even the most rigid of the Tunisian secularists, for example, would likely not argue that the call to prayer, which is heard throughout the day in every Tunisian city, town, and village, should cease. They might, however, reject the idea that the call to prayer should interrupt television or radio broadcasts—a practice introduced during the Ben Ali era—and they certainly would object to the notion that restaurants and other businesses should close for the specified prayer times, as is the case in certain Muslim countries of the Arab world. In contrast, the Salafis would want to see both of these practices strictly enforced.

Ferjani, who responded to Essebsi's remarks, spoke English. In his late fifties, Ferjani grew up in a very poor family in Kairouan, a city in the interior of Tunisia many consider the fourth holiest in Islam, after Mecca, Medina, and Jerusalem, but he did not become devout until late adolescence, when Ghannouchi was his teacher of Arabic. Under the Ben Ali government, Ferjani was jailed and brutally tortured for participation in Islamic Tendency, a political movement Ghannouchi had started in Tunis. Ferjani managed to escape to Britain with a borrowed passport, where he and his family lived for some twenty years before returning to Tunisia after the fall of Ben Ali. Ghannouchi, like many Islamist thinkers in exile from Arab countries, also lived in Britain during much of this period. While Ferjani studied English in secondary school, he would have mastered it during his years in England. He commented to one of the conference organizers that he had spoken in English to make clear to those assembled (especially Western conference attendees), and to the Tunisian people, that secularists who spoke French, such as Essebsi, had no corner on the market of modernity.

It is almost assuredly the case that each of these men understood everything the other two said, and that each man spoke using the language he was most comfortable using in an international academic conference. From this perspective, each man used the language that would permit him to project a particular identity—one of competence. But each man also chose to speak a language that symbolically linked him to aspects of the larger debates in Tunisian society about core values in the country's identity. In the minds of the Tunisian listeners, each of the languages used was associated with different things—either Islam and tradition, modernity as the French see it, or modernity in a more globalized sense, often associated with English. Additionally, each speaker used language in an exclusionary fashion, though perhaps not deliberately. It is quite unlikely that Ghannouchi or Ferjani, given their education and their years in England, would be comfortable delivering a formal address in French, just as Essebsi likely could not do so in MSA or English—facts everyone present, especially the Tunisians, realized.

Importantly, none of the three men used Tunisian Arabic, their native language. The situation was a formal one, and Tunisian Arabic, as noted, is associated with the things of everyday life; in fact, there are no words in the dialect for many of the concepts these men would have been discussing. When educated Tunisians talk about topics such as politics or philosophy, they often use the relevant word from MSA or French or English, at least for the moment, even while speaking Tunisian Arabic. At other times they will simply speak French or English, or engage in code-switching, mixing the languages they and their listeners share, a process mentioned above and illustrated in more detail in the next case study. Additionally, had these men spoken Tunisian Arabic, most of the Arabs from other countries and the Americans present would not have understood them, because these visitors would most likely have understood MSA, French, English, or even all three of them, but not Tunisian Arabic.

At this conference, as in multilingual contexts generally, the language a speaker chooses for a particular occasion adds a level of meaning to what is literally said; in other words, language choice lets the speaker project an identity that is relevant to the larger context and intent of what he or she says. In the case of a discussion of the future of Tunisia, the selection of language and what that says about the identity of the speaker are tied to contrasting and conflicting views of the world, and particularly of Islam and modernity.

Case Study 2: Language and the Internet in Tunisia

In Tunisia, as in nearly every other country around the globe, the Internet, and particularly Web 2.0—with its focus on social networking, user-generated content, and the creation of virtual communities—influences language and language use in complex ways. These changes provide opportunities for the creation of new identities at the local level that simultaneously invite participation at the international level. For example, websites of radio stations can attract listeners from around the world who may or may not understand the local languages(s) but enjoy the music or are simply curious. This section illustrates language use and choice in such situations by examining multilingualism in the website of Mosaïque FM, Tunisia's first private radio station, and Arabizi, the Latin-script version of Arabic that Tunisians and other speakers of Arabic often use when posting comments on websites like the one belonging to the radio station or on YouTube, or when texting one another.

Mosaïque FM

Started in 2003, Mosaïque FM is Tunisia's first privately owned radio station. It is especially popular among listeners aged twenty to thirty-nine, the favorite demographic of advertisers. As a commercial radio station, it features advertising, something that was not necessary when all Tunisian broadcast media were state-controlled, as was the case in many countries of the Arab world until quite recently.

The radio station's name is the French word for "mosaic," a metaphor scholars of North Africa sometimes use when they discuss aspects of the lives, identities, or histories of the region's peoples, because of the many cultural traditions that have shaped them. The name is also significant because all Tunisians are aware that as part of the Roman Empire, their country was home to many important Roman cities; indeed, the country boasts some of the world's most impressive Roman ruins. These cities included public buildings and houses decorated with mosaics, some of which are now in museum collections around the world, and others of which can be seen in their original location at the ruins.

Like many radio stations, Mosaïque FM maintains two websites, one for the French-language version (http://www.mosaiquefm.net/) and another for the Arabic-language version (http://www.mosaiquefm.net/ar). The content of the two versions of the website is identical, or nearly so, and both versions of the site use both languages and scripts. The name of the station, its logo, and the names of the logos for the four "web radios"—

A Roman mosaic of Ulysses and the Sirens from Tunisia, currently on display in the Bardo National Museum in Tunis. The museum is considered by many to be the second most important museum in Africa, after the Cairo Museum, and is best known for its collection of Roman antiquities, including mosaics. *(Wikimedia Commons.)*

the English term is used—are in Latin script. At the bottom of the web page, viewers find the current top twenty Western ("Top Occidental") and Eastern ("Top Oriental") hits. The Western song titles are in the Latin script, while the Arabic titles are generally in Arabic script. As is immediately evident, most of the Western hits are performed in English and seem a bit dated; in early August 2013, "Gangnam Style" by Psy, "Skyfall" by Adele, and "Diamonds" by Rihanna topped the Western list. On the French version of the website, songs new to either list are labeled "JDID," the Tunisian Arabic word for "new" written in Latin script, and an example of Arabizi, discussed below. Advertisements on both sites are often bilingual, sometimes using MSA and French, other times using Tunisian Arabic and French, and sometimes using all three. It is likely that English will soon be added to the mix, since advertisers are always seeking novel ways to push their products, and English in Tunisia is attractive not only due to its novelty, but also as a sign of cosmopolitanism.

    As noted, listeners can choose to listen to four streams of music on the web radio channels: *Tounsi*, popular Arabic-language music, much of it from Tunisia (*Tounsi*, as it is spelled using French orthography, is the Arabic word for "Tunisian"); *Tarab*, music in the tradition of what might be termed classical Arab music from the early part of the twentieth century; *Gold*, older popular Western music, much of it in English; and *DJ's*, beat-driven dance music. The use of the terms *gold* and *dj's*, Facebook's "LIKE" symbol, and the phrase "827,000 [or current number of] people like Mosaïque FM," along with the large number of English words used, especially in the pull-down menus, demonstrate the extent to which English continues to influence French around the world, including in Tunisia.

Like the websites of many radio stations, Mosaïque FM's site includes short articles as teasers for taped interviews with politicians, sports figures, and entertainers. The articles are written in Arabic—MSA, of course—or French, depending on which version of the website a viewer visits. Especially when dealing with political or religious topics, an interviewee might use Tunisian Arabic and MSA, often favoring the latter at least much of the time. However, in most cases, an interviewee is likely to speak Tunisian Arabic but frequently employ French words, expressions, or even entire sentences. For example, during the first minute of an interview on July 5, 2013, Manel Amara, a popular Tunisian singer, used a number of French words or expressions, including *ça va* (I'm fine), *exactement* (exactly), *tout simplement* (very simply), *donc* (so), and *les evenements* (the events). Later in the interview, entire sentences were in French.

The interview with Manel Amara on Mosaïque FM (http://www.mosaiquefm.net/ fr/index/a/ActuDetail/Element/23314-manel-amara-oui-je-suis-une-chanteuse-commerciale) shows the pop singer's liberal use of French in an interview conducted primarily in Tunisian Arabic.

Why would Amara use French some of the time, when it is possible to express all these ideas in Tunisian Arabic? In many places around the world, bilingual speakers engage in code-switching, the use of two or more languages in a single turn when talking with other bilinguals, and in so doing they create complex identities. Here, Amara is demonstrating first and foremost that she is Tunisian—how would you learn Tunisian Arabic if you had not spent a long time in Tunisia, likely having grown up there? Further, her Tunisian Arabic accent identifies her as being from an urban area in the northern part of the country. Equally important, she is demonstrating that she speaks French, and that she does so with an accent marking her as an educated North African. In other words, she does not sound exactly like a French woman her age speaking French might sound (though she comes very close).

Tunisians claim, probably correctly, that Tunisian women are more likely to engage in Arabic/French code-switching than are Tunisian men and that Tunisian women are more likely to adapt a French (in contrast to Arabic) accent when speaking French than are Tunisian men. Thus, the frequency with which a Tunisian code-switches and the accent he or she uses are tied to gender. In fact, it is safe to predict that were Amara with a group of close Tunisian female friends, the amount of code-switching would be higher.

The use of code-switching in Tunisia is also tied to where a person is from; code-switching is associated with urban areas, especially those in the north along the coast. There is far less code-switching in the interior of the country, in small towns, and in rural areas, a situation that can be accounted for historically by looking at where the French and French influence predominated during and after the colonial period. In fact, coastal areas in most countries, especially those where there is contact with people from other countries via trade or tourism, are generally more open or less conservative in many regards than are more isolated inland areas.

The sociolinguist Carol Myers Scotton (2005) has discussed how the highly educated in postcolonial societies often engage in code-switching as a form of "elite closure." This means that by code-switching, educated people not only make apparent that they are educated, but also they behave in a way that less-educated people cannot. Obviously, Tunisians with less education might be able to understand Amara, but they could not engage in the sort of back-and-forth switching that she does. Thus, again, this is a case where language choice can function in an exclusionary fashion, in this case across social classes.

Importantly, such code-switching enables speakers to construct what might be termed "both/and" identities. By speaking Tunisian Arabic (rather than Algerian or Omani Arabic), Amana demonstrates her local identity and her loyalty to that identity. Simultaneously, by using some French in the manner she does, she demonstrates that she belongs to a larger, more cosmopolitan world. Further, she switches in very Tunisian ways. Even though Moroccans, Algerians, and Lebanese—citizens of countries colonized by the French and where French continues to be widely spoken by the educated—code-switch using their national variety of Arabic and French, they do so in slightly different ways with respect to the grammatical constructions in which switching is likely to occur. Also important is the fact that, although Amara knows MSA, she does not use it in this case. As noted, MSA is associated with formal situations and serious, often intellectual, academic, or religious subjects, and in this interview she was not trying to deal with such issues or to create such a persona.

Monolinguals are often baffled by code-switching. They assume bilinguals switch because they do not speak both languages well. There are cases where bilinguals might know a word in one of their languages but not in the other, and there are cases where a word or expression in one language has no real equivalent in the other. In many bilingual communities, however, code-switching is the normal mode of interacting. In such contexts, asking a bilingual not to use both languages is like asking an able-bodied person to swim with one arm tied behind his or her back.

Interestingly, Tunisians report that the frequency of Arabic/French code-switching in the Tunisian media has risen considerably since the Jasmine Revolution, although it certainly occurred prior to those events. Less than two decades ago, however, such code-switching in the media was rare, and the government instructed broadcasters to avoid it and to encourage those they interviewed to do so as well. What has changed is not the extent to which Tunisians code-switch in daily life, but rather their attitudes toward its appropriateness in the media. Another factor is market pressure to create media that people wish to consume. Obviously, Tunisians are clearly interested in media where the language used resembles the way they actually use their languages in everyday life.

Arabizi: Tunisian Arabic Online

In the same way that the commercialization of the media and Web 2.0 are encouraging the public use of code-switching in contexts where it generally did not occur in the past in Tunisia and elsewhere, changes in technology across the Arab world are also influencing the written language, especially the written use of the dialect and, more particularly, the practice of writing it in Latin script. This way of transliterating spoken dialectal Arabic is often termed *Arabizi* (from *Arabi* [Arabic] and *Angleezi* [English]). *Transliteration* refers to the process of representing a language usually written in one script in a different script. This "chat alphabet" came into existence with e-mail and cellular phones before these technologies could accommodate the Arabic script.

Although many cellular phones, e-mail systems, and comment functions on websites can now accommodate the Arabic script, younger Arabs continue to use Arabizi, no doubt partly because they are used to it and partly because it connotes youth and coolness in a way the Arabic script does not. Arabizi is also beginning to show up in advertising across the Arab world, a fact that should surprise no one, since advertisers, as noted, are always looking for novel ways to sell products.

To make up for the fact that the Arabic script has letters for sounds that do not occur in English, users simply employ numbers that resemble the Arabic letter. Tunisians, for example, use the Arabic number 7 to replace the Arabic letter ح , the number 3 to replace the letter ع, and the number 9 to replace the Arabic letter ق. Arabizi has not been standardized, so there are slightly different systems of transliteration in use across the regions of the Arab world, as illustrated in the Wikipedia entry on "Arabic Chat Alphabet."

The screen shot on page 325 illustrates Arabizi as well as other phenomena that characterize written language practices in user-generated content on the Internet in Tunisia. These four comments were posted in response to an article about the return of Oussama Darrigi, a Tunisian-born soccer player, to a Tunisian team, Espérance Sportive de Tunis, from the Swiss team where he had been playing. The second and third comments are in Arabizi, while the other two comments are in European languages. The second comment says "Welcome to Bab Souika ♥," a poor Tunis neighborhood, where the Espérance Sports Club was founded in the 1910s. The third comment reads "God willing, Good Lord, Darigi is returning and won't leave like that dog Al-Qurbba did." The first comment is, in fact, an example of code-switching: *bienvenuto* is Italian for "welcome" while the *-nho* suffix attached to Darrigi's name is the Portuguese diminutive suffix, which here indicates endearment, as does the heart, of course. Thus, the message means something like "Welcome home, dear Darrigi." The fourth comment, in French, states, "There is no impossible in football."

Conclusion

This chapter has considered the roles that language can play at the level of the individual, the social group, the nation-state, and even transnational entities such as the Arab world. While the focus has been on a single country, Tunisia, bi- or multilingual societies are the norm across the Middle East, as illustrated in the bibliography below, and indeed in most of the world. In focusing on Tunisia, the chapter has provided specific analyses of the complex nature of Arabic across the Arab world; of the ways that speakers there, as everywhere, use language strategically in fashioning identities for themselves; and of the ways matters of language choice ultimately become part of larger societal debates about hot-button issues such as the role of religion in public life.

Comments written in Arabizi and other languages made in response to an article about sports posted on the Mosaïque FM Arabic-language webpage. *(Screen shot of Mosaïque's webpage.)*

In addition, some of the linguistic and social consequences of larger social forces have been highlighted, such as European colonization a century ago and globalization more recently. At the same time, the chapter demonstrates that Tunisia, like the countries of the region generally, has a complex history, one characterized by the presence of many languages and cultures, and that current conflicts there—religious, political, social, or linguistic—can be understood only in light of its past. Tunisians, like citizens of many countries around the world—find themselves struggling to hold onto and maintain the important parts of their past. However, which parts of that past matter, or should matter, is a hotly debated question—particularly in a world defined by rapid social change, increasing economic and technological interdependence, and the growing role of English, especially as the language of science, technology, and the global economy.

As is clear, the diglossic nature of Arabic continues to be renegotiated as national dialects come to be written in electronic media, a context that only recently came into existence. Likewise, as explained above, since the Arab Spring, Tunisian Arabic and Arabic/French code-switching are used far more often in the local media than was the case in earlier eras. At the same time, it would be too simple to make a causal argument, attributing this linguistic shift to political events alone. These changes could not have occurred without changes in the media, technological innovations, and economic liberalization, factors that are influencing countries and cultures around the globe. A few decades ago, much of the Arab world was committed at least ideologically to Pan-Arabism—the idea that all the countries of the Arab world were linguistically united and should seek stronger relations with one another. Today, however, the situation is different. There is strong linguistic evidence that Pan-Arabism is on the decline and that nation-state nationalism is growing as each country focuses on its own unique needs and desires, including distinguishing itself from other countries of the region.

The subtitle of this chapter, "Without Tunisian Arabic, We Are Not Tunisians," is the English translation of a slogan on a T-shirt a Tunisian gave me in the early 1990s. The language of the slogan is pure Tunisian Arabic, though it was written in Roman script, an early example of Arabizi. On the background of the T-shirt was a list, again in Roman script, of Tunisian words that were falling into disuse as the language changed. Such a nostalgic view of language and of Tunisian identity is not uncommon. In this case, in particular, it represents an effort to hold onto something profoundly local, an essential part of a country's identity, while simultaneously embracing a larger, rapidly changing, and more cosmopolitan world community—a challenge every country faces.

References and Further Research

"Arabic Chat Alphabet." Wikipedia. http://en.wikipedia.org/wiki/Arabizi. Accessed August 15, 2013.

Borjian, Maryam. 2013. *English in Post-revolutionary Iran: From Indigenization to Internationalization*. Tonawanda, NY: Multilingual Matters.

Chun, Elaine, and Keith Walters. 2011. "Orienting to Arab Orientalisms: Language, Race, and Humor in a YouTube Video." In *Digital Discourse: Language in the New Media*, edited by Crispin Thurlow and Kristine Mroczek, 251–273. Oxford: Oxford University Press.

Holes, Clive. 2004. *Modern Arabic: Structures, Functions, and Varieties*. Rev. ed. Washington, DC: Georgetown University Press.

Lewis, Geoffrey. 1999. *The Turkish Language Reform: A Catastrophic Success*. Oxford: Oxford University Press.

Maddy-Weitzman, Bruce. 2011. *The Berber Identity Movement and the Challenge to North African States*. Austin: University of Texas Press.

Myers Scotton, Carol. 2005. *Multiple Voices: An Introduction to Bilingualism*. Malden, MA: Blackwell.

Spolsky, Bernard, and Elana Shohamy. 1999. *The Languages of Israel: Policy, Ideology and Practice*. Clevedon, UK: Multilingual Matters.

Suleiman, Yasir. 2004. *A War of Words: Language and Conflict in the Middle East*. Cambridge: Cambridge University Press.

Walters, Keith. 2011. "Gendering French: Historicizing Tunisian Language Ideologies." *International Journal of the Sociology of Language* 211: 83–111.

About the Editor and Contributors

Lucia Volk is an associate professor of international relations and the codirector of Middle East and Islamic studies at San Francisco State University. Her research interests include the politics of memory, sectarianism, and nationalism. Her book *Memorials and Martyrs in Modern Lebanon* (Indiana University Press 2010) shows how political elites of different religious communities in Lebanon built public memorials to commemorate shared Muslim-Christian sacrifice.

Carel Bertram is an associate professor of humanities at San Francisco State University who conceptualizes place-related memory as the locus of identity for Ottoman and Turkish populations, including minorities and diasporas. Her book *Imagining the Turkish House, Collective Visions of Home* (University of Texas 2008) investigates how representations of Ottoman houses became memory markers that intensified, interrupted, or personalized a developing Turkish nationalism.

Rochelle Davis is an associate professor of cultural anthropology at Georgetown University, with research interests in refugees and conflict. In her book *Palestinian Village Histories: Geographies of the Displaced* (Stanford University Press 2010), she analyzes over 120 village memorial books composed by Palestinian refugees and displaced persons in Syria, Jordan, Lebanon, the West Bank, Gaza, and Israel.

Rachel Goshgarian is an assistant professor of history at Lafayette College and an expert on the multicultural Middle Ages and the Byzantine and the early Ottoman Empires. Her work has appeared in the *Turkish Policy Quarterly, Confraternitas,* and the *British Journal of Middle Eastern Studies*.

Maia Carter Hallward is an associate professor of Middle East politics and is jointly appointed to the PhD in International Conflict Management program at Kennesaw State University. Her research interests include nonviolence, civil society movements, the Israeli-Palestinian conflict, and the politics of religion. She is the author of *Struggling for a Just Peace: Israeli and Palestinian Activism in the Second Intifada* (University of Florida Press 2011) and *Transnational Activism and the Israeli-Palestinian Conflict* (Palgrave 2013).

Asli Ilgit is an assistant professor of political science at Gustavus Adolphus College, with research interests in the politics of identity, foreign policy, and discourse analysis. Her work has been published in *Mediterranean Politics, International Studies Review,* and *MERIP*, and she is the coauthor of a chapter in *Psychology and Constructivism in International Relations: An Ideational Alliance* (University of Michigan Press 2011), edited by Vaughn P. Shannon and Paul A. Kowert.

Mahmood Monshipouri is an associate professor of international relations at San Francisco State University and a visiting professor at the University of California at Berkeley, with research interests in globalization, identity construction, and human rights in the Muslim world. He is the author of *Human Rights in the Middle East: Frameworks, Goals and Strategies* (Palgrave 2011), as well as *Democratic Uprisings in the New Middle East: Youth, Technology, Human Rights, and US Foreign Policy* (Paradigm Publishers 2014).

Hootan Shambayati is an assistant professor of political science at Florida Gulf Coast University, with research interests in judicial politics and democratization in the Middle East. Some of his work has been published in the *Journal of Comparative Politics,* the *International Journal of Middle East Studies,* and the *Political Research Quarterly.*

Nadine Sinno is an assistant professor of Arabic in the Department of Foreign Languages and Literatures at Virginia Tech, and has published on contemporary Arabic literature, Arab women's writings, and transnational feminisms in the *Journal of Arabic Literature,* the *Journal of Middle East Women's Studies,* and *Interdisciplinary Studies in Literature and Environment.* She is also the translator of the Lebanese writer Nazik Saba Yared's novel *Canceled Memories* (Syracuse University Press 2009).

Keith Walters is chair of the Department of Applied Linguistics at Portland State University. A sociolinguist, he has published on numerous issues related to language and identity in Tunisia and North Africa more broadly. He is also coauthor of several textbooks used in undergraduate writing courses.

Nicole F. Watts is an associate professor of political science at San Francisco State University, with research interests in ethnopolitical and national movements, state-society relations, and Kurdish politics and mobilization. She is the author of *Activists in Office: Kurdish Politics and Protest in Turkey* (University of Washington Press 2010) and co-edited *Negotiating Political Power in Turkey: Breaking Up the Party* (Routledge 2012).

Russell Zanca is a professor of cultural anthropology at Northeastern Illinois University. His research focus is post–Soviet Central Asia, in particular Eurasian labor migration and globalization. He is the author of *Life in a Muslim Village: Cotton Farming After Communism* (Wadsworth Publishing 2011) and coedited *Everyday Life in Central Asia: Past and Present* (Indiana University Press 2010).

Index

Page numbers in **bold** refer to figures, page numbers in *italic* refer to tables.